THE CONSULTANT'S CRAFT

Improving Organizational Communication

THE CONSULTANT'S CRAFT

Improving Organizational
Communication

Sue DeWine

Ohio University

ST. MARTIN'S PRESS
New York

Development editor: Sylvia L. Weber
Managing editor: Patricia Mansfield-Phelan
Senior project editor: Erica Appel
Production supervisor: Pat Ollague
Art director: Sheree Goodman
Text design: Lee Goldstein
Cover design: Marjory Dressler

For information, write:
St. Martin's Press, Inc.
175 Fifth Avenue
New York, NY 10010

ISBN: 0-312-06151-X

Acknowledgments

Fig. 3.1, The Consulcube Figure from Robert R. Blake and Jane S. Mouton. *Consultation: A Handbook for Individual and Organization Development,* 2d ed. Reading, MA: Addison-Wesley Publishing Company, p. 11. Copyright © 1983 by Scientific Methods, Inc. Reproduced by permission of the owners.

Fig. 4.2, "Needs Assessment Tools," from Allison Rosset, *Training Needs Assessment,* Englewood Cliffs, NJ: Educational Technology Publications, 1987, p. 77. Reprinted by permission of the publisher.

Form 6.1, "Worksheet for Media Selection," by H. H. Sredal and W. J. Rothwell. Reprinted by permission of McGraw-Hill, Inc.

Fig. 6.1, "The Technology of Human Relations Training," reprinted from John E. Jones and J. William Pfeiffer (Eds.), *The 1979 Annual Handbook for Group Facilitators,* San Diego, CA: Pfeiffer & Company, 1979. Used with permission.

Parker case study in Chapter 6 reprinted, by permission of publisher, from *Executive Skills, 1981* © 1981. American Management Association, New York. All rights reserved.

Fig. 7.1, "Typology of Interventions," from Wendell L. French / Cecil H. Bell, Jr., *Organization Development: Behavioral Science Interventions for Organization Improvement,* 4/e © 1990, p. 122. Reprinted by permission of Prentice-Hall, Englewood Cliffs, New Jersey.

Acknowledgments and copyrights are continued at the back of the book on page 373, which constitutes an extension of the copyright page.

To my three significant others:
Mike, Leigh Anne, and James

CONTENTS

Chapter 5

HOW DO WE KNOW WHAT WE HAVE WHEN WE HAVE IT?
Data Analysis

PART III

TRAINING AND CONSULTING STRATEGIES AND TECHNIQUES

Chapter 6

USING TRAINING TECHNIQUES

Chapter 7
DESIGNING CONSULTING INTERVENTIONS 108

■ *PART IV*

CORRECTING COMMUNICATION FAILURES   137

Chapter 8

ISN'T ANYONE LISTENING?
Using Active Listening Techniques   138

Chapter 9

WHY ARE MEETINGS SO BORING AND
   UNPRODUCTIVE?
Managing Meetings   156

Chapter 10

CAN I HELP MY CLIENT FACE AN AUDIENCE?
Presentation Skills   192

Chapter 11

CAN THIS GROUP WORK AS A TEAM?
Team-Building Techniques   218

■ *PART V*

EVALUATING SUCCESS   293

Chapter 15

EVALUATING THE IMPACT OF TRAINING   294

Chapter 16

STRATEGIES FOR EVALUATING CONSULTING   310

PREFACE

One afternoon a woman of average means caught sight of Picasso in a restaurant. She had always admired his paintings but had never been able to afford one. She decided to be bold and ask him for a sketch: "Excuse me, but I have always been a great admirer of your paintings, and when I saw you in this restaurant I couldn't help but come up and tell you so. You would do me a great honor if you would simply sketch some scene from this restaurant on a napkin. I would treasure it forever." Picasso took the napkin and in less than three minutes he had sketched a scene from the restaurant. The woman was delighted. "I'm willing to pay you for this small sketch. How much would you want?" Picasso replied, "My fee is $50,000." The woman was astonished. "How could you charge $50,000 for a three-minute sketch?" she asked. "But my dear lady," he replied, "you are not paying for the three-minute sketch. What you are paying for is 60 years of experience!"

I have tried to put my knowledge and background as a consultant into this book, so that in buying the book you are also paying for my 25 years of experience. The examples and stories are true and happened to my colleagues and me in the course of trying to solve human problems in organizations. I have also tried to pass on what I have learned by teaching consulting and training to undergraduates for those 25 years, and to Ph.D. students for the last 15 years. However, you can't learn to be a consultant just by reading this book. You must add hundreds of hours of observation in organizations, with talented consultants, to the insights you learn here. I spent many hours observing Martha Langdom-Dahm and Gordon Lippitt. They were the first of many colleagues with whom I worked, but I remember them especially because we no longer have the opportunity to observe them in action but must remember the skill they demonstrated.

This book can serve as the primary text in an organizational communication or consulting course or as a companion text in organizational development, management, and human resource courses in communication and business schools. It will also be useful in adult education as well as public administration courses, focusing on human resource development. It will be helpful to the 50,000 trainers and human resource managers who are members of the American Society for Training and Development. Organizational managers who may be members of the American Management Association will also want to try these techniques and strategies.

The book is written from the point of view of the individual who will have to function in an organizational setting and wants to figure out ways to interact with others that will make him or her more effective. It is also directed to those individuals who will be, or are, in positions that require them to help others learn these techniques (e.g., trainers, internal consultants, or human resource managers).

Part One provides an overview and basic definitions. *Part Two* identifies specific assessment techniques used by communication specialists to help identify communication problems in organizations. *Part Three* presents a variety of training and consulting strategies, and *Part Four* identifies ways to correct communication problems encountered by the manager or communication specialist. Anyone who hopes to be an effective human resources or communication manager must be a model of effective communication behavior before transmitting any skills to others. *Part Five* presents evaluation methods for the trainer and consultant, and *Part Six* discusses professional development, so the consultant or communication manager is continually able to demonstrate desired skills.

This text is designed as a practical approach to solving communication problems for persons who will be, or are, managers and individuals responsible for human resources.

▌ *Acknowledgments*

This book was written in my office at Ohio University and at home in the living room, kitchen, and dining room. I took it with me when I taught in Hong Kong and on conventions in various parts of the United States. I wrote parts of it on a lap-top computer in hotel rooms and on planes. For a year and a half it was with me almost daily. I did not write it without help, however.

My husband, Mike, helped me remember some of the unique clients with whom I have worked, and he put up with my absorption with the book. He has always been the most supportive person in my life. My daughter, Leigh Anne, and my son, James, asked questions about the book that made me clarify my purpose. A number of graduate students and staff members assisted me by tracking down references and helping with library research: Tracy Corrigan, Jennifer Deatsch, Tara Emmers, Teresa Holder, Elizabeth Lozona, Robin Nichols, Anjali Ram, Scott Sheets, and Lisa Wallace. I would also like to thank Rita L. Rahoi, the coauthor of the appendix.

Joanne D. Daniels and Cathy Pusateri celebrated the initiation of this book in New York, and development editor Sylvia Weber and project editor Erica Appel helped give the book definition. One person in particular,

Wanda Sheridan, a colleague at Ohio University, was instrumental to the development of the book, especially in its initial stages. The following reviewers provided great insights and suggestions: Larry Albert, Morehead State University; Marta F. Belt, Hanover College; Phillip G. Clampitt, University of Wisconsin–Green Bay; Cal W. Downs, University of Kansas; Harold Gortner, George Mason University; Richard Hann, Manager, Human Resources, Douglass Aircraft; F. William Heiss, Virginia Commonwealth University; Ronald Perry, Arizona State University; Jill Rhea, University of North Texas; Roseanna Ross, St. Cloud State University; Donald Tobias, Cornell University; and Clay Warren, George Washington University.

Several colleagues read some of the early chapters and provided help in shaping the book: Anita James, Edward Baum, Ann Debrick, Valeria Perotti, and the winter, 1992 INCO #633 class. Two former students, Jill Rhea and Rosanna Ross, class-tested the book with their own students, and I greatly appreciate their students' feedback.

Finally, two special people provided guidance. My aunt Peg Porter, along with my mother, showed me how strong women can be. And my friend Lynda Swensen gave me constant support. Our discussions and our friendship helped shape my philosophy for working with individuals in organizations.

Of all my writing projects, I have enjoyed this one the most. Some of you reading this book may see yourselves in the stories about clients—I have tried to protect all identities. The stories I have told about clients reinforce for me the notion that no matter what positions they hold or personalities they possess, people everywhere want to enjoy being at work. Improving our ability to communicate with each other will indeed make our work more productive and rewarding.

SUE DEWINE

FOREWORD

by W. Charles Redding
Professor Emeritus, Purdue University
West Lafayette, Indiana

"Improving organizational communication," the subtitle of Professor De-Wine's book, epitomizes the reasons why it deserves our closest attention. To say that we live in an organizational world has become a truism. Thus, when any of the innumerable organizations touching our lives fails to function properly, we can expect to experience a variety of pains, both material and emotional, until the necessary improvements are made. Regardless of which particular organizational theory (if any) we happen to entertain, we must acknowledge one axiom: In every instance of organizational malaise that comes to mind, at some time and in some way, human communication behavior has been significantly involved. Indeed, there are those scholars who have persuasively made the case that a communication failure is at least one of the basic sources underlying *every* organizational failure.

As members of organizations, who among us can honestly report having never endured some sort of damage associated with such phenomena as insensitive supervision, confusing instructions, fruitless meetings, deceptive announcements, vicious defenses of "turf," biased (or entirely omitted) performance evaluations, misleading reports, empty promises, backstabbing tête-à-têtes with the boss, privacy-invading questions, sexist or racist harassment, scapegoating memoranda, clumsy explanations, paucity of information, conflicting orders, ambiguity (both intentional and unintentional), worship of inane regulations, refusal to listen to bad news, and rejection of innovative ideas—not to mention stubborn reliance upon autocratic, downward-directed messages in general? (Space limitations prohibit a complete inventory of evils.)

Yet to be considered are those problems we commonly experience in encounters, not as "insiders" but as "outsiders," with a host of organizations: government agencies, supermarkets, banks, labor unions, advocacy groups, insurance companies, professional societies, mail-order houses, educational institutions, publishers of journals, utility companies, manufacturers, and so on. As nonmembers of these organizations, we appear in such roles as customers, clients, suppliers, dealers, and, of course, taxpayers. Hence, we are all too familiar with the innumerable frustrations associated with the label "red tape," including unanswered inquiries, pedantic adherence to esoteric rules, incomprehensible prose, condescending (even insulting) statements, evasive explanations, refusals to accept responsibility, inconsistent assertions from different sources, violations of common courtesy, and so on.

Does this book claim to offer neat solutions to all these problems? Such an experienced and sophisticated consultant as Professor DeWine would vigorously reject any such suggestion. Indeed, one of the merits of the book is the author's emphatic insistence that communication failures in the organizational context are typically complex and rarely, if ever, amenable to formulary quick fixes. However, while carefully eschewing cookbook approaches, the author presents a great wealth of specific techniques designed not as magic cure-alls, but as helpful suggestions for the aspiring consultant.

I have not attempted a precise count of the number of times the reader is provided convenient lists of various items, such as principles, techniques, advisories ("tips"), self-assessment questions, and the like. Here is a sampling:

- "Principal skills" the consultant must have (Chapter 1)
- "Training skills"—31 of them! (Chapter 2)
- Pros and cons of data-collection methods (Chapter 4)
- "Classic errors" in data analysis (Chapter 5)
- Major training methods (Chapter 6)
- "Consulting interventions" (Chapter 7)
- Several supplementary lists of guidelines, procedures, and methods (Chapter 7)
- Reasons for meetings, and techniques for improving meetings (Chapter 9)
- "Emergency kit" for making oral presentations (Chapter 10)
- Self-administered "challenge readiness inventory" (Chapter 10)
- Criteria for evaluating the impact of training (Chapter 15)
- Criteria for evaluating the effectiveness of consulting interventions (Chapter 16)

As the foregoing titles suggest, this book is amazingly comprehensive. Perusing its pages, I thought of the varied consulting assignments I myself had undertaken over the years—all the while regretting that no such book was available to me as I was starting out in the 1950s. The more I reflected, the more I became convinced that almost no problem I have ever encountered has been overlooked by Professor DeWine. When we recall that she has had more than 25 years of experience as a consultant, this is hardly surprising. In fact the book, while not pretending to be more than a practical guide, even addresses some topics one would expect to find in a full-blown treatise—elements of what could be regarded as groundwork for a "proto-theory" of communication consulting.

I should like now to single out several features of the book that, in my judgment, merit special attention.

1. The practice of consulting is positioned in a frame of contemporary scholarship and research in the field known as "organizational communication." The reader is given to understand that consulting does not exist in a vacuum—as a bag of tricks totally unrelated to theoretical underpinnings.

The author does not devote a major segment of the book to a point-by-point exposition of basic concepts in organizational communication, but rather draws attention to a number of concepts, principles, and research findings, always taking care to demonstrate their relevance to consulting problems. The reader is left in no doubt that communication consulting can never be regarded as casual moonlighting for the dilettante but that it is serious business, requiring of the practitioner nothing less than a sophisticated understanding of research in human communication theory, organizational behavior, and management. Although the author is convinced that consultants will be more successful if they apply the principles she expounds, she gives absolutely no encouragement to those innocent souls who would like to believe that reading her book is a painless substitute for a thorough grounding in the appropriate disciplines.

2. Among both theorists and practitioners there has always been confusion regarding four significantly different, but overlapping, forms of helping interventions: teaching, counseling, training, and consulting. Unquestionably, in many consulting assignments, counseling, training, and teaching are all occurring simultaneously; in some other assignments, the consultant is acting almost exclusively as a teacher, as a trainer, or as a counselor. I am convinced that many unhappy episodes in consulting result from the failure, on the part of the consultant, the client, or both, to grasp the important differences that hold among these four activities. It is fortunate, then, that Professor DeWine has given careful thought (especially in Chapter 2) to this problem, emphasizing the crucial fact that consulting, when properly conducted, is one of the "helping" professions. She follows through in later chapters by focusing especially upon two of the most common tasks that consultants undertake: training and teaching. For both of these the reader will find a wealth of specific, down-to-earth suggestions.

3. The practitioner is advised how to "design consulting interventions" (Chapter 7), in terms of four basic categories: diagnostic, process

(including confrontation and negotiation), problem-solving, and decision-making. Any consultant who has neglected to think through the ramifications of these categories is headed for serious trouble.

4. A topic that may come as a surprise in a book about consulting is represented by Chapter 10, "Can I Help My Client Face an Audience? Presentation Skills." In some respects this chapter may be regarded as merely a summary of familiar principles of public speaking. But it is also much more. Three elements are especially noteworthy. The first offers an "emergency kit for presentations," an amazingly comprehensive inventory of devices for dealing with just about every glitch that has ever bedeviled a public speaker. It includes, for example, such items as paper towels, extension cords, rolls of masking tape, transparency pens, headache medications, magnifying glasses, scissors, flashlights, envelopes with stamps, single-edge razor blades, and dimes (for removing jammed slide trays).

The second presentation tool is a "speaker's checklist." Among scores of items are these: coat racks in "secure" locations, tables for hand-outs, ready access to restrooms, window blinds, a marked script or cue sheet for projectionists, lectern lights, easels, and tape for door latches (not to recapitulate Watergate, but to preserve silence during late arrivals!).

The third is a self-administered "challenge readiness inventory" (borrowed from a Synergy Group newsletter). It invites prospective speakers, using a ten-point scale, to rate their predicted "comfort levels" when confronted by 16 speaking situations. Sample questions are: "Present a proposal or sales talk with appropriate documentation to a client group"; "Deliver a 5-to-10-minute, all-purpose, amusing, and motivating talk to groups from 3 to 3000"; and "Present a one-minute television editorial on the benefits your industry brings to society."

Devices such as these vividly illustrate Professor DeWine's rare ability, derived from her many years of experience "in the trenches," to provide detailed, hands-on advice to beginners as well as veterans in the consulting profession.

5. The author's treatment of feedback, a staple of communication textbooks, is unusually helpful when it offers excellent guidelines for giving and receiving feedback. I have learned, from painful personal experience, how thin the ice is when a consultant sets out to provide survey findings to a client organization whose members cannot tolerate bad news. Professor DeWine's suggestions should help practitioners to deal with such hazardous situations.

6. An especially provocative chapter (13) is devoted to a question frequently asked but seldom answered (at least in print): "How do I cope with difficult people?" The chapter, not surprisingly, offers no surefire formulas. Indeed, its candor is commendable for acknowledging that consultants must face up to the inevitability of failure in their dealings with a

certain number of difficult people. Given this constraint, Chapter 13 offers sage, experience-based advice.

7. The concluding chapter (16) contains absolutely essential material; namely, criteria for evaluating consulting interventions. Four points of view are considered: the consultant's effectiveness, the consultant's own satisfaction, the client's satisfaction, and long-term outcomes of an entire project. Since every aspect of consulting demands careful consideration of ethics, it is noteworthy that many of the criteria in this chapter require the consultant to confront ethical issues.

8. Finally, the book is jam-packed with *specific real-life examples,* drawn from Professor DeWine's 25 years of consulting experience.

I now ask the reader to recall that, as an academic field, "organizational communication" is young. Organized graduate curricula have been in existence only since the 1950s (in fact, many were established as late as the mid-1970s). Ironically, a case could be made that communication *consulting* has a longer history than does the academic field of organizational communication itself. Both professorial and nonacademic entrepreneurs were offering their services as communication consultants (under a variety of labels, to be sure) at least as far back as the 1920s. In fact, Dale Carnegie—thought to be the first communication consultant—got his start as a speech instructor at a New York City YMCA in 1912. The 1920s saw the appearance of textbooks (including Carnegie's in 1926), advertised as teaching aids to be used in helping business and professional clients to improve their on-the-job communication skills. After the Second World War, skills training, aimed as it was at individual effectiveness, expanded into efforts to improve the functioning of an entire organization. However—until now—there has been no comprehensive guidebook for those who serve as communication consultants to organizational clients.

In a paper published some years ago (1979), discussing communication consulting as one of the helping professions, I warned that the consultant "occupies a role which always has the potential of doing irreparable damage to many persons," adding that even surgeons are "in a position to hurt fewer individuals than are many organizational consultants." I still hold this opinion, but, with the sage guidance Professor DeWine offers in this book—in which she reveals all her trade secrets—I have no hesitation in predicting that communication consultants will be far more likely to do good, and far less likely to do harm, than would otherwise have been the case.

Keeping all this in mind helps one to appreciate the special importance of this book. To say that it fills—and fills admirably—a long-standing void is to indulge in understatement.

INTRODUCTION

by Richard H. Brown
Vice Chairman, Ameritech

A friend of mine, a high school teacher, once commented to me: "Just because you tell them something doesn't mean they know it." He knew that teaching, like all communication, is more than a random toss of the ball. If there's no catch, there's no communication. Business author Brent Filson highlighted this important truth when he wrote, "Communication isn't simply moving information. It's moving people by using information; it's transmitting a conviction from one person to another." Sue DeWine's book, *The Consultant's Craft: Improving Organizational Communication,* certainly follows this adage. It's not just about information; it's about affecting people. Every part of this excellent text on organizational communication is firmly grounded in the way people think, how they react to information, and how they interact with each other.

My experience as a business executive absolutely supports this approach. There are many ways to describe a business enterprise. For example, there is a legal description, such as you would find embodied in its articles of incorporation. There are material descriptions that describe the business in terms of its capitalization, its assets, or its sales revenues. There are functional definitions that tell you what the business does, what needs it meets, and what products or services it provides. But if you are looking to understand what a business truly is, and how it really works, I believe the most pertinent starting point is to define it from the human angle. Simply put, before it is anything else, a business is a group of people organized around a common goal.

When a business is understood this way, the universal importance of organizational communication becomes clear. It is not only a discipline for specialists, but a core element of leadership. After all, whether you're talking about the CEO or a shop foreman, leadership is at base a matter of influencing people to agree on and pursue a goal. The leader knows that people do the job and that motivation is essential if people are to do it well.

This is where you will most often find the difference between a mere manager and a manager who is also a leader. The leader is always aware that the job is being done by people. Leaders tend to be behavior- and people-centered, whereas mere managers can often be mechanistic and thing-centered. In his seminal work, *American Spirit: Visions of a New Corporate Culture,* Lawrence M. Miller tells us that leaders appeal to their people for contributions to customers, to the public interest, and to the long-term goals of the corporation, but managers tend to push the team with quantified, short-term objectives. Leaders give energy to an enterprise by defining purpose, and managers steer the energy. Leaders define success in terms of product and service achievements, and managers define it by numbers.

At the all-important point where decisions have to be executed and goals have to be achieved, leadership becomes essentially a matter of communicating—communicating the goal and communicating the enthusiasm needed to achieve the goal. Certainly this means that the most effective leader will be a consummate communicator. But it also means a leader must promote good communication among all the groups and individuals in the organization. There must be communication up and down and across the business. Leadership, therefore, implies some expertise in the techniques of using information to move people. As I see it, the greater the number of managers in a business who are good communicators, the better the leadership in that business, and the better its performance is likely to be.

As its title implies, *The Consultant's Craft* is a book for consultants and about consulting. The perspective throughout tends to be that of an outside consultant who works with a business on an ad hoc basis to address specific communication issues. But Professor DeWine makes it clear from the beginning that this is also a book for those managers within a business whose official responsibility is to ensure good communication in their organizations and for executives who know that human resources are the key to an organization's success. I would go further, and say that this is a book for every manager. Is each of us not responsible for some aspect of the process of communication? And should we not all know and use, at least to some extent, the techniques of organizational communication? To my mind, *The Consultant's Craft* is indeed a treatise on the process of communicating, but it is also by extension a treatise on a key aspect of management and leadership.

This book can serve as a corrective for the belief that internal communications is one of the "soft" disciplines, to be handled by the corporate communications or human resources department or perhaps by an outside consultant, but certainly not by those with the more "serious" task of running the business. Explicitly or implicitly, every part of the book supports the thesis that good communicating is critical to good management and good business performance. No one can read this and come away thinking that communication is separate and apart from the other facets of managing a business, or believing that it is anything other than "serious," or convinced that it is "someone else's job." In fact, at one point the author suggests that communication skills could become part of the management performance appraisal process.

Similarly, the manager who thinks effective communicating is always easy will be in for a surprise. Professor DeWine's analysis of problems and her comprehensive treatment of solutions illustrate the attention to depth and detail that must go into the process of communicating. The reader will gain new respect for the science of communication, as it becomes clear how complex and demanding it can be. Important communication decisions will be less likely to be tossed off casually, or made on the basis of whim or fancy.

My perspective in reading *The Consultant's Craft* was that of a businessperson, and so is my reaction to it. I am not a consultant. But if I were a consultant—or a student preparing for a career in organizational consulting—I am sure I would be just as pleased with this book. Professor DeWine has compiled a summary of the best in current thinking on her topic, and at the same time she has created a thoroughly detailed, hands-on manual, rich with illustrations and examples from her long experience as a consultant. It can serve as a textbook for the novice or a reference for the practitioner.

American business has come a long way since the days when hierarchical authority structures and mechanistic measurements were the norm for management. Today, most managers have learned they must attend to human factors, to motivation, to the quality and process of information flow. Professor DeWine's book is testimony to the progress that's been made in this regard and a contribution to further progress.

THE CONSULTANT'S CRAFT

Improving Organizational
Communication

PART *I*

Overview

*T*his section of the book provides some basic definitions of the individuals for whom this book is written. Who in the organization is likely to be working on human communication problems? If you are hired as an outside consultant, how do your activities affect internal managers who may be working on the same problems?

Chapter 1 presents an extended example of a manager with whom I worked and the human communication problems he faced in the first few days of his new job. Chapters 2 and 3 identify the differences between training, consulting, and other helping professions. Throughout the book personal examples and stories are told about clients with whom I have worked for the past 25 years. I have also included self-assessment instruments, evaluation forms, short articles, and intervention materials that I expect readers to pull out and use in a variety of settings.

Part I provides the foundation for sections to follow. Once you can identify how this material applies to you, it is more apparent how the techniques discussed can be utilized.

Chapter *1*

WHY ARE HUMAN COMMUNICATION SKILLS SO IMPORTANT?

"We're not sure exactly how the innovative process works. But there's one thing we do know: the easy communications, the absence of barriers to talking to one another are essential. Whatever we do, whatever structure we adopt, whatever systems we try, that's the cornerstone— we won't do anything to jeopardize it."

Senior Hewlett Packard Manager
Quoted in: In Search of Excellence *(p. 218)*

*O*rganizations are plagued with a variety of persistent communication problems. In 25 years of consulting activity, I have worked with organizational members who did not clearly communicate expectations for new employees, gave miscues about work to be done, were involved in bitter interpersonal battles, did not know how to give positive *or* negative feedback, modeled poor listening behaviors for others, misused group decision-making techniques, and were generally described as poor communicators. Of course it is easier to identify these problems in others than in ourselves! My job as a consultant is not only to help solve these problems, but to develop the skill in others to solve them themselves. In that sense the techniques and strategies discussed in this book are useful for the consultant and manager as well. In fact, any individual in the organization with better-than-average communication skills can intervene and help resolve such dilemmas.

The following case study demonstrates the need for planned communication systems within organizations. This example is based on an actual situation in which David Andrews[1] was hired to supervise a staff of seven as a district manager of a nationally known insurance agency. One week prior to assuming the responsibilities of his job, he had occasion to talk privately with his predecessor about the agents he would be supervising. Chuck Johnson, the outgoing district manager, talked openly about the strengths and weaknesses of each agent.

Jake Miller was in his early 50s, a good worker, very cooperative, and made above-average sales. He was happy working at this level and had no desire to move into management.

3

Chris Rand was 43 and overloaded with work. He had a large family depending on him and many personal demands that made his work less than effective. Lately, his sales had dropped off considerably.

Larry Johnson worked in a remote district and did not have much contact with the main office. He was 27 and the other agents viewed him as a "loner" and not really a member of the team.

Mike Thompson was near retirement. He used to be the top salesman in the district, but in the last 2–3 years his sales had dropped off considerably. He did not seem to be as interested in his job as he was in a ranch his family had recently purchased.

Janet Curry was the best salesperson. At age 38 she had achieved the highest sales record, kept clients longer, and had a more stable relationship with both her clients and the other agents. She was a good trainer and was willing to share information with new employees.

Nita Whitberg, in her early 20s, was the newest agent and the least knowledgeable. She had been with the company less than a year and was just beginning to make stable client contacts. At a recent district meeting she asked the salary figures of each of the agents to compare with her own income. This request led to a heated debate followed by her isolation by the other agents.

Tony Antal, 48, had recently been demoted from district manager to sales rep. He had mismanaged his sales force in another district, lost 50 percent of his sales force in a two-year period, and some agents accused him of unethical practices. He was resentful and angry and thought David Andrews would try to tell him how to do his job.

Chuck's final words to David were, "You've got a job on your hands. This group's average sales have dropped considerably over the last three years. If I were you, I'd fire most of them and recruit young, bright, more qualified people who want to get ahead. After all, your success in this job is directly tied to their output. They don't put out, and *you're* out!"

Try to place yourself in David's position as some of the more difficult problems he is facing are identified. In this case, David must focus on a unique set of human performance and communication issues that he may or may not have been trained to handle. He does have the good fortune of being able to call on a support staff member in the central office whose job is to help district managers deal with human resource management issues. He must, however, also learn to handle these problems by himself.

Individuals in the organization who are able to assess communication variables effectively and who can design methods for smooth information flow throughout the organization will be the organizational leaders of the future. These individuals may either be in staff positions, like the staff consultant available to David, or may be people like David himself who are in line management positions and have acquired communication skills to deal with human relations problems described in the opening of this chapter. Throughout this text these individuals will be referred to as "communication specialists" or "communication managers." Communication managers spend a great deal of their time dealing with people problems.

Many authors have indicated the importance of controlling information in the organization. As Goldhaber, Dennis, Richetto, and Wiio reported in 1979, ". . . we are experiencing a revolution in which decision-making power is rapidly shifting from traditional decision makers (the line organization) to traditional knowledge workers (the staff organization). We propose that those responsible for interpreting that organizational environment have emerged as the true controllers of the organization and that the future will, if anything, further solidify their organizational power" (p. 4). Later, Goldhaber (1986) again asserted, "Communication is essential to an organization. Information is vital to effective communication. Persons who control information control power" (p. 6).

Clearly, the acquisition and use of organizational information will determine, in large measure, the amount of influence any one individual may have. In other words, the more you know, the more likely it is that you can be effective.

With the advent of new communication technologies, the focus on information power is even more striking. In fact, Everett Rogers suggested this will change the structure and power base of the entire organization. "The new information technologies allow the restructuring and/or de-structuring of organizational communication" (Rogers, 1988, p. 443). Thus, new technologies such as computers increase the importance of information power sources. These information power sources can be anywhere in the organization where individuals are knowledgeable about the flow of messages and can change the system when communication patterns are causing a decrease in organizational effectiveness.

Communication consultants are particularly well-suited to increasing organizational effectiveness because so much is dependent on how well organizational members are able to communicate and use relevant information (Schein, 1985). Thus the process of developing or increasing one's ability to assess and intervene in the communication system can be enhanced by examining the variables involved in organizational communication. It will be easier for David Andrews to build a team among his sales force if he has some idea of the communication process generally.

Organizational Communication and the Communication Manager

Organizational communication has been defined as "The study of the flow and impact of messages within a network of interactional relationships" (Tortoriello, Blatt, & DeWine, 1978, p. 16). The organization is a complex network of relationships in which individuals must make sense of their job tasks. Communication is the process through which that sense-making occurs.

Communication in any environment is an interactional process in which persons share meaning verbally and nonverbally. The communication manager must be very sensitive to the fact that communication is *irreversible, unrepeatable,* and *reciprocal.* Consequently, the communication manager in the organization will understand that once a message has been sent and received, he or she can neither erase the effect of that message nor ever repeat the message in exactly the same way. Because communication is a dynamic, ever-changing process, one can never move backward. Finally, people tend to respond in a manner similar to the way others talk to them. Consequently, the communication process builds on the interaction of two or more people.

For example, I worked with a manager who told her assistant, "You worked out much better than I expected!" The assistant was offended because he felt that meant she did not have a high opinion of him initially. There was no way the manager could take back what she had said; her only course was to listen carefully, demonstrate understanding of the assistant's feelings, and send additional supportive messages. Those first words could not be erased, but they could be neutralized. We are not able to repeat a communication experience. The reciprocal nature of the interaction, with the sender becoming the receiver of feedback, makes the process continuous.

In an **organization** there is a sense of interdependence among members who occupy positions in a hierarchy attempting to achieve common goals. A hierarchy may be quite informal but there is always some division of labor and some sense of who makes the final decisions. In any organization communication is affected by a complex network of individuals within a unique organizational environment. David Andrews' agents are independent salespersons, each with his or her own clients. Yet, they work in an organizational structure and depend on individuals in that structure to provide support services such as a data base for client information, a processing center to handle the policies they sell, adjusters to assess clients' future claims, and a company wisely investing its money so that clients will be covered for losses. They need each other and yet still need to be independent. It is David's job to help them interact effectively.

Organizational communication is the process by which messages are sent, the monitoring of what types of messages are sent, the values associated with those messages, the amount of information conveyed, the rules and norms under which messages are sent, and the organizational variables affecting the process like structure and outcome measures. It is those very structures and outcome variables that make organizational communication different from family communication, for example.

Values are communicated along with the content of a message. For example, the first non-family member to head a small, previously family-owned company unintentionally sent messages that suggested he did not accept the same set of values held by the family. When he did not renew sponsorship of a local Little League baseball team he unwittingly sent a message that he was not interested in the community and the employees' families. Employees saw this as a sign of a "hard-nosed" manager who did not care about their welfare, when quite the opposite was true. Each message we send carries with it a set of values we are communicating.

Communication managers/specialists spend a large portion of their job managing human interactions and developing human potential in the organization. They are information managers in that they monitor the process by which messages are sent and received. Their job title may be the "manager" or "administrator" who has the ability to monitor this process or they are "staff personnel" whose primary job function is to develop human potential in the organization. They also work with managers to develop their potential for solving human communication problems. David Andrews is a communication manager. There may also be an individual in the corporate office in a staff position who is responsible for developing human resources. "The consultant must work jointly with the manager so that the manager can learn to see the problem for him- or herself, share in the diagnosis and be actively involved in creating a solution" (Coghlan, 1988, p. 27). Andrews must work closely with any staff personnel provided by the company to assist with human resources.

Application of Organizational Communication Principles

In the opening case, a number of communication issues are present. Individual goals seem to be in opposition to group goals, causing defensive communication, information overload, isolates in communication networks, and motivational problems. In addition, violations of communication rules and climate norms have caused tension among the staff members.

The process of assessing the impact of such variables, and developing programs for improving the communication process, is the focus of this book. In later chapters, effective methods for determining what communication variables are disrupting the exchange of messages between persons in the organization will be identified. A communication manager or consultant needs these skills to enter or intervene in the system and create change.

Intervention

The term **intervention** refers to an action taken by an individual or group of persons, designed to interrupt and change some ongoing human process. For example, one staff I worked with had established a pattern of behavior in the office that was very cold and unresponsive. They did not talk to each other informally or even greet one another. In order to "intervene" and change that process, I asked that every staff member go out of his or her way each morning to greet every other co-worker.

Attitudes follow behavior. I believe you must change behavior first, and then attitudes. This simple suggestion obviously did not solve all the interpersonal problems plaguing this group, but it began a process where people paid more attention to the way they dealt with each other. It was an attempt to *intervene* in the system and begin the change process.

In the case of David Andrews, one intervention was suggested: fire and rehire. In one sense, the manager then loses two valuable components—the time invested in training these individuals, and their present knowledge of the company and its product. Sometimes this loss is less damaging than the potentially negative impact the individual might have on the system. The manager might also choose to ignore the problem under the belief that the best way to help people is to get out of their way and let them solve it themselves.

Another solution may be for the manager to restructure job responsibilities so that those who are capable of handling larger responsibilities are given increased assignments, and those less capable are isolated so that their impact is minimized. Communication managers look at the total system and how human communication is presently operating. After carefully assessing communication needs, they design and implement intervention strategies to combat nonproductive behavior.

Assessment

In the case of David Andrews the organizational communication manager (who might be David himself, an internal staff member, or an outside consultant) would assess the flow of communication among the agents using a number of techniques and instruments described in later chapters. For example, a communication audit might be administered. A **communication audit** can determine where communication problems exist and is similar to a financial audit in that each one uses a battery of techniques and instruments (see Chapter 7 for further discussion of audits).

A communication audit might identify problems of several staff members in communicating within the group. Chris Rand, for example, is suffering from information overload. He is an individual who evidently has exceeded his tolerance level of information he can effectively process. A communication manager would work with Chris to give him some specific techniques for handling information more effectively.

As an example, David might identify for Chris the types of information that are most important and, regardless of any other items that come to him, must be handled first. Chris also needs to learn how to delegate tasks and allow someone else to handle some assignments.

A communication manager might suggest ways in which a person who has little interaction with the core group in an organization could be integrated more successfully. Some recognition of Larry Johnson's "distance" problems might make him willing to travel to the main office more frequently. If the central staff makes an effort to have contact with him in his own territory, their action will more likely be reciprocated.

Nita Whitberg is an example of a person who breaks communication rules or norms. By asking publicly for information that normally is not discussed openly (salaries and wages), she has unwittingly caused others to mistrust her. In this case, David needs to make better use of Mike Thompson's years of experience. If David were able to match a person with a lot of experience about the way in which "things get done in this organization" with a new employee, one who needs to be socialized into the organization's unique interaction patterns, he would be accomplishing two things. One, he would be establishing a role model for Nita, who is new to the organization, and two, he would be "retrieving" some of Mike's expertise that is currently being lost to the organization.

Another likely mentor for Nita is Jake Miller, who gets along well with other organizational members. A communication network analysis might reveal that Jake interacts with other agents on a regular basis and gets most of his information about new insurance benefits from them. It might also reveal that he serves mainly in the role of liaison, in that he links most agents to each other. David could develop some new channels of communication that would allow Nita more access to this network through Jake.

David definitely needs to do some staff development and make better use of resources available to him. Janet Curry is the most successful agent. Working with Janet to become a part of the staff development program as a trainer/coordinator would make better use of her skill and help others to learn from her.

Tony Antal would appear to be David's most difficult individual. There seem to be questions about his ethical standards and the way in which he has handled business in the past. If David were going to fire anyone Tony would probably be his first choice. On the other hand, Tony has yet to be fired by the central office, which indicates to David that the conclusion about his previous behavior has not been entirely negative. Some of the techniques discussed later in the book may well give the communication manager help in assessing the depth of this particular problem. It is certainly one that needs his immediate attention.

In essence, communication managers recognize that "information is power" and the ability to successfully handle important messages in the organization will increase an individual's visibility. Training others to handle communication problems will also enable the communication manager to have greater control over organizational outcomes.

Communication managers also recognize that there are *no simple answers when dealing with human behavior.* Communication managers can only *provide choices* and generate a better understanding of *probable consequences* of our actions. When I actually worked with the individuals presented in the case study, changes occurred only after a complex assessment process. Specific assessment processes will be covered in the next several chapters.

▋ *Skills Needed by the Communication Manager*

Within an organization, communication managers need people-oriented skills with a focus on human resource development. Huse (1980) articulated this focus when he talked about the organizational development manager. If one replaces the phrases "organizational development consulting" and "change agent" with "communication manager," the emphasis remains the same:

> Certainly, OD [Organizational Development] consulting is as much a person specialization as a task specialization. The change agent must not only have a repertoire of technical skills but must also have the personality and interpersonal competence to be able to use himself or herself as an instrument of change. Regardless of technical training and/or accreditation, the consultant must be able to maintain a boundary position, coordinating be-

tween various units and departments and mixing disciplines, theories, technology, and research findings in an organic rather than mechanical way. The practitioner is potentially the most important OD technology available (p. 452).

Eight Principal Skills

To be successful with human resource management, communication managers must have eight skills. These skills enhance an individual's interpersonal competence (Huse, 1980).

First, communication managers must be *eclectic* in that they choose from a number of "systems" or "doctrines." In this sense, the effective communication manager does not have one way of working with people, but instead is sensitive to the needs and values of others. Effective managers choose from a variety of styles that will mesh best with those around them. This is not to say that individuals can change their basic personality structures as they move from group to group in the organization. Communication managers, however, need to have a contingency style of communication and make modest adaptations to the situation.

Second, communication managers must see themselves as *facilitators* of change. In this way, they assist or help the change process but may not serve as the agent of change. They prod where necessary and "back out" of the system when their presence would inhibit action taking.

Third, communication managers must be *situational experts.* This means they must be able to develop new problem-solving strategies that are generated *out of the situation* rather than being predetermined. Managers must be "tuned in" to the needs and special issues being expressed in each situation, and creative enough to be able to adapt human development processes to the particular needs of that setting.

Fourth, communication managers must have *assessment* skills. They must have at their disposal survey methodologies, interview and observational techniques, and other tools for assessing the communication system at work, and they must know which tools will be most effective in a particular situation. In order to improve the communication system one must have a good understanding of how communication presently flows throughout the organization.

Fifth, communication managers must be a cross between *process managers* and *lay technicians.* To monitor the process effectively, managers must have a good understanding of the technical components. This does not mean that they are skilled technicians, but they should have a lay-man's comprehensive understanding of how various technical compo-nents unite in the system to affect the whole.

Sixth, communication managers must be able to *identify internal re-sources.* If the "natural resources" of the organization are not utilized, then the organization is not able to develop human potential on its own. Com-munication managers must be keenly aware of expertise among organiza-tional members that may have not been tapped.

A seventh, very important characteristic for managers is the ability to *network* throughout the system. In this capacity, communication managers must have a good sense of what they do and do not know, as well as the ability to create a network among other managers and using resources un-covered in the system. This helps to establish a support system through-out the organization that will help human development processes con-tinue to be productive.

The eighth skill requires that communication managers must recog-nize when a part of the system no longer needs their continuous support and assistance, and when termination of the relationship with either a subunit or a system is appropriate. Communication managers who con-tinue to be facilitators when the group or unit has taken over those func-tions on its own can be destructive to the process.

Communication managers are always training organizational mem-bers to take over the job they are doing at any one time. We can summa-rize these abilities by saying a **communication manager** must be:

An eclectic practitioner

A facilitator

A situational expert

An assessor

A process specialist/lay technician

A resource identifier

A network developer/user

A temporary associate

The consultant may have all these characteristics and still not be suc-cessful unless the organization is supportive and the consultant is per-ceived as credible.

To test your ability to recognize these skills in yourself, a self-assess-ment checklist has been developed for your use (see Form 1.1). As you begin to "assess" your own capabilities and improve/increase your abil-

■ **SELF-ASSESSMENT CHECKLIST FOR ORGANIZATIONAL COMMUNICATION SPECIALISTS**

Mark each statement on a scale of 1 to 5 in terms of how characteristic that quality is of the way in which you behave in the organizational setting.

1	2	3	4	5
not at all characteristic	occasionally characteristic	neutral	somewhat characteristic	very characteristic

1. _____ I tend to use a contingency style of leadership, meaning I use whatever style is most appropriate for the group or individuals involved.

2. _____ I am most often a *facilitator* of change rather than causing change to come about or operating on my own.

3. _____ I am most comfortable creating new approaches to problem-solving from the situation itself rather than planning what method to use prior to identifying the level and depth of the problem.

4. _____ I have the skills necessary to assess the communication system within the organization. I know what instruments to use to collect what type of data and can successfully analyze that data so that recommendations can be generated.

5. _____ I have enough technical knowledge of the organizational system so that I can understand the language of the system and can relate my knowledge to their specific technical problems.

6. _____ I am a process manager in that I am extremely sensitive to the *way* in which things are accomplished in the organization. I am able to process for others how interactions are conducted.

7. _____ I have a good ability to assess what I don't know and can successfully link others to resources that may be useful to solving their problem when I am unable to help myself.

8. _____ I am able to identify internal resources for a group so that they can make the best use of the human potential available to them.

9. _____ I have a knowledge of intervention techniques that can be used to improve communication once problem areas have been identified.

10. _____ I can recognize when I am no longer needed by the system or unit of the system and am sensitive to smooth termination of

(Continued)

■ **SELF-ASSESSMENT CHECKLIST FOR ORGANIZATIONAL COMMUNICATION SPECIALISTS** *(Continued)*

that working relationship while still allowing for follow-up on my part and a continuation of internal support system on their part.

A *score of 45–50* indicates that you perceive that you possess these skills to an extensive degree. Your next step is to check with others to determine if their perception of your skills in these areas matches your own.

A *score of 35–44* indicates an above average perception of demonstration of communication manager skills. You need to identify those areas most in need of development and concentrate your efforts there.

A *score of below 35* indicates a low perception of communication manager skills. The fact that you are reading this textbook is an indication of your attempt to increase these skills or it may also be an indication that you don't feel these skills are necessary to the communication manager. As you continue to read, attempt to apply these skills to yourself and your own particular working environment. Use those skills and techniques that seem most useful and effective in that particular environment.

If these are skills you are just learning, a low score should be expected. Return to this self-assessment after you have finished the book.

ity to work as a communication manager, this knowledge of the "status quo" will help you determine what areas to work with first.

Activities of Communication Managers

Farace, Monge, and Russell (1977) have developed an interesting outline of actual activities that are typical of the communication manager's job in the organization. These activities include:

- interacting with other managers to develop communication strategies and policies.
- supervising the planning and production of internal and external communication programs.
- devising communication programs for organizational units to facilitate production.
- modifying and expanding the job-performance appraisal system to reflect communication skills.
- preparing manuals outlining policies and procedures and developing and implementing communication training programs.

These are all programs that can be developed and implemented by an internal communication manager with or without the help of external managers. *External communication managers* are experts in the field of communication who are not a part of the organizational system but who come into the system on a temporary basis to assist with some specific communication program.

There are advantages and disadvantages to both internal and external communication managers. A discussion of some of the approaches taken by both internal and external communication managers will help clarify the roles for each.

Internal and External Communication Specialists: A Comparison

Communication managers may be permanent members of the organization working internally or are external consultants called in to provide expertise which the company is lacking. Both roles have several things in common aside from their focus on the management of human resources.

Common Factors

First, *both the internal and external communication managers must work with others who are a permanent part of the system.* They need access to information sources and rules and norms under which communication normally occurs.

Second, *both can be called in or imposed on* the organizational members by forces outside those immediate groups. As a consequence, they can both sometimes suffer from individuals' perceptions that they are "spies" for upper management, especially if there is mistrust between upper management and the group with whom the consultants are working. After all, if upper management hired this person to work with the group, that person must have been told what to look for, they reason. It will be important for both the internal and external communication manager to establish a high level of trust with the client members.

Third, *both will need to play multiple roles* and may need to shift from time to time from trainer to advocate to planner. The ability to be flexible in a variety of contexts is critical for the communication manager. Finally, *both want to be successful!*

Differences between Internal and External Consultants

The major advantage for internal managers is that they have *quicker and easier access to sources of information* within the system. They already know much about the communication system and how it works. At the same time, this knowledge may bias their outlook. Someone from outside, who is not a part of the permanent system, can be *more objective* and is able to look at a situation without considering how the situation is currently affecting her or his own daily work environment. Internal managers may well be a part of the problem and cannot view it without letting their biases affect the eventual outcome.

A second major difference between the external and internal communication manager is that the *internal manager must live with any changes* made in the system, while the external manager can walk away from the situation. This may make the internal manager more cautious.

The perception the organizational members have of both internal and external managers may be both positive and negative. On the one hand, the *internal manager is a known quantity*, while the external manager's ability to work with the group may be untested.

At the same time, this very familiarity of the internal manager often leads *organizational members to view external consultants as having more skills and expertise* and thus credit them with more ability to deal with problems.

An internal manager having the same skills and expertise may be so familiar to the organizational members that his or her abilities and attributes may, at times, be taken for granted. As Lippitt and Lippitt (1986) point out, "Familiarity can lead the client system to stereotyped preconceptions of the inside consultant's particular responses, which may be quite incorrect" (p. 19).

Because the outsider is seen as the expert with no "stake" in the outcome, organizational members may be more open about what issues are unresolved than they will be with the insider. This may create high expectations for the outsider as the "savior." If the organization expects the outsider to "save" the company, an inappropriate dependency may result. After all, if the outsider is that critical to the daily operation of the company, then perhaps additional staff with those skills should be added to the organization permanently, rather than on a short-term basis.

One organization I worked with had a consultant fly in every Friday morning, direct a two-hour workshop, and fly out that same afternoon. They were paying $5,000 a week for this two-hour session. He had been doing this same workshop every Friday for 18 months. It finally dawned on the client that they no longer needed to depend on this outside consultant for the Friday workshops and over the 18 months they had developed the expertise among their own staff to conduct the workshop themselves!

Because of internal managers' permanent link to the organization, their ability to control the involvement of others, particularly individuals higher in the hierarchy, is quite limited. An *external manager* sometimes has *greater power to get others involved* in the intervention process to improve communication systems.

> It is more difficult for the inside consultant [or communication manager] to request the participation of high power figures in the client system and the involvement of parts of the system that are uncommitted but crucial. The outside consultant often has great leverage with respect to involvement (Lippitt and Lippitt, 1986, p. 28).

The final stages of assessing and improving a particular unit or portion of the communication system involves the evaluation of the intervention and termination or de-escalation of the process. An *internal manager has a better opportunity to observe firsthand the impact of the intervention used* and to evaluate its success. If changes in the communication system occur as a result of the assessment and intervention processes, an internal manager is more likely to be aware of that change than the external manager who has removed him- or herself from the environment.

At the same time, because an *external manager* can leave the scene,

there is *a much smoother and more defined termination stage* with the organizational members who have been directly involved in one part of the
assessment/intervention communication process. The working relationship that the internal manager has with all other organizational members may constantly have to be redefined as he or she moves throughout
the organization assessing various component parts of the communication system. Figure 1.1 summarizes the advantages and disadvantages
of both the internal and external communication manager in the organization.

Preferences for External or Internal Assistance

Spechler and Wicker (1980) supported the need for and use of internal
consultants. They referred to these internal change agents as "internal
consulting groups," and identified several ingredients which they said
must be present in order for such managers to succeed in the organization.

First, *support from top management must be evident.* Top management
must be willing to commit time, money, interest, and resources to change

Internal Communication Specialist		External Communication Specialist
+	Knowledge of client system	−
−	Objectivity	+
−	Greater flexibility due to low impact of problem on daily routine	+
+	Known quantity	−
−	Seen as valuable resource	+
+	Leverage with respect to involvement	−
+	Access to evaluation and success intervention	−
−	Smooth termination	+

FIGURE 1.1   Pluses and Minuses for the Internal and External Organizational Communication Specialist

efforts. Without support from the top of the hierarchy, the chance that an effort for change will be successful is significantly reduced, and in many cases rendered impossible.

Second, *internal managers* in human resources management *must have a broad-based scope and mission* including some of the following activities:

> . . . to provide data for use by management in planning, directing coordinating, and controlling the enterprise; to conduct or coordinate studies needed by management in the formulation of policies and long-range plans; to assist management in developing and implementing policies; to assist management in establishing sound organizational plans, including objectives, functions, responsibilities, authorities, and relationships; and to recommend, coordinate, and perform the analysis, planning, design, and installation of the systems (Spechler and Wicker, 1980, p. 27).

For communication managers, these activities would all have some relationship to human resources development.

Third, Spechler and Wicker also stated the *internal manager must be located on the organization charts* so that the operating management has a great sense of control over the change process. Where the consulting group is located on organization charts will be an indication of how seriously top management takes its function.

Fourth, there *must be a "change orientation"* within the organization, which means organizational members must be willing to look at themselves critically and adopt new systems if necessary. In addition, the internal managers *must be professionally qualified* and willing to maintain a *continuous education of themselves.* Spechler and Wicker pointed out such managers may be seen as a threat and thus will need to sell their programs by using a well-developed marketing program. There must be an *emphasis on performance measurement* since these specialties could be a great aid to the organization in developing a strong performance appraisal system. Often these conditions do not exist and while that may prevent overall company change programs, individual consulting can be done with less-than-ideal support.

Finally, the organization must be *willing to evaluate the success* of the internal managers' programs based on an analysis of the costs and benefits of the work performed. This evaluation should be a part of the design from the very first step so that every stage of the process can be included.

It should be obvious from the previous discussion that both the internal and external communication managers have the potential for advantages and disadvantages associated with their particular role. This text and the techniques and materials discussed can be used effectively by individuals in either of these two roles.

It is my personal belief that in order to mitigate the negative results of either role, and to magnify the positive attributes of both, an internal/external communication manager *team* should be developed whenever possible. This requires the internal communication manager to be continually aware of those outside the organizational system who might be helpful in developing specific communication assessment/intervention programs. Communication managers, both internal or external to the organization, need a variety of skills to make their job more likely to have successful outcomes.

Because of the communication explosion of the last 25 years, organizations are realizing that their own communication is big business. Many top level executives believe if business is to survive and enhance public opinion, it must have the capability to respond effectively. How well a company meets its communication needs determines not only its public image, but also the bottom line on its annual reports. Top level management is beginning to understand the need for devoting as much careful attention to internal and external communication as they devote to product management and capital investment. Successful executives are developing a new awareness of the need for industry to communicate with many more elements of society than ever before. They also recognize the vital role that communication plays in the day-to-day management of a company. Once there is widespread recognition of the need to communicate effectively to influence the public and political climate in which business operates, the communication manager's position will be even more critical to the functioning of the organization.

Note

1. The names have been changed to protect the privacy of the people involved.

▌ *Suggested Readings*

Daniels, T., & Spiker, B. (1991). *Perspectives on organizational communication* (2nd ed.). Dubuque, IA: Wm. C. Brown.

Farace, R. V., Monge, P. R., & Russell, H. M. (1977). *Communicating and organizing.* Reading, MA: Addison-Wesley Publishing Co., Inc.

Jablin, F. M., Putnam, L. L., Roberts, K. H., & Porter, L. W. (1987). *Handbook of organizational communication: An interdisciplinary perspective.* Newbury Park, CA: Sage.

Lippitt, G., & Lippitt, R. (1986). *The consulting process in action* (2nd ed.). San Diego, CA: University Associates.

Chapter 2

WHAT ARE TRAINING AND CONSULTING?

Some Definitions

- ■■ **HELPING PROFESSIONS**
- ■■ **TRAINING SKILLS**
- ■■ **CONSULTING SKILLS**
  Definitions of Consulting
  Approaches to Consultation

". . revenues for the traditional core of the [management consulting] business . . . have reached $10 billion annually and are growing more than 20% a year in the U.S. and even faster overseas. That's just for appetizers."

Anne Fisher, 1989, Fortune

"In 1986 IBM discovered it was spending $900 million a year on employee education and training . . ."

Patricia A. Galagan, 1989,
Training and Development Journal

*H*uman resource training and consulting are big business. The reason is that managers probably spend more time coping with human relationships and individual behavior problems than they do making decisions about company policies, system maintenance, and organizational outcome issues related to products and services. These human relationships are the core of the organization. Without strong working relationships the company cannot exist. Training and consulting, as discussed in this book, refer to ways in which human behavior can be modified both from inside the organization, by managers, and from outside the organization, by external consultants.

◼ Helping Professions

Training and consulting are part of the helping professions. Teaching and counseling are other examples of helping professions. All four focus on assisting others to function more effectively in their personal and professional lives. A comparison of the four will clarify the unique focus for training and consulting.

Training is the direct delivery of skills, through some formal process, to enhance human performance. These skills can be technical knowledge applied to the organization's product or service or human relationship skills applied to working with, and directing the work of, others.

23

Consulting is entering into a system (or intervening) to stop the progression of some destructive human process and to improve the ability of the organization to function. The destructive process may be affecting the organization's ability to produce quality products, provide prompt services, or function without high turnover and disputes.

Both of these activities (training and consulting) can be delivered by internal employees or external trainers/consultants. The activities of both can be adapted by internal managers as well. Parts Two, Three, and Four of this book will provide specific techniques and suggestions that could be used by anyone facing human relationship problems in the organization and wishing to improve its general work climate. Individuals actively working on human relationship issues and becoming skilled at managing communication issues will be referred to as "communication managers."

Figure 2.1 provides a comparison of training and consulting to various other types of helping activities. It is critical for the communication manager to understand how the focus shifts, who is involved in the process, how psychological distance changes, and if expectations increase depending on the type of help being presented.

As helping professions, consulting, training, teaching, and counseling all focus on human behavior and attempt to enhance individual performance. While they have these things in common they also differ in dramatic ways so that the process of each is quite different.

Focus is the specific aspect of human behavior the communication manager is addressing. A communication manager may be a teacher, a

Theoretical issue	Consulting	Training	Teaching	Counseling
Focus	issue	skills	knowledge	people
Number of players	3 or more	3 or more	2	2
Distance	distant	sometimes close sometimes distant	sometimes close sometimes distant	close
Follow-up	constant	not responsible	not responsible	sometimes occurs, sometimes doesn't
Definition of problems	together	client defines	teacher defines	sometimes client sometimes counselor
Focus of problems	work-related	work/personal	personal	personal
Entry issues	great	minimal	medium	great

FIGURE 2.1   The Training/Teaching Matrix

counselor, a trainer, or a consultant. A *teacher* is trying to enhance the *knowledge* level of the students; a *counselor* wants to help an individual cope with *emotional stress*; a *trainer* is *imparting skills* so that a job can be completed more competently; and a *consultant* is assisting individuals to address *work issues* that when resolved will result in better performance and a more positive organizational climate.

The *number of players* changes across these various activities. Consulting and training involve at least three people: the trainer/consultant, the participant, and the individual(s) with whom the participant is working. Usually the goal of training and consulting is to help individuals work more effectively with others and to pass along the skills learned so that the performance of those they work with may be improved as well. For example, a training session for managers on time management ultimately is designed to have the managers not only improve their own time management skills but to assist those they manage to do the same. Teaching and counseling involve a more direct delivery of help with just two people directly involved: the teacher/counselor and the person receiving the help or education. Although the teacher usually lectures to a group of 15–40, the relationship is between that teacher and each individual student in the class.

Psychological distance determines how intense and intimate the relationship may get. Counseling is the most interpersonally intense of all the helping activities. Because the counselor and the client are dealing with emotional and personal issues, the process is necessarily a direct connection between the counselor and client. The intensity of this relationship may cause clients to transfer some of their emotional reactions to the situations they find themselves in, to inappropriate feelings of closeness to the counselor.

Teaching and training involve a mixture of more and less distance between the helper and the person being helped. In both cases there are times when the trainer and teacher are imparting knowledge, and the psychological distance is great. There are also times when both the trainer and the teacher are asked to assist an individual to improve his or her performance and, in working with the individual, the teacher or trainer may uncover personal problems preventing the person from performing well.

In consulting, the relationship is usually more distant since the consultant is assisting with the resolution of problems that will involve many others beyond those with whom the consultant has direct contact. Often, the consultant is helping the teacher or the trainer determine how to cope with the issues raised by the individuals with whom they must work!

The *follow-up* expected of the trainer and teacher is low. It is expected that the individual who is trained is responsible for her or his own learning and usually the teacher or trainer is not expected to follow up on the day-to-day use of that knowledge. In sharp contrast, the consultant is often hired especially to follow up on problem solving and to determine how effectively managers are applying solutions to problems. The counselor does not own the problem; however, his or her involvement in the solution is a mixture of direct and indirect. On a continuum from follow-up being expected to no follow-up at all, the consultant would be placed on the high end of the continuum, the teacher and trainer on the low end, and the counselor in the middle.

Who defines the problem can be a very important determination to make early in the relationship. In training, the client usually defines the problem. A trainer is asked to develop a workshop on supervisory skills and does so. In this case the client has determined that supervisory skills need to be improved. Even when the trainer conducts a needs analysis, this assessment is very abbreviated compared to the problem assessment conducted by the consultant. In fact, often the client and the consultant together focus their entire effort on identifying problems. The teacher is similar to the trainer in that one person defines the problem, only in this case it is the teacher. The teacher, in consultation with state, district, and school guidelines, determines what material will be covered in each class setting.

Depending on the type of counseling being conducted, there may be a mixture of client/counselor definition of problems. For example, a counselor using the approach developed by Sigmund Freud, which was very analytical in nature, would define the problem without collaboration with the client. "Psychoanalysis" is a system of psychology which stresses the unconscious and requires the counselor to analyze for the client what the problems may be. A counselor following the approach developed by Alfred Adler would define the problems in consultation with the client. "Adlerian Psychology" is a personality theory in which "two equals cooperatively tackle the education task" (Mosak & Dreikurs, 1973, p. 74). Finally, a counselor using Carl Rogers' approach of acceptance and supportiveness would help the client to define the problem him- or herself. "Client-Centered Psychology" has as its central hypothesis that "the growthful potential of any individual will tend to be released in a relationship in which the helping person is experiencing and communicating realness, caring and a deeply sensitive nonjudgement understanding" (Meador & Rogers, 1973, p. 119).

Another significant difference is the *nature of the problem*. In counseling the nature of the problem is personal; in consulting it is work-related. If a consultant finds the client pursuing personal issues, the consultant should refer the individual to a counselor or focus on only those aspects of the personal issue that affect work performance. Both training and teaching may be a mixture of the two however, neither should be acting as psychological counselors unless specifically trained to do so.

Finally, *entry issues* may vary depending on the needs of each situation. Entry issues are those questions that come up during the very first encounter with the client or the persons with whom the manager is working. Since the trainer is usually with the participants for a short time, entry issues are minimal and mostly relate to building credibility so the skills that are delivered will be accepted. The teacher is with the student for a longer period of time, and thus must build credibility over a period of weeks in order to maintain interest. Since the counselor deals with emotional personal issues, and the consultant addresses sensitive organizational problems, both must spend a great deal of time building the trust level of the client so that the client will be open and share information necessary to aid diagnosis. Knowing these differences, individuals engaged in training and/or consulting must possess certain unique skills. These unique skills are examined in the rest of this chapter.

■ Training Skills

There are specific kinds of skills needed for a director of training that vary from consulting skills. One of the best sources to identify those skills is the American Society for Training and Development (ASTD). In November of 1981, the National ASTD Professional Development Committee and the ASTD National Board of Directors commissioned the ASTD Training and Development Competency Study. The charge of the study was "to produce a detailed and updated definition of excellence in the training and development field in a form that will be useful to and used as a standard of professional performance and development" (McLagan, 1983, p. 2). "After consulting with numerous experts and ASTD committees, one of the products of the study was a definition of training which is the following: Identifying, assessing, and through planned learning, helping develop the key competencies which enable individuals to perform current or future jobs" (McLagan, p. 25).

Thirty-one competencies were identified for the training professional (McLagan, 1983, pp. 38–68). Those competencies were:

1. *Adult learning understanding*—knowing how adults acquire and use knowledge, skills, and attitudes. Understanding individual differences in learning.

2. *AV skill*—selecting and using audio/visual hardware and software.

3. *Career development knowledge*—understanding the personal and organizational issues relevant to individual careers.

4. *Competency identification skills*—identifying the knowledge and skill requirements of jobs and tasks.

5. *Computer competence*—understanding and being able to use computers.

6. *Cost benefit analysis skill*—assessing alternatives in terms of their financial and strategic advantages and disadvantages.

7. *Consulting skill*—helping individuals recognize and understand personal needs, problems, alternatives, and goals.

8. *Data reduction skill*—scanning, synthesizing, and drawing conclusions from data.

9. *Delegation skill*—assigning task responsibility and authority to others.

10. *Facility skill*—planning and coordinating logistics in a cost-effective manner.

11. *Feedback skill*—communicating opinions, observations, and conclusions so that they are understood.

12. *Futuring skill*—projecting trends and visualizing possible futures and their implications.

13. *Group process skill*—influencing groups to both accomplish tasks and fulfill the needs of their members.

14. *Industry understanding*—knowing the key concepts and variables that define an industry or sector (i.e., critical issues, economic variables, inputs, outputs, and information sources).

15. *Intellectual versatility*—recognizing, exploring, and using a broad range of ideas and practices. Thinking logically and creatively without undo influence from personal biases.

16. *Library skill*—gathering information from printed and other recorded sources. Identifying and using information specialists and reference services and aids.

17. *Model-building skills*—developing theoretical and practical frameworks which describe complex ideas in understandable, useful ways.

18. *Negotiation skill*—promoting win-win arguments while successfully representing a special interest in a decision situation.

19. *Objectives preparation skill*—preparing clear statements which describe desired outputs.

20. *Organization behavior understanding*—seeing organizations as dynamic, political, economic, and social systems which have multiple goals; using this larger prospective as a framework for understanding and influencing events and changes.

21. *Organization understanding*—knowing the strategy, structure, power networks, and financial position of the specific organization.

22. *Performance observation skills*—tracking and describing behaviors and their effects.

23. *Personnel—HR field understanding*—understanding issues and practices in other HR areas (organization development, organization job design, human resource planning, selection and staffing, personnel research and information systems, compensation and benefits, employee assistance, labor-union relationships).

24. *Presentation skills*—orally presenting information so the intended purpose is achieved.

25. *Questioning skill*—gathering information from and stimulating insight into individuals and groups through the use of interviews, questionnaires, and other probing methods.

26. *Records management skill*—storing data in an easily retrievable form.

27. *Relationship versatility*—adjusting behavior in order to establish relationships across a broad range of people and groups.

28. *Research skills*—selecting, developing, and using methodologies for data collection and analysis.

29. *Training and development field understanding*—knowing the technological, social, economic, professional, and regulatory issues in the field; understanding the role Training and Development (TD) plays in helping individuals learn from current and future jobs.

30. *Training and development technique understanding*—knowing the techniques and methods used in training; understanding their appropriate uses.

31. *Writing skills*—preparing written material which follows generally accepted rules of style and form, is appropriate for the audience, [is] creative, and [which] accomplishes its intended purpose.

These skills are needed by both the trainer and the consultant. These actions are referred to as "interventions." Entering into an ongoing process and causing change to occur is intervening. An *intervention* is a specific technique used by the trainer or consultant to cause that change to occur.

Redding (1979) identified two ends of a continuum of consulting interventions. At one extreme are those things classified as training which are specific, technical, hands-on skills. At the other end are those things categorized as consulting, which are broad-based, conceptual skills. The first type of intervention includes assisting with the improvement of an organizational in-house publication, or presenting a workshop or seminar to improve specific skills. Redding suggested these activities fall under the skills-oriented area of human resource development.

The second type of intervention includes working on organizational problems such as conflict between line and staff, communication climate, or the development of an employee communication program. As Rudolph and Johnson (1983) pointed out, "Even though Redding's approaches categorize consulting into two neat packages, obviously times exist when consulting activities shift along the continuum from one area to another. An employee's attitude survey, for example, could be identified as an intervention step in an organizational development project rather than an activity in the skills areas of human resource development" (p. 2). While skills may shift from one end of the continuum to the other, consulting has its own unique set of behaviors and activities.

Consulting Skills

Previously, consulting was defined as intervening into an organization to stop some destructive process. In addition, consulting is a *temporary helping process* that should be *voluntary* and focuses on solving a *work-related human or organizational problem*. The key words in that definition are "temporary" meaning consulting is not a permanent part of the organizational life, "helping" since it is essentially a problem-solving process, "voluntary" meaning people should not be required to participate as a condition of employment, and "work-related" suggesting that it focuses on work rather than personal issues.

Definitions of Consulting

Lippitt and Lippitt (1986) defined consulting as "A two-way interaction process of seeking, giving, and receiving help aimed at aiding a person, group, organization, or larger system mobilizing internal and external resources to deal with problem confrontations and change efforts" (p. 1). This definition attaches significance to the internal as well as external resources that are available and the need to draw upon those resources to solve problems for the organization.

Rudolph and Johnson (1983) identified the difference between organizational development and human resource development. Organizational development deals in the broadest context with the totality of planning, organizing, leading, and controlling compared to human resource development, which is more narrowly focused dealing with the functions of a manager from a situation-oriented, technical, educational, and/or problem-solving perspective. They suggested "Communication consulting is most often viewed as a component of human resource development even though dealing with the management process. The primary job of the communication consultant is to apply communication principles and concepts to specific situations as one means of helping the organization meet its objectives relative to its human resources" (p. 5).

To focus on communication specifically as a consulting activity may be ignoring a great deal of potential data, or it may mean centering the activity on that which is most important to all other actions. Goldhaber (1986) suggested that communication consulting is part of the larger area of organizational development while Pace and Faules (1989) discussed human resource development and suggested that this is really the area for communication consulting. Pace's position is more narrowly focused.

The perspective of this book is articulated in Daniels and DeWine (1991). That treatise clearly identified communication as the central activity of organizational processes. " . . . power, leadership, and all the other requisite variables with which consultants work are created and sustained in the language and discourse of organization members" (p. 2). Katz and Kahn (1978) added to this conclusion when they suggested, "Communication is the very essence of a social system or organization" (p. 428). Thus, from my perspective, the manager, consultant, trainer, or communication manager who attempts to change human behavior does so by using communication as both the tool to intervene and the target of the change effort. Communication becomes both the tool and the target for solving human problems. An examination of approaches to consultation is appropriate, starting with communication as the central activity in human resource development.

Approaches to Consultation

Sherwood (1981) identified two approaches to consultation: 1) The client presents the consultant with a problem for solution, to which the consultant provides a recommended solution or alternatives; and 2) The client asks the consultant to both define the problem and to offer recommended solutions. Sherwood suggested this latter case is the *physician's* approach: a client presents a set of symptoms and the consultant must first make a diagnosis and then prescribe a remedy. Rather than either of these approaches, Sherwood recommends a collaborative approach to organizational consultation where the organization, not the boss, is the client in all the following phases.

1. Identification of problems.
2. Conceiving solutions or actions.
3. Implementation.
4. Follow-up.

"To say that the organization is the client means that the consultant works together with the boss to define a meaningful organizational unit, one that includes the boss, with which the consultant will work" (p. 5).

Sherwood goes on to point out that traditional approaches to consulting often assume that the client has already effectively identified the problem or that it is the consultant's responsibility to decide the nature of the problem. In a collaborative approach, the consultant works with the client to arrive at a joint understanding of problems facing the organization. He reminds us that consultation must remain a management responsibility.

Lippitt and Lippitt (1986) defined the consultation relationship as a voluntary relationship between a professional helper and a help-needing system, in which the consultant is attempting to give help to the client in the solving of some current or potential problem, and the relationship is perceived as temporary by both parties. Also, the consultant is an outsider, and not a part of any hierarchical power system in which the client is located (p. 17). Lippitt and Lippitt identified seven stages of the consulting relationship:

1. Developing a need for change.
2. Establishing a consulting relationship.
3. Clarifying the client problem.
4. Examining alternative solutions and goals.
5. Transforming intentions into actual change efforts.
6. Generalizing or stabilizing a new level of functioning or group structure.
7. Achieving a terminal relationship with the consultant and a continuity of change ability (p. 19).

These stages help prepare the consultant for demands in the development of the consulting relationship.

Writers often refer to organization development (OD) as the major focus of consulting activities. OD is concerned with increasing the competence and health of an entire organizational system or subsystem. It typically involves diagnosis of organizational problems and implementation of meaningful and lasting organizational change. In the course of stimulating organizational change OD specialists may call upon different intervention strategies such as team building, career planning, process consultation, and role analysis (see French & Bell, 1990).

OD differs from training and development in that the latter is concerned primarily with improving the self-awareness, skills, and motivation of individual organizational members. Although an OD effort might involve employee development, it would do so only as a part of its larger objective of improving the competence of the units comprising the total organization (Deckhard, 1969). Some of the intervention techniques that are used by OD specialists are also used by trainers for developing individual managers (Wexley & Latham, 1981, p. 9).

The strategies used by trainers are discussed in Chapter 6 and those used by consultants in Chapter 7. I began this chapter by contrasting training and consulting with two other helping processes: teaching and counseling. Skills needed by trainers and approaches to consulting help identify when each of these activities is most appropriate.

Since this book is directed toward the communication manager, either as an internal or external helper, and as a trainer or consultant, we need to explore the specific career options and activities of such a position next, in Chapter 3.

■ Suggested Readings

American Society for Training and Development. (1988). *Practical guide for technical and skills trainers: Vol. 1 & 2.* Alexandria, VA: American Society for Training and Development.

Blake, R. R., & Mouton, J. (1989). *Consultation* (2nd ed.). Reading, MA: Addison-Wesley Publishing Co. Inc.

Lippitt, G., & Lippitt, R. (1986). *The consulting process in action* (2nd ed.). San Diego, CA: University Associates.

Schein, E. H. (1988). *Process consultation Volume I: Its role in organizational development* (2nd ed.). Reading, MA: Addison-Wesley Publishing Co. Inc.

Chapter 3

WHO ARE COMMUNICATION MANAGERS?

Job Descriptions

"You can have brilliant ideas, but if you can't get them across, your brains won't get you anywhere."

Lee Iacocca, 1984,
Iacocca: An Autobiography

*T*he importance of communication and the need for individuals to pay special attention to it cannot be overstated. Communication managers or specialists ensure that the importance of communication is not overlooked. As defined here, communication managers/specialists are those individuals in the organization whose primary focus is developing the human potential to communicate. This focus may be due to an individual's formal authority, as is the case for a training and development specialist or a human resource consultant, or as part of a general management position when the person in that position believes human resources are one of the most important factors in the organization's success.

Paying attention to the communication process means focusing on a key ingredient of the organizational environment. Consultants, trainers, managers, and executives who are communication managers focus on the *process* human beings use to complete a task. Thus, communication managers would work within the framework of management consulting, and the umbrella term, organization development. Activities that assist with the development of human potential include, but are not limited to, the following: conflict resolution, team building, and decision-making practices among managers and staff and within work teams.

■ *The Case for Communication Managers*

The need for communication managers is supported by Rosabeth Moss Kanter in her book, *When Giants Learn to Dance* (1989). In her discussion of organizational changes in the 1990s she suggested that misinformation is one of the results. "Communication is haphazard [during organizational restructuring] and some managers do a better job than others keeping their people informed. Rumors are created and take on a life of their own especially when it is not clear who has the right information. Some of the rumors are potentially destructive" (p. 62). She discusses "emotional leakage" when managers are so focused on the task to be done that they neglect or ignore the emotional reactions engendered by the change. Any change consumes emotional energy, especially if the restructuring is perceived negatively. People become preoccupied with those changes, the mood becomes somber, morale sinks, and it is hard to maintain the usual pace of work. All of this speaks to the need for high communication competence in order to maintain a positive environment as well as cope with a changing one.

> Management tasks are different under a post-entrepreneurial system in which responsibility is delegated downward to reduce management layers or managers work with outside partners rather than inside employees. In these more participative circumstances, people need to spend more time selling ideas rather than commanding. They need to spend more time explaining goals, keeping staff or allies up to date with timely information, [and] making sure they understand where their responsibilities fit in the whole task (Kanter, p. 275).

Evidence suggests the greatest proportion of an executive's time is spent communicating in short fragments on a large variety of topics. With the increase of participative decision making, communication becomes a prerequisite to successful organization outcomes. Now more than ever before communication managers and consultants, with communication as their focus, are critical to the success of corporate endeavors. In the post-entrepreneurial corporation, communication demands, and therefore time demands, are up. There is a positive correlation between effective communication and an integrated, synergistic organization. In order to meet these new demands, communication consultants/managers/specialists will need a variety of skills to bring to each new situation.

Skills for Communication Managers

Management theorists and scholars have developed lists of skills that communication managers need to perform effectively. As you read the following discussion, identify those skills you feel you already possess and those you need to improve. Look for common characteristics identified by all the authors.

Boyer

Boyer (1987) suggested the following as necessary skills for organizational consultants, which are needed by communication specialists or communication managers as defined in this book:

1) cognitive skills in such areas as organizational theory, design and change, small group and interpersonal behavior, and individual behavior; 2) interpersonal skills for developing and maintaining relationships with organizations and individuals with widely diverse backgrounds, values, and styles; and 3) personal skills needed to use one's person as an instrument of change (p. 149).

Skills two and three above suggest the need to focus on communication behaviors that must be changed in the organization as well as the consultant's personal style of communication as a role model. While the communication manager must focus on communication as a principal element in the organizational environment, communication skills must also be demonstrated constantly to others. Thus, as expressed in an earlier paper, communication becomes both the "target" and the "tool" for organizational change simultaneously (Daniels and DeWine, 1991).

Schein

Schein (1978) identified three areas of competence for consultants: "analytical competence, interpersonal competence, and emotional competence." The communication manager must be able to analyze human resource issues and clearly describe those problems to the client. What Schein has added to this picture is the concept of "emotional competence." Since communication managers are often the catalysts that bring about change, they may find themselves in the middle of a storm of controversy. They must have enough emotional maturity to walk away from the situation with their ego intact and without residual negative feelings.

Lippitt and Lippitt

Lippitt and Lippitt (1986) identified abilities that a communication manager or consultant must have in order to be successful. They include the ability to do the following (Lippitt and Lippitt, p. 169):

Diagnose problems

Develop objectives

Interpret and evaluate results

Manage planned growth and development

Help others learn how to learn

Help others adjust comfortably to change

Handle confrontation and conflict

Work creatively with clients

Maintain and release human energy

Be self-renewing

Be proactive

Communicate effectively

Lippitt and Lippitt also suggested that the consultant must be flexible, innovative, have inner motivation, extreme perception and sensitivity toward others, ability to deal successfully with ambiguity, extreme honesty, genuine desire to help others, profound respect for others, optimism and self-confidence, sincerity, and charisma. It sounds like someone who must be perfect! Certainly these are desirable traits, but unrealistic to expect in all settings.

Wexley and Latham

Wexley and Latham (1981) identified a series of basic requirements for a person to be a human resource specialist in an organization:

- The individual must be an expert at demonstrating the skills to be imparted,
- The individual should have knowledge and ability to use various learning principles and training methods,
- The individual must be well-grounded in organization, task, and person analyses, as well as experimental design, criteria development, and statistics, and
- The individual must possess certain personal qualities that facilitate learning, for example: being organized and being flexible.

The next step is taking these skills and applying them to a variety of issues and circumstances one finds in any organization. Blake and Mouton's (1989) approach provides a framework for doing that.

Applying Skills to Resolve Issues: The Consulcube Model

Blake and Mouton (1976, 1989) developed a model that identifies not only skills needed by consultants but likely issues and circumstances under which one might be addressing those issues in a consulting relationship. We know that communication managers and consultants may be asked to resolve sensitive organizational problems.

Redding (1979) stated, "It is common knowledge that some communication consultants deal with extremely sensitive and high-risk problem situations; for example: line-staff conflicts, superior-subordinate malfunctions, participative decision making, employee publication practices, etc." (pp. 348–49). He goes on to caution that communication consultants need a broad perspective in order to deal with such sensitive issues: "The consultant who lacks a sophisticated grasp of systems approaches will almost certainly either waste the time and money of the client with innocuous trivia or dangerously mislead the client into believing that '*in vacuo*' tinkering will solve profound problems" (p. 349).

Levels of the Organization

Blake and Mouton's "consulcube" provides the type of framework called for by Redding (see Figure 3.1). First, the consultant will enter the organization at a particular level by working with an individual, a group, among groups, throughout the organization as a whole, or between organizations (identified as "units of change" in the Blake and Mouton model). Any intervention into a system creates change. Certain interventions are more effective at the micro versus macro level in the organization.

Intervention Approaches

Blake and Mouton have identified five broad categories of interventions: acceptance, catalytic, confrontation, prescriptive, and theory and principles. The **acceptance style** of intervention is one in which the consultant acts as a sounding board for the client—similar to Carl Rogers' counseling style of helping individuals. The consultant accepts the problem as the client presents it and tries to be responsive to the client's needs. An example from my own consulting business is a group with whom I had been working for some time providing communication skills training. They called and asked that I help them cope with the violent death of one of their co-workers. My intervention was to be an accepting listener. I could not suggest "solutions" but only provide a sounding board for their frustration and sadness.

The **catalytic style** is similar to the use of the word in chemistry: the catalyst enables other chemicals to react with one another. The consultant who uses a catalytic style of intervention causes individuals to interact and communicate with one another in order to solve problems. When I worked with a group of women who felt they were not being heard by their male bosses, I ran a workshop for the entire group in which I spent

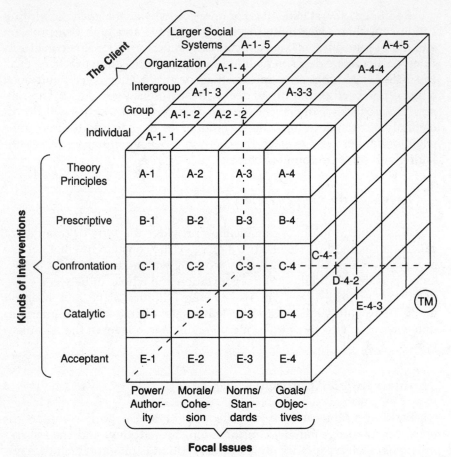

FIGURE 3.1   The Consulcube™   From *Consultation: A Handbook for Individual and Organization Development* (Second Edition), by Robert R. Blake and Jane Srygley Mouton. Reading, MA.: Addison-Wesley Publishing Co., Inc., 1983, p. 11. Copyright © Scientific Methods, Inc. Reproduced by permission.

most of my time focusing on the process and simply calling their attention to the way in which they were all interacting. My presence alone caused some interaction to occur about why they needed an outside communication manager at all! I served as a catalyst to generate communication between the males and females about their styles of interacting with one another.

A **confrontation intervention** is one in which the consultant directly confronts contradictory information or behaviors. "A consultant who operates in a confrontational mode pinpoints for the client inappropriate, invalid, or unjustified values and gets him or her to face up to a reality in the values domain which was previously unrecognized, ignored, disregarded, or rejected" (Blake and Mouton, p. 224). A CEO who says he has an "open-door policy" and is not available four days out of five, may have to be confronted with the information about his lack of accessibility versus what he would like for others to believe about his style.

Prescriptive interventions are those that provide the answer for the client. This is a doctor-patient model where the communication manager collects the data and makes a diagnosis. "A prescriptive consultant not only identifies what the real need is but also specifies the actions necessary if the client is to escape from self-defeating behavior cycles" (Blake and Mouton, p. 296). Its success depends on the client's *willingness* and *ability* to follow the diagnosis. Clients may be *able* to perform the tasks requested, but refuse to do so, because they are not convinced those tasks are necessary or helpful. Or they may be *willing*, but lack the necessary skills to carry out the recommendation from the communication manager.

I once recommended to a client that they needed to have regular staff meetings so that everyone would understand new policies. They were willing to do so, but the leaders of the group lacked the skills necessary to run an effective meeting, and these meetings soon evolved into wasted time (see Chapter 8 for details on running effective meetings). They were *willing*, but *unable* to carry out the recommendation. Another client, who had the ability and resources to implement a performance review process, needed to be convinced that this was a necessary process to implement before he would be willing to carry it out. He was *able*, but *unwilling* to implement the suggestion.

Finally, Blake and Mouton identify *"theory and practice"* as a type of intervention. With this approach, the consultant or communication manager uses a theoretical approach to understanding issues. "Theory-based interventions engage a consultant in those activities necessary to assist a client in acquiring a theory basis for governing individual action. The client is freed from blind reliance on common sense and conventional wisdom and is enabled to see situations more objectively by avoiding the distortions that subjective attitudes, beliefs, and untested convictions can produce" (p. 381). I find this to be the least used of the five types of interventions.

Categories of Issues

The third dimension of the consulcube involves the identification of four broad categories of issues with which consultants must deal: *power/ authority; morale/cohesion; norms/standards;* and *goals/objectives.* These categories are broad enough that most human relationship problems can fit under one or more of them. Decisions being made by top level officials, without input from those who must implement the decisions, might be an issue of power and authority. Adding a large number of new members and losing old members of a work team may lead to a problem of morale and cohesion. An individual who acts inappropriately in an office setting may be ignoring norms that have become a part of the organization's culture. Finally, I frequently find that various individuals in the organization have separate goals that sometimes conflict with the organization itself, leading to problems of goals and objectives.

Application of the Model

The consulcube is formed by placing these three dimensions along three planes of a cube, creating squares that cross "level of the organization," and "potential issues," with an "intervention approach." Some crossings are not appropriate. For example, usually when the issue is "morale," "confrontation" would not be the most appropriate intervention to use. Nor would working with the total organization provide many opportunities for an acceptance style of interaction. However, other squares help guide the consultant when choosing an appropriate method to approach the problem. For example, a problem of individual morale might call for an acceptance intervention while some power issues must be confronted directly by the consultant.

In choosing an appropriate intervention, most often I use a collaborative model of consulting. As Kurpius (1978) suggested, "When following the collaboration mode the consultant's goal is to facilitate the consultee's self-direction and innate capacity to solve problems. As a result, the consultant serves more as a generalist than a technical expert. His [her] major efforts are directed toward helping people develop a plan for solving problems" (p. 19). With this philosophy, the client and the consultant determine together what the issue is, how it can be solved, and what both the client and the consultant can do to resolve it. This type of joint diagnosis insures a greater likelihood of acceptance for the solution.

The communication manager is an individual who focuses on the potential for increased human performance and uses a variety of skills to tackle many organizational problems. I have used the terms communication manager, communication specialist, and communication consultant interchangeably in this chapter. All three terms will be referenced throughout the book. All three refer to individuals who focus attention on the development of better communication throughout the organization.

These first three chapters have served to provide a framework for what follows. Understanding the role of the communication manager in the resolution of common communication problems will guide the following discussion. The next part of this book identifies communication problems by discussing how to conduct needs assessments and analysis, and what intervention strategies can be applied to those problems. Part three provides solutions through specific communication techniques. I hope these will help you learn new "frameworks" in which to place problems as well as alternative ways of coping with them.

■ *Suggested Readings*

Bell, C. R. (1985). Diagnosis: Frameworks for consultants and clients. In C. R. Bell & L. Nadler (Eds.), *Clients and consultants: Meeting and exceeding expectations* (2nd ed.) (pp. 152–64). Houston, TX: Gulf Publishing Co.

Goldhaber, G., Dennis, H., Richetto, G., & Wiio, O. (1979). *Information strategies: New pathways to corporate power.* Englewood Cliffs, NJ: Prentice-Hall.

Kanter, R. M. (1983). *The change masters.* New York, NY: Simon and Schuster.

Kanter, R. M. (1989). *When giants learn to dance.* New York, NY: Simon and Schuster.

Redding, W. C. (1979). Graduate education and the communication consultant: Playing God for a fee. *Communication Education, 28,* 346–52.

Rudolph, E. E., & Johnson, B. R. (1983). *Communication consulting: Another teaching option.* Annandale , VA: Speech Communication Association.

PART II

Identifying Communication Problems

Part II explains the first step in solving human communication problems in organizations: identifying the problem. You can't apply solutions until you understand fully the dimensions of the problem with which you are dealing. The very first thing a consultant or communication manager must do is a needs assessment to determine individual as well as organizational needs.

This section of the book is divided into two chapters: Chapter 4 discusses data collection techniques, and Chapter 5 explains some simple data analysis procedures. Data collection and analysis absolutely must be a part of the consultant's repertoire of skills. The techniques are not difficult to acquire; however, the reader who has no background in data analysis at all may want to explore the suggested readings for more details about statistical design. This discussion will give you a good start toward learning the techniques.

Chapter 4

CONDUCTING NEEDS ASSESSMENTS

"Don't try to play hard ball if you haven't got a glove!"
quoted in Zemke and Kramlinger,
1984, p. 4

Your recommendations to the client must be supported with facts and observations that are believable, or you shouldn't be in the business of making recommendations. The way in which you collect data is the subject of this chapter and the analysis of data is discussed in the next chapter.

One of the consultant's most significant contributions is to be a neutral observer of organizational life. Organizational members are caught up in the processes of the organization and therefore are not able to disengage themselves in order to make clear, unbiased observations.

> I sat in the chair opposite the CEO's desk and watched as he talked. "This was a family-owned business for 43 years. It has been on the open stock exchange only for the last five years. We still have a strong sense of family around here." I noticed a framed comic strip on the wall and pictures of his family on the low cabinet behind his desk. Before he had finished talking a custodian walked in without being announced, said "Good morning," and walked out with the trash can. "While I am not related to the founder in any way, we have several family members on the payroll. Besides that, many of our employees are related to one another." As he showed me the organization chart he began to point out different relationships that existed between various managers in the plant. His secretary called him to tell him "John" and "Howard" were on their way to talk to him about a new employee educational program. All the time I was in his office, during our first interview, I was collecting data on the way in which his view of the "organizational family" was exhibited in daily routines. These observations were later used to help identify areas explored in other interviews and questionnaires.

The consultant's job is not only to identify the problem but to separate it from symptoms and uncover solutions that frequently lie buried in the minds of organizational members. In this sense, the consultant or communication specialist acts like a detective. Steele's (1985) comparison of consultants and detectives highlights the importance of diagnosis for both. One of the major activities of both a detective and a consultant is an extensive search for clues and evidence. Both the consultant and the detective have two reasons for collecting evidence. One is to understand what has occurred and the second is to make a case.

Second, both the detective and the consultant have temporary involvement in a system or group of people. They establish a network of relationships for the duration of the case. A consultant or detective may be quite central to several of these relationships and may be very important at the time, but then that consultant or detective moves on to a new case.

Third, both a consultant and a detective are independent of the group they are studying and yet there are many attempts by individuals to incorporate them into the group. Both have to have a keen sense of intuition and a sense of the dramatic. They are on center stage and they must control the timing of events. The first step, for both of them, is recognizing a problem when they see one.

How Do We Know When a Problem Exists?

To the degree there is a gap between "where we are" ("A") and "where we want to be" ("B"), we have a problem area. The challenge is planning how to get from "A" to "B." The wider the gap, the greater the distance we must travel to achieve our goals. Thus, one of the first steps for the consultant is to describe the organization in its current state, and second, help the organization determine its immediate and long-term goals.

We also know a problem exits when, as Davis (1986) suggested, behavior moves out of the range an observer would normally view as being reasonable in the circumstances. This may be behavior by a single individual or by groups of people. Of course, what is "reasonable" to one person may be "out of range" to another! There must be some agreed upon standard of behavior to which employees will be held accountable.

Davis goes on to point out five pitfalls in problem identification that are quite useful for consultants to remember:

1. *Mistaking symptoms for the underlying problem.* Symptoms may point to the existence of a problem but if you waste time solving the symptoms you may not touch the actual issue.

2. *Accepting without question the opinions of others* concerning the prob-

lem. Because the people you talk with may very well be a part of the problem, you must not be in a hurry to reach conclusions until the evidence triangulates, or doubles back on itself and supports earlier versions of the story.

3. *Assuming the problem is a person.* It is unrealistic to believe the problem is exhibited by a single person. If the consultant focuses on only one person without examining the surrounding people, events, and environment, then the analysis is quite isolated.

4. *Killing the messenger* as a reaction to bad news. Sometimes the messenger is mistaken for the bad news itself. To the degree individuals in the organization blame the messenger, future reports will be less likely to filter up through the organization.

5. *Overlooking multivariable causes.* The consultant needs to look at all contributing variables listed above, plus more.

These general guidelines suggest the need to keep searching for answers even when the problem solver thinks all symptoms have been answered. Making assumptions that lead to untested solutions is dangerous. My rule of thumb is to keep collecting data until it starts to "double back" on itself, that is, it becomes repetitive. I also have learned that part of what the client is paying me to do is to help articulate issues. The first contact usually mentions some vague need to improve "communication." That could mean anything from writing clearer memos to examining dysfunctional interpersonal relationships to reworking unclear job descriptions! The consultant usually begins with a series of questions that need answers.

Bell and Nadler (1985) suggested 13 questions that the consultant might explore in order to develop an organizational diagnosis:

1. Is there a well-defined, widely communicated statement of organizational mission or purpose?

2. Do employees have clear work goals or objectives?

3. Is there an organizational structure that provides for adequate span of control and balanced allocation of resources?

4. Are there training activities that provide employees with the competencies needed?

5. Is there a process for ensuring the right people are in the right work roles?

6. Does the organization have effective ways of ensuring that employees get performance feedback?

7. Do employees have a way of determining the priority of their work objectives to enable them to put the greatest energy on the most important tasks?

8. Is there a method for communicating management information needed to achieve work objectives?

9. Does the organization have a process that allows employees to contribute to the development of work objectives?

10. Are there methods for employees to be appropriately rewarded for their contribution?

11. Do employees have the tools and aids they need to perform their work?

12. Is there a process that ensures employees have the freedom they need to perform their work efficiently?

13. Are job descriptions existent and up-to-date and communicated to employees? (pp. 156–57).

These questions can serve as the basis for building a series of inquiries into organizational life. The communication consultant will tend to focus on issues related to organizational relationships and the ability to send and interpret messages, while a financial consultant may focus on the balance sheet. The talented consultant will know that when issues arise that need to be addressed by persons with expertise other than their own, additional individuals should be called on to help solve problems. No consultants should attempt to solve problems for which they have no training or expertise.

Sampling Procedures

When the consultant is working with a large organization (i.e., more than 100 employees) it is unreasonable to expect that every person can be interviewed or included in the data analysis. This would take unlimited funds and time, both of which are highly valued commodities. Therefore, the consultant must determine a method for **sampling** the population that will ensure that the individuals included in the sample are representative of the rest of the group. First, you need a list of all the names of organization members.

If you sampled only the daytime workers in a plant, or you talked only to the managers, or only long-time workers, imagine the slanted view you would get of the organization. There are two principal ways to select subjects: random sampling and stratified sampling.

Random Sampling

The "random" in "random sampling" does not indicate a haphazard approach to selecting subjects. In order to make sure that the procedure is indeed **random sampling**, every person in the population must have an equal chance of being selected. Therefore, you cannot start with the beginning of the alphabet and stop when you have enough because that means those whose names begin with letters at the end of the alphabet did not have an equal chance of being selected.

The most correct way to select subjects is to use a table of random numbers which are included in any standard statistics book. This table will indicate which numbers to use given the total number of subjects you want. They have been generated by a computer to be absolutely random and would select subjects in the population at all points.

Another convenient way to select random subjects is to determine how many subjects you want (5 to 10 percent of the population is reasonable with large organizations) and divide that number into the total number of organization members. The result will indicate how many people to skip. For example, if you are working with an organization of 500 people and you want a 10 percent sample, or 50 people, divide 50 into 500 and the result is 10. This means you should select every 10th person to be included.

The final test of random sampling is to compare your sample demographics with the population demographics. If there are 60 percent females and 40 percent males in the total population, then your sample should approximate that distribution. Also check length of employment, age, salary level, positions, and previous training. Since you hope to generalize to the total population, the sample must be as similar to that population as possible. Otherwise, you can draw conclusions only about this unique small subset of the total group.

Stratified Sampling

The second major sampling technique is called **stratified sampling**. If you want special subgroups represented in the sample, you could divide the population into those subgroups and then do random selection from within the subgroups. For example, if you want to make sure you included an equal number of long-term employees and new employees, you could divide the list of organization members into these two groups and then draw an equal number of subjects from each group, randomly.

■ *Data Collection Methods*

The questionnaire and the interview are probably the most frequently used methods for collecting data about the organization. While these are the most used, they are not always used correctly and may not be the best ways to get at the information needed. This section outlines suggestions for developing questionnaires, interview guides, observation techniques, critical incidents, and organizational outcome data. The next chapter identifies the best ways to analyze the data collected with each of these techniques.

The Questionnaire

Consultants develop questionnaires by identifying broad categories to be studied and then constructing questions within these categories. Well-executed questionnaires are a useful form of data collection but they are not the best source of data in every situation. The communication consultant must know when, as well as how, to use questionnaires. The first step is to develop a content matrix.

CONTENT MATRIX

The first step in developing a questionnaire is to define the broad general categories of interest or concern. The questions are generated by developing a matrix of possible areas to explore. Researchers identify these areas from past research; practitioners identify them from past research as well as preliminary discussions with corporate leaders about areas of concern.

For example, an employee survey on satisfaction with the decision-making processes used in the organization might include the following categories of interest:

	Effectiveness of decision	My involvement	Follow-up
Upper management's decision-making practices	#1	#2	#3
My unit's decision-making practices	#4	#5	#6
My immediate supervisor's decision-making practices	#7	#8	#9

FIGURE 4.1   Content Matrix for Questionnaires

Depending on the desired length of the questionnaire (and the shorter the better!) the matrix in Figure 4.1 would generate at least nine questions covering three levels of decision making in the organization across three characteristics of decision making. This matrix ensures that each aspect listed vertically is analyzed by each characteristic listed horizontally. Thus, a question in square #1 might read: "How effective are decisions made by upper management?" compared to a question in square #9, "Does my manager follow up on decisions in a timely fashion?"

STRUCTURING OF QUESTIONS

The second step in developing the questionnaire is to structure the questions following these guidelines:

1. *Ask only one question at a time.* For example, a question like this: "Does your manager make effective decisions, and do you feel upper management follows up on decisions made at lower levels?" provides no useful data. You do not know which is the more salient bit of information in the question: my manager or upper management's follow-up practices.

2. *Use simple and unbiased wording.* A question written like the following: "Do you feel there is a lack of adequate follow-through on decisions made by upper management?" is not only one-sided, but confusing.

3. *Try to avoid negative wording.* Some negatively worded items are necessary to control for response biases; however, double negatives and leading questions are out of bounds. "Do you not believe that decisions are poorly made in this organization?" is confusing and misleading. However, it is much clearer if respondents are asked the degree to which they agree or disagree with the statement, "Decisions seem to take a long time to be made in this organization."

4. *Use questions that can be easily tabulated for computer scoring but also allow space for comments* particularly when you are asking for answers that are not objective. You are losing a great deal of information if you do not allow respondents to make clarifying comments.

The structure of the questionnaire is very important. Place a few easy and interesting questions at the beginning to gain respondents' interest, your most important questions in the middle, and demographic items at the end. You do not want the demographic items up front in case they make the respondent hesitant to answer for fear of revealing who they are. At the end of the questionnaire, they can always choose not to respond to some demographic questions and not affect content items.

The consultant should always create at least two different questionnaires with the items in a different order. Since respondents get tired of answering questions, the last questions on the questionnaire may be answered with less thought or not at all. You don't want the same questions to always be responded to in this way. Therefore, with different orders respondent fatigue will be distributed across items more equally.

As mentioned earlier, some items must be worded negatively so that respondents do not respond routinely. Also, the same information must be asked for more than once to check for validity of answers. When scoring these negatively worded items, remember to reverse the score on those items or you will have "garbage"!

While there are several types of forced-choice questions, I prefer making statements and using **Likert-type scales** for responses. These are five-point scales on which respondents can indicate their opinions or beliefs in a quantifiable way. The following is the standard scale in use:

1—strongly agree

2—agree

3—neither agree or disagree

4—disagree

5—strongly disagree

Other anchor points that have been used successfully include:

almost never true, rarely true, occasionally true, often true, almost always true

very characteristic, somewhat characteristic, neither characteristic nor uncharacteristic, somewhat uncharacteristic, very uncharacteristic

inadequate, somewhat inadequate, adequate, more than adequate, excellent

not at all, to a slight extent, to a moderate extent, to a large extent, to a very large extent

Additional types of scaling include rank ordering (used when you want to determine which answers are most important to respondents) or yes/no questions. I find yes/no questions to be the least useful since they limit, to such a great extent, the amount of information you receive.

Advantages and Disadvantages of Questionnaires

The advantages of using a questionnaire are that it is the easiest and least expensive way to collect large amounts of data and include diverse populations in a short period of time. Questionnaires can also be standardized so that the data can be easily quantified and summarized. Finally, you can ensure anonymity for the respondents.

The disadvantages are the lack of "rich" data, particularly if forced-choice items are used. Also, if you are surveying a population that is frequently tapped for questionnaire completion, you may get a low response rate. At one time it was felt by researchers that unless you received about an 80 percent response rate, your data were so nonrepresentative of the population as to be unusable. Indeed, some types of surveys need close to 100 percent response for any meaning to be extracted from them. However, today one feels fortunate to receive a 30–40 percent response rate from randomly mailed surveys.

Interviews

The interview provides a rich source of data for the consultant. In fact, interviews are the way in which the consultant begins any data collection. From the first meeting with the client, the consultant should be using good interviewing techniques to try to uncover the areas of concern for the organization.

The Interview Guide

The first step is to develop the interview guide. This set of questions can be developed in a way similar to the construction of the content matrix used for questionnaires, although the questions are usually more open-ended. *The interview guide can be used to help determine areas of concern and thus use open-ended questions, while the questionnaire should be used more to confirm issues and thus uses more closed questions.*

In developing the questions, follow the same guidelines for language as recommended for questionnaire items, plus, invite the subject to talk. A question such as, "Does upper management follow up on decision making in this organization?" will not invite as much comment as, "What is your sense of how decision making takes place in this organization? Cite some examples that illustrate your response."

An interview guide should include the main questions asked as well as indicate follow-up questions that might be used to probe for more information. For example, a main question might be, "How frequently do you like to receive feedback about how you are doing your job?" with a series of possible follow-up questions such as "Is once a week too much? Would you rather receive this information in written form or face-to-face?"

THE OPENING STATEMENT

Second, the interview must develop the "opening statement." This includes not only the purpose for the interview but answers questions the respondent may be thinking but will not ask. Rossett and Arwady (1987) identify these concerns on the part of the respondent as questions of *intent, competency, propriety, and broader impact.* Respondents want to know why they are being interviewed, whether the interviewer is an expert, who will have access to this information, and what will be done as a result of the interview. One of the most difficult situations is one in which previous interviews have brought about no noticeable changes. Respondents will be discouraged about participating once again, only to find that their comments do not matter. Worse still is the situation in which previous data collection techniques have brought about the disappearance of jobs!

NOTE TAKING

Third, the interviewer must develop some form of note-taking procedure. Audio- or videotaping the interview is the most comprehensive way of collecting the data and is used frequently when a complete data set is desired. The three principal drawbacks are: the intimidation felt by the respondents even when they give their permission, the overwhelming amount of information, and the labor-intensive transcription process that takes place later. The cost as well as cultural considerations often prevent companies from using this method.

Using some form of brief note taking during the interview can work well. The interviewer would be wise to leave time between interviews to more completely fill out the notes taken. If notes are not amplified immediately, facts will begin to fade, and one can easily confuse respondents' answers.

AVOIDANCE OF BIAS-INDUCING BEHAVIOR

Fourth, the interviewer must be aware of any behaviors that will cause biases on the part of the respondent. The rule of thumb is to be as unobtrusive as possible. This refers to the interviewer's appearance as well as suggesting, in any way, agreement or disagreement with the respondent's answer.

A FAVORABLE ATMOSPHERE

Finally, select a time and place that enhance your chances of getting open, honest responses to your questions. This means a private space, free from distractions, at a time that is convenient for the respondent. If you are interviewing a person during the busiest part of the day or week, the respondent's mind will be on the tasks left to do that day, rather than on your questions. Let your interviewees determine the best time for the interview.

Practice interpersonal responsiveness by beginning the interview with some nonthreatening questions that help you to know the person with whom you are speaking. Starting with ridiculous comments on the weather is insulting. Both the interviewer and the interviewee know why they are there, and while the first questions should not be the most difficult or controversial, they should indicate your intent not to waste time and should clearly point out the purpose of the interview. Form 4.1 shows a sample interview guide used to collect information on decision making in the organization.

The open-ended questions are followed by probing questions for examples and details of their general conclusions. It is in the examples that you will acquire some of the richest data and information. You might simply say, "Could you give me an example of that?"

ADVANTAGES AND DISADVANTAGES OF INTERVIEWS

The advantages of the interview include adaptability and richness of data. These are also the major disadvantages. Adapting the interview to each interviewee makes it very difficult to compare data across subjects, and the richness of data may make the analysis stage so overwhelming as to render the consultant unable to draw conclusions. The selection of a questionnaire or interview will be determined by a number of factors, such as length of time to complete data collection and the detail needed to answer the questions of interest. Rossett and Arwady (1987) have developed a chart that summarizes the advantages and disadvantages of both (see Figure 4.2).

Observations

Observations of individuals on the job are probably the most realistic, though time-consuming, activity in which a consultant can participate. Davis (1986) suggested four methods of observation: 1) observe by walking around and taking notes on people and activities; 2) observe from a

■ SAMPLE INTERVIEW GUIDE

Good morning! My name is Sue DeWine and I am working with the Human Resource Department to study the decision-making process at your organization. I am a researcher and consultant from Ohio University and I have worked with companies like yours for the past 25 years.

I would appreciate your candid remarks since no names will be attached to any information collected. The more open you are the better able I will be to help determine how to improve the decision-making process.

I will be writing a report and making recommendations to the Vice President for Human Resources when I have completed the interviews. Each participant will receive a summary of those results and at any time you may contact me if you have questions or concerns about the process we are using.

First, tell me how long you have been in this business and your length of employment at this organization.

During your time with this organization, how would you characterize the decision-making process used here? For example, when are you consulted about decisions being made?

With whom do you consult when you have decisions to make?

What do you particularly like about working here?

How would you like for things to be different about the way in which decisions are made?

| FACTORS | INTERVIEWS | | | PRINT SURVEYS | |
| | In Person | | Telephonic | Small n | Large n |
	Indiv.	*Sm. grp.*			
Anonymity of sources	None	None	None	Some	High
Cost	Depends on number distance, length	Depends on number distance, length	Depends on length, number and cost of calls	Low	Usually high especially in devpt of instrument
Follow-up questions	Good opport'y	Fair opport'y	Good opportunity	Some or none	None
Response rate	High	High	Usually high	Depends on quality of questions & anonymity	Usually low
Ease of analysis	Depends	Depends	Depends	Easy with preparation	Depends on quality of questions & data analysis preparation
Risk	Some	High; need group skills	Some	Some; print endures	High; many people receive & print endures

FIGURE 4.2   Needs Assessment Tools   From A. Rossett & J. W. Arwady, *Training Needs Assessment*, Englewood Cliffs, NJ: Educational Technology Publications, 1987, p. 77. Reprinted by permission.

fixed location without being seen; 3) observe from a fixed location with the knowledge of the subjects that they are being observed; and 4) observe and also interact with the person (or persons) being observed. The interaction will focus on asking for more information about a certain task.

The first step is to determine the purpose of the observation and the length of time necessary to make the observation. Early in the process a decision must be made about how much information the person being observed will be given. If not at the beginning, then at some later point in time it is very important that individuals be fully informed about the intent of the process. I personally would not agree to observe individuals without their knowledge. I find that once I am around long enough, they ignore me and my presence is not disruptive.

Second, a method for taking field notes must be developed. Field notes require coding schemes that will be useful to you at a later date. For example, the time of day and the amount of time passed during each observation may be important. As with interview notes, it is absolutely critical you spend some time immediately following the observation clarifying your own notes. Otherwise, they will be more useless than useful to you.

Third, you must become as unobtrusive as possible. This means you cannot enter into the interaction taking place to offer suggestions or solutions to problems you observe! Nor should you do anything that will call attention to your presence (by wearing clothes that are obviously out of place with the culture or by responding nonverbally to things you observe by laughing or chuckling at humorous events).

In order to be a good observer you must distinguish between the content of what you see and hear and the process of the event. In Chapter 6 the technique of process observation is discussed. This is the most frequent type of observation in which you will engage and takes a great deal of skill and talent. You must be a naturally curious individual with keen insight, patience, and tact.

Critical Incidents

Critical incidents are extensive examples individuals are asked to write out. Zemke and Kramlinger (1989) have outlined a step by step procedure for collecting critical incidents. John C. Flanagan, a World War II military psychologist was actually the designer of this data collection tool. He was asked to determine why so many training planes were crashing. He decided to ask pilots exactly what they had done incorrectly and described the process as "soliciting war stories." In a sense, when you use critical incidents in the organization you are "soliciting war stories" about life in that organization.

> Critical incidents are reports or descriptions of things people in the study population report having done or have been observed doing by others. These incidents are classified by supervisors or other knowledgeable subject matter experts as effective or ineffective in achieving the desired job results. These descriptions can take the form of stories, anecdotes, reports, or observations related by superiors, peers, subordinates, or by qualified observers. The incidents can be analyzed bit by bit, collectively, or both (Zemke and Kramlinger, p. 129).

Having organizational members tell stories about life in the organization will provide the consultant with an understanding of issues that no other method will generate. Many organizational researchers are now studying organizational culture by living in the organization for a period of time and asking for stories from its members. Being a good listener is the key to the effectiveness of this technique.

Organizational Outcomes

Organizational outcome data include all the publications produced by the organization as well as personnel files and records. It could even include what Greiner and Metzger (1983) refer to as "routine data." The following is a sample of some of the routine data they collected and conclusions it led to.

> An analysis of memos circulated in the top management revealed the power structure of the organization through the listing of names of recipients at the bottom.

> A client claimed that his plant was promoting good young managers out of the plant to other parts of the company. An analysis of the personnel records showed this not to be the case; in fact, managers with high appraisal ratings were being kept back, and those with low ratings were rotated out.

> A CEO who was well-read in management theory lectured the consultants on how participative he was in running the company—until the consultants examined his calendar pad to find that he remained in his office 95 percent of the time and seldom held a meeting.

> A consultant hired to design an alcoholism program for a company found the participants for the program by analyzing time clock records to see who was chronically late on Mondays.

All of these techniques lead the consultant to insights about issues organizational members may face and be unwilling, for a number of reasons, to articulate. In the end, the consultant should use a variety of methods to arrive at the clearest picture of where the organization is and where it wants to be. In the next chapter the methods for analyzing the data are described. Often the consultant collects a great deal of material and then doesn't know quite what to do with it!

■ *Suggested Readings*

Downs, C. (1988). *Communication audits.* Glenview, IL: Scott, Foresman & Co.

Downs, C., DeWine, S., & Greenbaum, H. (in press). Organizational communication instrumentation. In R. Rubin & H. Sypher (Eds.). *Instrumentation in communication.* New York, NY: Longman Press.

Greiner, L.E., & Metzger, R.O. (1983). *Consulting to management.* Englewood Cliffs, NJ: Prentice-Hall.

Rossett, A., & Arwady, J.W. (1987). *Training needs assessment.* Englewood Cliffs, NJ: Educational Technology Publications.

Zemke, R., & Kramlinger, T. (1989). *Figuring things out: A trainer's guide to needs and task analysis.* Reading, MA: Addison-Wesley Publishing Co., Inc.

Chapter 5

HOW DO WE KNOW WHAT WE HAVE WHEN WE HAVE IT?

Data Analysis

- **CLASSIC ERRORS IN DATA ANALYSIS**
- **EFFECTIVE DIAGNOSIS**
  Objectivity
  Feedback versus Handback
- **FREQUENCIES AND HYPOTHESIS TESTING**
- **CONTENT ANALYSIS AND GROUNDED THEORY**
- **MULTIPLE APPROACHES**
- **CONSULTANT'S TIPS FOR ANALYZING RESULTS**

"All statistics do . . . is help you crunch large amounts of information into usable numbers."

> *Ron Zemke and*
> *Thomas Kramlinger, 1984*

*I*ndividuals without statistical training are sometimes intimidated by the language of statistics. I have always believed that a few simple rules for data analysis, spoken in "plain English" can be followed by anyone, and will allow anyone to interpret the data that have been collected. The techniques discussed in this chapter are designed to help you avoid making some of the following mistakes about data available to you.

■ Classic Errors in Data Analysis

Metzger (1989) identified what he called classic errors in data analysis. These lead to false conclusions about how to solve problems before you really know what the problem is!

Slot machine management—when managers lose hope they often enter a "valley of despair." In the valley, it appears that the only way out is to be extremely decisive, so they start making a lot of decisions quickly, as if loading nickels into a one-armed bandit, but they seldom line up three cherries, and these frantic efforts only make things worse.

Freudian hydraulics—as people's normal impatience gets worse and worse, it can become a powerful psychological force that makes people absolutely unable to wait, so they try to make something, *anything*, happen and push unrealistically hard until it does. Such approaches take a heavy toll.

The charge of the light brigade—this is management's propensity to keep right on doing whatever is running the firm into the ground simply because management has so much invested in the existing systems of values and tenets that it cannot face the enormous impact of its error. It is an ego trap of immense proportions (p. 176).

■ *Effective Diagnosis*

It is critical once the data are collected that very careful analysis takes place so that hasty conclusions and solutions are not implemented. Greiner and Metzger (1983) identified qualities that the consultant must have in order to carry out an effective diagnosis. Most important is the quality of objectivity. I have often worked with clients who were so desperate to find a solution, any solution, that they grabbed the first plausible explanation they stumbled upon. Often they were correcting a symptom, not a cause. Consequently, the solution did not fix the problem but provided only temporary relief.

Objectivity

Consultants cannot believe every opinion expressed to them by client employees. Nor can they take sides with executives. They need to be independent and step back from the "trees" to see the "forest." Second, they must have an intense curiosity. "Consultants must be nosey, looking behind symptoms and superficial explanations. They are puzzle solvers who must love the challenge of a messy and ill-defined problem." Third, they must demonstrate the art of being able to see a pattern running through many pieces of evidence. Most client problems rarely have simple explanations. Finally, the consultant must treat each situation as if it is new and unique, not as an exact replica of their last engagement (Greiner and Metzger, 1983, pp. 29–30).

What makes this process difficult is the fact that while the consultant and client are collecting data they are generating it and changing it at the same time. In other words, the minute we begin to examine an organization, it begins to change and we contribute to that change! Therefore, we must always be aware of our own actions as we collect and analyze the data.

Feedback versus Handback

The consultant's job is not over until the client has some useful action steps to take. Don't confuse data feedback with data "handback" (Bowers and Stambaugh, 1986, p. 45), which occurs when

> . . . tabulated information simply is returned to supervisors and managers who don't know how to use it effectively. Data handback produces pernicious and irrelevant effects. Feedback needs to be a thorough and systematic process supported by trained facilitators in order for it to work well.

You cannot hand a group a summary of their survey results and expect them to handle it well without outside help (p. 45).

For example, in one communication audit the head of the unit being audited was identified as an isolate and the cause of much of the frustration among staff members. At the same time a division in the group was causing decision making to be almost impossible. To "handback" that information without first preparing the unit head and providing a plan of action steps to correct these problems would serve only to make the problem more awkward. Thus, the feedback must take the form of positive steps that can be implemented by the group members.

Table 5.1 shows the data analysis techniques I suggest for each of the data collection methods discussed in Chapter 4, so the consultant will be able to provide "feedback," not "handback."

■ *Frequencies and Hypothesis Testing*

The scales used on the questionnaire will determine the type of analysis possible. For example, most demographic data produce a **nominal scale** meaning you are simply counting the number of items or observations in any one category. Suppose you want to conduct a workshop on gender issues in the organization, and you want to know the number of females at each level of the organization. By asking the respondents to indicate their sex and level of employment, you would simply count the number in each category.

In a second type of scale, an **ordinal scale,** data can logically be placed in rank order. For example, when studying gender one might ask men and women what their preferences are for sending messages in the organization (e.g., memos, meetings, interviews, e-mail, newsletters, etc.). Each response is ranked by the subject from lowest to highest preference. The

---

■ TABLE 5.1

MATCHING DATA ANALYSIS TECHNIQUES TO DATA COLLECTION METHODS

Data Collection Method	*Data Analysis Technique*
Questionnaires	Frequencies tables, Central tendency figures, Range, Variance, Hypotheses testing
Interviews and critical incidents	Content analysis
Observations	Behavioral frequency counts, Grounded theory
Outcome data	Multiapproaches

number of observations for each sex can be counted but the categories themselves cannot be added or multiplied.

The third type of scale is an **interval scale** in which distances between the responses have meaning. The Likert-type scales defined earlier are used for interval data, where "strongly agree" is defined as higher on the scale than "agree." For example, one might ask respondents to indicate how effective they think various forms of communication are: "Sending memos is an effective way to communicate with people in this organization" with responses ranging from "strongly agree" to "strongly disagree." Different from either nominal or ordinal scales, these data can be added, subtracted, multiplied, and divided.

A **frequency table** simply lists the number of responses for each item while **measures of central tendency** describe one characteristic of the data. The **mode** identifies the most frequent number in a series of numbers, the **medium** indicates the middle number in a series of numbers, and the **mean** is the average of a series of numbers. For example, suppose subjects were asked how often they talked with their supervisors during an average week. The answers for the nine fictional subjects were the following: 2, 2, 3, 4, 4, 5, 5, 5, and 9. The mode is 5, the medium is 4, and the mean is 4.33. Probably the most meaningful statistic is the mean, or the average number of times individuals talked with their supervisor during a week. It can be calculated only for interval data. **Variance,** or the way the numbers vary around the mean, and **range,** or the highest and lowest numbers, are simply other ways to indicate the variability of the data. The range in our example is from 2 to 9.

In order to test hypotheses, one can use simple **t-tests,** which are statistical tests for the difference between two sets of scores. **Analysis of variance** tests for differences among three or more scores. There is a chance that the mean (or average) score for two groups will be different by a few points but not be statistically significant, thus these tests provide a valid answer. The reader is referred to the suggested readings section at the end of this chapter, which includes a short article written for HRD practitioners and a text with a brief "statistics emergency kit" (Maiorca, 1991, and Zemke and Kramlinger, 1989). These two sources are the simplest, yet most complete, description of basic statistics I have found.

Content Analysis and Grounded Theory

Content analysis is a systematic analysis of text. For example, journalism researchers might collect editorials written during a certain period of time, by major newspapers, on a particular topic. Adjectives used, topics included, or arguments presented might be counted and summarized. Conclusions could be reached about the treatment various newspapers gave to political topics or candidates.

A recent research study (Hale, Cooks, and DeWine, 1992) analyzed the transcription of the Clarence Thomas hearings for appointment to the Supreme Court. Specifically, Hale, Cooks, and I conducted a content analysis of the senators' questioning of both Thomas and Anita Hill. We made comparisons between the language used, arguments presented as a preoration to their questions, and themes the congressmen reinforced by the style and content of their questions. We discovered significant differences in the way in which these two people were introduced, allowed to answer, and treated during the hearing.

Usually in content analysis, categories are predetermined and examples are found in text that fit those categories. In **grounded theory**, the categories emerge from the text itself, thus the theory or conclusion is "grounded" or based on the data, not predetermined.

Examples of occasions when a consultant might use the grounded theory technique include the following:

- an analysis of promotional material used by the organization in order to determine how it presents its goal or mission.
- an examination of critical incidents written by employees and identifying themes expressed by a majority of the respondents.
- content analysis of performance appraisal forms before and after some intervention into the organization.

This technique sounds simple and easy to do, and yet I believe it is the most difficult. When one has an abundance of data, finding insightful and meaningful themes is the goal.

Behavioral frequency counts involve simply listing, in a logical order, behaviors that are observed for one particular person or one specific task. Then a category scheme can be applied or developed in similar fashion to content analysis or grounded theory. This is not based on perception but actual observed behavior.

Multiple Approaches

Outcome data are that information collected by the company that will ultimately reveal how human behavior has changed as a result of some intervention. Absentee rates, turnover percentages, number of manufacturing errors, and safety records are examples of outcome data. There are two important steps to analyzing these data: first, getting access to them, and second, understanding the conditions under which they were collected. For example, absentee data need to be considered in the light of times of the year and general wellness of a community. Outcome data can provide very clear evidence of the impact of interventions on actual goals for the organization or they can be "garbage," depending on how many other variables can be controlled.

■ Consultant's Tips for Analyzing Results

The following are techniques I have used for collecting and analyzing results. There are many pitfalls along the way to a good data analysis and these suggestions may help you avoid some of them.

- *Keep a log of ideas and observations as the project progresses.* Your own chronological notes will be extremely useful to you as the project progresses.
- *Highlight notes in the margins of the flow diagrams.* As a part of your field notes you may be diagraming information and work flow. Notes that help you understand your diagrams will be critical.
- *Don't give your client more of a presentation than is required to inform, persuade, or initiate action.* Sometimes a consultant will overwhelm the client with information. It is better to provide only enough data at a time that can be fully understood and acted upon.
- *The written report should include nine sections:*
  1. The executive summary
  2. Project background
  3. Objectives and scope
  4. Methods
  5. Analysis
  6. Findings and conclusions
  7. Recommendations
  8. Expected benefits
  9. Implementation guide (O'Shea, 1986, pp. 239–40).
- *Enhance the readability of your report.* You should:
  - Write short reports.
  - Arrange material for emphasis.
  - Avoid long, complex paragraphs and sentences.
  - Avoid jargon.
  - Use active voice and direct, descriptive words rather than euphemisms.

- Use pictures and graphs.
- Use numbers selectively (O'Shea, p. 245).

If the written report is not clear, clean, and crisp, your recommendations may be ignored. The way in which the ideas are presented determines how much "noise" is present when the client is listening to your suggestions.

Kelley (1981) points out several pitfalls that inexperienced consultants often run into in collecting data. When consultants encounter these problems, their data are suspect, and their analyses may be based on inaccurate or incomplete information.

1. They fail to discuss with the source the purpose of the data collection; consequently, the source provides inaccurate or inappropriate information.

2. They fail to understand the source and its biases. Every source has an awkward and limited perspective.

3. They fail to understand how the source gathered its own data. This contributes to the source's bias and may affect the data's validity.

4. They fail to plan ahead in order to obtain what is needed the first time. Returning to the scene because of an oversight creates an air of incompetence.

5. They fail to document everything they read, see, or hear immediately. Memory is short.

6. They fail to reflect on the data gathering process. Are they covering each facet of the problem? Are there data gaps? Are they jumping to conclusions that bias their efforts? Are the data well organized? (p. 169).

In the final analysis, the consultant must draw on years of experience working with human beings in organizations in order to make an accurate assessment of conditions as they exist. Listening carefully to clients will enable the consultant to provide them with many answers and possible solutions they are unable to suggest themselves for a variety of reasons. This stage of the consulting process is essential for any follow-up intervention. Interventions without careful data analysis will fail and may leave the organization worse off than before the consultant or communication specialist entered it.

Once the needs assessment has been completed, the next step is to plan an intervention or training proposal. This must come from the data analysis itself rather than being preplanned or superimposed. The old adage about a boy who receives a new hammer and goes around looking

for things to bang on is never more true than when individuals have training or consulting interventions in mind and attempt to make them fit
whatever data have been collected.

In Chapter 6 a variety of training techniques are discussed. The reader
must keep in mind that you cannot simply pull a technique out of context
and apply it, like the hammer, to anything in sight. The technique or intervention must be carefully selected based on what the data reveal about the
organization and the people in it.

■ Suggested Readings

Maiorca, J. J. (1991). Basic statistics for the HRD practitioner. In W. Pfeiffer & W. Jones (Eds.)
    The 1991 Annual: Developing human resources (245–65). San Diego, CA: University Associ-
    ates.
Zemke, R., & Kramlinger, T. (1989). Figuring things out: A trainer's guide to needs and task analy-
    sis. Reading, MA: Addison-Wesley Publishing Co., Inc.

PART *III*

Training and Consulting Strategies and Techniques

Part III provides a collection of some of the most effective training and consulting techniques I have encountered. I have tried to include all the information necessary so that you could implement these techniques after reading their description. However, reading about a technique and actually performing it may be very different.

Chapter 6 reviews eight major categories of training methods while Chapter 7 discusses numerous consulting techniques under seven broad categories. These are techniques I have used, along with hundreds of others, for more than 25 years. The ones I have included are the ones that have been consistently effective. No matter who the group is (top-level executives, first line employees, university faculty, high school students, government workers, social service employees), these strategies have helped them become more aware of human communication problems and how to solve them.

Chapter 6

USING TRAINING TECHNIQUES

"The old idea was that the schools cooked you until you were done, and then you went to work. Now, you've got to be constantly cooking. If companies want to be continuously innovative to meet competition, they must engage in continuous, career-long training of all employees."
John Hoerr, 1990

*T*raining is big business. The American Society of Training and Development has 27,500 members, from every state in the U.S., whose professional careers are in the field of training. Training has become another arm of the educational system (DeWine, 1987a) and is also a very demanding activity.

I sometimes think adults have a shorter attention span than young children. I recently watched a group of children in a room filled with Lego blocks of all sizes become absorbed for over an hour in building imaginary high rises, yet I have also often watched trainers lose adult audiences' attention after only 30 minutes. The difference is involvement. No one was lecturing to those children about how to put the blocks together. They were learning by doing. Adults get as bored as children when they are talked *at* rather than invited to get involved more actively in the learning process. Adults are just *usually* more polite about it.

This chapter presents a variety of techniques to get participants "involved" in the training process. These techniques range from simple strategies that make lectures more exciting to complex simulations. Ultimately, the success of any training technique depends on the skill of the trainer. The selection of a technique depends on overall program objectives, amount of time available, costs of implementing the technique, facilities, and availability of equipment and materials. One of the basic tools of training is the lecture.

◼ Lectures

The word "lecture" conjures up a stern father trying to explain to his child the difference between right and wrong, or a professor reading from her yellowed notes to a class of students, half of whom are sleeping. Yet the lecture can be one of the most effective ways to get important information across to the trainees, but it should be used sparingly and with some creativity.

Limitations of Lectures

Wexley and Latham (1981) described the purpose of lectures as the "attempt to train employees by focusing primarily on their cognitions" (i.e., thoughts and ideas) (p. 127). The major disadvantage to the lecture is the one-way nature of the presentation, where information flows only from the trainer to the trainee. The learner becomes a passive listener. Wexley and Latham criticized the lecture technique for being "deficient for teaching job-related skills that can be transferred from the learning situation to the actual work situation. What can be transferred from the lecture to the job must almost always be limited to cognitive principles, rules, and factual information" (p. 128). They also suggested that the lecture technique may be threatening to individuals who have limited educational, social, or economic backgrounds.

Finally, the lecture typically ignores differences among trainees' abilities, interests, backgrounds, and personalities. When selecting a training format, the trainer must consider the participants' learning styles as well as the complexity of the material being presented.

Advantages of Lectures

Smith and Delahaye (1987) identified advantages and disadvantages of using lectures in training programs. Advantages are the low cost and the fact that most adults have been taught by this method and are familiar with it. The lecture can conserve time, allows the trainer to present information in an orderly fashion, and can accommodate a large audience. It does require speaking ability on the part of the trainer and those trainers who are comfortable with this style of delivery can capture the participants and make them want to learn and participate in the training session.

Features of Dynamic Lectures

The most important principle of developing dynamic lectures is to keep them short. In a training session a lecture usually shouldn't last more than 15–30 minutes. If more cognate material needs to be presented, break it up into smaller sections. Trainers are fond of calling this activity a "lecturette."

The lecture needs all the elements of a good public speech: an *attention step* that makes the audience want to hear more, *a need step* that tells them specifically why this information is relevant to them, *a variety of appeals* including logical, emotional, and ethical, and *a conclusion* that summarizes the primary objective and makes one final appeal. The presentation should be filled with examples and illustrations tying the trainees to the topic. Chapter 10 provides more specific information on public presentations which is relevant to short lectures in training sessions as well.

Audio-Visual Aids

We know that audio-visual aids, when used properly, can enhance a training program. For example, Sredl and Rothwell (1987) suggested about 80 percent of learning occurs through sight alone, 10 percent through hearing, 5 percent through touch and 5 percent through smell and taste. "The more that senses are stimulated, the more that information is reinforced and likely to be retained. Simulating more than one sense at the same time dramatically increases recall" (p. 124).

Form 6.1 presents a worksheet for selecting media. The issues to be considered are quite helpful and should give any trainer the best guidance for selection of media.

Effectiveness of Audio-Visual Aids

Wexley and Latham (1981) suggested audio-visual techniques should be considered in the following situations: 1) when there is a need to illustrate how certain procedures should be followed over time, 2) when there is a need to expose trainees to events not easily demonstrated in live lectures (i.e., a visual tour of a factory, open-heart surgery), 3) when the training is going to be used organization-wide and it is far too costly to ask the same trainers to travel from place to place or assemble everyone in one location, and 4) when audio-visual training is supplemented with live lectures or discussions before and after the sessions. "Well-developed audio-visuals can arouse strong, drive-producing responses especially when effective instructors are employed. Audio-visuals also clue or attract trainees' attention by using their unique features, like instant replay, slow motion, animated cartoons, time lapse photography, and close-ups" (p. 134).

The guidelines on page 81 are suggested to determine if the use of videos or films will enhance the learning situation (The American Society of Training and Development, 1988).

■ WORKSHEET FOR MEDIA SELECTION

Directions: As you consider choice of media, work through the questions on this worksheet. Check an answer in the center column to each question in the left column. Finally, at the end of the worksheet, make a media selection.

Issues to Consider	Yes (√)	No (√)	See Remarks (√)	If Yes, Eliminate (or Consider Carefully) Use Of:	If No Eliminate (or Consider Carefully) Use Of:
1. Will instruction be delivered to a group?	( )	( )	( )	• Computers for instruction • Printed material • Audiotape, unless properly amplified • Videotape, unless projected on large screen	• Blackboard • Ceramic board • Felt board • Magnetic board • Overhead • Opaque • Rear screen projection • Slides
2. Do learners have any preferences for certain media? Are they opposed to certain media?	( )	( )	( )	(Fill in as appropriate)	
3. Are instructional objectives primarily cognitive?	( )	( )	( )	(Fill in based on your preferences)	• Computer-based instruction • Overhead • Blackboard • Felt board • Ceramic board • Magnetic board • Opaque • Rear screen projection • Slides
4. Is there a great deal of time available for preparing media materials?	( )	( )	( )	(Fill in based on your preferences)	• Film • Professional audiotape • Professional videotape • Computer-based instruction • Slides

(Continued)

■ WORKSHEET FOR MEDIA SELECTION *(Continued)*

Issues to Consider	Yes (√)	No (√)	See Remarks (√)	If Yes, Eliminate (or Consider Carefully) Use Of:	If No Eliminate (or Consider Carefully) Use Of:
5. Is funding available for the most expensive media-based materials?	( )	( )	( )	(Fill in based on your preferences)	• Professional films, audiotapes, videotapes • In-house computer instruction
6. Are facilities adequate for most any kind of media?	( )	( )	( )	(Fill in based on your preferences)	(Fill in as appropriate)
7. Are raw materials available such as blank videocassettes?	( )	( )	( )	(Fill in as appropriate)	(Fill in as appropriate)
8. Is in-house talent, skilled in all types of media, available?	( )	( )	( )	(Fill in as appropriate)	(Fill in as appropriate)
9. Is necessary equipment available (or obtainable)?	( )	( )	( )	(Fill in as appropriate)	(Fill in as appropriate)
10. Will frequent revision be necessary?	( )	( )	( )	(Fill in as appropriate)	(Fill in as appropriate)
11. Other (specify:_____ _____)	( )	( )	( )	(Fill in as appropriate)	(Fill in as appropriate)
12. Other (specify:_____ _____)	( )	( )	( )		

(Continued)

79

■ **WORKSHEET FOR MEDIA SELECTION** *(Continued)*

SELECTION OF MEDIA
Which one medium or group of media would be appropriate?

REMARKS
Are there reasons to take different action? If so, explain and tell how any anticipated problems will be overcome.

From H.J. Sredl & W.J. Rothwell, *The ASTD Reference Guide to Professional Training Roles and Competencies, 1&2,* New York: Random House Professional Business Publications, 1987, pp. 129–131. Reprinted by permission.

- Does the program meet your needs analysis requirement; does it tie into the learning objective in the training session, or is it merely entertaining?
- Is the program style and approach appropriate for the age group, cultures, experience, and education level of your learners?
- Is the program attention-getting and, if appropriate, motivating, or is it dull?
- If characters and situations are shown in the program, are they realistic or ridiculous, does the dialogue sound natural or contrived?
- Does the program portray a work environment similar to that of your learners?
- Are the job problems portrayed in the program similar to those encountered by your learners, or are the problems shown irrelevant?
- If the program is about job behaviors, does it include examples of both desired and undesired behaviors?
- Does the program include enough information on how to improve job performance?
- Does the program include only a digestible amount of information, or would learners suffer from information overload?
- Is the program terminology consistent with that used in the rest of the training session?
- Does the program periodically summarize information and emphasize the essentials?
- Is the program conducive to postviewing discussion?
- What could the program accomplish in training that could not be done more simply or inexpensively with another film, video, or training method?
- Is the program accompanied by print materials that support the program content?
- Is the program accompanied by information validating the effectiveness of the program?
- Is the film or video in good physical shape, will it run smoothly?

Cautions in Using Audio-Visual Aids

Arnold and McClure (1989) listed a few simple rules for using audio-visual aids in training presentations:

1. Confine audio-visual aids to a single concept.

2. Make sure that every participant in the training session can see and/or hear the audio-visual aid.

3. Maintain control of your audio-visual aid by planning ahead for its use.

4. Watch out for Murphy's law: "If something can go wrong, it will."

Ribler (1983) identified the significant costs incurred when using audio-visual media:

> The cost estimates for audio-visual materials are based on the use of professional support. If, for example, you were costing a film, we include a scriptwriter, a director, at least one technician, and studio time costs. The same would be true if we were considering video tape or video disks . . . . Costs for initial production of audio-visual materials are many times higher than for written materials. For that reason alone the decision to produce them should be carefully considered. The cost for changing these kinds of materials after they have been completed is also very high. So stable materials should be selected, as well as material that is to be presented to large numbers of people over a broad geographical area or at intervals in a few locations. The decision to include these kinds of audio-visuals in a training program should be taken seriously and made only if the costs can be justified . . . . Making large investments in materials that cannot be completely justified can do more harm to your presentation than good (pp. 157–58).

I use the simplest form of audio-visual aids possible. They are aids, not the main focus of the presentation. When they become noticeable then probably they are inappropriate. I use flip charts most often because they are simple and transportable, and they provide visual evidence of the group's accomplishments.

There are many sources of information about the use of audio-visual aids. One of the best is the ASTD Info Line (Spruell, 1987), in which a series of criteria are identified to help trainers select the most appropriate aids for any training session.

■ *Video- and Computer-aided Training*

The advent of technology into the training room has dramatically changed some training programs. Computers are now being used for decision-making meetings, and video conferences have become a cost-effective way to bring people together. Companies are beginning to realize the usefulness of videoconferencing for introducing new products and policies. These can be brought into the field office without bringing all the field managers into a central location.

John Hancock Financial Services of Boston has relied on business television networks to bring its 17,000 employees closer together.

> This company—whose insurance business alone has $32 billion in assets—has used an in-house television studio for more than 20 years. Yet by upgrading its equipment to handle live transmissions, John Hancock's group and retail insurance companies . . . have realized advantages in savings in travel costs, reaching 30 times as many people for each class, and a decreasing need to take seminars on the road to regional locations for weeks at a time (Gerwig, 1991).

The traditional classroom is no longer the only place training can take place. As Romiszowski and deHaas (1989) pointed out, distance learning can take place via computers with the advantages of:

> . . . classrooms open 24 hours a day and you never find a closed door when you want to speak to your tutor. It means a more democratic environment for group interaction, in the sense that all people are equal because they have the same possibilities and tools to communicate their thoughts. Interruptions can be made at any time. Even reactions to past messages belong to the possibilities (pp. 8–9).

Some of the newest uses of computers and video involve group decision making. Computer-mediated decision making tends to remove the impact of status and position power in small group discussions. It also has the potential to remove some of the fear of being evaluated immediately. It equalizes verbal contributions so those who are less verbal have an equal chance of being "heard"; however, it may introduce unequal treatment due to writing styles and abilities.

Some suggestions for using technology in training and consulting include the following:

- Discuss with the client the potential change in communication messages when they are sent via technology rather than face to face.
- Use techniques that will help make the training more personal even though the participants may be seeing you on a large screen instead of in person. The instructor will have to work harder at calling people by name and making personal comments which indicate the instructor knows the class members.
- Try to offer options to the students that will make them feel more a part of the class rather than audience members. For example, they might want the class broken into short lectures with certain

times for interaction with the instructor and personal phone conferences.

- If possible, visit each site at least once so students have personal contact with the instructor.

- Encourage small group interaction and group presentations so that the participants feel a sense of commitment to each other.

Trainers need to be competent to use video conferences and computer-mediated training techniques if they want to be able to meet the demands of modern businesses.

Self-assessment Instruments

Many trainers will use **self-assessment instruments** as a part of the training program. These tools range from personality inventories to opinions about how the group or organization is currently functioning. These self-assessment instruments can be found in a variety of places, but one of the best resources is the instrumentation books and annual handbooks published by University Associates (Pfeiffer and Jones, 1972–1993). A recent review of organizational communication instruments provides another resource that includes the instruments (Downs, DeWine, and Greenbaum, in press).

Benefits and Hazards of Self-assessment Instruments

The benefits of using self-assessment instruments include helping participants to understand group or individual behavior theory, providing feedback about one's own behavior from a nonpersonal source, allowing nonthreatening comparisons with "norms" or the rest of the group, and providing a common language for future discussions.

The hazards of using self-assessment instruments include the fear some people have of being "exposed" and not wanting to talk about their own behaviors, presentation of more feedback than individuals want or are able to handle, development of a "nit-picking" session on the instrument itself, and the facilitator's presentation of the results as the "only answer."

Effective Use of Self-assessment Instruments

To avoid these pitfalls, the facilitator must set the appropriate climate. Introduce the instrument as merely a "snapshot" of individuals' behavior at one point in time. Clarify that there are no right or wrong answers and that this instrument only provides a "mirror" to hold up and see how much is reflected. When consultants start using instruments to guide all behavior and all future interventions, dangerous assumptions are operating. Instead, these instruments must be used to stimulate discussion about what is going on in the group and how each individual may or may not be reacting to that group. Instruments should never be used as a strict category system in which to place individuals for future reference.

The underlying principle of the instrument must be explained. Try to select instruments that do not imply there is one "right" way to be. The administration of the instrument must be clear and without confusing directions. Make the scoring of the instrument as simple as possible with score sheets set up so that very little instruction must take place.

The results should be interpreted in the context of the focus of the particular group setting. Avoid playing "dime store psychologist." Your job is not to psychoanalyze anyone but merely to have each individual think carefully about his or her own behavior.

If the group gives you permission, posting the results can be very revealing. It is not necessary to post individual results, but in the aggregate, individuals can see where they fit into the overall group picture. It is critical that the facilitator spend enough time discussing the results so that participants can use the information to improve their ability to function in the group.

Case Studies

A **case study** is a narrative or short story about some organizational issue. Case studies can be rather simple, including only the basic information, or very complex, including a complete financial report and history of the organization. The use of case studies in training sessions provides real life examples of problems or issues the trainees are asked to analyze. The case study approach to learning was originally developed by the Harvard University Business School.

Types of Case Studies

According to Ronstadt (1980) Harvard M.B.A.s prepared between 500 to 700 business cases before graduating. The case studies include the following types:

1. *Highly structured or technical problem-solving cases.* These are short case studies with a small amount of information. The best solution

is often available, and the student or reader applies some kind of formula to find an answer.

2. *Structured vignettes.* These are used in introductory management courses at the graduate and undergraduate level. They may vary in length. A best solution usually does not exist, but the student is expected to identify and apply several concepts to solving the case.

3. *Long, unstructured cases or problems/opportunity-identifying cases.* Here the reality of the situation is reflected by supplying all or nearly all of the relevant information.

4. *Ground-breaking cases for advanced M.B.A., doctoral, or executive management classes.* The business situation is totally new, and not all problems have been identified.

Effective Use of Case Studies

A retired professor from Harvard who was in part responsible for the development of this training technique suggested the following eight tips when using case studies:

- Take responsibility for classroom leadership. This should not turn into a massive nondirective interview.
- Do not let the participants "beat a dead horse."
- If a sideline discussion is important, let it be developed if time is available.
- Insist that participants state positions and conclusions.
- Indicate when analysis is moving in the right directions.
- As facilitator, serve as a "sounding board" for ideas and analysis.
- Ask participants to list major topics and then insure they are covered in the discussion.
- State the objectives of the case study and be enthusiastic (Christensen, 1987, pp. 9–15).

There are many case study books available for training settings (see: Sypher, 1990). Cases should be selected for the main issue they present and the degree to which that issue addresses problems the group may be facing (James and DeWine, 1990). They can be used with individuals or in groups. There is seldom a right or wrong answer but rather they are used to have participants consider factors important to making decisions.

Tracey (1989) suggested that the major advantage to using case studies is that "the products of thinking in case studies are more relevant to the experiences of the trainees because they must inject their own perceptions, attitudes, and feelings into the case" (p. 258).

Maier, Solem, and Maier (1975) have identified important contributions of the case method to training including the following:

- It discourages making snap judgments about people and behavior.

- It discourages believing in or looking for the correct answer.

- It graphically illustrates how the same set of events can be perceived differently.

- It destroys any smug generalizations one might have about right versus wrong answers, management prerogatives, the attitude of labor, the best methods of discipline, the younger generation, the place of women in management, and many other issues.

- It trains one to discuss things with others and to experience the broadening value of interaction with one's equals.

- It stresses practical thinking so that such considerations as cost, convenience, deadlines, attitudes of top management, and the feelings of other persons prevent solutions from becoming idealized.

- It causes doubt as to whether there really are basic human relationship principles (pp. 1–2).

Two excellent examples of extended case studies that address organizational communication issues are those by Goodall (1989) and Tompkins (1992). In both books, each chapter represents a different case study or a different segment of the same case. Their insights and observations are thought-provoking. Parts of these books would be very useful in a training session that focuses attention on communication issues. To appreciate the case study technique from a trainee's perspective, try working through "B. Parker and Company" on pages 99–106 at the end of this chapter. The content of this case will also give you insights into communication problems that a consultant might face.

Tracey (1989) pointed out the major disadvantage of using case studies: "A considerable amount of time is required for trainees to read, digest, and discuss all the materials in a case report" (p. 258). Case studies can be fairly simple, like the one at the end of this chapter, or so complex and detailed that they take over 200 pages to explain!

■ *Small Group Activities*

Dividing training participants into small groups of 5 to 7 people allows a more personal experience with other types of training techniques. For example, a simulation involving five people will allow everyone in the group to participate in either the discussion or in the actual role plays in the simulation. As long as you are in a group of 20 to 40 people, many people will be passive audience members. Small group activities personalize the training experience for all participants.

Bunker, Nochajski, McGillicuddy and Bennett (1987), in their review of literature on training designs, concluded that "to be effective, skills training requires practice according to criteria, followed by performance feedback. When a new skill is learned, a small group may be a safe place to try it out" (p. 229). Many training techniques are "tried out" in group settings. Placing participants in small groups will make them feel more involved in the process.

First, a small group will foster interpersonal relationships among the group members. This will increase the possibility that group members will know each other better and feel more comfortable with each other. People tend to want to help someone they like accomplish tasks. Thus, the group becomes more cooperative. This makes consensus easier to reach. It is also possible that as they get to know one another they will increase their dislike for each other as well! However, I have found that during the initial stages of a group there is a "halo effect" in operation. The halo effect suggests that people will give each other the benefit of the doubt in initial interactions and will suspend judgment in an effort to get along.

At the same time, groups have to watch out for "groupthink" (Janis, 1972). **Groupthink** occurs when a group becomes so dependent on its own information that members do not allow outside information, especially if it is contrary to their own thinking, to enter into the discussion.

Small groups members must be careful that they do not defend one group member against another, that they do pay attention to the process they are using to making their decisions, that they don't allow so much social interaction that it interferes with accomplishing the task, and that interpersonal conflicts are not under the surface and never dealt with.

Ellis (1988) suggested the consultant or trainer needs to "guide rather than influence the group's activity" (p. 54). The facilitator must not present the ultimate solutions to the group because then the facilitator, rather than the group, "owns" the solution. Nor, at the same time, can the facilitator sit back and simply let the group move in any direction. "Guiding rather than influencing" is a good guideline to follow.

■ *Structured Experiences*

Structured experiences are exercises intended to allow individuals to try out behaviors in a relatively "safe" environment. Experimental learning is most useful where intellectualization is not as effective as actually placing people in true-to-life settings.

Structured experiences should not be used by inexperienced trainers, and yet that is the activity of choice for many training consultants. The problem with using "games" is that many trainers do not know how to analyze them properly once they are completed. A very well thought out and carefully orchestrated debriefing should occur with every structured game and, in fact, often will take longer than the game itself took to complete.

Porter (1987) suggested a five-stage process for completing the debriefing following an activity. These stages are: experiencing the activity, data gathering, interpreting, generalizing, and applying (p. 69). During the data gathering stage, participants are asked what happened during the activity, including thoughts and feelings, and what people did or said. The third stage, interpreting, asks individuals to "make sense of the data reported in the preceding phase" (p. 70). The next stage, generalizing, is "drawing out what the participants have learned and relearned" (p. 70).

The last stage, application, may be the most significant of all the stages. Here the trainer is asking participants how this experience can be used in their everyday lives and how their new knowledge might influence or affect the way they behave on a day-to-day basis. Sometimes the trainer will use this stage to help participants make commitments to what they will do with what they have learned, on the job or in their personal lives. In my own experience, processing the activity is much harder and demands greater skills than running any activity. If the trainer is not highly skilled at drawing out insights and helping people to understand their own experiences, the activity remains just a game.

A facilitator should spend approximately twice as much time discussing the activity as was spent participating in the activity. This discussion first asks participants to explain to the whole group what they were asked to do during the simulation. People always want everyone to know why they were acting the way they were and that the behavior is not typical of how they normally would react. Only after everyone has had a chance to explain what he or she was doing can you get the group to focus on the meaning of the activity. What did they learn from this activity that they can now apply to work or personal settings? How did they feel when people acted a certain way and how does that translate into everyday life? This discussion is absolutely necessary, or the participants will end up thinking, "This was an interesting activity and kind of fun, but what does it have to do with anything else?"

■ *Role Play*

A **role play** is a description of a problem "acted out" by two or more individuals. It can bring out the "ham" in people, but for those who are more apprehensive, I would never use the term "role play"! Some will see this as "silly."

Maier, Solem, and Maier (1975) identified two role-playing procedures. One is the multiple role-playing procedure, in which the entire group attending the training session is formed into role-playing groups, the size of the groups depending on the number of participants required for the particular case. All groups role-play simultaneously. This maximizes opportunities for the members of the audience to try out new attitudes and behaviors and provides data from several groups so that the results can be compared.

The other procedure that Maier, Solem, and Maier identified is single role playing, in which only one role-playing group performs while other members of the class participate as observers. An advantage to this is, since all persons observe a single performance, it is possible to discuss the details that led to a particular effect. Also, participants in the role play profit from the analytical discussion of their behaviors since they are often unaware of the effect of their actions on others. Finally, observers can develop sensitivity to the feelings of the performers.

There are also modifications of these two basic types:

Role reversals: participants begin the role play in one role and half way through are asked to switch places with another participant and assume a different role. This is especially effective at helping individuals to experience another point of view.

Alter egos or doubles: one person plays a role and a second person stands behind the participant, providing advice and suggestions. In this way, the second person becomes the "alter ego" of the role player and helps the performer remember his or her role.

Rotation or fish bowl: I have found it quite useful to have individuals rotate through roles or have the entire group watch a role play (as if the participants are in a "fish bowl") and then ask the observers to make suggestions for the role players. For example, one role player is trying to use a new conflict management technique. I may stop the interaction and ask the observers if there are other things the person

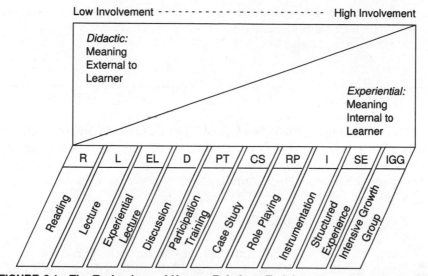

FIGURE 6.1   The Technology of Human Relations Training   From J. E. Jones & J. W. Pfeiffer, Role Playing, *The 1979 Annual Handbook for Group Facilitators,* San Diego: University Associates, 1979, p. 182.

might say or do to help resolve the role play. I may ask someone who has a particularly good suggestion to take the place of the role player and act it out. This gets the entire group involved while providing one common experience for all to analyze.

Role plays should be strictly voluntary, as forcing a normally shy individual to "act out" will cause extreme stress for that person as well as those watching the experience! Don't force someone who is not inclined to be "on stage" to do so. Provide opportunities for one-on-one role plays or discussions about the situation for those individuals who are reluctant to perform in front of a group.

The importance of debriefing cannot be overemphasized. The facilitator must "make the point" or the whole exercise becomes fruitless. The debriefing should normally take as long as or longer than the activity took to perform.

Figure 6.1 outlines Jones and Pfeiffer's (1979) identification of the extent to which role playing, as well as other activities, are either more or less didactic versus experimental. At the extreme end of the continuum are "intensive growth groups." These activities involve many of the others described earlier; however, they also involve counseling, and I would not suggest that any trainer who has not had graduate-level training in counseling and/or psychology use this technique. Even then, the training should be specifically for this type of activity. Don't try it if you don't know what you are doing!

Simulations

In **simulations,** participants are asked to "act out" complex cases and roles in order to analyze an organizational problem. Simulations are attempts to create real social settings where individuals can have a true-to-life experience. The goal is to gain insight into one's own behavior.

Purposes of Simulations

Caplan and Darth (1987) summed up the purpose behind the use of simulation in training: "The idea behind laboratory education is quite simple: to provide a setting in which participants can exhibit behavior and in turn reflect on and learn from that behavior" (p. 137). Laboratory education, simulations, or hands-on experience was developed as an alternative to more didactical methods in which an expert delivers information that is absorbed by the listeners. It is also an alternative to the case method, in which the instructor leads a discussion based on a post-mortem of an actual case. As Caplan and Darth suggested, laboratory education was "invented expressly to serve the purpose of creating a living laboratory in which participants put their own behavior under a microscope" (p. 237).

Examples of early simulations used by trainers certainly include the T-group (training group) from NTL (National Training Laboratories). After 40 years of use, it still offers advantages, despite the image problems this technique has had over the past two decades. During the 1950s and '60s T-groups, or sensitivity training, was sometimes seen as therapy groups run by nonpsychologists. An unskilled trainer asking probing, personal questions can do a great deal of damage.

An example of a current simulation is "Looking Glass" (McCall and Lombardo, 1979). "Looking Glass" is a hypothetical medium-size glass manufacturing corporation, complete with annual report, financial data, and glass products. The simulation creates an air of authenticity. The fictional company consists of three divisions, whose environments vary according to the degree of change. The simulation lasts six hours and is intended to represent a typical day in the life of the company. It begins by giving each participant an "inbasket" full of memos and materials. Contained in the collective inbaskets of the 20 participants are more than 150 different problems that participating managers must attend to. The problems vary in importance. During the simulation, problems often take the form of discrepancies between "what participants intend to do and what they discover later they actually do" (p. 147).

McCall and Lombardo point out limitations of this technique because a simulation removes participants from the present environment, and whatever is learned from the simulation must be adapted to the individual's current circumstances. Second, it is powerful, meaning that it exposes participants to an intensity that many of them may not be prepared for, and it is highly demanding in terms of staff preparation and time.

Boyer (1987) described a simulation approach for developing consultation skills. He suggested the advantages of using a simulation are that it "permits some simultaneous training in cognitive interpersonal and personal competence without the time commitments and complications that may accompany a practicum approach" (p. 149). A practicum approach is usually more like a semester-long class in which students take on roles for several weeks at a time in a true-to-life organization.

Boyer suggested that cognitive approaches typically emphasize cognitive skills more than interpersonal or personal emotional skills. They are easier to design, control, and implement. Simulations do provide substantial opportunities for participants to develop interpersonal and personal competence. The simulation approach may serve as a transition between the cognitive and practicum approaches. It is less labor-intensive, yet permits simultaneous development of cognitive, interpersonal, and personal skills. In addition, it can be used with less experienced participants.

A Sample of the Simulation Technique

The activity in Form 6.2 was developed for a graduate consulting class. Each participant takes a turn at playing the role of "consultant" with the same cast of characters. The interactions are videotaped for later review.

Designing and Directing Training

Like their clients, trainers need training and practice to ensure that they perform their work well. In "practicing what they preach," trainers build on a body of knowledge about the design and direction of training activities. They also develop their own talents and skills.

■ THE CONSULTATION SIMULATION

The Organization

Mead Mental Health Clinic is a district-wide community service agency serving a district of four counties. Its services include counseling and psychological services, career planning, crisis intervention related workshops, and outpatient and inpatient care. It also provides educational services to inpatients, including continuing education for adults and regular educational services for school age patients. On the staff are 39 professional workers and 72 hourly wage workers.

Background of the Problem

Mead Mental Health Clinic has long recognized that employees who are satisfied with their jobs enable a company to be successful. This philosophy, rather than a specific problem, led to the establishment of two-way communications. Over the years, the philosophy and the programs which reflect it have evolved to meet employees' changing needs, encompassing a variety of face-to-face, written, and other methods of communication. Every April and May since 1946, the Mead Mental Health Clinic has held a series of two-hour "jobholders meetings" in which management reports to employees on the company's financial health, business planning, wages and benefits, and other areas of general interest. Employees in turn, are free to question any member of management, including the top administrator of the center. Some questions are submitted in writing, some are asked from the floor. Some are signed, some are anonymous. Whatever the question, a top-level administrator gives a spontaneous reply.

The Problem

The employees who attend these meetings respond very favorably to them. However, only 60 percent of the professional workers and 25 percent of the hourly wage workers attend. Top management would like to increase the percentage of attendance in hopes of increasing participation in decision making and policy development. *You have been called in as a consultant to help them attain this goal.* You have had two previous meetings with top management which includes: Center Director, Director of Clinical Services, Director of Educational Services, Supervisor of Nursing Staff, and Director of Personnel.

(Continued)

94

■ THE CONSULTATION SIMULATION *(Continued)*

Meeting Participants

Mr. Stan Leiber, Center Director: overall administrator with particular responsibility for financial operations. He enthusiastically supports this project and made the initial contact with the consultant.

Dr. Victoria Quarterly, Director of Clinical Services: a counseling psychologist, who is skeptical about the success of the project as well as the effect of having an outsider come in as a consultant.

Ms. Margaret Coffman, Director of Educational Services: would like to be supportive of this project as long as it is not going to eliminate any of her present educational programs or increase her workload.

Mr. Fred Williams, Supervisor of Nursing Staff: wants equal attention given to problems of the nurses as well as equal respect given to their input into decision making.

Dr. Chris Dotson, Director of Personnel: having designed three consultation workshops he believes he can solve any problems the center has with no outside help. He feels he already knows why the attendance is at its present level and if given the proper resources, feels he could solve the problem.

Design

Students are divided into groups of six with one person designated as the "consultant." Every 10 minutes students change roles until everyone serves as the consultant. While one group is being videotaped, another group is watching on closed circuit TV. Each group also reviews its own tape.

Guidelines for Designing and Directing Training

Bunker, et al. (1987) reviewed a large body of published material on training design and concluded the following guidelines based on categories of important principles of design.

The first category is initial activities. These initial activities were viewed as critical since adults need to "know the schedule, the rules of the game, and who the staff and other participants are" (p. 227). These activities were seen as setting the climate for the entire workshop and establishing the staffs' role with the participants in the workshop.

The second category is establishing a collaborative participant-staff relationship. Their review indicated many authors emphasized that adults must be responsible for their own learning (Pfeiffer and Jones, 1973). I recommend the staff should put themselves in the participant's roles when designing a training event in order to understand the nature of a collaborative relationship.

Third, levels of activity and participation are planned. Many authors suggest that the degree to which there is active participation on the part of the attendees is something that needs to be decided early in the event. An underlying assumption is that "involvement and shared leadership increase commitment which in turn increases learning" (Bunker, et al., p. 228).

Fourth, the trainer must maintain energy in the workshop. The level of energy on the part of the staff carries over and is expressed by the participants. Staff members should vary the activity type, length, and intensity so that participants do not get bored. All trainers must pay attention to building in time for breaks for the physical, as well as psychological, needs of the participants.

Fifth, the trainer must plan strategies to reduce resistance. Several authors deal with resistance as a part of the process of learning and of the change process and explain that it must be carefully understood. Finally, a variety of sequence patterns were recommended from less difficult to more difficult or from less risky to more risky. Most suggested that as the program progresses the trainer should gather data on how it is affecting the participants.

Lippitt and Lippitt (1986) suggested ten assumptions as guides in designing learning sessions:

- Every client group is unique.
- Within each group, participants show differences in readiness.
- The consultant should recognize the network already established within the client group and support its influence.

- The consultant should encourage learning through the formation of teams of peers.
- Client learners should have a major role in planning the design.
- The consultant should demonstrate how to build resources.
- The consultant should build mutual feedback processes.
- The design should promote follow-up.
- The design should teach methodological skills so that client learners can apply their training without having to rely on the consultant.
- The consultant's challenge is to help the client tie information to a variety of applications, like action planning, management plans, and risk taking.

Lippitt and Lippitt (1986) also identified traps to avoid in training designs. Some of the traps involve personnel, both the training staff and the client. Relying totally on one expert is a bad idea, as is allowing the participation of an inadequately prepared, unknown, and uncomfortable resource person. Not obtaining any data about the client before the session, not involving the client in the planning, and not sharing the agenda can prevent the session from meeting the client's unique set of needs. Not dealing with the learners' feelings or allowing the expression of individual preferences, and using haphazard grouping patterns can also be damaging. Inattention to the details of the physical set-up of the training site (for example, the seating arrangement, the working order of equipment, and the legibility of visual aids) or to the schedule (failing to devise a definitive way to begin the session, allowing long coffee breaks, having no plans for transitions) may have a negative effect. Even after a successful session, failure can result in the long run from skipping plans for follow-up or preparing inadequately for the recording and distribution of follow-up materials (pp. 108–109).

It is important that the trainer pay attention to all the small details that make a session go well. In a sense, it is like planning a mini-conference, with plans for food, seating, lighting, travel arrangements, and social programs. I always pay a great deal of attention to the environment in which I will be working because I believe the shape of the room, the places where people are sitting, lighting, and sound can all have a great impact on the success of the meeting. But sometimes all the planning in the world will not prevent problems.

A colleague and I were planning a full day retreat for a medical association. This was the first time I had worked with this consultant and

I wanted to be sure we had thought of every detail. We arrived at the hotel the night before, and at 10:00 P.M. found the room with the name of the organization on the door for the next morning. The room was not arranged as we had instructed and so we dismantled the room and spent till 11:30 P.M. rearranging it to fit the needs of this session. We found someone in housekeeping to provide new tablecloths to fit the new arrangement and were very pleased with the result. As we wearily approached the elevator, congratulating ourselves for coming in a night early and avoiding a disaster, we noticed on the bulletin board for the next day that the room we had just rearranged was scheduled for a pharmaceutical company! They no doubt had had the room arranged just the way they wanted it! Attending to every detail can still get you in trouble! We told the desk clerk the next morning that there must be some error on the bulletin board and actually the two rooms were switched and then spent the rest of the morning wondering, along with the group leader, why the hotel would have switched the rooms at the last moment! At the right opportunity, I will fess up!

The Consummate Trainer

Spaid (1989) has outlined 10 characteristics of what he called the "consummate" trainer. The consummate trainer:

- has experience in virtually all tasks and techniques of the entire range of training methodology and can carry out these activities at an acceptable level of proficiency, but prefers and performs some of them exceptionally well.
- orchestrates the parts of training with an acute awareness of the impact of the whole.
- is flexible and versatile and open to change, from one training session to another and from one subject to the next.
- takes risks and can submerge ego for the good of the group and the training.
- can generate excitement in training, through a sense of drama.
- has a sense of humor, which is applied to self as well as to others.
- does his or her own homework and keeps on learning.
- exhibits patience, with learners and with self.
- has enough independence and toughness of mind not to be overcome by fads and untested theories.

- respects wisdom, as not knowledge alone or experience alone, but each informing the other (pp. 18–19).

If the trainer has all these characteristics, then he or she will be part magician, vaudeville act, teacher, counselor, and comedian. But most of all, he or she will be an outstanding trainer.

■ WHAT WOULD YOU DO?
B. Parker and Company

The following case study gives you a chance to practice the concepts you've learned . . . After reading each section of the case, think about what's going on. Analyze why things are happening the way they are. Then go on to read and answer the review questions. Compare your answers with the next part of the case, which describes what happened as a result of what came before, or the action that was taken in that particular instance. Remember, the action taken and the decisions made in this case are not necessarily the only possible or justifiable ones. Rarely is there only one right answer to any business problem.

B. Parker and Company is an advertising firm located in Boston. It was founded in 1931 by Brendan Parker II and is presently run by his son, Brendan Parker III. Initially, the company handled only print media—newspapers and magazines. But as television and radio became more popular and more influential as an advertising medium, B. Parker and Company branched into T.V. and radio advertising. By 1963, B. Parker and Company had become one of the most sought-after firms in Boston. Over the years, B. Parker's creative department had collected a network of talented in-house and freelance writers and graphic artists. Their newspaper ads were catchy and bright, their T.V. and radio commercials witty and appealing. This year the company is celebrating its fiftieth anniversary.

Brendan Parker III is eloquent without being loquacious, and well-spoken with no hint of arrogance. He speaks well with others and presents his ideas clearly. He also listens carefully to what others have to say, and always with a sympathetic ear. It's an attribute and a skill that the entire company profits from.

Planning a Meeting

Brendan Parker was reasonably satisfied with the company's present rate of growth and its prestige, but he felt it was time to get involved in bigger things. He wanted the company to plan on bidding for new accounts in the advertising market dominated by the larger New York agencies. He decided to lay the groundwork for the new marketing push by meeting informally with the company's managers to gather their reactions and pool their ideas.

(Continued)

These included the production manager, Michael Fox; the creative manager, Lee Codman; the marketing manager, Lauren Casey; the finance manager, Sean Dennison; and the sales manager, Jane Monoson.

As B.P. sat down to prepare the memo announcing the meeting, the intercom buzzed. "Yes, Vanessa," he answered to his secretary.

"Mr. Parker, Jeb Stuart from Rockwell is on the line. May I put him through?"

"Vanessa, tell him I'm busy right now, but that I'll get back to him just as soon as I can. That'll give me a chance to glance through the Rockwell file."

As B.P. replaced the receiver, he picked up a file from his desk. B. Parker and Company had been having problems with this account from the beginning. Rockwell was what B.P. referred to as the "blue-blooded killer." It was an old company located in Connecticut. Rockwell was meticulous in its approach to everything, and its managers were perfectionists to the core. Although B.P. admired these traits, he found his dealings with Rockwell tedious. He knew it was an account that had to be handled delicately. It was an important account, one that would add to the prestige of his company if it was successful in its bid for the account.

After quickly reviewing the file, he called back Jeb Stuart.

"Hi, Jeb. Brendan here. Sorry I wasn't able to talk with you immediately. How are things going?"

"Fine, Brendan, fine," Jeb replied. "But questions concerning your campaign have cropped up in the minds of a few people here. They're matters of policy rather than approach, so I thought it best to speak with you personally."

"Right, Jeb. What seems to be the problem?"

Jeb and Brendan went on to discuss the problem for the next 20 minutes. In the course of the conversation, Brendan decided it would be best to meet personally with Jeb and other members of Rockwell. Except for the policy reservations Jeb referred to, Rockwell seemed ready to accept B. Parker's proposed advertising campaign. Brendan was determined to quell any remaining reservations Rockwell might have. The two men finished their conversation after agreeing that Brendan would meet with Jeb in Connecticut that afternoon.

Brendan buzzed Vanessa and asked her to book him on an early afternoon flight to Connecticut. He then quickly finished his memo to his managers. Brendan's memo is shown in Exhibit A.

Review Questions

1. Is Brendan Parker's message effectively conveyed by his memo? Why or why not?

2. Brendan Parker decided to hold an informal meeting. Does the tone of his memo reflect this? Is the tone formal or informal?

(Continued)

EXHIBIT A   **Brendan Parker's Memo**

TO: All Managers
FROM: Brendan Parker
RE: New Marketing Strategies
DATE: March 15, 1981

There will be a mandatory meeting for all managers on Friday, March 17, at 3:00 P.M. in the informal conference room on the thirtieth floor. After a thorough appraisal of each department's performance, I have decided it is time to re-evaluate our position in the marketplace. You will be expected to provide input to help reshape our marketing policies.

---

3. Is there any difference in the message Brendan Parker is *sending* and the one the managers are *receiving?* How do you think the managers will interpret the message?

4. Is the memo clear? Will there be any questions in the readers' minds when they've finished reading it? Will the managers attending the meeting be prepared for what Brendan Parker wishes to discuss?

5. How could this memo be improved, if at all?

Jane Monoson Gets Worried

After receiving the memo, Jane Monoson immediately went to Lauren Casey's office.

"Did you get the memo?" Jane asked as she walked into Lauren's office.

Lauren nodded and said, "It was just put on my desk. I'm not quite sure what to make of it. I didn't think our position in the market was threatened in any way. Of course, our bid for the Batchelor account could have been rejected. B.P. was really counting on it—it's worth $2 million. B.P. always holds meetings if an account falls through."

"Oh, no," Jane moaned. "I gave that account to that new young exec, Paul Winthrop—the fellow we pulled in from the Wilmar Agency. Maybe I shouldn't have put him in charge of something so big so soon."

"I wouldn't worry too much yet, Jane," Lauren replied.

Jane stood up and said, "No. I'd better talk with Paul—see what kind of feedback he got from the people he's worked with at Batchelor's. Paul would have a better idea of what's going on with that account than anyone. Besides, I don't want to go to this meeting completely defenseless. Listen Lauren, I'd better see you later. I want to catch Paul before he heads out to lunch."

Jane returned to her office and phoned Paul's office. The call was put through to Madge, the account executives' secretary.

"Hi Madge, it's Jane. Is Paul anywhere in the building?"

(Continued)

"Sorry, Jane," Madge replied. "Paul just stepped out for a luncheon meeting. Can I leave him a message?"

Jane thought for a moment. "Yes, tell him to see me as soon as he returns. It's about the Batchelor account. A big problem has surfaced, and I have to talk to him."

Madge took down the message and reassured Jane she would pass it on to Paul immediately.

Review Questions

1. Brendan Parker's message has obviously been misinterpreted by Lauren and Jane. Where did the communication process break down? More specifically, at what point in the sender-receiver system was the weakness?

2. What do you think of Jane's reaction? Is she acting too hastily? Should she have waited until after the meeting before acting? Why or why not?

3. Should Jane have passed the message to Madge? Or should she have waited to speak with Paul personally?

4. What possible interference problems could there be in the transmittal of Jane's message?

The Anxiety Spreads

After failing to reach Paul, Jane decided to try B.P. personally. Maybe he can calm my fears, she thought to herself. She picked up the phone and called Vanessa, B.P.'s secretary.

"Hi, Vanessa, it's Jane. Is Brendan around?"

"Sorry, Jane," Vanessa replied. "Mr. Parker just left for a meeting with a client. Very urgent business, so I hear."

Jane groaned silently to herself. B.P.'s "urgent business" had to do with the Batchelor account, she thought. After thanking Vanessa, Jane phoned Michael Fox, the production manager.

"Mike, did you get the memo? What do you think B.P. wants? I tried calling B.P., but—"

"Jane! Slow down! I've seen the memo. We all have. I thought it was just a general meeting—an open forum. But after talking with the others, I'm beginning to worry. Sean, for one, is sure it means trouble. Now it sounds as though you think that, too."

"Mike, I think it's about the Batchelor account. I've been trying to get ahold of Paul Winthrop, who's handling the account. But Madge says he's at lunch. I'll see what I can find out from him when he gets back, and I'll keep you posted."

Almost two hours later, Paul Winthrop returned to his office, elated after his meeting with J.P. Stance, the executive representing the Batchelor Company.

(Continued)

"How're ya doing, Madge?" he greeted the secretary as he burst into the office. "A sunny day to match my feelings. Just about settled the big one—seems to be no competition out there. Dear J.P. did everything but sign the contract. All she's got to do is convince one more big wheel that we've got the talent they need, and the account is ours. Can't wait to tell Jane."

Madge sighed and said, "Paul, I hate to be the bearer of bad news, but Jane phoned while you were out. I don't know—maybe she spoke with that one big wheel J.P. Stance hadn't. Whatever it was, she sounded frantic. Said there was a major problem with the account. She wanted to see you as soon as you returned. Paul, really, I'm sorry."

Paul looked stunned. "Madge, I can't believe it! J.P. almost had her pen in her hand! She must know what's going on over at Batchelor's. I really didn't think she'd play games with me." He sighed. "I should have known. My first big one, on the line. I'd better see Jane right away."

A Measure of Relief

Paul rushed to Jane's office, apprehensive and nervous. He knocked on her door and walked in when he heard her "Come in." Right away he knew something was wrong from the look on her face.

"Have a seat, Paul," Jane said tiredly. "I'm not quite sure how or where to begin. I'm not even sure what to pin my concerns on. But I've been worried all day."

"Did you talk to that big wheel at Batchelor's—Mr. Bentley? I really didn't think J.P. would run me through the mill. I mean, Jane, she did everything but sign the papers! Listen, I reviewed our campaign again with her during lunch. She said that Batchelor was in dire need of our kind of exposure. Jane, she was almost pleading with me, instead of me with her! I really don't understand. I mean—"

"Paul, hold on! I haven't spoken with Bentley since our last meeting together at the Plaza. I called you because *I* wasn't sure of the status of the account. You see, I got this memo today from B.P. He seems concerned about our position in the marketplace. I immediately assumed our newest big account had been shot down. B.P. always holds meetings after a potential client falls through."

"Well, if that's all it is," said Paul, annoyed, "it's a good thing I didn't call J.P.! I was thinking about it before I came to see you. I really could have blown the account. Listen, do you mind my asking exactly *what* the memo said?"

"Why not?" Jane replied. "At this point, a second opinion may help."

Paul read the memo and handed it back to Jane. "Jane, granted, the memo sounds serious, but I think you're jumping the gun. I'd talk with the other managers—see what their reactions are. Listen, I'd better return to my office. I want to put a few polishing touches on the Batchelor presentation I was about to throw out the window."

(Continued)

Jane gave Paul an apologetic look. "Paul, I'm sorry. I suppose I was passing my worries on for nothing. Anyway, I should have waited to talk with you personally. And I probably should've kept my mouth shut until after the meeting. Well, I'll let you know what happens. And keep smiling. It sounds like you've done a great job with this account."

Review Questions

1. What breakdowns in the communication process do you see thus far?
2. What problems will these breakdowns present? What problems do you think will arise at the meeting?
3. What obstacles have hampered effective communication? What problems with interference (internal and external) have occurred?

The Meeting Begins

Two days later, Brendan Parker was in his office editing his notes and polishing his ideas for the meeting he had arranged. His secretary, Vanessa, walked in with a letter that needed his signature. B.P. smiled. He was in fine spirits.

"Well, Vanessa, looks like a great St. Patrick's Day. The Batchelor and Rockwell accounts went through smoothly. Batchelor's was so pleased with Winthrop's final presentation. With these accounts under our belts, I think we're ready for the New York competition. We'll show them Boston's brains are the brightest. Oh—by the way, don't let me forget to send a personal note of congratulations to Paul Winthrop. He did a tremendous job. Hmm— it's time for the meeting, isn't it? Have all the managers gathered in the conference room yet?"

"Yes, Mr. Parker. I was just going to bring in coffee. Do you have a cup, or should I bring an extra?"

"No, I'm all set, Vanessa. Thanks. Tell them I'll be in in a few minutes. I've got to make one more phone call."

All the managers had gathered in the conference room ahead of time and were impatiently waiting for Brendan to arrive. Sean Dennison, in charge of finance, was nervously drumming his pen on the table. He turned to Michael Fox, who was sitting next to him, and said, "I wish B.P. would get here, already. I've gone over these notes so many times the figures seem blurred."

Michael smiled sympathetically. "I know, Sean. At this point, we're all a little on edge. But I still say that if it were a serious problem, surely at least one of us would already know about it."

Jane was sitting across the table, nodding her head in acknowledgement of something Lauren had said.

"You know, Lauren," Jane said, "the Batchelor account is really a smashing success. I feel horrible about Paul. I really had him terrified."

"Well, Jane, mistakes can happen," Lauren replied. "We often look for answers too quickly—even when we're unsure of what the question is."

(Continued)

Lee Codman, sitting next to Lauren, was resting his head in his hands. "God, I'm exhausted," he said to no one in particular. "First I was charging around the office trying to abate fears and calm nerves. Then I had to do an aboutface and start congratulating everyone for their stupendous efforts on the Batchelor account."

Lauren looked at Lee and said, "You *look* tired. But then, we all do. We've all been a little jumpy the past couple of days. Look at Sean. He's walking the floor like an alley cat. Stop pacing, Sean," Lauren called out. "You're making me nervous."

Just then, the conference room door opened and Brendan Parker came striding in, sporting a huge grin. "Happy St. Patrick's Day from the happiest Irishman in Boston today. We're here to—" Brendan looked around at all of the managers gathered in the room. His grin turned to a look of bewilderment as five haggard, anxious faces stopped him in mid-sentence.

Review Questions

1. What has happened? Why is Brendan so confused? What are the managers demonstrating through their body language?
2. Think back on the events over the past two days at B. Parker and Company, and list the communication problems that have plagued:
   (a) Paul and Jane.
   (b) Brendan Parker and the managers.
3. Consider the communication style of each of the managers and Brendan. Which individuals could stand some improvement in communications skills? Specifically, how and in what areas should they improve?

B.P. Vows Improvement

"Why all the glum faces?" Brendan asked as he approached his chair at the head of the table. "We need more spirit in this room! We'll soon be high rolling with the big New York agencies!"

"What?" Jane cut in.

The managers looked at one another and then at Brendan.

"You mean we're expanding our market?" Lee Codman asked.

"Yes," Brendan replied. "You've all done incredible jobs. Your departments have competent, talented people. B. Parker has put together a strong, talented group—one that's ready to meet New York head on."

Jane laughed softly, shaking her head in disbelief. "Brendan," she said, "we're here for the wrong reasons. Or, I should say, we're here prepared for battle. A lot of us assumed that you called this meeting because something awful had happened."

Brendan looked around the room. The looks on the other managers' faces confirmed Jane's statement.

"Well, I don't know what to say. You all received my memo," Brendan said. "How did you get such a wrong impression?"

(Continued)

Sean refused to be blamed for misinterpreting the memo. "Well, Brendan," he said, "when you wrote that we were going to 're-evaluate our position in the marketplace,' most of us assumed that you were referring to a major change in company policy, all right. But you have to understand there was no positive tone in your memo—no optimism or excitement."

"That's right, Brendan," Lee agreed. "We just weren't sure. And, of course, the situation became magnified when we started talking to one another."

Brendan pulled the memo he had written out of his folder. After reading it over, he said, "O.K. I can see your point. No guidelines. No definite statement. It is ambiguous. But why didn't you come and see me instead of whispering among yourselves? My door is always open—always has been."

"Is it really?" asked Lauren, boldly speaking up. "You've been inaccessible—out of town—until today. And in the little time you are here, it's not that easy to see you."

Brendan looked around at the nods and expressions of assent that punctuated Lauren's statements. "Looks like you're not the only person who feels that way, Lauren," he said soberly. He thought for a moment. "Maybe before we start talking about making headway in New York, we ought to talk about improving our position right here, among ourselves. After all, I believe that openness is really important to a creative company like ours. It's the flow of ideas and the criticisms and changes that we make that keep us alive. Maybe we should take steps to improve communication in this company. So tell me: How do you think we can make the organization more receptive to accurate and free communication? And what can I do personally to keep misunderstandings like this one from happening again?"

Review Questions

1. How would you answer Brendan's questions if you were one of the managers?
2. Do you agree with Brendan's statement that communication is important to a creative company? Why or why not?
3. Would you say that B. Parker and Company's problems stem from the fact that the company is too open, or not open enough? Could it be both? Explain your answer.

Source: American Management Association (1978). *Executives Skills*, pp. 13–16. Reprinted by permission.

Suggested Readings

Goodall, H. L. (1989). *Casing a promised land: The autobiography of an organization detective as cultural ethnographer.* Carbondale, IL: Southern Illinois Press.

Mirvis, P. H., & Berg, D. N. (1977). *Failures in organization development and change: Cases and essays for learning.* New York, NY: John Wiley & Sons, Inc.

Pace, R. W., & Faules, D. F. (1989). *Organizational communication* (2nd ed.). Englewood Cliffs, NJ: Prentice-Hall.

Pfeiffer, J. W., & Jones, J. E. (1972–93). *Annual Handbook for Group Facilitators.* San Diego, CA: University Associates.

Tompkins, P. K. (1992). *Organizational imperatives: Lessons of the space program.* Los Angeles, CA: Roxbury.

Chapter 7

DESIGNING CONSULTING INTERVENTIONS

- **ORGANIZATIONAL DEVELOPMENT AND INTERVENTION**
- **CATEGORIES OF INTERVENTION**
- **DIAGNOSTIC INTERVENTION**
  Communication Audit
  Survey Feedback
- **PROCESS INTERVENTIONS**
  Process Observation
  Confrontation Meetings
  Negotiation
- **PROBLEM-SOLVING INTERVENTIONS**
  Wants and Musts
  Best, Worst, Most Likely
  Is and Is Not
- **DECISION-MAKING INTERVENTIONS**
  Forced Field Analysis
  Synectics
  Nominal Group Technique
  The Delphi Technique
- **DESIGNING AND DIRECTING A CONSULTATION INTERVENTION**

"The problem with most (consultants) is that they don't understand their jobs. They try to take the horse to water and make it drink it. Their job is to make the horse thirsty."

author unknown

Consulting interventions are not designed to *make* clients change their behavior. They are designed to encourage others *to examine* how they are functioning and *consider changes.* Intervening into an ongoing system suggests major changes that will have a ripple effect throughout the organization. For that reason, one should intervene very carefully and only after consideration of the possible impact of that intervention, negative as well as positive.

Lippitt and Lippitt (1986) suggested: "One should not intervene to influence a group unless the impact will be at least neutral, if not positive, for each individual in the group" (p. 47). Stepping into an organization and simply being there, changes the nature of how individuals interact with each other.

You cannot ask an "innocent" question. "How are things going?" suggests that people ought to stop and think about how this organization functions. As any teacher knows, when you ask for assessment, you are bound to get it! It is highly unlikely that you will ever receive a response like, "Everything is just great! I love it here!" Even if people feel very positive about their work setting, when they are asked to assess it they search until they find something to say about how it could be better. Therefore, when you ask the question you must be prepared to do something with the answer. Intervening into an ongoing system implies change. To intervene, and do nothing, is to make life worse than it was.

> "Sue, we want you to talk to our staff about their low morale and then give us some recommendations," said the two chief operating officers of the organization. "With the first interview I conduct, you will be raising expectations by the employees that something will change. Don't invite me in unless you are prepared to make some immediate changes that indicate you have heard what they have

tried to tell you or I will just make the situation worse! Higher expectations with no results are much harder to live with than low expectations with no results."

That is how I begin most initial conversations with potential clients. People expect to see some results from their participation in a change effort and they expect those results to show up rather quickly. This does not necessarily mean a major shake-up in the organization but may in fact mean some small step that can be taken immediately to demonstrate that employees have been heard.

Intervening is sometimes asking the most obvious questions and making statements that seem so simplistic that they make you wonder why you are needed. Yet, when individuals are caught up in the politics of the situation, they are unable to ask those questions of themselves. Questions such as, "Why are you doing it that way?" and comments such as, "It doesn't seem to be working," and "That doesn't make sense to me, please explain it to me," can lead to productive analysis of an ongoing process."

■ Organizational Development and Intervention

Organizational development is a form of direct intervention into the human potential of the organization. Beckhand's (1967) definition of organizational development remains the most appropriate: ". . . an effort which is planned, organization wide and managed from the top to increase organization effectiveness and health through planned interventions in the organization's processes, using behavioral science knowledge" (p. 20).

French and Bell (1990) defined an organization development (OD) intervention as: " . . . sets of structured activities in which selected organizational units engage in a task or a sequence of tasks where the task goals are related directly or indirectly to organizational improvement. Interventions constitute the action thrust of organization development; they 'make things happen,' and are 'what's happening' " (p. 113).

They go on to suggest some general guidelines which I think are quite useful for designing interventions. The intervention activity should be structured so that

- The relevant people are there. The relevant people are those most affected by the problem being resolved.

- It is oriented to the problems and opportunities generated by the clients themselves.
- The goal and the way to reach the goal, are clear. Few things demotivate an individual as much as not knowing what he or she is working toward or how the activity contributes to goal attainment.
- Successful goal attainment is highly probable. Expectations of practitioners and clients should be realistic.
- It contains experience-based learning as well as conceptual/cognitive/theoretical-based learning. Learning through experience can be made a permanent part of the individual's repertoire when it is augmented with conceptual material that puts the experience into a broader framework of theory and behavior.
- The climate of the activity is such that individuals are "freed up" rather than anxious or defensive. Setting the climate of interventions so that people expect "to learn together" and "to look at practices in an experimenting way so that we can select better procedures" is what is meant by climate setting.
- The participants learn how to solve a particular problem and "learn how to learn" at the same time.
- Individuals can learn about both task and process. The **task** is what the group is working on, that is, the stated agenda items. The term **process** refers to how the group is working and what else is going on as the task is being worked on.
- Individuals are engaged as whole persons, not segmented persons. This means that role demands, thoughts, beliefs, and feelings, not just one or two of these, should be called into play (pp. 114–15).

Categories of Intervention

Blake and Mouton (1976) also identified major interventions in terms of their underlying themes. These included:

- *Discrepancy intervention* which calls attention to a contradiction in action or attitude that leads to exploration;
- *Theory intervention* which uses behavioral science knowledge and theory to explain present behavior and assumptions underlying the behavior;

- *Procedural intervention* which represents a critiquing of how something is being done to determine whether the best methods are being used;

- *Relationship intervention* which focuses attention on interpersonal relationships (particularly those where there are strong negative feelings) and brings the issues to the surface for exploration and possible resolution;

- *Experimentation interventions* in which two different action plans are tested for their consequences before a final decision on one is made;

- *Dilemma intervention* in which an imposed or emergent dilemma is used to force close examination of the possible choices involved and the assumptions underlying them;

- *Perspective interventions* which draw attention away from immediate actions and demands and allows a look at historical background, context, and future objectives in order to assess whether or not the actions are "still on target";

- *Organization structure intervention* which calls for examination and evaluation of structural causes for organizational ineffectiveness;

- *Cultural intervention* which examines traditions, precedents, and practices—the fabric of the organization's culture—in a direct, focused approach.

There are many schemes for classification of interventions. Some divide them into diagnostic activities, team and individual activities, education and training, coaching and counseling, career counseling, and structural activities. French and Bell (1990) categorized interventions according to their focus on the individual or the group and on task versus process issues. This is shown in Table 7.1. I have categorized interventions, according to the procedures used to actually carry out the intervention, into the following six areas:

- *Diagnostic interventions:* communication audits, survey feedback
- *Team-building interventions:* interpersonal interactions
- *Process interventions:* process observation, confrontation meetings, negotiation
- *Planning interventions:* strategic planning
- *Problem-solving interventions:* defining problems, force field analysis, synectics
- *Decision-making interventions:* nominal-group technique, Delphi

■ **TABLE 7.1**

FRENCH AND BELL'S TYPOLOGY OF OD INTERVENTIONS BASED ON TARGET GROUPS

Target Group	*Types of Intervention*
Interventions designed to improve the effectiveness of INDIVIDUALS	Life- and career-planning activities Role analysis technique Coaching and counseling T-group (sensitivity training) Education and training to increase skills, knowledge in the areas of technical task needs, relationship skills, process skills, decision making, problem solving, planning, goal-setting skills Grid OD phase 1 Some forms of job enrichment Gestalt OD Transactional analysis Behavior modeling
Interventions designed to improve the effectiveness of DYADS/TRIADS	Process consultation Third-party peacemaking Role negotiation technique Gestalt OD Transactional analysis
Interventions designed to improve the effectiveness of TEAMS & GROUPS	Team building—Task directed 　　　　　　—Process directed Grid OD phase 2 Family T-group Responsibility charting Process consultation Role analysis technique "Start-up" team-building activities Education in decision making, problem solving, planning, goal setting in group settings Some forms of job enrichment and MBO Sociotechnical systems and Quality of Work Life programs Quality circles Force field analysis
Interventions designed to improve the effectiveness of INTERGROUP RELATIONS	Intergroup activities—Process directed 　　　　　　　　　—Task directed Organizational mirroring (three or more groups) Structural interventions Process consultation Third-party peacemaking at group level Grid OD phase 3 Survey feedback

(Continued)

■ TABLE 7.1

FRENCH AND BELL'S TYPOLOGY OF OD INTERVENTIONS BASED ON TARGET GROUPS (Continued)

Target Group	Types of Intervention
Interventions designed to improve the effectiveness of the TOTAL ORGANIZATION	Technostructural activities such as collateral organizations, sociotechnical systems, and organizational restructuring Confrontation meetings Strategic planning/strategic management activities Grid OD phases 4, 5, 6 Survey feedback Interventions based on Lawrence and Lorsch's contingency theory Interventions based on Likert's Systems 1–4 Physical settings

Source: From W. L. French & C. H. Bell, *Organization Development: Behavioral Science Interventions for Organization Improvement,* Englewood Cliffs, NJ: Prentice-Hall, Inc. 1978, p. 122. Reprinted by permission. Not all of the interventions listed above are discussed in this book. The reader is directed to the original source for further elaboration.

The rest of this chapter provides examples of specific interventions in the diagnostic, process, problem-solving, and decision-making categories. Chapter 11 details team building and includes a variety of interventions to be used with groups. Team building is such a pervasive intervention today that an entire chapter needed to be devoted to its explanation along with examples and techniques. Strategic Planning is another major intervention that I use most frequently. For that reason I have devoted an entire chapter to the change process, resistance to change, and planning for change. Chapter 13 details strategic planning models and techniques.

■ Diagnostic Interventions

In Chapter 4 I discussed the development of questionnaires and the criteria by which to measure their validity. Any diagnostic intervention should also meet these criteria. The first diagnostic intervention combines survey research with feedback sessions and major organizational recommendations that make it a comprehensive intervention.

Communication Audit

A communication audit is one diagnostic intervention that has been used by the communication discipline for some time. The International Communication Association (ICA) Communication Audit is the most well known and still widely used package of diagnostic intervention tools.

> For many of us, the word audit elicits fear or irritation because of its association with the Internal Revenue Service. Basically, however, an audit is merely a process of exploring, examining, monitoring, or evaluating something. Accountants audit our financial records, physicians audit our health, professors audit our learning progress, and managers review, or audit, our level of performance. . . . A communication audit differs from other audits only in that it focuses primarily on communication, and, therefore, there are certain methodologies that may be applicable to it (Downs, 1988, p. 3).

The International Communication Association is a professional organization dedicated to the study of communication processes in a variety of contexts. The Organizational Communication Division of ICA devoted more than five years to the development of the Communication Audit. The Communication Audit is actually a package of instruments used in the assessment of employees' perceptions of the communication process in their organization. The ICA Communication Audit has been used extensively in research and consulting in the years since its development. The advantages of the ICA Communication Audit are well documented: overcoming the use of single instruments, limited situationalism, small unrepresentative samples, lack of standardization and norms, and limited measurement of actual behaviors, to name a few of the claims made by the audit's developers (Dennis, Goldhaber, and Yates, 1978; Falcione, Goldhaber, Porter, and Rogers, 1979; Goldhaber, Yates, Porter, and Lesniak, 1978).

In an extensive study of the audit's use (DeWine, James, and Walence, 1985) data suggested several conclusions about the ICA Communication Audit. First, the audit does appear to have the ability to identify or highlight communication problems and potential solutions within an organization. Aside from an awareness of obvious problems the audit appeared, for a majority of the people who used it, to provide viable alternatives, confirm the directions or courses management had charted, initiate creative thinking or, in some instances, inspire administrators not to change the environment at all. Second, the data demonstrate that managers maintain their own form of organizational reality. The administrators will select and accept issue analysis and recommendations from an audit according to their own perceptions of organizational reality and what is most appropriate for their organizations, regardless of the nature of the recommendations. The recommendations may function as a force to propel communication behaviors to a higher level of consciousness for the purposes of observation, assessment, and modification.

Sections of the audit cover the following areas:

Amount of information activity received about topics

Amount of information desired about these topics

Amount of information actually sent about topics

Amount of information desired to be sent about these topics

Amount of follow-up by people now

Amount of follow-up needed

Amount of information received from sources

Amount of information desired from these sources

Timeliness of information received from key sources

Organizational communication relationships

Satisfaction with organizational outcomes

Amount of information received from channels now

Amount of information desired from channels now

The questionnaire, in a revised format (DeWine and James, 1988) is included in its entirety below. In addition to this questionnaire, a communication diary, communication network analysis, and a critical-incidents form as well as interview schedules complete the "package" of diagnostic tools (Goldhaber and Rogers, 1979; Downs, 1988).

Survey Feedback

Survey feedback is one of the oldest and most frequently used diagnostic interventions. The consultant or manager systematically collects data about the organization and its members and then presents the data in a feedback session. Groups at all levels of the organization are involved in the data collection, analysis, and feedback. This is different from a research project, in which the data may be isolated from the day-to-day workings of the organization. From the moment you begin collecting the data, you are in fact changing the organization since organizational members are assisting with the collection process. French and Bell (1990) pre-

■ TABLE 7.2

TWO APPROACHES TO THE USE OF ATTITUDE SURVEYS

	Traditional Approach	*Survey Feedback or OD Approach*
Data collected from:	Rank and file, and maybe supervisors	Everyone in the system or subsystem
Data reported to:	Top management, department heads, and perhaps to employees through newspaper	Everyone who participated
Implications of data are worked on by:	Top management (maybe)	Everyone in work teams, with workshops starting at the top (all superiors with their subordinates)
Third-party intervention strategy:	Design and administration of questionnaire, development of a report	Obtaining concurrence on total strategy, design and administration of questionnaire, design of workshops, appropriate interventions in workshops
Action planning done by:	Top management only	Teams at all levels
Probable extent of change and improvement:	Low	High

Source: From W. L. French & C. H. Bell, *Organization Development: Behavioral Science Interventions for Organization Improvement*, Englewood Cliffs, NJ: Prentice-Hall, Inc. 1978, p. 122. Reprinted by permission.

sent a comparison between the characteristics of survey feedback and the traditional use of attitude surveys in Table 7.2. The major difference is the involvement of organizational members in the survey feedback throughout the process versus only top management involvement in the traditional attitude surveys.

■ *Process Interventions*

Process interventions may take one of three forms: process observation, confrontation meetings, or negotiations.

Process Observation

When the focus is on the process the group uses to carry out their tasks, then the intervention is most likely to be process observation (PO). PO is one of the cornerstones of communicative consulting. An individual who is able to objectively observe the group process, accurately and fairly report it back, and help the group cope with the things they discover about themselves, is truly a talented individual.

The following discussion comes as close as possible to describing how to carry this out; however, the best way to learn how to do it is to observe a master facilitator. I have spent hundreds of hours watching others manage groups effectively and ineffectively. I learned just as many helpful hints from those who did it poorly as I did from those who did it quite well. I often am negotiating a contract that includes an observer or person in training so that others may have carefully protected experiences while they are learning how to perform this extremely delicate intervention.

Process observation is the ability to watch group interaction, at both the verbal and nonverbal levels, in order to make accurate inferences about the health of the group's communication. In addition, observations must be presented to the group in a nonthreatening way. The goal is to help the group build a positive climate in which a cohesive team may be formed.

The key is to observe actual behavior (either the person's exact wording or nonverbal cues) and record it accurately. The second step is to reflect on what one is observing. Avoid classifying the behaviors as either "good" or "bad." The question to ask is, "What is this person doing that will help or hinder the group process? What could they be doing differently to enhance the efforts of the group?"

When the process observer is presenting feedback, the self-esteem of individual members should be enhanced. This may mean giving some feedback outside the group setting to a person who has some behaviors to correct. Also, focus should be on the group problem, not on individual people. The person's behavior is a problem, not the person. The group is there to solve a problem, not to evaluate people. Chapter 9 provides more details on the skills of providing feedback.

Greiner and Metzger (1983) discussed the difference between process consultants and content consultants. "Process consultants are the psychologists of the consulting trade whereas content consultants are the specialist surgeons. The process consultant offers no specific answers but rather asks lots of questions" (p. 20). On the other hand, the content consultant "takes direct action to verify the causes of a problem and then writes a report to support a set of specific recommendations. Content consultants believe they are better able to see the 'forest' for the 'trees' because they are independent and objective outsiders" (p. 21). In reality, either extreme is likely to be less effective than a combined approach. As Greiner and Metzger put it, "Most clients are not interested in hiring a psychiatrist to 'shrink' them, nor are they receptive to a professional lecture" (p. 22). Thus, process consulting must be used as a part of a major intervention process.

Gabarro and Harlan (1976) defined process intervention and divided it into three distinct classes. The first is **conceptual inputs** whose objective is to provide members of the client group with an organizing principle. This principle can help them see the distinctions between typical and optimal behavior.

Second is **coaching** which Gabarro and Harlan defined as the process of assisting members of a client group to practice using new behaviors with which they want to become proficient. Coaching interventions are most effectively made either during the early, standard setting phases of the consultive process—when they can shape the kinds and sequence of interpersonal communication early. Here the consultant would work closely with individuals to help them understand the consequences of their own behaviors to the group and for themselves.

Finally, process observation can be used to heighten the client group members' awareness of the significance of the distinction between **content and process dimensions** of transactions occurring within a group. It may increase the group's awareness of the implications and consequences of members' actions and provide a model of behavior that demonstrates how one can facilitate a group's movement in the direction of it objectives.

Metzger (1989) concluded:

> Nowadays as we have seen, the traditional content based consulting approach is no longer readily accepted by many clients. Given the sophistication of most management teams today, it is unrealistic to think that consultants should personally take charge and direct the solution for the client, while educating the client's managers on how this or that problem should be resolved. Such consulting approaches correspond to the old paradigm of mechanistic management (p. 49).

Thus, the best approach may be to focus on the human process that group is using to carry out organizational tasks.

Schein's (1987) two volumes on process consultation provide one of the best sources on actual techniques used in process interventions. He explained the concept of process as "How things are done rather than what is done. If I am crossing the street, that is what I am doing, but the process is *how* [italics added] I am crossing: walking, running, dodging cars, asking someone to help me across because I feel dizzy, or some other way" (p. 39).

Schein (1988) clearly defined the kinds of interventions that a process consultant would be most likely to use starting with agenda setting, managing interventions, questions that direct attention to process issues, meetings devoted to process issues, and conceptual inputs on process related topics. Actual solutions to management problems are not even listed because they would not be considered valid interventions in a process consultation model. A consultant who permitted him- or herself to become interested in a particular management problem in sales, marketing, or production would be switching roles from that of process consultant to that of expert resource. Becoming an expert resource can make a consultant lose effectiveness as a process consultant.

Schein goes on to say: "The process model starts with the assumption that the organization knows how to solve its particular problems or knows how to get help in solving them, but that it often does not know how to use its own resources effectively either in initial problem formation or in implementation of solutions" (p. 29).

The process model further assumes that inadequate use of internal resources or ineffective implementation results from process problems. People fail to communicate effectively with each other, or develop mistrust, engage in destructive competition, punish things that they mean to reward and vice versa, fail to give feedback, and so on. "The job of the process consultant is to help the organization to solve its own problems by making it aware of organizational processes, the consequences of those processes, and the mechanisms by which they can be changed" (Schein, p. 193).

Confrontation Meetings

A process consultant is needed to run a **confrontation meeting** between two groups or single individuals. It should be done in a "laboratory-type" setting where two conflicting groups come together and work through their tensions and frictions that have built up over an extended period of time.

The first step is to set the climate for an open exchange of opinions, which may indeed differ. A series of activities will help establish this climate.

Second, each group meets separately to identify how they perceive the other group and how they think the other group perceives them. Then the two groups are brought together and their perceptions are shared.

In one instance I was asked by the head of the unit to work with a group of mid-level female managers who "seem to think they are being mistreated although I can't for the life of me understand why. We have given two of them recent promotions and salary increases but it doesn't seem to satisfy them." I met with the women, then met with the top management team (all of whom happened to be male) and then had the two groups come together for a confrontation meeting. I asked the females to meet in one room and list all their perceptions of the males, and the males to do the same about the females. Then I also asked them to identify what they predicted would be the other group's perception of them.

When these four lists were compared, we discovered that: the women thought the men would perceive them as not as serious about their work while the men did indeed see them as serious about their work, as evidenced by the belief that higher salaries would correct the problem. We also discovered that the men thought the women would perceive them as mistreating them when the women actually saw the men as unaware of how their actions were slowing down the progress of the group. Higher pay for two women was not solving the problem of lack of respect for all of them.

During the confrontation meeting I acted as the facilitator, reading the lists as they were developed and asking questions for clarity. It was an eye-opening experience since both sides learned that their perceptions of how the other group viewed them were often wrong. Only after the two groups confronted their own misperceptions could we begin to work on pulling this team together again. As a result of these meetings, promotions took place and changes in personnel policy were developed. I can't say that internal attitudes changed because I don't believe any external force can cause attitudes to change; however, work behavior patterns did change, for the better.

The facilitator must be aware that feelings may be more intense during this session than in previous sessions. Second, if no action is taken as a result of the confrontation meeting, morale will be even lower.

Negotiation

Often, the consultant or communication manager ends up being the mediator or negotiator in interpersonal relationships, group conflict, and decision making. The communication consultant needs the same characteristics that are required for legal mediators who are trying to reach a settlement between disputing parties. Keltner (1987) identified 10 skills needed by the mediator:

Credibility and integrity of the mediator is the most basic tool of the mediator. The mediator must be accepted as a person who can be trusted, who thoroughly knows the process involved, and relates well to the parties.

Empathy means the mediator must establish rapport with the clients by trying to see the situation from each perspective. It is important that the mediator not have a predetermined outcome for the situation in mind.

Listening is a basic skill. The mediator must not only listen for feelings but for content and to evaluate as well. This means the mediator must be able to read nonverbal cues as well as verbal cues.

Feedback is a skill discussed in Chapter 9. The ability to provide information to clients without increasing their defensiveness is critical. Using feedback to see if you have received an accurate understanding of the individual's message is important to the establishment of positive relationships.

Interrogation is the use of questions as an important part of the data-gathering process. It is also a part of the persuasion that goes on during a mediation process when the question itself may suggest a course of action.

Timing for the mediator means knowing when to move forward, when to allow the other person to go on with their analysis, and when to make an analysis. The mediator needs to have a sense of when it is time to push the parties to resolution. If they are "pushed" too soon, the mediation will be unsuccessful.

Speaking skills or the ability to converse informally with the parties in a clear, friendly, and useful fashion is important. The mediator must hold the attention of the clients.

Message carrying or taking ideas from one party to another requires careful work. Some messages must be transferred as precisely as possible and others must be attenuated or modified in order not to upset delicate relationships being established.

Nonverbal communication is an ever present part of the negotiation process. The observation of facial expressions, use of space, eye contact or lack of it, personal appearance, and other forms of nonverbal cues will be very useful to the mediator in order to determine the attitudes of the parties.

Persuasion is sometimes the final skill needed as the mediator tries to get resolution on the part of two disputing parties. If the parties are going to reach a settlement, they must change the rigid positions they start out with.

Keltner goes on to identify seven stages in the mediation process:

1. *setting the stage* (establishing rapport and credibility);
2. *opening and development* (identifying ground rules and building trust);
3. *exploration of the issues:* isolation of basics (when the relative importance of issues is decided and clients state opening positions);
4. *identification of alternatives* (identification of other options);
5. *evaluation, negotiation, and bargaining* (matching needs with criteria previously established);
6. *decision making and testing* (when parties begin to make commitments);
7. *terminating the process* (mediator reviews the decisions made).

These steps become quite helpful when the session begins with little agreement or movement on either side.

■ *Problem-solving Interventions*

The most difficult step in problem-solving interventions is defining the problem. The difficulty arises in part because of a confusion between symptoms and the problem. The following three techniques can be used to help identify those problems.

"Wants and Musts"

Ask the group to generate a list of problems or issues related to one problem. Use normal brainstorming techniques of not allowing any evaluation while the original list is being generated. After the list is developed, explain to the group that not all the items they have raised may be able to be addressed in this session. In fact, it is my experience that a group is usually not able to address every item that may have been raised. It turns out that the group is ready to live with some issues if the most *critical* issues can be addressed. Next, go over each item on the list and ask the group the following question: "Is this an item that *must* be addressed in order to solve this problem or is this an item we *want* to address if possible but it is not as critical?" "Musts" are discussed immediately and "wants" are left for a later meeting or time.

"Best, Worst, Most Likely"

Often, when groups are trying to solve a problem, they are prevented from moving forward because of unrealistic fears of the things that might happen as a result of implementing a solution. Have the group identify the "worst" thing that could happen if this solution is implemented, the "best" and the "most likely" outcome. Once the group has listed the worst possible outcome, and you then address what is more likely to happen, the group often is able to handle the "worst" and understands what is more probable.

"Is and Is Not"

When defining the problem, it is sometimes useful to identify what it is not, or what it will not involve. For example, when a group was talking about low morale, they were talking about people being discouraged from trying new programs and policies. They were *not* talking about people treating each other fairly or unfairly, they were *not* talking about low trust, they were talking specifically about innovations and the system's inability to respond quickly to new ideas.

Watzlawick, Weakland, and Finsch (1974) suggested the notion of reframing a problem in order to solve it. They explained, "To reframe, then, means to change the conceptual and/or emotional setting or viewpoint in relation to which a situation is experienced and to place it in another frame which fits 'facts' of the same concrete situation equally well or even better, and thereby changes its entire meaning" (p. 95). They proposed a four step approach to solving problems:

1. A clear definition of the problem in concrete terms
2. An investigation of the solutions attempted so far
3. A clear definition of the concrete change to be achieved, and
4. The formation and implementation of a plan to produce this change (p. 110).

In the first step, the translation of the problem into concrete terms turns a vaguely stated problem into concrete ideas and permits the critical separation of problems from pseudo problems. Second, a careful examination of any attempted solutions shows what kind of change should not be attempted and also reveals what maintains the situation in its current state. Finally, the tactic chosen to solve the problem must be translated into the group's own language.

■ Decision-making Interventions

The difference between problem solving and decision making is that **problem solving** is a process to determine the reason or cause of a problem so that one can make appropriate decisions. **Decision making** is the process of selecting among a variety of alternatives which one would best solve the problem that has been identified.

Some typical types of decision making include: decision by majority with voting or polling taking place; decision by minority, wherein a few somehow manage to influence the larger group; formal authority in which one individual, because of position, makes the decision for the group; and decision by consensus, in which the group continues discussing the issue until everyone can "live with" the decision. Some specific interventions that assist with the decision-making process include the following techniques.

Forced Field Analysis

Lewin (1951) originally developed **forced field analysis**, the concept of identifying those forces that drive a group or individual to make a certain decision and those forces that are preventing that decision from being made. A group must know what the desired condition is and then must be able to identify what is preventing them from reaching that desired condition.

In order to change the current condition, Lewin suggested that driving forces could be increased, restraining forces could be reduced, or both. Lewin advised against simply adding more driving forces because that may increase tension and resistance. Thus, the best approach is to work on the most important restraining force and attempt to reduce it. Sometimes a detailed form helps a group complete all necessary steps for this analysis (See Form 7.1).

At a corporate board meeting, I helped top executives identify what was preventing them from performing as a team. The strongest restraining force was the fact that the previous CEO had encouraged competitiveness among his senior officers. In fact, each officer was evaluated on how he was able to increase his return on investment at the expense of other units in the organization. The main driving force was their loyalty to the company. Increasing their loyalty to the company would not overcome the block to working collaboratively, but reducing the competitiveness would.

Synectics

Prince (1970) and Gordon (1961) founded the Synectics Incorporated in the late '60s and early '70s to promote the development and study of an intervention called **synectics**. Synectics groups are currently functioning, as are groups using some of the basic ideas developed as a part of this

■ FORCE FIELD ANALYSIS

Change Effort Analysis

Step A.

We will use the Force Field Analysis concept to analyze your problem. This concept states that:

■ Any function or item to be changed can be thought of as an ongoing process-in-equilibrium.

■ The process may be described as operating at a particular level on a continuum running from "less" to "more," or "not so good" to "very good." This may be portrayed thus:

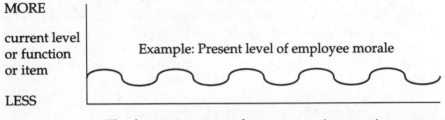

MORE

current level or function or item

Example: Present level of employee morale

LESS

■ The function or item always occurs in a tension-system (or field of forces)—a system of forces opposing each other and stabilizing at the present level of the function. Different forces will have different strengths or importance and may be so indicated by the *length* of the arrow.

    ■ The forces pushing the function in the direction of MORE are called "driving forces."

    ■ The forces pushing the function in the direction of LESS are called "restraining forces."

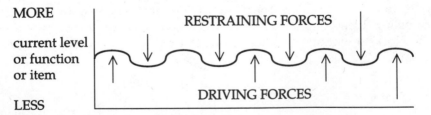

MORE

current level or function or item

RESTRAINING FORCES

DRIVING FORCES

LESS

■ A quasi-stable equilibrium exists when the strength of the forces tending to lower the level (restraining forces)

(Continued)

are in balance with (or equal to) the forces tending to raise the level (driving forces).

■ Three processes are involved in changing the level of the function or item to a more desirable level:

- ■ Diagnosis. Identifying all forces—driving and restraining—currently maintaining the present level.

- ■ Unfreezing. Changing the different strengths of the individual forces.

- ■ Refreezing. Stabilizing the forces at the new, desired level.

Step B.

Construct a force field analysis for your change effort. Identify all the driving and restraining forces you can. These can be:

- individuals
- groups
- forces and factors like tradition, pleasure, fear, etc.
- yourself. You may be both a driving and a restraining force.

The key at this stage is *full* identification of driving and restraining forces—often you will discover allies and restrainers you did not suspect.

Less   **More**

Driving Forces	Change Effort	Restraining Forces
------------------------>	{	<-----------------------
------------------------>	{	<-----------------------
------------------------>	{	<-----------------------
------------------------>	{	<-----------------------
------------------------>	{	<-----------------------
------------------------>	{	<-----------------------
------------------------>	{	<-----------------------

(Continued)

127

■ **FORCE FIELD ANALYSIS** *(Continued)*

Step C.

Now assess the relative strength of each of the forces. One technique that might be helpful would be to apportion 100 points to the driving forces and 100 points to the restraining forces. You cannot be fully discrete or accurate, but try to be as realistic as possible. It is conceivable, for example, for a single force to receive a weighting of as much as 90.

Step D.

Three basic strategies for effecting change present themselves:

1. Add to the driving forces. This is generally less desirable since adding driving forces usually marshals more opposing forces and increases tension.
2. Remove, or reduce, restraining forces. This is usually more desirable—it is less obvious.
3. Add to the driving forces and work to eliminate or/and reduce restraining forces. This is probably the most frequently employed strategy.

We will concentrate on reducing or eliminating the restraining forces. It is fully recognized, however, that in your change effort you may find it highly desirable to consider adding to the driving forces.

You cannot normally attack all the restraining forces simultaneously. Some restraining forces are so rigid that they are almost impervious to change. Review the restraining forces you have identified.

- Which should you dismiss as not being amenable to change?
- Which of the restraining forces are most ready to change?
- Which of the restraining forces are not only amenable to change, but also have been assigned a significant weighting?

Step E.

Consider the restraining forces you have identified as significant and vulnerable to change. We are now concerned with considering which of these restraining forces we should attempt to change. The following kinds of questions should be considered relevant to each force.

(Continued)

■ FORCE FIELD ANALYSIS *(Continued)*

- Who in our system has access to the force I am trying to change?
- Which force, if I can change it, will have trigger-linkage—multi-causality?
- What are my resources for giving the kind of help that seems to be needed now or that may develop?
- Where do I and my group of change agents have the most leverage?

Force Field Analysis-Action Planning Steps

Step A.

From where do you feel the support for this change in your organization must come? (Rank)

_____ top management

_____ professional personnel

_____ middle management

_____ supervisors

_____ hourly workers

_____ external consultants

_____ external crisis

_____ internal crisis

_____ other

Step B.

What are the best roles for you to assume in the change effort?

_____ an educator

_____ an advisor

_____ a technician

_____ an advocate

_____ a trainer

_____ a mediator

(Continued)

■ **FORCE FIELD ANALYSIS** *(Continued)*

_____ an expert on procedures

_____ a do-er

_____ other

Step C.

What new resistances can be expected and how can they be countered?

Step D.

Who are part of the "driving forces," and who needs to be involved/informed so that you don't alienate any of your supporters?

Step E.

Are you clear with reference to the action steps:

- What exactly is to be done and in what sequences?
- How is it to be done?
- Who is to do it?
- Where is it to be done?
- When is it to be done?

Step F.

How can or should you terminate your role as a change initiator? When will the change be considered completed?

intervention. The purpose of the intervention is to provide individuals with a system for arriving at creative and innovative solutions to problems. It is a highly structured process that takes a group through several steps leading to solutions previously not imagined.

The two essential concepts to the process that can be applied in any group setting are: *making the strange familiar* and *making the familiar strange.* Individuals usually feel threatened by something strange and unknown to them. Thus, an unusual concept must be made familiar so that concrete solutions can be considered. For example, one group was trying to design a solar-powered camping oven that would fold up. Some members could not imagine how such an item could fold up until someone described it as an "umbrella," a common article.

Nominal Group Technique

Nominal group technique (NGT) is a technique developed by Andrew H. Van de Ven and Andre L. Delbecq in 1968 (Van de Ven and Delbecq, 1971, 1974). The purpose of the technique is to provide groups with a decision-making process that does not initially put people "on the spot," as brainstorming can do. There are six steps involved in this process:

1. Individuals suggest solutions to a problem independently and in writing.

2. Ideas are presented to the group members through a format that disassociates the idea from the person. The ideas are all listed on a flip chart and the leader goes through them without identifying the ideas' authors. Evaluation of the ideas should not take place at this stage.

3. The ideas of all the group members are then discussed for clarification and now pros and cons may be presented. Again, the ideas have been separated from the people who proposed them so less defensiveness will occur since the "cons" are about ideas, not the person him- or herself.

4. The group arrives at a decision by secret ballot. The members are asked to rank the ideas that have been proposed. This system reduces conforming pressures that often are present in an open discussion.

5. The preliminary vote is discussed. Each member can comment on selected items and raise any questions or issues for the group to consider.

6. A final vote is taken, again by secret ballot.

The advantages of this technique include:

- It ensures that ideas are collected from every member as opposed to brainstorming or any oral method of discussion during which only the most vocal members of the group usually speak up.
- The ideas are problem-centered and all related to solving the problem rather than topics that get the group off track.
- It separates the idea from the person thus reducing defensiveness.
- It forces all members to work and produce their share of the effort.
- The technique can accommodate a large number of participants.
- It forces equality of participation.
- It allows participation from all hierarchical levels.
- It is less costly and quicker than some other methods of problem solving.

Disadvantages include:

- Members may be "voting" on ideas they do not fully understand.
- The group is missing the "synergy" that sometimes occurs when group members talk together. One idea may lead to another if the discussion is allowed to continue.
- Some members may dislike writing ideas and have more difficulty expressing themselves in writing than orally.

The Delphi Technique

"Organizations employ a variety of strategies for bringing stability and certainty to their environments" (Pfeffer and Salancik, 1978, p. 70). One technique for increasing stability and reducing uncertainty, is the Delphi Technique.

Delphi is used to predict future events and reduce uncertainty. Delphi was originated at the Rand Corporation in 1948. It was initially developed to provide the Air Force with information on the targets for a Soviet nuclear attack. Since the 1960s the Delphi has been used in a variety of settings and to help solve human communication problems.

Delphi is: "a method for structuring a group communication process so that the process is effective in allowing a group of individuals, as a whole, to deal with a complex problem" (Linestone and Turoff, 1975); "an intuitive methodology for organizing and sharing expert forecasts about the future" (Weaver, 1971); and "an attempt to elicit expert opinion in a systematic manner for useful results" (Sackman, 1975).

Once a problem is formulated, an expert panel is selected and a questionnaire is developed. The "solution testing" involves submitting the results of the questionnaire to the panel as many times as it takes to gain consensus or until a minority opinion can be articulated. Then the group opinion of the panel is written and disseminated. The first version of the questionnaire is usually open-ended questions. The second questionnaire is usually scaled items developed from the open-ended responses. Panel members are asked to prioritize their responses in light of the summary of the group response. In the last round the lowest ranked items are dropped. The process continues until consensus is reached.

An example of a successfully used Delphi was a small city government trying to prioritize the purchase of city equipment. The discussion had dissolved into factions advocating the purchase of equipment for the fire or police department. The arguments were no longer rational and had become personalized attacks against various members of each department.

A Delphi technique was introduced to first collect information from experts in the field about the quality of equipment necessary for various tasks and the expected cost for acceptable equipment. This removed the discussion from personal attacks to factual information about equipment needs. Once the information was collected a second Delphi was used with the government officials, feeding back the information obtained and asking for their judgement about priorities. A list was developed for the purchase of equipment according to greatest need. Even after the decision was made, some of the interpersonal problems remained and were dealt with at a later time.

The advantages include having a panel of experts on a particular subject, having an opportunity to receive the opinion of every panel member, and, like NGT, allowing anonymous input. It is best used for complex issues and questions that require much thoughtful consideration. Like NGT, it keeps people focused only on the main issue at hand. It does, however, eliminate group dynamics and any chance of "synergy" that might occur in a face to face group. Some panel members may be pressured to agree with the majority opinion and thus "groupthink" may occur.

Designing and Directing a Consultation Intervention

After an extensive study of the impact of various human potential interventions on measures of productivity and job performance, Nicholas (1982) found a 71 percent improvement in turnover and 57 percent improvement in absenteeism when compared to organizational structural changes or job redesign. In addition, of the human resource interventions applied, structured laboratory training efforts reported the greatest impact on hard outcome measures, "showing an overall change in 80 percent of the measured variables" (p. 536). Clearly, interventions into human interactions have great impact on the organization's success. Designing an intervention requires an understanding of the steps of the consulting process.

Lippitt and Lippitt (1986) identified the following phases in consulting: 1) initial contact and entry, 2) formulation of a contract, 3) identification of problems, 4) goal setting and action planning, 5) action, and 6) completion of the contract (continuity, support, and termination) (p. 12). Interventions would be implemented at stage five.

One way to evaluate the success of an intervention is to look at the criteria Peters and Waterman (1984) used to identify excellent companies. These criteria could also be applied to identifying outstanding consultants as well. The eight attributes that emerged to characterize the distinction of excellence are captured in the following phrases: 1) a bias for action, for getting on with it, 2) close to the customer, 3) entrepreneurship, 4) productivity through people, 5) hands-on, value-driven, 6) stick to the knitting, 7) simple form, lean stuff, and 8) simultaneous loose-tight properties (pp. 13–15).

Having a "bias for action" means being analytical in one's approach to decision making but not being paralyzed by that fact. "Close to the customer" suggests keeping in touch with the clients and understanding what their needs are. It is surprising how many consultants enter the client system with ready-made solutions that may not address the client's needs at all. "Entrepreneurship," number 3, means being innovative. For the consultant "productivity through people" implies fostering an attitude that human beings are the single most important investment for the corporation. "Hands-on, value-driven" is explained through the words of Thomas Watson who said, "the basic philosophy of an organization has far more to do with its achievements than do technological or economic resources, organizational structure, innovation and timing" (Peters and Waterman, p. 15). "Stick to the knitting" means, "never acquire a business you don't know how to run" (p. 15). The consultant should be very careful about claims he or she makes about individual competencies. "Simple form, lean stuff" implies simple but eloquent designs for the system and for operating the organization. "Simultaneous loose-tight properties" combines a centralized and decentralized approach to interacting in the organization.

Table 7.3 on page 135 will help you select which of the preceding interventions you might feel most comfortable integrating into your own client/consultant relationships. It identifies 14 criteria to compare inter-

■ TABLE 7.3

INTERVENTIONS COMPARED

	Audits	Survey	Team-Building	Process Observation	Confront. Mgt.	Negotiation	Planning	Synectics	Forced Field	Nominal Group	Delphi
Expediency	L	L	A-H	H	H	A-h	L	H	H	H	L
Skill Consultant	A	A	A	H	H	H	H	H	A	A	A
Skill Client	L	L	H	L	A	L	A	H	A	A	H
Size of Group	H	H	L	L	L	L	A	L	A-H	L-A	A-H
Cost—$$	H	H	A	L	L-H	L-H	A-H	A-H	L	L-H	A-H
Cost Emotional	L	L	A-H	A-H	H	H	A	A	A	A	L
Risk Level	L	L	A	A	H	H	A	H	A	A	A
Formal vs. Spontaneous	F	F	F-S	S	F	F	F	F	S	S	F
HR vs. OD	OD	OD	HR	HR	HR	HR	OD	HR	HR	HR	OD
PS vs. Awareness	Aw	Aw	Aw	Aw	PS	PS	PS	PS	PS	PS	PS

Key: H = High, A = Average, L = Low, F = Formal, S = Spontaneous, OD = Organization development, HR = Human resource, PS = Problem solving, Aw = Awareness raised ventions. "Expediency" refers to how urgent the situation is and consequently how quickly the intervention should be implemented. Some interventions require a high level of skill on the part of the consultant, while others cannot be used unless the clients are fairly skilled at human interactions.

For example, Delphi technique requires experts in a particular field to participate. Size of the group, the organization's goals, and the financial costs are clear; however, you must also consider something less obvious. Emotional costs, such as the self-disclosure needed in a confrontation meeting, might be quite high. This is similar to risk level, which could mean making yourself vulnerable. The physical environment, as well as the formality of the situation, may be more supportive of certain types of interventions.

A human resource (HR) problem versus an organizational development (OD) problem will call for very different types of interventions. For example, role plays are effective for HR problems while Delphi is more effective for OD issues. Finally, some interventions (e.g., confrontation meetings) simply make individuals *aware* of problems while others (e.g., forced field) work at solving problems. In short, the best intervention is the one you feel the most comfortable using, the one most acceptable to the client and the one best suited to the particular situation.

Subsequent chapters will address special communication problems you are likely to face.

■ Suggested Readings

Bell, C. R., & Nadler, L. (1985). *Clients and consultants: Meeting and exceeding expectations* (2nd ed.). Houston, TX: Gulf Publishing.

Blake, R. R., & Mouton, J. (1976). *Consultation* (2nd ed.). Reading, MA: Addison-Wesley Publishing Co., Inc.

French, W. L., & Bell, C. H. (1978). *Organization development: Behavioral science interventions for organization improvement.* Englewood Cliffs, NJ: Prentice-Hall.

Lippitt, G., & Lippitt, R. (1986). *The consulting process in action.* (2nd ed.). San Diego, CA: University Associates.

Schein, E. H. (1987). *Process consultation Volume II: Lessons for managers and consultants.* Reading: MA: Addison-Wesley Publishing Co., Inc.

PART IV

Correcting Communication Failures

When a group asks me to work with them, chances are they are experiencing intergroup conflict and weak communication skills. This section of the book contains a wealth of stories and examples from my consulting practice. These seven chapters cover solutions to the most typical communication problems that I have encountered. Chapter 8 provides specific techniques for increasing listening ability, Chapter 9 suggests some simple but powerful strategies to improve meetings, while Chapter 10 explains how to help others prepare dynamic presentations. Chapter 11 includes team-building strategies, and Chapter 12 discusses one of the most important skills for a consultant: how to provide feedback in a nonthreatening manner. Chapter 13 describes everyone's nightmare: dealing with difficult people and conflict situations. Finally, Chapter 14 addresses the problems encountered when any change is introduced in a system.

This section is very practical and skills-oriented. The techniques are fully described, and you are encouraged to apply all of my "trade secrets" to enhance human communication in organizations!

Chapter 8

ISN'T ANYONE LISTENING?

Using Active Listening Techniques

- **WHY IS LISTENING IMPORTANT?**
- **TYPES OF LISTENING**
- **POOR LISTENING**
  Myths about Listening
  Poor Listeners: Who Are They?
  Why Does Poor Listening Exist?
- **ACTIVE LISTENING: WHAT IS IT?**
- **CONSULTANT'S TIPS ON LISTENING**

> *"One advantage of talking to yourself is that you know at least somebody is listening."*
>
> Franklin P. Jones

> *"Listening errors are estimated to cost businesses upwards of $1 billion each year."*
>
> George Headrick, 1983

One of the most poignant examples of poor listening skills occurred among staff members who had been participants in a year-long communication training program. The unit director called me one day and said, "We'd like for you to spend some time with us this week. We need help dealing with a crisis that has occurred in our office." When I inquired about the nature of their problem, I was told that one of the employees had been stabbed to death in a parking lot on a public street and the staff was having a very difficult time coping with the loss of this colleague. What they really wanted was grief counseling. I spent an entire afternoon in a series of discussions and activities designed to allow them an opportunity to express their grief and their sadness.

Finally, near the end of the day one individual said, "I've been trying to tell people all week how angry I was and I haven't been able to do that," and then she gave us examples of what she had said to indicate her anger. However, people tried to appease her by saying: "We understand that you are very sad. We are too." She went on to say, " I was not sad. I was angry, because I had invested so much time in this colleague, helping him develop and be a more effective office worker. Now I feel like all that time and energy is wasted. Then I feel guilty for not feeling sad! This is what I've been trying to say and no one has heard me! Coping with this guilt had been awful. I've felt so alone."

Her colleagues were not listening carefully. They were hearing only what they thought she should be saying but they weren't actively involved in the process of listening or they would have heard her anger and identified with her frustration on an entirely different level.

The word "listen" is derived from two Anglo-Saxon words: *hylstan,* meaning hearing, and *hlosnian,* meaning to wait in suspense. Listening is a combination of hearing sound and waiting in suspense for psychological involvement with the speaker or source generating the message. Consequently, it goes beyond simply hearing sound waves to include psychological involvement with the speaker and his or her message.

Listening is defined as: "a unitary-receptive communication process of hearing and selecting, assimilating and organizing, and retaining and covertly responding to oral and nonverbal stimuli" (Wolff, Marsnik, Tacey, and Nichols, 1983, p. 8). Each of those steps is critical to the process of listening. The listener firsts selects out those stimuli to which he or she will pay attention (the first occasion for distortion to occur!). The story about the two men's approach to listening suggests this.

Two men were walking along a crowded sidewalk in a downtown business area. Suddenly one exclaimed, "listen to the lovely sound of that cricket." But the other could not hear. He asked his companion how he could detect the sound of a cricket amidst the din of people and traffic. The first man, who was a zoologist, had trained himself to listen to the voices of nature, but he did not explain. He simply took a coin out of his pocket and dropped it on the sidewalk whereupon a dozen people began to look around them. "We hear," he said, "what we listen for."

Cited in Burley-Allen (1982).

Then those stimuli must be arranged in such a way that the listener can make sense of them. Otherwise the listener can be overwhelmed with information that is too much to manage.

Some of those stimuli are then retained for future reference (another occasion for distortion to occur, since we tend to remember things according to our own biases). Finally, the listener, if actively involved in the communication process, will then respond verbally or nonverbally to the messages that have been heard. If any one of these steps is incomplete then the process fails.

One group I worked with had a great deal of difficulty with "collective memory." Each one of them would remember ideas and decisions from meetings with a slight twist to them. Even when they had a recorder to write up summaries of the meetings, they still disagreed about the summary! As the meetings drew to a close, they would be so anxious to be "done with" a controversial issue that they didn't really listen to the summarizer who tried to make sure they all heard the same decision. Only later would they then step forward and argue again about the issue.

The dialogue from these meetings would go something like this:

Summarizer: "So we all agree the new policy will require two signatures on requisitions before final approval can be granted."

Person who disagrees with policy: "Yes, we've agreed" (meaning: this will simply be a rubber stamp and any two signatures will do).

Person who agrees with policy: "Yes, I think we've debated this enough and we agree" (meaning: at last we will be firm about getting two supervisory signatures before any purchase is approved—we're finally cracking down!).

Only when the first requisition is presented for approval do they discover they don't really agree. Two things are happening: first, they are not willing to put energy into resolving their differences and second, they are not carefully listening to the summarizer to make sure the "agreement" is spelled out in enough detail so that misunderstanding does not occur later.

Of all the skills of human communication, the one we take most for granted is listening. We assume that listening ability is acquired automatically as we grow older. Research reveals that we probably spend more time each day involved in listening than we do in using any other communication skill. We spend less time developing and refining that skill, however, than any of the other communication skills. The burden of making people listen has always rested on the sender of the message. That responsibility should be placed equally on the listener as well. As listeners, it is extremely important that we identify and improve our listening habits.

■ *Why Is Listening Important?*

In a recent study Sypher, Bostram and Seibert (1989) concluded that "listening is related to other communication abilities and to success at work. Better listeners (as measured by a listening comprehension test) held higher level positions and were promoted more often than those with less-developed listening abilities" (p. 301).

Being a good listener is clearly identified with good management skills. A survey of personnel directors in 300 organizations found that effective listening was ranked highest among the skills defined as most important in becoming a manager (Robbins, 1989). Some of the most successful CEOs with whom I have worked made me feel they were carefully listening to each idea I raised.

Consultants understand the value of listening. In fact, it is probably the single most important skill I use when assessing organizational needs. If you listen very carefully to what employees are telling you, the answers to their problems exist among all the verbiage. Solutions are all present, waiting to be discovered among the hidden agendas, the "fronts," and the language used to "position" themselves. Peters suggested:

> My correspondence occupies many a file cabinet after years of dealing with managers in turbulent conditions. The most moving letters by far are the hundreds about "simple listening." In fact, if I had a file labeled "religious conversion"—that is, correspondence from those whose management practices have truly been transformed—I suspect that 50 percent of its contents would deal with just one narrow topic: going out anew, with a "naive" mind-set, and listening to customers (1988, p. 16).

Steil, Barker, and Watson (1983) reported that the majority of our time each day is spent listening: 14 percent of the day we spend in writing, 17 percent in reading, 16 percent speaking, and 53 percent in listening (p. 3). They go on to report "Listening is a communication skill that we rarely receive formal training in; yet, listening is the skill we develop first and use most often. Instead of training, our listening behaviors are developed by watching and listening to others" (p. 5).

Types of Listening

Wolvin and Coakley (1985) discussed several different types of listening including discriminatory listening, comprehensive listening, therapeutic listening, critical listening, and appreciative listening. Each of these listening skills requires different techniques and focuses on a different form of communication.

Discriminatory listening is listening to distinguish the aural stimuli. This type of listening is basic to the other four. It is developed early in a person's life, and the importance of auditory discrimination is documented in research on the language acquisition of children.

Comprehensive listening is listening to understand. The comprehensive listener is successful if the message received is as close as possible to that which the sender intended. One variable directly related to comprehensive listening is memory. We cannot process information without bringing the memory into focus.

Wolvin and Coakley suggested that in order to improve comprehensive listening, a listener must capitalize on the amount of time difference between how quickly someone speaks and how quickly one can think and connect back to what is being said. They also made suggestions on listening for main ideas by paying attention to the transitions speakers use when they are introducing a main idea like "I want to make one impression on you and that is . . . , " or "Today we are going to discuss . . . , " or "Simply stated, the issue is . . . . " These transitions are signals that the speaker is about to present a main point.

Therapeutic listening is listening to provide a troubled sender with the opportunity to talk through a problem. The skills or techniques needed for therapeutic listening are focusing attention, demonstrating attending behaviors, developing a supportive communicative climate, and listening with empathy. The listener must be willing to enter the other person's world whole-heartedly, for a few moments in time.

Critical listening is listening to comprehend and then evaluate the message. The critical listener makes a decision to accept or reject the message on the basis of sound criteria. Particularly as consumers of the mass media, all people need to be critical listeners. Skills needed to be a critical listener include identifying the dimensions of source credibility, recognizing the influence of credibility, evaluating inductive and deductive arguments, detecting and evaluating reasoning fallacies, evaluating evidence, and recognizing emotional appeals.

Finally, **appreciative listening** is used by one who listens to obtain sensory stimulation or enjoyment through the works and experiences of others. Since appreciative listening is highly individualized, there are no criteria by which to draw a formula for the appreciation of anything for all people.

Communication managers will most often be engaged in comprehensive and therapeutic listening. When you are trying to solve people problems, you are most often listening for facts and feelings. You are also responding to individuals to let them know they have been heard and understood, even if you don't have a solution for them. Many times, they simply need a sounding board and once they have talked their way through the problem, without being interrupted with another person's own problems, they can figure out the solution on their own!

Myths about Listening

Wolff, Marsnik, Tacey, and Nichols (1983) identified ten misconceptions about listening:

Listening is a matter of intelligence.

Good hearing and good listening are closely related.

Listening is an automatic reflex.

Daily practice eliminates the need for training in listening.

Learning to read will automatically improve listening.

Learning to read is more important than learning to listen.

The speaker is totally responsible for success in oral communication.

Listening is essentially a passive activity.

Listening means agreement.

Consequences of careless listening are minimal. (pp. 30–39)

First, listening in and of itself, has no relationship to intelligence. Listening means paying attention to each point the speaker is making. If the listeners do not understand the language or the concept, then their careful involvement in the communication process will allow them to ask pertinent questions for understanding. The intelligent person may have the capacity to understand the concepts but not listen to them, while the active listener hears each point and if it is not understood, asks for clarification.

Second, good hearing simply means that the auditory signal has reached the listener's ear. There is no guarantee that the message got through. One may have good hearing but poor listening ability.

Third, listening is not automatic. We think if we sit quietly we will simply "absorb" the message without effort. Good listening, like any other skill, must be activated. We can actually measure how involved a person is in the listening process. In an actively involved listener the heart rate will increase, blood pressure will rise slightly, and body temperature will go up.

Many people also think because we listen each day, we are receiving daily training in this communication skill. I drive a car every day but I don't get any better at following directions unless I make a conscious attempt to improve. As long as I play golf, I will continue to slice to the right until I get some lessons that will help me correct that swing. No amount of hitting the ball will change that unless I'm willing to pay attention to what I am doing wrong and try to correct it.

The next two misconceptions in the list above both indicate the importance we have placed on reading as the most important communication skill. Yet in today's fast-paced world, we receive more messages orally than in written form. Reading and listening are two very different skills and require diverse styles of "attending" to stimuli.

The seventh and eighth items suggest that the listener plays a passive role in the communication process, and the speaker is totally responsible for the success of the communicative event. The listener does nothing and is not held accountable! These misconceptions make listening a much easier job than it really is. Obviously, communication is a cyclic, not linear, process.

Poor Listening

Unfortunately, most of us assume we are good listeners! Brownell (1990) asked subordinates to evaluate the listening ability of their managers. Over 50 percent placed their managers in the "poor" category. At the same time, ". . . virtually all managers in this sample perceived themselves as 'very good' or 'good' listeners (a small percentage placed themselves in the 'fair' category) even though those managers received low ratings from their subordinates" (p. 412).

Ask managers how they interact with their subordinates and they will probably tell you they have an "open-door" policy, which implies they are ready to listen to whoever walks in. Ask the people who report directly to them and you will get a very different story: "My boss is constantly interrupted by the phone while we talk"; "My supervisor is distracted by what is on the desk during our conversations"; "My boss smiles, nods his head, gets a glazed look in his eyes, and then never responds to what I've just said to him" are a few of the complaints I have heard. Our perceptions of our own listening ability are often inflated. We need to ask others if they feel they have been listened to after talking with us!

We must decide at the beginning of the communication process that we want to be that involved in it. We "clear our minds" as if we were sweeping aside everything on the top of our desks. We should prepare to listen psychologically by placing ourselves in the other person's world for a few minutes. This means setting aside all our personal concerns and ideas for the time being, which is not an easy task. We also have to prepare to listen physically by maintaining eye contact, leaning forward, and positioning our bodies toward the person talking. This reminds both communicators that the focus is totally on the person talking.

One of the reasons individuals are hesitant to quit talking and listen is that they are afraid it will somehow convey agreement with what is being said. Silent listening, we are afraid, will be taken for silent support. We feel a desperate need to get our next point in, lest someone forget what our position really is! In other words, our focus is often on ourselves and "covering" our position rather than on the other person.

The final myth is that poor listening has minimal impact on the communication process. One has only to read case studies of poor listening to discover the depth of impact such communication behaviors may have: divorces, labor negotiations, missed directions costing companies hundreds of thousands of dollars, all point to the fact that the consequences of careless listening can be great.

One of our assumptions is that we are all good listeners. We are usually surprised when someone tells us we aren't listening! We heard the person but maybe we weren't really listening. The following section identifies some of the weak listening habits all of us have probably exhibited at one time or another.

Poor Listeners—Who Are They?

Poor listeners are you and I, anytime we haven't made the other person's thoughts our priority. Montgomery (1981) identified some of the most common poor listeners. Do any of these apply to you?

The unfocused listener is the person who is thinking of something else with wandering eyes and wandering head.

The fact-focused listener always has a mindful of little tidbits of information but may be completely lost as to what the facts prove or what the speaker is trying to get across.

The inattentive listener makes listening difficult if not impossible by slouching in his or her chair or over a table or on a counter as though lacking the energy to really pay attention.

A finicky listener calls the speaker or subject uninteresting and makes the burden of listening and understanding focus on the speaker. This person focuses on tiny details and misses what the person is trying to say.

An emotional listener highlights another bad habit of listening. This is a person who gets overly excited about things that are heard because of a word that has been misunderstood or some negative impact of the speaker.

The fake listener pretends to pay attention and to get the message, smiling, nodding, even looking intently at the speaker, but this listener's mind has detoured and may be a thousand miles away.

A note taker tries to write down every word the speaker is saying. Even with shorthand it would be difficult or impossible to do that. Good note takers sometimes miss the major message.

The unaware listener, instead of anticipating the points the speaker is making and mentally summarizing them, sits and lets the words go in one ear and come out the other. Unless you are working actively at listening, you aren't really listening (pp. 30–60).

All of these types of listeners have been present from time to time in my seminars and retreats. Often, there are several of them present at the same time! At one retreat I conducted for a large professional organization, one person made rather dramatic pleas for solidarity and then undermined consensus during the breaks. The fake listener sat in the front row, nodding and smiling but, when asked to by his supervisor, couldn't recall a single idea expressed that day. Another listener continually sidetracked the group with his off-the-cuff and off-the-topic comments! A communication specialist needs some techniques to handle these poor listeners in a group, some of which I have included at the end of this chapter under "consultant's tips."

Steil, Barker, and Watson (1983) identified the differences between bad listeners and good listeners:

- The bad listener tunes out dry subjects. The good listener looks for benefits and opportunities and asks what's in it for me.
- The bad listener tunes out if delivery is poor. The good listener judges content, skips over delivery errors.
- The bad listener tends to enter into an argument. The good listener doesn't judge until the message is complete.
- The bad listener listens for facts. The good listener listens for central themes.
- The bad listener shows no energy output and fakes attention, while the good listener's whole body works hard, actively exhibiting attention.
- The bad listener is distracted easily while the good listener fights to avoid distractions and knows how to concentrate.
- The bad listener resists difficult, expository materials, seeks light, recreational material while the good listener uses heavier material as an excuse to exercise the mind.
- The bad listener reacts to emotional words while the good listener does not get hung up on them.
- The bad listener tends to daydream with slow speakers while the good listener challenges, anticipates, summarizes, and listens between the lines (pp. 72–73).

Communication specialists must not only guard against becoming poor listeners themselves but will need to model effective listening behaviors to train others as well. If you are interested in improving the communication process for the groups with whom you work, you will need to develop techniques for helping others become better listeners.

Why Does Poor Listening Exist?

We are all prone to poor listening habits for a variety of reasons. Burley-Allen (1982) discussed physical barriers to effective listening including the time of day and fatigue. There are moments in every day, and entire periods of time, when because of your own physical or psychological condition, you are unable to tune into someone else's problem. If the environment you are in does not provide privacy and freedom from distractions, it is very difficult to maintain the level of interaction desired as well.

Anxiety may also cause us to be poor listeners. If we are listening to defend ourselves against possible attack and are anxious about what may be said next, then we are not involved in active listening but rather are engaging in "defensive" listening. Defensive listening means we hear only those things we think are unfair or unjustified in order to respond to them. Kurtz (1990) talked about "chain reactions" involving an attack, a poor listener, and a reaction rather than listening to understand or clarify.

Timm (1986) also suggested that we are poor listeners because of self-centeredness and self-protection.

> Self-centeredness refers to the degree of "vested interest" we may have in our own point of view. When a difference of opinion arises among people, our vested interest in our ideas can create a listening barrier . . . . In other words, we are "listening" through a predetermined set of biases, looking for flaws in our "opponent's" views rather than seeking common understanding. We develop a mind like a steel trap—closed (p. 251).

Self-centeredness is difficult to control. Listeners must be more interested in the other person than in themselves. That is something few of us are able to do on a regular basis. We can, however, enter another person's world temporarily, as an active listener.

Poor listening also becomes very obvious among groups as well. Groups who have a low level of listening show the following characteristics: dominance by a few members, cross-talk (several members talking at once), ideas lost (no mechanism for catching and retaining points), repetitive contributions, wording inputs (individuals use much speaking time for little content), turned-off members, and inability to handle consensus decision making (Francis and Young, 1979, p. 87).

■ Active Listening—What Is It?

The term **active listening** means the ability to pick up, define, and respond accurately to the feelings expressed by the other person. When active listening is employed, speakers perceive that they are being understood. This perception allows them to explore and express their feelings, identify ideas as their own, and to rely less on defensive behavior.

> Active listeners listen with their ears, their eyes, and their mind. They take in the objective information by listening to the literal words that are spo-

ken. But every spoken message contains more than words. Speakers also communicate subjective information—their feelings and emotions—through other vocal sounds and nonverbal signals. These include verbal intonation like loudness, emphasis, hesitations, voice inflections, and the rate of speaking. Nonverbal signals encompass the speaker's eye movements, facial expressions, body posture, and hand gestures. By listening for feelings and emotions, as well as for literal words, you can grasp the total meaning behind the speaker's message. Yet no matter how good you become at listening for total meaning, there still remains the potential for misunderstanding (Robbins, 1989, p. 31).

What Robbins is suggesting is that even when a person uses active listening skills, the possibility of misunderstanding still exists. However, active listening significantly reduces this possibility. Active listening conveys trust and is one of the most effective ways for the listener to help the speaker feel comfortable with the interaction.

Dr. Thomas Gordon (1977), author of *Parent Effectiveness Training*, was one of the first authors to introduce the concept of active listening. An active listener is fully engaged in the communication process even when not talking. The active listener listens for unspoken words and ideas. Gordon also indicated the twelve most commonly expressed nonaccepting responses which defeat the active listening process.

1. ordering, directing, commanding ("You have to . . . ")
2. warning, admonishing, threatening ("You better not . . . ")
3. moralizing, preaching, exhorting, imploring ("It's your duty.")
4. advising, giving suggestions, or solutions ("What you should do is . . . ")
5. persuading with logic, lecturing, arguing, teaching ("Experience says that . . . ")
6. judging, criticizing, disagreeing, blaming ("You'd be foolish to . . . ")
7. praising, agreeing, evaluating positively, buttering up ("You're such a good . . . ")
8. name calling, ridiculing, shaming ("How naive can you be?")
9. interpreting, analyzing, diagnosing ("Your problem is . . . ")
10. reassuring, sympathizing, consoling, supporting ("Tomorrow will be better.")
11. probing, questioning, interrogating ("Why did you . . . ?")
12. distracting, diverting, kidding, avoiding withdrawing, humoring ("Hey, have I told you . . . ") (pp. 60–62)

It is very seductive to listen to someone else's problems and be asked for advice. We all think we can see so clearly what others ought to do with their lives. Often, however, the person is not really asking for advice but simply empathy. The above responses tend to judge the other person's ideas as good or bad rather than simply accepting them. Gordon's list of nonaccepting responses is a good reminder of what type of responses get in the way of active listening. Bite your tongue if you hear yourself using any of them! Avoiding use of the word "why" will eliminate a number of occasions when you appear to be challenging someone's feelings or ideas.

Ask questions that do not get the person off track but instead, help focus on the issues rather than the "symptoms" of the problem. The active listener asks questions for clarification rather than explanation or justification. Those questions must come at appropriate times so that the listener is not interrupting. A variety of authors have discussed at length the ability to ask such questions so that the listener can summarize the "whole picture" for the speaker (Montgomery, 1981; Steil, Barker, and Watson, 1983; Robbins, 1989; Wolff, Marsnik, Tacey, and Nichols, 1983).

Listening is a craft that must be developed. It is much easier *not* to develop that skill, so one has to be motivated to do so. Finally, people must create the most supportive climate in order to encourage effective listening.

Gibb (1961) identified the kind of supportive climate that a good listener wants to establish: a climate that is descriptive rather than evaluative and problem-oriented rather than controlling, one of spontaneity rather than strategy, empathy rather than neutrality, equality rather than superiority, and finally, one of provisionalism rather than certainty.

▍ *Consultant's Tips on Listening*

First, communication specialists must check their own psychological well-being before entering into an active listening process. If you are unable, psychologically or physically, to listen to someone, you do that person a great disservice by pretending to listen. It would be much better to let the speaker know you are unable to help at that time but would be willing to assist in identifying someone who could. You could also make specific plans right then to meet with the client when you feel you will be better able to be an active listener.

Also, check on your general listening behavior. Ask others if you wait to hear someone out or do you tend to interrupt. Be prepared to accept their answers without feeling you must defend yourself! Ask others if you dominate small groups and how often you play the role of "interviewer" in a two-way conversation. If you don't like the answers you get, read this chapter again!

Second, move to a place that will provide some privacy and comfort for the person talking with you. In private conversation, people want to feel secure that the intended listener is the only listener. This may be something as simple as closing a door or moving to a quieter part of a large room. Ask the other person whether he or she is comfortable talking where you are or would prefer to move elsewhere.

In personal conversations, listen for feelings first. People who are upset about something initially need to let off steam before they are ready to talk about solutions. If you get the "yes but" response, you know they are not ready for answers! Besides, they need to come up with their own answer. If you give them the answer, then it will be your solution, not theirs, and if it doesn't work, guess who gets blamed!

Fourth, the communication specialist must have a vocabulary for listening. You must be ready to respond immediately and will need a variety of messages that indicate you have heard the other person and are trying hard to listen carefully. Francis and Young (1979, p. 87) identified a number of useful responses to establish active listening behavior.

Checking: "Can I repeat what you said in order to check my own understanding."

Clarifying: "It seems to me that this is what you mean . . . . "

Showing support: "I hear you. Please carry on."

Building on: "Building on your last point, I would add. . . . "

Structuring: "Shall we look at the symptoms, try to define the problem, and then discuss possible solutions?"

Fifth, watch out for "traps." For example, it is easy to get trapped by **cognitive dissonance** which is the tendency to "dismiss or not allow into consciousness any information not consistent with what we believe or want to believe" (Kurtz, 1990, p. 7). If you are hearing something you do not want to believe personally, it is very difficult to maintain your active-listener role. For that moment, you need to set aside your own opinions and listen only to support the other person.

Finally, listen with intensity, empathy, acceptance, and willingness to take responsibility for completeness (Robbins, 1989) rather than listening to argue a point of view that may or may not be consistent with your own set of values. Empathy is not the same thing as sympathy. Rather than feeling sorry for someone you are simply trying to place yourself in the other person's position—not to agree or disagree—but merely to understand his or her point of view.

You can transfer listening skills to your clients by providing descriptive feedback. Cite specific examples of when they have demonstrated those skills. Then ask clients to repeat information you have shared. This will put them in the habit of paraphrasing and listening closely. Some of the training techniques discussed in Chapter 6 could be used to develop a workshop on listening for your client.

Form 8.1, the listening quiz, is designed to help you pay more attention to your own attitude toward listening. Monitor your own listening behavior for one day and ask others for feedback. How often during a typical work day are you an active listener? Are you like the person in the following poem, wondering if the person listening to *you* is "missing"?

■ CONVERSATION

i have just
wandered back
into our conversation
and find
that you
are still
rattling on
about something
or other
i think i must
have been gone
at least
twenty minutes
and you
never missed me
now
this might say
something
about my acting ability
or it might say
something about
your sensitivity
one thing
troubles me tho
when it
is my turn
to rattle on
for twenty minutes
which i
have been known to do
have you
been missing too?

Source: Reprinted from *Dragonflies, Codfils & Frogs* by Ric Masten, p. 59. © 1977 Ric Masten.

■ LISTENING QUIZ

Directions: Mark each statement true or false.

_____ **1.** People tend to pay attention to what interests them.

_____ **2.** People tend to expect or anticipate what they are familiar with.

_____ **3.** Sometimes people distort things so they hear what they want to hear.

_____ **4.** Listening is a natural process.

_____ **5.** A person's training, experience, and knowledge affect what that person perceives.

_____ **6.** Hearing and listening are the same.

_____ **7.** Listening is a skill.

_____ **8.** Most people have a short attention span and have difficulty concentrating on the same thing for too long.

_____ **9.** Listening requires little energy; it is "easy."

_____ **10.** The speaker is totally responsible for the success of the communication.

_____ **11.** An effective listener keeps an open, curious mind.

_____ **12.** Speaking is a more important part of the communication process than listening.

_____ **13.** When a listener's emotional level is high, he or she will be an effective listener.

_____ **14.** When a person is involved with internal distractions, he or she will not be able to listen to what the speaker says.

_____ **15.** Being critical and judging a speaker is not an effective listening skill.

Suggested Readings

Burley-Allen, M. (1982). *Listening: The forgotten skill.* New York, NY: John Wiley & Sons, Inc.

Montgomery, R.L. (1981). *Listening made easy: How to improve listening on the job, at home, and in the community.* New York, NY: AMACOM.

Steil, L.K., Barker, L.L., & Watson, K.W. (1983). *Effective listening: Key to your success.* Reading, MA: Addison-Wesley Publishing Co., Inc.

Timm, P.R. (1986). *Managerial communication: A finger on the pulse.* (2nd ed.). Englewood Cliffs, NJ: Prentice-Hall.

Wolvin, A.D., & Coakley, C.G. (1988). *Listening.* Dubuque, IA: Wm. C. Brown.

Chapter 9 ═══════════════

WHY ARE MEETINGS SO BORING AND UNPRODUCTIVE?

Managing Meetings

■ **WHY MEET?**
To Announce Organizational Changes
To Increase and Improve Solutions
To Gain Acceptance of a Decision through Participation
To Cultivate Members as Individuals

■ **WHEN SHOULD A MEETING NOT BE CALLED?**

■ **ROADBLOCKS TO EFFECTIVE MEETINGS**
Groupthink
Procedural Issues

■ **TECHNIQUES FOR MAKING MEETINGS MORE PRODUCTIVE**
Directing Traffic
Separating Topic from Procedure
Identifying Roles

■ **GROUP LEADERSHIP**

■ **PREPARATION FOR MEETINGS**
Learning about Participants
Attending to Logistics
Planning a "Grand" Meeting

■ **CONSULTANT'S TIPS FOR SUCCESSFUL MEETINGS**

"People can be motivated to be good not by telling them that hell is a place where they will burn, but by telling them that it is an unending committee meeting. On judgment day, the Lord will divide people by telling those on his right hand to enter his kingdom and those on his left to break into small groups."

author unknown

*I*t has been reported that one corporation holds all its top-level meetings without chairs, requiring individuals to stand during the entire meeting. The goal is to force people to be quick with their comments, making the meeting more productive and efficient. This technique may not work with all groups; however, the goal is a noble one.

I recently worked with a group of individuals who scheduled a three-hour meeting every Wednesday morning, whether there was something to discuss or not. Every Tuesday afternoon, half of the staff met to plan what would be said in the Wednesday morning meeting. Consequently, the Wednesday meeting was a repetition for half of the attendees and for the other half it was a briefing on mostly routine information with no input from them. Two individuals in the group used a strategy to make the Wednesday meetings more productive. They requested that the meeting be moved to 11:15 because they had prior commitments earlier in the morning. Their strategy was to hold the meeting as close to the noon hour as possible so the meeting would only last 45 to 50 minutes. This strategy worked. There was less side conversation and less repetition of information. The important issues were the ones that came up first and got dealt with, and the meeting was over before any unnecessary discussion could occur.

Why are meetings so boring? One reason is that those who make up the agenda are often not in touch with the needs and interests of those who must attend the meeting! Frequently, I have discovered a staff spending 1–2 hours dreaming up items for an agenda the day before a meeting that others will attend. The meeting then turns into an information briefing, when most of the information could have been communicated in written form and saved everyone valuable time. This doesn't mean team briefings shouldn't occur. The team briefing can be very useful; however,

157

when it occurs, meeting participants should know the intent of the meeting is to provide information, not to solicit opinions.

The other major reason meetings are boring is that a few people use meetings as an opportunity to promote some agenda or issue of their own, and the person in charge of the meeting does not limit the amount of time any one individual may control. These are just two of the issues this chapter will address and for which it will provide easy and simple solutions.

Why Meet?

Recent research suggests that most managers spend 2–3 days a week tied up in unproductive meetings. As much as 30 person days and up to $71 million are wasted each year on meetings that solve nothing (Mosvick and Nelson, 1987). As the article written by Isadore Barmash for *Newsweek* points out, many people have a very pessimistic view of the potential outcome of meetings. When people come to meetings with such negative expectations, they are bound to fail! If meetings are such a waste of time, why do people keep holding them?

To Announce Organizational Changes

We hold meetings when the rapid changes in the marketplace make it necessary for managers to keep employees informed on a regular basis. These environmental changes have also caused a great deal of reorganization compelling individuals to meet to discuss and understand how reorganizing the system will affect their day-to-day jobs. In this highly technical environment changes in products, services, and marketing are so rapid it behooves the managers to keep employees constantly in touch with these changes.

Kanter (1989, 1983), and other writers who discuss future changes in corporate America (Naisbitt, 1982; Naisbitt and Aburdene, 1990), have indicated that the hierarchies of organizations are collapsing. Organizations are becoming more flat, with decision making at the lowest level of the hierarchy. An organization is described as "flat" when there are few hierarchical levels from the top of the organization to the bottom. If there are fewer hierarchical levels then more people at each level are involved in decision making. Consequently, more meetings among those who must make decisions are necessary. The increase in *participative management* has encouraged group interaction and deliberation.

■ A NEW ECONOMIC INDICATOR

So much has been written about the decline in our nation's productivity and so many reasons advanced that one wonders why we haven't solved the problem.

But we haven't, and we won't unless we identify the real culprit. I, for one, know what it is; and it's as elusive as only the truly obvious can be.

Meetings.

It doesn't really matter where, be it government, business or education, but meetings are held at the drop of a memo. They are wasteful, and mostly painful. I am reasonably certain that if there were an organization called the National Commission on the Study of Multiple Encounters, its findings would be devastating. It would discover, I am sure, that there were 3.8 trillion meetings held at American companies last year. Of that number, 70 percent lasted 45 minutes or more, and about 75 percent included 10 participants or more. If the NCSME pursued its research properly, it would also find that the growth trend of meetings has exceeded major economic indicators such as the gross national product, the rate of inflation, interest, unemployment—and productivity.

Meetings, I therefore suggest, have become our national pastime, yet one is hard put to see any advantage to them other than someone's decision to hold a meeting so the group can for a time avoid doing the job it is paid to do. In that sense, meetings are relaxing. The irony is that no one does.

The trouble with meetings is that too much is considered and too little is resolved. Meetings are self-perpetuating. They last twice as long as they should. They are an excuse and are often intended to impress others with the patent effort to induce employee participation. Meetings are a euphemism, a ploy really to evaluate the three P's—people, programs and politics. Meetings are deceptive. Meetings aren't held to hear what everyone has to say, but for everyone to hear what one has to say.

Well, if the National Commission on the Study of Multiple Encounters could figure it out, the number of hours spent on meetings in the United States, based on the numbers I estimated earlier, is almost incalculable, as is the number of employees involved. It would come to trillions of man- or woman-hours annually that can be translated into lost productivity. So revealing would the findings be that they might be considered a new economic indicator—the American meetings rate, seasonally adjusted.

By Isadore Barmash. From *Newsweek*, September 9, 1985, p. 12. Reprinted by permission.

To Increase and Improve Solutions

Another reason for holding meetings is individuals are able to identify more and better solutions to problems although some individual creativity may be stifled. There is much research to suggest the advantages of several people contributing to the problem solving instead of developing solutions in isolation, particularly with complex tasks. There is greater motivation to perform well in a group setting since others are judging one's actions. A number of studies also suggest that groups will consider more ideas which is likely to improve the quality and originality of the decision (Schultz, 1989, p. 8). Since opportunities for communication have increased, the group's decision-making ability is enhanced as well (Gouran, 1982). In the introduction to their book, Poole and Hirokawa (1986) indicated:

> There is a world of difference between making a decision alone and making a group decision. The unique chemistry of social interaction can distill the best that each member has to offer, creating a resonance of ideas and a synthesis of viewpoints. A different chemistry can stop the reaction and contaminate the product with erratic reasoning or low commitment. Communication is the catalyst for this social chemistry and, as such, it is widely recognized as a key force in group decision making (p. 15).

It is clear that group interaction changes the way in which solutions are generated and those solutions become more than just the sum of the individual efforts. In another research program, Hirokawa (1987) found four communication characteristics that distinguish the interaction in high- and low-quality decisions. High-quality decisions came from groups characterized by "vigilance" or careful, thoughtful, and systematic discussion of the pros and cons of solutions. Second, high-quality decisions were generated when the group practiced "second guessing" or challenging questionable information introduced by group members. Third, these groups participated in more accurate information processing, which means that group members actively rejected faulty information. Finally, the high-quality decisions came from groups characterized by the absence of what Hirokawa called "improbable fantasy chains." This refers to unrealistic hypothetical scenarios and stories. In short, low-quality decisions were made when the group relied on flawed information in arriving at their decisions. Thus, given the above conditions, groups have the ability to generate better solutions than individuals.

To Gain Acceptance of a Decision through Participation

Meetings also encourage a "buy in" to solutions. We know the more individuals participate in the generation of the solution the more likely they will be to implement it. When individuals have helped determine the solution they have already made a commitment to make sure it works. All of the management literature of the 1980s pointed to the need to make employees a part of the process of decision making in corporations. "People are psychologically committed to ideas that they help generate in meetings, which goes beyond the product itself" (Napier and Gershenfeld, 1987, p. 421).

The CEO of one company formed a cross-sectional group to examine quality issues in the company. As a consultant, I was asked to facilitate the initial meetings of this group and train them in effective decision-making processes. They were charged with eliminating any procedures or policies that were "blocking" effective communication. At first, the committee members came into the group meetings defending their personal attachment to policies and sub-groups. Over a period of several weeks, when the meeting facilitator continued to emphasize the goal of the group, they eventually "bought into" the idea that some policies and procedures may have been slowing down their ability to work together effectively. Eventually, the group recommended the elimination of 50 percent of the policy making groups that had been formed over the years and dramatically streamlined procedures for approval of new services. When their recommendations were presented to the rest of the management teams, these teams were outraged. Since they had not been a part of the long discussions, they had no commitment to making such long-term changes. At that point, the total organization had to be brought into the decision-making process so that all members of the management team could experience some level of commitment to implement these new steps, otherwise the recommendations would fall on deaf ears. To the degree that individuals are involved in the decision making process, they will be willing to implement the final decision.

To Cultivate Members as Individuals

Group meetings also provide us with opportunities to display our skills to co-workers and superiors. This is often the time in which our ability to solve problems can be recognized in front of others. It is important that the work team has a good sense of the skills of each individual so human resources are used appropriately. Often meetings serve critical symbolic functions. Celebrating organizational members' successes and congratulating group achievements, are important to the climate established in the organization.

Finally, since our work life and our personal life are more blended today than ever before (see Chapter 17), meetings serve to satisfy our personal and social needs as well. We do much more than work on tasks in the work environment. We form friendships, meet future mates, and have many of our social interaction needs satisfied. While these are not the primary reasons for calling meetings, they are critical factors in our work life.

Although the preceding reasons for calling meetings are compelling, managers and consultants need to know when it is inappropriate to call a meeting because some other form of communication will work better.

When Should a Meeting Not Be Called?

The most effective leaders/group facilitators know when *not* to call a meeting as well as when one is necessary. Consider the following criteria for not calling a meeting:

- When information can be distributed in written form or by voice mail
- When a decision has already been made
- When individual or programmed learning is best
- When key people can't be there
- When there is no real agenda
- When time and information are inadequate

As you look down the list above, can you recall meetings you have attended when one or more of these conditions existed? How did you feel during the meeting? Most individuals feel frustrated and angry that their time has been wasted. First, a meeting should not be called if information can be more easily distributed through written memos. This allows individuals to review that material at times most convenient to their schedule instead of pulling everyone together at one time to listen to someone read information to them.

Second, if a manager tells a group that they have the power to make decisions, that manager can't later admit the decision has already been made. The meeting leader needs to make the intent of the meeting clear to the participants. That intent may be to advise the leader/supervisor, make recommendations, or to actually decide an issue. The attitudes and actions of the group members will vary greatly depending on the objective of the meeting. A leader gets into trouble when individuals come to a meeting expecting to have a role to play in a decision only to find out the leader does not want their advice after all! Don't ask for others to make decisions if you aren't ready to accept a decision that may not be your choice!

FIGURE 9.1 *Calvin and Hobbes* copyright 1991 Watterson. Reprinted with permission of Universal Press Syndicate. All rights reserved.

■ THE USES OF MEETINGS

I learned not long ago of a meeting at a small plastics manufacturing firm. Present were a division manager, six department heads and the heads of three sections. The topic: Should a replacement be hired for a recently injured secretary, or should a typist be secured from a temporaries service and kept on a week-to-week basis?

It took 50 minutes to reach a consensus on that question. Actually, the decision should have been made privately by the division manager or by the manager of the one office involved.

What was decided is not important. The effect of such meetings on the company is. Because of the length of the discussion about the secretarial replacement, time ran out before a second topic could be considered. A decision on it was not reached until another meeting weeks later. The topic: Should a new fluorescent lighting system for the plant be installed? Involved were not just one office but four departments—not to mention a $28,000 investment.

It should not be that way. First of all, meetings are expensive. When 12 people, each paid $15 to $25 per hour, meet for two or three hours, the cost for one session may easily exceed $500. Such a price is justified when it is necessary to bring representatives from engineering, production, finance and marketing together to solve a legitimate problem. But when the session is held to get a consensus on whether coffee breaks should be taken at 10 A.M. and not at 10:30, or whether the copying machine should be moved 50 feet, blowing $500 worth of time on a meeting is unconscionable.

Second, when a manager calls meetings to decide on items that are inconsequential or that he should handle himself for other reasons, the importance of future meetings is diluted. People will find reasons not to attend whenever they can—a pity, because there will be some vital meetings that require input from everyone invited.

And third, when meetings are called by a manager who wishes to spread responsibility, a signal is given to his subordinates: "This is a policy you may wish to follow when you become a manager. Always cover yourself."

These situations tend to reduce initiative and harden the organizational arteries.

By Norman B. Sigband. Reprinted by permission, *Nation's Business*, February 1987, copyright 1987, U.S. Chamber of Commerce.

Third, a meeting or training session should not be called when the topic can be covered in a more effective way. Sometimes people need different ways in which to learn. A training session is not always appropriate for the individuals or the subject matter. I have observed trainers attempt to teach computer skills without benefit of hands-on experience on the part of the participants. You can't just talk about computers and expect others to learn how to use them. In addition, one-on-one training may be better than a room full of novice individuals all attempting to hit the same key on the keyboard at the same time. Consequently, a meeting called for the purpose of training must be the most appropriate way to deliver that skill.

Fourth, if the goal of a meeting is team building then the "team" must all be present or the meeting should not be called. You can't build a team when key players are not there. At the same time, individuals who are not going to be members of the team should not be present either. A client asked me to conduct a team-building session for one unit in the organization. When I asked about who the "team" would be I discovered they had planned for two individuals to come who were in the process of leaving the organization. One of these individuals had been a source of much conflict and everyone appeared to be relieved that he was leaving the organization. To have this individual attend a "team-building" meeting was inappropriate. I asked that anyone who was not a permanent member of the team be excused from the meeting.

Fifth, meeting participants seem most frustrated when no agenda is provided and no attempt is made to develop one at the beginning of the meeting. A meeting should not be called unless the meeting leader lets participants identify what items they feel need immediate attention. An "expectations check" is a system used to check on the needs of the group before the meeting begins. The leader simply asks, "Are there any items someone feels must be addressed before this meeting ends today?" This can be done ahead of time through written memos or orally at the beginning of the meeting. The leader must take responsibility for limiting the discussion and getting the group to quickly agree on those items of top priority. The group decides which issues must wait until the next meeting and which must be discussed at this meeting. Finally, if the meeting leader has issues that must be addressed, all information relevant to those issues must be available to group members prior to the meeting.

■ *Roadblocks to Effective Meetings*

Once you have determined that a meeting needs to be called, you need to be sure the purpose of the meeting is clearly articulated and that adequate information has been provided. As you think of things that can go wrong in the meeting itself there are two major areas for concern: psychological issues relevant to the group process and procedural issues.

Groupthink

First, one needs to address group behavior issues. Janis (1972) wrote about the phenomenon of "groupthink." This theory identifies some of the most difficult road blocks to effective group meetings and group decision making (see Chapter 11). Groups can fall into the trap of believing that they are invulnerable by discounting negative information, ignoring ethical considerations, pressuring dissenters into conforming with the group norm, believing unanimity exists when it doesn't, and appointing "mindguards" who watch for any comments or ideas that seem out of the mainstream of the group's thinking. In short, these behaviors protect the group from attending to any information or ideas that contrast with their own personal views.

> I worked with one group who sent their "mindguards" to me as an "advance team" to make sure that I "got the picture" before I worked with the group. We sat in a cafeteria prior to the meeting I was to facilitate and I was surrounded by three individuals in the group who had been long-term members. These representatives wanted to be sure that I had an accurate history of the group to help me understand the issues they were now facing. One individual spoke first: "These young guys just don't understand how hard we have worked to establish a marketing strategy that will work. They come in with all these new ideas with no thought for our past efforts." The next fellow became agitated and, without realizing it, was revealing their unwillingness to hear any idea different from their own when he said, "The next time one of these young kids tries to put something over on us I'm going to set him straight!" These individuals were completely unwilling to hear any idea that had not originated with them. Ultimately, the job of the facilitator was to make the group aware of their nonproductive behaviors. These groupthink behaviors are psychological blocks to productive meetings.

Procedural Issues

Procedural issues as well must be taken into account. Two authors surveyed over 1,000 managers to determine what goes wrong in meetings (Mosvick and Nelson, 1987). They discovered the following actions topped the list of complaints:

1. Getting off the subject (reported by 204 managers)
2. No goals or agenda (190)
3. Too lengthy (187)
4. Poor or inadequate preparation (94)

5. Inconclusive (88)
6. Disorganized (86)
7. Ineffective leadership/lack of control (38)
8. Irrelevance of information discussed (37)
9. Time wasted during meeting (37)
10. Starting late (36) (p. 19)

These complaints are not difficult issues to deal with. They don't indicate differences in philosophy or conflict as being the most obvious problems. Rather, the complaints of these managers have to do with procedures for running meetings. If leaders followed a few simple rules most of these issues could be eliminated.

■ Techniques for Making Meetings More Productive

Given this variety of issues the meeting facilitator needs to focus attention on what makes a meeting work. Five basic problems present themselves to the meeting facilitator. He or she must: decide how to direct traffic, determine if the group is talking about how to discuss a topic or what topic to discuss, identify who does what during the meeting itself, develop strategies for handling information overload, and determine the goal of the meeting.

Directing Traffic

Directing traffic simply means some system must be in place to ensure group members do not interrupt each other and all individuals are given a chance to speak. In large meetings (over 50), **parliamentary procedures** are necessary to control the flow of business. These procedures control how motions can be placed before the group and how discussion can be limited. The group must know how to deal effectively with matters brought before them.

The following are the basic "survival steps" necessary to function in a parliamentary procedure environment. Parliamentary procedure is useful because it provides an orderly way to move through officer reports, and second it allows every member an opportunity to present ideas in the form of motions for debate.

Four types of motions can be presented. A **privileged motion** takes priority over all other motions and is not debatable, thus an immediate vote is taken once the motion has been seconded. An example would be a motion to adjourn, take a recess, or attend to the comfort of the group in some way.

Incidental motions deal with the procedures the group is using in the meeting. These must be voted on before main or subsidiary motions. Examples of incidental motions would include suspension of the rules or a point of order.

Subsidiary motions apply to or amend main motions. They must be voted on before the main motion but are "outranked" by incidental or privileged motions. These types of motions would include postponing the discussion or vote until a future time, amending a main motion, limiting debate on a main motion, and calling for the "previous question" (asking for a vote on the main motion).

Finally, the **main motion** is the statement of an item of business. These motions are actually the activity of the group but are voted on last, after any amendments or questions about procedures and privileges of the group have been decided.

If the group is using parliamentary procedure, then the chair must make sure these procedures are followed: no one makes a motion without being recognized, having the motion seconded, and having the floor opened for debate and discussion (no discussion takes place if the motion does not receive a second). The debate is controlled by not allowing interruptions, and the motion is reread when the discussion is finished. Only then does the chair call for the final vote.

Table 9.1 provides a brief summary of motions and their requirements. This can serve as a quick guide for large meetings. Knowing how to use these procedures will facilitate carrying out the business desired. The most likely place these procedures will be used is in large association meetings and democratic institutions. In business and industry, decision making does not take place on a scale so large as to require the use of parliamentary procedure.

In smaller groups, parliamentary procedure may get in the way of informal discussion, which can be carried out among 20 or fewer people. Still, the group leader needs to set some ground rules and ensure that all participants are heard. For example, one rule might be that everyone has a chance to present ideas only once before voting or deciding on an issue. Or the group could require a "first reading" prior to voting. In this case, the group hears about a suggestion or motion at one meeting but does not vote on it until the next meeting. This gives everyone a chance to think carefully about the idea before being asked to vote. The decision to use parliamentary procedure should be based on the following guidelines: the procedures should not get in the way of open discussion, should control debate, and establish an efficient system for dealing with the work of the group. The ultimate goal is to avoid chaos!

■ TABLE 9.1

PARLIAMENTARY PROCEDURE:
TABLE OF MOTIONS

Motion	Vote Required	Debatable	Amendable	Needs Second	Interrupt Speaker
PRIVILEGED MOTIONS:					
Fix time of next meeting	Majority	No	Yes	Yes	No
Adjourn	Majority	No	No	Yes	No
Recess	Majority	No	Yes	Yes	No
Question of privilege	Chair decides	No	No	No	Yes
Orders of the day	Chair decides	No	No	No	Yes
SUBSIDIARY MOTIONS:					
Lay on table	Majority	No	No	Yes	No
Stop debate (previous motion)	⅔	No	No	Yes	No
Limit or extend debate	⅔	No	Yes	Yes	No
Postpone to definite time	Majority	Yes	Yes	Yes	No
Refer to committees	Majority	Yes	Yes	Yes	No
Amend	Majority	Yes	Yes	Yes	No
Postpone indefinitely	Majority	Yes	No	Yes	No
MAIN MOTIONS:	Majority	Yes	Yes	Yes	No
INCIDENTAL MOTIONS:					
Appeal	Majority	Yes	No	Yes	Yes
Division (for vote count)	Chair decides	No	No	No	No
Divide question	Majority	No	Yes	No	No
Withdraw motion	Majority	No	No	No	No
Point of order	Chair decides	No	No	No	Yes
Suspend rules	⅔	No	No	Yes	No
Object to consideration	⅔	No	No	No	Yes
Parliamentary inquiry	Chair decides	No	No	No	Yes
TO REOPEN AND BRING BACK BUSINESS:					
Take from table	Majority	No	No	Yes	No
Reconsider	Majority	Yes	No	Yes	Yes
Rescind or repeal	⅔	Yes	Yes	Yes	No

Source: Doyle, M.E. and Strauss, D., 1986, *How to Make Meetings Work*, Berkley Publ. Co., N.Y.

Separating Topic from Procedure

Sometimes a group spends more time discussing how to proceed than discussing the topic itself. Obviously the procedure used is important however, if the group gets too caught up in a procedure discussion it is likely to accomplish very little. I have seen groups informally express agreement on an issue but then not be able to figure out how the process they were using would allow them to do what they wanted. *Procedures are useful only if they enhance a group's ability to get done what they want.* When the procedure becomes the issue the group needs to be reminded of its basic goal or mission.

Identifying Roles

Who does what? This question addresses the roles individuals play in the group. For example, there is usually one *historian* in every group who reminds the group of their past history, who they are, and what they have done before. Sometimes this behavior is very helpful in that it serves as a group conscience. Other times it can be blocking behavior because the person may constantly remind the group that a solution has been tried before and did not work. While the historian's perception may be accurate, idea generation requires that the group not evaluate the idea until all ideas are expressed.

Other group roles include the *person who initiates* discussion. This person gets the discussion started and often serves as the sounding board for others. Usually someone is assigned to be the *recorder* for the group. Everyone needs to know who is *"in charge"* of the meeting. This person will constantly test the group's willingness to move on to another topic or make a final decision on the topic under discussion. These of course are not official roles but are personality traits that are manifest during the course of the meeting.

Schein (1988) identified a series of roles individuals play in the group process. Every meeting will have a mixture of these various roles and member behaviors (see Chapter 11 for further discussion). **Task functions** are those behaviors that help the group concentrate on specific jobs. Someone gets the discussion started by making the first comments. Others will provide and ask for information and opinions. Still others will perform clarifying roles of pulling information together and testing to see if the group agrees on an issue. **Maintenance functions** are those behaviors that help the group stay together and deal with the interpersonal relationships of the group. These behaviors focus on resolving conflicts, being a "gatekeeper" or providing a way for all members to talk, providing encouragement to others and setting the standards for the group. **Boundary management functions** are those activities that link the group to other groups. "Scouting" other groups or individuals for information and negotiating roles within the organization are important tasks for group members to perform.

There are also a series of blocking behaviors that prevent the group from moving forward. A person who is always negative no matter what the idea is, the dominator who has something to say on every topic, the person who constantly seeks attention, and individuals who remain silent can be some of the most difficult people to deal with. Chapter 13 discusses some techniques for dealing with these difficult people.

The role of group leader is a unique set of tasks. Besides learning to deal with these individual personality types, the leader has a set of tasks for that role as well.

■ Group Leadership

Doyle and Straus (1986) suggested that the "meeting facilitator" is really a "meeting chauffeur." That analogy accurately suggests the major role for the meeting leader. The leader directs the group's activities and ensures that the group gets to its destination safely. If the group leader wants to participate in the discussion then another individual should take over running the meeting for that period of time. The meeting leader must be the facilitator, not the dominant voice. In a sense, the meeting leader is more aware of the process the group uses to get their work done than the content of their discussion. Thus, the leader's primary jobs include: 1) helping the group stick to the subject, 2) making sure everyone gets a chance to speak, 3) acting as a harmonizer and preventing others from being attacked, and 4) as Doyle and Straus suggest, monitoring "short-term memory" by placing ideas on a flip chart and "long-term memory" by making sure minutes are provided as a follow up to the meeting.

The group leader must also decide *how much information is enough.* Sometimes a group leader, in an attempt to make sure everyone is fully informed, will provide too much information. Individuals feel overloaded and unable to sort through the mass of data that has been presented. An advisory board can often help the group leader examine the information and condense it into easily consumed data so that individuals can make reasonable judgments.

The most important thing we have learned about leadership, after years of study, is that it is situational. **Situational leadership** means leaders must adapt to the particular environmental and individual needs of the moment. A person cannot change their basic personality; however, one can make slight modifications so that when the group needs a leader who is focused on task versus one who is focused on the relationships in the group, the leader can pay more attention to that issue. A "leader" is a person who is directing the activities of others, while "leadership" is a behavior that can be exhibited by anyone in the group. A group can be "leaderless" (without a designated leader) but will not function without "leadership" (behaviors exhibited by various group members which provide direction for the group). Therefore, leadership roles are important for everyone to understand.

Some authors have referred to a new leadership style as **transformational** (Tichy and Devanna, 1986). They define it as a style of leadership that is "systematic, consisting of purposeful and organized searches for changes, systematic analysis, and the capacity to move resources from areas of lesser to greater productivity" (p. 27). This form of leadership is needed as corporations undergo dramatic change in markets and economic conditions in the United States, and reinforces the need for a situational style that adopts to various conditions.

Finally, the group leader must decide the goal of the meeting. If it is a decision-making meeting, then the suggestions given above will apply. If, on the other hand, it is a briefing, the leader needs to make the intent very clear. Briefings provide many useful services to the group including:

- Providing managers and supervisors with information they can share with employees
- Guaranteeing that supervisors, rather than the grapevine, will be the primary source of information
- Building loyalty because employees are trusted and confided in
- Creating regularly scheduled occasions for work groups to get together to discuss business
- Increasing employees' understanding of business problems and concerns and their ability and desire to offer solutions
- Giving all employees permission to speak openly by structuring and institutionalizing face-to-face discussion
- Maximizing management's opportunities to deal with employee concerns before they cause morale problems and affect productivity (Johnson, 1990, pp. 55–56).

With the decision to hold a briefing or a problem-solving session the leader establishes a normative behavior for the group which will guide the interaction throughout the meeting. Rules that guide the "traffic," determined ahead of time, will decrease interruptions.

Preparation for Meetings

The meeting facilitator needs to do a good deal of preparation for a meeting, even to the point of arranging the chairs. The first order of business is to find out about the participants so that the meeting can be planned to accomplish the goals they are assembling to address. By attending to logistics, the facilitator will help the participants focus on their business and avoid irritating distractions. The facilitator who knows how to prepare for a meeting can run an elaborate conference as effectively as a smaller gathering, but success requires systematic planning.

Learning about Participants

Napier and Gershenfeld (1987) suggested a list of questions the meeting leader ought to ask about the participants in order to be fully prepared for facilitating the discussions.

1. Whom does each of the participants represent within or outside of the organization?
2. Why have these individuals been chosen and not someone else?
3. What are each individual's organizational interest and needs? What does each of them want from the meeting? What hidden agendas might be influencing the life of the group?
4. What is known about each individual's personal goals and needs? Is his or her ego on the line? Do any have a stake in certain outcomes in addition to the organizational needs they represent?
5. Do the participants come with individual biases toward the leader, other members, the task at hand, or the general format of the meeting?
6. What are the personal skills and strengths available in the group that can be utilized if necessary?
7. What are the personal limitations and idiosyncrasies present in the group that might block the task at hand?

History of the Group:

1. How did the participants leave the last meeting? Were they pleased? Did they experience success? Or failure?
2. As a result, what are the expectations of this meeting?
3. What were the sources of pleasure experienced at the last meeting, of accomplishment or other rewards?
4. What were the sources of tension, frustration, or conflict?

Realistic Goals:

1. What are the real task priorities of the members?

2. How is it possible to best utilize the resources available in meeting these priorities?

3. What needs to be done to ready the group to work on the task so they can hear each other and focus on goals?

4. What do the individuals know when coming to the group?

5. What information do they not know but need to have in order to work effectively on the priorities at hand? (Napier and Gershenfeld, 1987, p. 428).

This type of detailed assessment of the group members and their past behaviors and expectations, will greatly enhance the likelihood for suc-

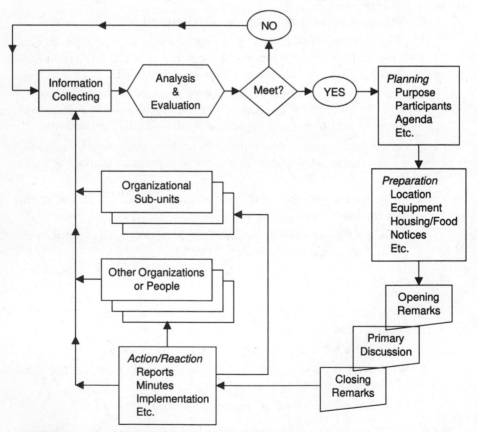

FIGURE 9.2   The Problem-Solving / Decision Meeting Cycle   Reprinted by permission of Ed Baum. All rights reserved.

cess at the meeting. Not having access to this information will mean the meeting planner is likely to repeat information they have already covered, or raise or lower expectations unrealistically.

Attending to Logistics

Often it is the smallest of details that can make a meeting less effective. The meeting leader should make sure the room is large enough, that the chairs and tables are arranged appropriately for the activity being conducted (e.g., conference tables if notes will be taken), and that all facilities are available to provide for the participants' needs (e.g., lunch arrangements). One meeting leader, who had failed to attend to these details, found he had a disaster on his hands when the meeting started 35 minutes late because the audio-visual equipment had not been tested and did not work, the room got too hot, and a loud buzzing noise came from the lights throughout the meeting. In addition, two people sat on chairs in the hallway because the room was too small, the lunchroom was not prepared for as many participants as attended, and lunch took 1 hour and 45 minutes to serve! Busy people hate wasting time.

Following the meeting there are as many details as in the preparation stage. Minutes should be sent to all participants, any follow-up actions must be taken as soon as possible, and the next meeting should be planned. Figure 9.2 visually represents the business meeting cycle. Note that the planning stages and follow-up stages are represented as a complete circle. The follow-up steps from one meeting affect organizational subunits which in turn become the source of information for the next meeting.

The checklist provided in Form 9.1 will help the meeting planner review details to attend to not only prior to the meeting, but during and following the meeting as well. These are the kinds of details that will make participants eager or reluctant to come to the next meeting.

Planning a "Grand" Meeting

A conference or convention takes the same skills as running a business meeting, with the addition of 1,001 small details. Figure 9.3 lists some of those details and the amount of advance time needed to plan for each one. From determining a theme for the conference (#11, at 29 weeks) to mailing announcements (#34, at 13 weeks) to last minute details at the conference site, a conference planner must be extremely organized. The reactions of five hundred (or more) participants who are "unhappy campers" because dinner took one and a half hours to be served,

■ **MEETING LEADER'S CHECKLIST**

Preparing for the Meeting

_____ 1. Establish the reason for calling the meeting.

_____ 2. Develop the agenda.

_____ 3. Select the right people to attend.

_____ 4. Select the date and time.

_____ 5. Confirm date, time, and agenda with key people.

_____ 6. Notify all people who will be attending, and include starting and closing times.

_____ 7. Reserve a room.

_____ 8. Distribute agenda and materials for review, if needed.

_____ 9. Select person to chair the meeting, if appropriate.

_____ 10. Set up meeting room with needed equipment.

_____ 11. Prepare handout materials.

_____ 12. Request secretary to attend.

_____ 13. Arrange for refreshments, if desirable.

Opening the Meeting

_____ 14. Begin the meeting on time.

_____ 15. Introduce participants, if necessary.

_____ 16. Instruct recording secretary, if necessary.

_____ 17. Set the appropriate climate.

(Continued)

■ **MEETING LEADER'S CHECKLIST** *(Continued)*

_____ 18. Review the agenda and announce the objective.

_____ 19. State any problems to be solved, or decisions to be made during the meeting.

Conducting the Core of the Meeting

_____ 20. Encourage participation and orchestrate the roles of all group members.

_____ 21. Focus on subjects at hand.

_____ 22. Establish and follow an agreed-upon decision-making process.

_____ 23. Model appropriate roles and communication skills.

_____ 24. Listen for new ideas.

_____ 25. Ask for information and clarification.

_____ 26. Seek others' advice.

_____ 27. Guide discussion toward the goals and objectives of the meeting.

_____ 28. Test for consensus.

_____ 29. Follow the agenda.

_____ 30. Remain flexible.

_____ 31. Do not allow any one person to dominate.

_____ 32. Control pace and keep to time frame.

_____ 33. Clarify decisions.

_____ 34. Record significant decisions.

(Continued)

■ MEETING LEADER'S CHECKLIST *(Continued)*

_____ **35.** Assign responsibilities and dates for implementing decisions.

_____ **36.** Summarize steps needed to implement decisions.

_____ **37.** Announce the next meeting, if appropriate.

_____ **38.** Close the meeting on time.

After the Meeting

_____ **39.** See that minutes of meeting are completed and distributed to all participants.

_____ **40.** Follow up on implementation of decisions made during the meeting.

_____ **41.** Announce and prepare for the next meeting, if necessary.

_____ **42.** Evaluate the meeting, either formally or informally.

_____

Reprinted by permission of Ed Baum. All rights reserved.

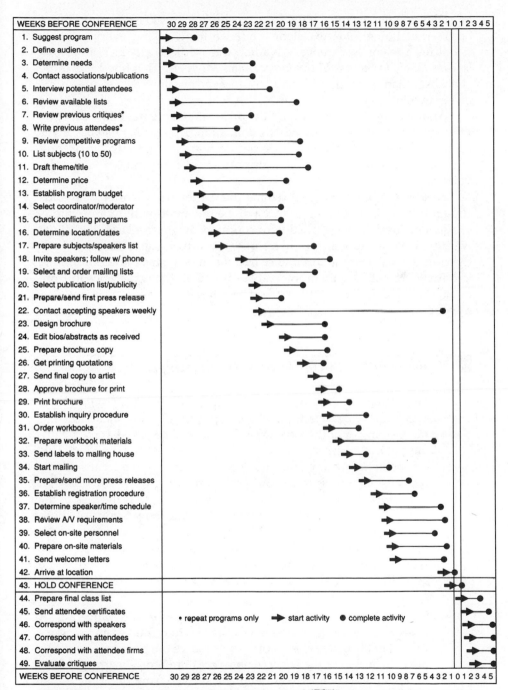

FIGURE 9.3 Forty-Nine Steps to a Successful Conference From *How to Market Training Programs, Seminars, & Instructional Materials* by Don M. Schrello. © 1988. Reprinted with permission of The Marketing Federation, 109 58th Ave., St. Petersburg Beach, FL 33706. 813/367-4934.

or room assignments got mixed up, or the key speaker was a dud, can be overwhelming! One excellent reference for checking every possible detail for a major conference is Nadler and Nadler's (1987) *The Comprehensive Guide to Successful Conferences and Meetings*. This book has more checklists than a meeting planner could ever possibly dream up on his or her own!

Another important resource is the professional organization, Meeting Planners International. Its monthly publication, *The Meeting Planner*, gives extensive coverage to convention sites and materials, and its journal and national convention provide other opportunities for members' career development.

Besides the organizational details the conference planner who adds something special to the conference will be rewarded with more requests to run meetings! I have worked with conferences where a laser light show was the finale, a nationally known star was a surprise speaker, and where the closing session of the conference had the meeting facilitator interviewing attendees telling human interest stories about the conference in front of 1,000 people, Phil Donahue style. These are the conferences people remember.

■ Consultant's Tips for Successful Meetings

- First, *those who are going to be involved in the meeting should always help build the agenda.* Either their input should be solicited before the meeting or at the very least they should be asked at the beginning of the meeting if there are items that need to be added. This can be done quickly and efficiently and still give all participants the sense that their ideas and needs are going to be addressed, if not at this meeting then at some future meeting. It is the task of the group leader to help the group determine how many of those items can be handled in any one meeting. The leader *must* ensure that those items not addressed at this meeting are handled at the very next opportunity or participants will soon learn it does no good to suggest items for discussion because they never come up again!

- Second, *a process observer should be assigned* for every meeting. A **process observer** is someone who agrees to refrain from being involved in the discussion in order to observe the process. For example, it is the job of the process observer to remind the group of the time they have left, when they have strayed from the topic under discussion, and when individuals have been interrupted and have not been allowed to complete a thought. They also could be put in charge of maintaining talk time by reminding individuals of the limit the group has agreed they will apply to any one individual. Forms 9.2 and 9.3 present sample observation sheets to help direct the observers' attention to important variables. (See the section of Chapter 11 called "Schein's Categories" for help in using Form 9.3.) These forms could be used by the chair of the meeting or another individual. After the process observers have experience with the technique, they will no longer need any forms to remind them of behaviors on which to focus their attention. A consultant often serves in this role, at least initially.

> One group asked me to facilitate a series of meetings designed to develop better communication among group members. In particular, complaints from female employees had the all male management team worried. Women complained their ideas were not taken seriously among other issues. We began the retreat by asking how individuals demonstrated respect for one another. A lively discussion was generated about people's strong belief that everyone should be respected! About 40 minutes into a rather intellectualized discussion of what respect means, the process observer made one simple observation about the level of participation in the group. "For the last 40 minutes the males have been actively involved in this discussion. Have any of you noticed that none of the women have commented? What do you think is happening here?" What followed was the beginning of an open discussion on the interaction style of the people in that room.

The process observer has to have a keen sense of timing, make objective statements about observed behavior, and be prepared to facilitate intense discussion that may follow. It is then possible that the process observer can make the group aware of procedural problems as well as dramatically increase group members' awareness of interpersonal issues. This can change the direction of the entire meeting and heighten the potential meeting outcomes.

■ Third, as much as possible the *leader should remain neutral.* You cannot express your own opinions and still fairly run the meeting allowing all points of view to be heard. When the leader feels compelled to express personal feelings, opinions, or expert advise, then

■ PROCESS OBSERVER FORM

Observee: _____

When I respond to each question, I will mark (√) next to the appropriate letter and then record the exact words used by my Observee to support my data.

 I. How does my Project Director select a Co-worker?

    A. ( ) Asking.

    B. ( ) Inviting.

    C. ( ) Demanding.

    D. ( ) Sending an "I" message ("I need help, etc.").

    E. ( ) Sending a "You" message ("Will you help?" etc.).

    Words or statement used by my Observee: _____

    _____

 II. How does the team Project get chosen?

    A. ( ) Imposed by one member.

    B. ( ) Shared decision.

    C. ( ) Suggestion followed by agreement.

    Words or statement used by my Observee: _____

    _____

 III. How do the plans develop?

    A. ( ) Mutual sharing of ideas.

    B. ( ) One person informs the other to do certain things.

    C. ( ) Another way (specify).

    Words or statement used by my Observee: _____

    _____

 IV. How does my Observee communicate?

    A. ( ) Uses "Yes, but" phrases.

    B. ( ) Uses "No, that won't work" phrases.

    C. ( ) Uses "I've got a better idea" phrases.

(Continued)

PROCESS OBSERVER FORM *(Continued)*

D. (   ) Uses descriptive phrases. ("Will you clarify for me?")

E. (   ) Uses supportive phrases. ("I like your idea . . . ")

F. (   ) Interrupts others.

G. (   ) Listens and doesn't interrupt.

H. (   ) Answers questions which others ask of him or her.

I. (   ) Does not answer questions directed to him or her by others.

Words or statement used by my Observee: _____

_____

Observer Question

V. How did I communicate my feedback to my Observee?

A. (   ) Sent "I" messages.

B. (   ) Gave accurate, observable data.

C. (   ) Gave process observation feedback.

D. (   ) Gave process interpretation feedback.

Personal comment: _____

_____

_____

© *Learning Development Systems Publication.*

■ PROCESS OBSERVER ROLE FORM

Directions: Write each person's name in the column marked Observee. Process observe each member for role behaviors. Indicate the primary roles each member functions within by selecting the letter next to the role title. [Explanations of the role titles follow this form.] Write the letter in the column marked Code. Write the exact words and/or give an accurate description of the action in the column marked Behavior. Try to be precise, accurate, and clear in your observations.

MAINTENANCE ROLES	TASK ROLES	INDIVIDUAL/BLOCKING ROLES
A. Harmonizer	E. Information Seeker	I. Silent One
B. Helper	F. Information Giver	J. Negativist
C. Quality Controller	G. Clarifier	K. Dominator
D. Follower	H. Summarizer	L. Judge
		M. Attention Seeker
		N. Quibbler

Observee Name	Code—Letters	Behavior—Exact Words/Describe Actions
1. _____	_____ _____	_____ _____
2. _____	_____ _____	_____ _____
3. _____	_____ _____	_____ _____
4. _____	_____ _____	_____ _____
5. _____	_____ _____	_____ _____

(Continued)

■ **PROCESS OBSERVER ROLE FORM** *(Continued)*

6. _____

Explanations of Roles

Maintenance Roles

A. Harmonizer
   1. Attempts to clear up disagreements.
   2. Deals with conflict in a nonthreatening manner.

B. Helper
   1. Encourages others to speak and share ideas.
   2. Shows warm and friendly attitude toward each member by making genuine supportive statements such as, "I'd like to support you."

C. Quality Controller
   1. Analyzes the data and tries to help group understand information presented.
   2. Applies standards to data to evaluate.
   3. Suggests ways of keeping group on target by checking progress toward goal.

D. Follower
   1. Listens to another's ideas and nonverbally decides to accept them.
   2. May have own ideas but is willing to accept another way of achieving goals.
   3. Willing to follow to keep group active and moving toward solution.
   4. At times, firmly supports another's idea verbally.

Task Roles

E. Information Seeker
   1. Asks for facts/opinions/suggestions.
   2. Seeks information on the issue/topic/agenda point.

F. Information Giver
   1. Offers facts/suggestions.
   2. Responds to questions asked by other members.

(Continued)

■ **PROCESS OBSERVER ROLE FORM** *(Continued)*

G. Clarifier
   1. Interprets facts and clears up confusing statements.
   2. Asks questions for better understanding.
   3. Checks to see that questions are answered satisfactorily.
   4. Keeps one point on the agenda at a time.

H. Summarizer
   1. Pulls together related ideas.
   2. Calls for discussion after suggestions.
   3. At times, writes facts on newsprint.
   4. Makes closure on agenda points. Example: "I'd like to summarize. . . . "

Individual/Blocking Roles

I. Silent One
   1. Usually shy; answers questions with a Yes or No.
   2. Not inclined to enter discussion.
   3. Sometimes, uses specific nonverbal messages to control group.

J. Negativist
   1. Usually replies to comments with "yes, but . . . " or "It won't work."
   2. Makes comments on every topic.
   3. Uses nonverbals to reinforce verbal message (facials and body gestures).

K. Dominator
   1. Interrupts others to talk.
   2. Talks at great length on every topic.
   3. Attempts to control group by asserting an authoritative tone.

L. Judge
   1. Evaluates every comment in absolute terms.
   2. Gives advice even though it is not solicited.
   3. Uses phrases: "That's correct" or "I think you should do it this way."

M. Attention Seeker
   1. Monopolizes the discussion by "showing off."
   2. Used nonverbals to attract attention.
   3. Interrupts others to gain center focus.

N. Quibbler
   1. Argues about small details. Example: "The bill was $2.97 and not $2.95."
   2. Corrects speech imperfections, "You didn't pronounce the 'g' at the end of the word 'going'. "

a temporary leader should take over while the meeting leader assumes the role of a group member. If the role of chair and advocate get confused, the meeting will quickly disintegrate into a briefing by the chair of decisions that have already been made. Those types of meetings are sometimes necessary; however, they should be called "briefings" and group members should understand they will not be coming to a meeting in order to express their ideas. Nothing is more frustrating than to attend a meeting expecting your ideas will be heard only to discover the intent of the meeting is for you to listen and not be heard.

> A search committee was charged with hiring a new school administrator. The behavior of the chair was neutral and aided the discussion of other members until one particular name came up for discussion. Even though he admitted he knew the candidate personally (the candidate was a special friend of his son's) the chair continued to lead the discussion. Interspersed in his procedural statements controlling the discussion were expressions of opinion about the candidate. For example, he stated: "I think the comment on this candidate's lack of experience is unfair given the record of our other finalists." He then proceeded to attack each candidate making statements like, "Since she's not married, who would do the entertaining for her position?" and "This individual already holds this type of position, so why would he want to make a lateral move? We would be better off with our final candidate who is looking to move up." Finally he said, "I think we have an excellent candidate here; are there other comments?" It was clear he had already made up his mind and was going to control the discussion to ensure that his preferred candidate was selected.

A meeting leader should never become an advocate. If the meeting leader wants to voice an opinion, someone else should take over during that discussion thus separating the role of meeting facilitator from advocate of one particular viewpoint. Otherwise, leaders have an unfair advantage because they can control the discussion while at the same time making their own statement.

■ Fourth, *use a system that allows everyone to win.* "Loss aversion theory" suggests that the negative impact of losing is much more significant than the positive influence of winning. People are more concerned with negative consequences than potential advantages (Mosvick and Nelson, 1987, p. 59). An individual may receive much praise but what is remembered is one negative comment. Consequently, the leader needs to use descriptive feedback (see Chapter 12) so that individuals do not feel they are being attacked. Descriptive feedback simply describes a behavior or event without evaluating or attempting to interpret its meaning. I may say, "You were 15 minutes late to the last meeting and were 30 minutes late today. I get frustrated when I know you have missed important information." This is very different from saying, "You are always late. It shows you have no concern for others." Or saying, "I think you are always late because you simply don't plan ahead." The first alternative gets the message across without evaluating the person and lets the listener know how the behavior is affecting him or her as well. The second and third alternatives evaluate, blame, and interrupt, encouraging greater defensiveness on the part of the listener.

■ Finally, in the decision-making process, *ideas should be separated from the people.* This allows the ideas to be critically assessed without individuals feeling they personally are being evaluated. A simple technique would be to have all ideas expressed first and then, after the ideas are no longer associated with any one individual, evaluate each idea. The use of these simple brainstorming techniques will go a long way toward ensuring protection of individual egos!

Essentially, the meeting leader must decide the goal of the meeting and act accordingly. If you want ideas, *really* want people to express their views, then you need to set up meeting perimeters that will allow that to happen. If, on the other hand, you have already made up your mind and feel there are no alternatives, at least do your participants the courtesy of telling them ahead of time that you will be briefing them on your decision. Don't insult their intelligence by inviting their ideas and then making it perfectly clear that you do not want to hear them!! And be prepared for "Murphy's Laws of Meetings."

■ MURPHY'S LAWS OF MEETINGS

- Rooms inspected in advance prior to your meeting will diminish in size by one-half between selection and use.

- A request for a "U-shape" table arrangement will be modified to a "W" to take into account the large columns which appeared overnight.

- The phrase "comfortable, stackable chairs" is a contradiction in terms.

- Material essential for pre-meeting preparation will not reach the participants. When it does arrive, it will not be read.

- By the time you arrive at your meeting with all necessary materials, pre-punched holes will heal, clear printing will fade, collated materials will regroup, and felt pens will cast off their caps.

- Handouts will be 10–20% short, or enough will be left over to wallpaper a medium-sized ballroom.

- Ventilation and temperature controls will be part of the room decor and not intended to be functional.

- Guest speakers will bring a presentation prepared for a completely different group.

- When serving refreshments, one-half of the group will complain that there is not enough. The other half will observe that there is too much. All will complain about gaining weight.

- The PA system in use in an adjoining room will be piped into your meeting room as a convenience.

- For any equipment you bring, the extension cord will be 2 feet too short.

- For any situation not listed above, simply assume that your worst nightmares will be proven true.

P.S.   This is the third time I had to type this sheet. The copy machine ate the first two!!!!!!!!

Author Unknown

▌ *Suggested Readings*

Janis, I.L. (1972). *Victims of groupthink* (2nd ed.). Boston, MA: Houghton Mifflin Co.

Mosvick, R. K., & Nelson, R. B. (1987). *We've got to start meeting like this.* Glenview, IL: Scott, Foresman & Co.

Nadler, L., & Nadler, Z. (1987). *The comprehensive guide to successful conferences and meetings.* San Francisco, CA: Jossey-Bass, Inc.

Chapter 10

CAN I HELP MY CLIENT FACE AN AUDIENCE?

Presentation Skills

The number one fear of Americans, above snakes and fear of death, is fear of giving a public speech.

from the Book of Lists

"The capacity for oral expression, whether in conversation or in more formal contexts of communication, is a skill needed for both the clarity and pleasure of communication. Our neglect of the spoken word sharply distinguishes our society from that of ancient Athens, where elegance was the rule."

Joseph Katz
Chronicle of Higher Education

"The one universal skill of successful consultants is the ability to organize and express ideas."

T. J. O'Shea, 1986

*M*ost business leaders realize that presentation skills are critical to the success of any manager and yet few actually have those skills or demonstrate them on a regular basis. In the business world many people view themselves as highly competent individuals in a number of areas but do not tend to see themselves as effective speakers. "I received a pilot's license at the age of 40; I jumped from a plane as a sky diver a year later; I've tried many dangerous challenges, but I just cannot face an audience" (Makay and Fetzer, 1984, p. 35). The reason so many of us fear public speaking is we are afraid we will make fools of ourselves in front of a group.

As a consultant you may be asked to help a client improve his or her presentation skills. At the same time you must constantly be improving your own style since you will often be judged by your presentations. I have probably given hundreds of speeches during my career, and on those occasions when I was *not* nervous about it, I gave a less than stellar performance. Being nervous is an indication that you are excited about the occasion and want to do well. The trick is to learn how to turn that nervousness into energy and dynamic performances. I once had a colleague who was a theater major and she was backstage throwing up before every performance, and yet on stage she was brilliant! Overcoming stage fright begins by anticipating those occasions when you will most likely be called on to give a public presentation.

When Will I Ever Have to Give a Speech?

Most speaking occasions will fall into two broad categories: internal presentations and company speeches to the public. Both can be critical to a manager's career. It is your job as a communication specialist to assist the manager with this communication task. The following suggestions can be communicated to your clients as well as be implemented when you make presentations yourself.

Speaking Internally

The 30-minute presentation you have been asked to give to corporate leaders could be the most important 30 minutes of your career. In those 30 minutes you can demonstrate you are self-confident, articulate, knowledgeable, and persuasive, or you can demonstrate you are nervous, unsure of yourself, and not clear about what you want your audience to do. Consultants must sell their services and present findings in a clear and uncluttered way. They must also help corporate leaders do the same thing.

Organization members are constantly asked to make internal presentations to colleagues, supervisors, and subordinates. In all cases, these speakers are being asked to sell themselves. If the speaker wants acceptance of a new policy, listeners have to trust the speaker before they will believe the policy is in their best interest. When the speaker is giving directions, listeners have to believe the speaker is knowledgeable enough to provide the details they will need. If the speaker wants the boss to try out a new idea, the speaker must convince the boss that it is worth listening to.

One new manager with whom I worked was asked to brief his subordinates on a new product line. His anxiety increased as the day came closer; however, he was well-prepared and had practiced some techniques to make his presentation more effective. He found out later his superiors were using this occasion to help determine his potential to move into an upper management position. On the day of his talk, he checked on the overhead and found out it had a burned out bulb that he replaced. He practiced presenting his talk in the room where it would occur and discovered he could not see his notes easily, so he had a small light placed on the lectern. Finally, as people filed into the room before his presentation he greeted them at the door and learned five people were in the wrong session. Consequently, he avoided three disasters because he thought ahead and was prepared for potential problems. A good speech alone will not get a person a promotion, but a bad one can prevent upper management from selecting that person to play a more important role as an official company representative.

Speaking Externally

Corporate leaders are asked repeatedly to represent their organization in the public arena. Although current managers are more independent than the typical "organization man" of the 1950s, they still must understand the "party line." As Osborn (1991) suggested in reporting on Leingerger and Tucker's, *The New Individualists*, the "organization man" with his faith in hierarchy and bureaucracy, no longer exists in this generation. Employees are more committed to what they do, to their professions, and to their work, but not their company (p. 2). It will be even more important that corporate leaders, and the consultants working with them, understand the public relations nature of their talks.

Thrash, Shelby, and Tarver (1984) provided six strategies for external talks with an advocacy focus for the company. How a company responds to attacks and what it does to turn negative publicity around may very well spell success or failure for that corporation. The following six strategies can be effectively used for corporate advocacy.

Withdrawal from confrontation is used specifically to stop the escalation of the debate. The "no comment" is typical of this approach. You use it when it is worse to respond to attacks than to try and answer them. It should be used carefully because it can easily have more negative consequences than positive. For example, the "attacker" gets to present the case without the opposite position being heard.

Sleight of hand focuses the audience's attention on something else, just as do the magic tricks from which this term was derived. This allows the company spokesperson to obscure a controversial issue. It may be viewed as ethically questionable since after the tricks are over, the objections will still stand.

Challenging opposing facts and arguments is a strong position when you are able to refute the arguments as presented. You can weaken the attackers' position by proving their evidence is flawed, but the attacks may still have done their damage even if you are able to refute all issues.

Redefining the issues may be necessary if the facts presented by the attacker are true. You may need to point out the issues are not relevant or are misdirected. Sometimes this means identifying questionable assumptions about the facts made by the attackers.

Presenting the company position adds an important dimension to a presentation that has already exposed the opponent's arguments as invalid. It is important the audience understand fully what the company's stance is on the issues raised. You will need to identify the company position specifically, back it up with facts, explain the reason for the position, and explore the advantages and disadvantages of it. It is always better to identify the disadvantages yourself rather than have the opposing side state them in exaggerated terms.

Finally, you can adopt a *proactive approach* which anticipates the public's reactions and tries to resolve them before they are presented in a negative framework. Answering arguments before they become points of contention will result in fewer public relations problems for the company to handle (Thrash, Shelby, and Tarver, 1984, pp. 156–57).

While internal and external speaking have different goals, the speaking techniques used may be the same. Whether you are speaking internally or externally, a simultaneous first step with defining your purpose is knowing your audience.

Knowing and Understanding Your Audience

According to Mark Twain, "It takes three weeks to prepare a good ad-lib speech." Very few people can speak elegantly on the spur of the moment. Preparing yourself with information about the people to whom you will be speaking is essential. As Howell and Borman (1988) suggested, communication events are joint ventures. "In a sense, people may say to one another, 'shall we communicate?' in much the same way that they might ask 'shall we dance?' " (p. 19).

How Will They React to the Content?

Before making a presentation speakers need to think about the audience and adapt the content and delivery of what they are going to say to the particular needs and interests of the audience members.

What are your goals for the presentation? What do you want your audience to know, believe in, or do as a result of your speech? Like readers of office memos, listeners to a speech need to know exactly what you want them to do as a result of receiving the message. How many memos bury the action step requested at the end of several paragraphs of background information? Often, people stop listening and/or reading long before they figure out what you are trying to communicate to them.

Do your audience members have the same background and level of experience as your own? The use of jargon and technical language can be an effective shorthand way of communicating to an audience, all of whom share a common understanding of the language. Complex, technical information may be essential as well for a highly trained and select audience. For an audience who may not have the same training or background as yourself, the use of jargon, technical language, or complex information is not impressive; it is frustrating.

How much information do they already have on your topic? It is better to provide a short, simple summary of background information to make sure everyone has at least some common ground from which to understand your points. This background material, however, must be short, short, and shorter!

How were they selected to attend the presentation, or have they volunteered? A volunteer audience is very different from a group who is required to be there. If your audience did not select on their own to listen to you, you must develop an extended "need" step. This is your justification for why they need to listen. How will these ideas influence their daily lives? For example, if the topic is "teamwork" the audience may resent being told they must listen. Maybe they think they already function as teams! The speaker must convince them, early in the presentation, that information they are about to hear will make their jobs, or work lives, more pleasurable in some way.

What Form of Presentation Will Deliver the Message?

The size and composition of the audience and the physical facility determine the suitability of the form of presentation. Ask yourself the following questions.

Has the audience attended presentations similar to yours? How have they responded to such presentations? In other words, is this audience used to sitting and listening to formal presentations? Do they do this frequently? And do they seem to enjoy it? If they are "action-oriented" individuals who are *not* used to listening, you must provide some entertainment and high motivation for them to stay with you. Find out how they have reacted in similar situations. Are they likely to want to ask questions after the presentation, or, if you ask for questions, are you more likely to be met with a resounding silence?

How many people will be in the audience? Whether or not you chose to use a microphone, stand behind a podium, or move among the audience members will be determined by the size of the audience. Your nonverbal gestures will have to be exaggerated with a larger audience. You can deal with 40–50 people as if they are still a small group, but any group approaching 100 might as well be 1,000! Once you are unable to see every face, and the audience is unable to hear you without amplification, then it doesn't matter how much larger the group gets since you will be using mass audience techniques anyway.

Will they be able to see visual aids clearly? Are there obstructions in the room that will prevent audience members from seeing anything you may display? It is always helpful to have some sense of how the audience may respond to certain types of visual aids. For example, if I believe I may have English teachers in the audience, I tend not to use visual aids. Since you can't put complete sentences on a screen and make them big enough to see, you use shortened versions which are often seen as unacceptable to these guardians of the English language! Using visual aids may be critical to your presentation. In Chapter 5 I discussed in detail the advantages and disadvantages of various visual aids and their use. This would be useful information to review for a public presentation. The items listed in the "emergency kit" on pages 199–200 have been absolutely vital to speakers in the past and will be quite useful to you.

Do some of the participants have special learning needs? For example, does anyone have visual, hearing, or mobility difficulties, and how can you accommodate these learners?

I once conducted an entire seminar using flip charts posted around the room, only to discover two of the participants were legally blind and could not see a single word I wrote! A simple question before the presentation would have saved them, and me, the embarrassment of having to prepare transcripts of my presentation.

How much time will you have for the presentation and will you include a question and answer period? Absolutely the worst thing you can do is go overtime. Even if you have given only half of your speech, once you are over the amount of time the audience has agreed to stay, you have

EMERGENCY KIT FOR PRESENTATIONS

Paper towels

Small box of pushpins

Plug adapter (3-prong to 2-prong converter)

Extension cord(s)

Extension for slide projector remote control

Roll of masking tape

Small roll of transparent tape on dispenser

One box of assorted markers

12 manila file folders (When open to 19 by 12" they make a good emergency chart.)

Transparency pens for writing on viewgraphs

1 box of transparencies (black on yellow)

Soft chalk (white and colored)

Eraser

Hand towel

Wet napkins

2 collapsible pointers

4 night-lights (for rooms having only off/on lighting)

1 8½ by 11" meeting pad

1 pocket-sized memo pad

2 pens

1 pack of 3 by 5" index cards

Calendar

Assortment of stomachache, headache, and/or cold medications

Box of throat lozenges

Various sizes of company logos

Corporate telephone directory

Small slide viewer or magnifying glass

6 translucent sheets with pockets for slides (in case major rearrangement or sorting is required)

White-out (for whiting out errors)

Single-edge razor blade

Scissors

Pocket knife

2 large clips (to hold charts in case easel is broken)

(Continued)

> **EMERGENCY KIT FOR PRESENTATIONS**
> *(Continued)*
>
> 12 blank black slides
> 12 clear slides
> Dime (for removing jammed slide trays)
> Tweezers (for removing jammed slides)
> Cricket (for slide change where no other signal is available)
> Pocket flashlight
> 12 envelopes with stamps
> Express-mail or package service envelope and form
> 30 pieces of 8½ by 11" white card stock to fold in half for name tents.
> Stick-on name badges
> Small American flag (in case you are accused of "flag waving")
>
> *Source:* Adapted from T.C. Smith, *Making Successful Presentations: A Self Teaching Guide* (New York: John Wiley & Sons, Inc., 1984).

lost them anyway! It is very tempting to squeeze in just a few final thoughts at the end. DON'T DO IT! Your audience will thank you. Err on the side of brevity.

These questions form a good checklist for the speaker prior to facing the audience. Insist on getting the answers before preparing your presentation. If you are unable to secure the information you want about the audience, you can ask a few quick questions in the beginning of your presentation and request a show of hands that will give you some "gross" information about who is in the audience. In that way you can at least make some minor adaptations based on the information you get. For example, you can quickly access the number of males and females, number of supervisors and nonsupervisors, etc.

What Is the Audience's Attitude toward You and the Event?

Finally, you need to have a sense of your audience's attitude toward you and the event. Margaret Bedrosian (1987) has identified some of the audiences you might be facing.

The audience might want you to win. This audience represents about 98 percent of the people you will be talking with. They don't want to waste their time and they are hopeful you will do a good job. The "halo effect" is the phenomenon that allows us to give a person extra chances to succeed initially. If you do not succeed they will be disappointed too. However, there is that other 2 percent!

The audience might want you to fail. There is that other 2 percent of the people who would like to see you fail. Who knows why, nor is it important. For some perverse reason, their image of themselves improves as your credibility goes down. If you try to satisfy this small portion of the people listening, you will lose the rest of your group. Forget them! They have their own motivations to deal with.

The audience expects polish. Remember, we have significantly increased our expectations for presentations. Our audiences have been raised on Sesame Street and MTV. They expect "flash." They will no longer accept a person's apology for not being a public speaker. They demand a polished performance. They expect you to be graceful, articulate, funny, timely, relevant, knowledgeable, and unbiased against any of the demographic groups represented among them. They expect you to be able to handle hostile questions without taking out your emotions on them. In short, they expect a lot!

The audience is easily bored. As Bedrosian pointed out, we are victims of the "million-dollar minute" mentality. Advertisers bombard us with short, dynamic messages. Audiences want to get the message in the shortest amount of time possible. Their attention span has shortened by about 90 percent in the last 20 years! You might as well assume they will start out bored and that your job is to wake them up so they will listen to a few short points.

The audience wants specifics. People respond best to human interest stories that connect them to the presentation. I once talked about my father and his determination to succeed in this country and then connected it to a challenge facing the audience. Telling a personal story about my family did two things: made me more "human" and suggested how they might be personally connected to the point I was trying to make. Remember that your audience is less involved in your topic than you are. Your job is to give them enough specific information and examples to make them want to learn more.

The audience will want to know what to do next. Unless you are giving an after-dinner speech with the sole purpose of entertaining, you will need to give your audience some specific actions to take. Do not expect them to figure it out on their own. Be clear about wanting them to vote, adopt your proposal, change their behavior, write to their legislators, or consider your new program.

Tell them what to do, and if possible, link that recommendation to something they are likely to do in the next 24 hours. This helps create in them a "timed-release" reminder of their intention to act. Use phrases such as "Tomorrow morning when you face yourself in the mirror as you brush your teeth, say to yourself, 'This is the day I . . . ' " or "The next time you set foot in an automobile ask yourself if you should . . . " or "Tonight when you take off your shoes and your feet revel in having their delicious freedom back, say to yourself . . . " (Bedrosian, 1987, p. 58).

How Long Should the Presentation Be?

The title of one article says it all, "Less Talk is More Convincing" (Whalen, 1990). How often have you heard people complain that a speech or presentation was too short? More often, their reaction is like that of the individual in the cartoon in Figure 10.1: if the speaker says one more thing, we may scream! We have already learned more than we ever wanted to know about a particular topic! If you can't say it in 15 minutes or less, write it.

My most difficult public speaking situation was the time I faced 8,000 parents and college students in a large convocation center made to hold 15,000. These graduation ceremonies were for M.A.s and Ph.D.s. Everyone is there to celebrate this moment of achievement for loved ones and no one wants to listen to a commencement

speaker. The best thing you can do for them is be brief. I said that at the beginning of my speech and received applause. I also said if they would stick with me, hear only three points I wanted to make, I would promise to be brief. I actually had strangers coming up to me for five years afterwards telling me they remembered those three points!

Structure

After analyzing your audience, you must begin to develop the structure of the speech. The organization of the presentation begins with the first impressions the audience has of the speaker.

First Impressions

The impression the group will have of you and your presentation starts with any information they are given prior to your appearance. Usually, in a formal speech, this means the introduction. The introducer can do you a favor by providing a brief, but impressive, review of your accomplishments and credentials. Or, the introducer can inadvertently destroy your credibility by trying and failing to be funny, by identifying you with the wrong organization or project, or by misrepresenting your accomplishments.

The choice you must then make is between correcting (and embarrassing) the introducer, joking about yourself, or ignoring the bad introduction and depending on the introduction to your speech to set things straight. I usually ignore all but the most blatant mistakes. I also try to poke fun at myself in the beginning to try and balance the more elaborate introduction I have just received. You can avoid this problem altogether by writing your own introductions. Program planners will thank you and you will be sure the correct information is presented!

The audience's first impression of you continues as you approach them. What you wear, how you walk, the formality of the situation (which you may not have any control over), and the first words out of your mouth will have great impact on the audience's willingness to listen. In a smaller audience, even your handshake will leave an impression.

Opening Remarks

The beginning of the presentation must capture the audience's interest, convince them to listen, overview for them what will follow, and connect you to the topic. If one of these elements is missing then you have given the audience an excuse *not* to listen. There are a variety of ways to capture the audience's attention.

Startling Statement

"If we decide today to implement the following new policy, we can save the company $500,000 by the end of the month."

Such a statement is designed to make the listeners want to hear more. You have "teased" them with just enough information to suggest the rest of the presentation may be of particular interest to them.

Poignant Example

"A customer in northern Ohio called the office yesterday to thank us for our new voice activated dialing system. She has a 12-year-old son who is completely disabled and was unable to talk to his friends unless someone was there to dial and hold the phone for him. Until this new dialing system was installed, he could not have a private conversation with a friend. Imagine being 12 years old and having someone—especially your mother!—listen in on all your conversations."

Here the speaker is trying to arouse the listeners' emotions. You want the example to remind them of the human side of an enterprise. In this case, it was designed to remind the listeners of the real value of developing new technology. Connecting an idea to everyday happenings helps to recognize the value of new products, services, or ideas.

Joke

"With an introduction like that, how can I help but fail! *No one* can live up to such high expectations. Even God gets a day off every week!"

Jokes can easily backfire. Sometimes the most innocent comments can offend someone. The reference to God in the preceding example might be offensive to certain individuals. Plus, you cannot guarantee the joke is one people will laugh at. A "pregnant pause" following a joke is deadly. You must determine your success rate with humor prior to using it. I usually do not tell standard jokes, although I do use a lot of humor in my presentations. The form of humor I am best at is telling jokes about myself or teasing someone in the audience I am familiar with and know will not be offended by it. Use humor sparingly and when in doubt, *don't!*

Impressive Statistics

"Cars that come off the assembly line on Fridays have twice as many problems as cars produced on any other day of the week. Each Friday, 14,500 workers are absent from work in our plants across the country and other workers must cover for their jobs. This means at least one in every 15 workers is unhappy on Fridays because they are having to cover for someone else. Unhappy people make mistakes."

To be used effectively, statistics must be impressive, rounded off to the next nearest whole number or round number and applied to concepts that are easily understood. In the example above, the speaker took the 14,500 figure and made it more meaningful by pointing out how likely you would be to encounter these unhappy workers! After you have the audience's attention, your next task is to say something worthwhile in the body of the speech.

Organization

Any pattern can be an effective way to organize a speech. Some common structures are: cause-to-effect, chronological, topical, and problem-solution.

CAUSE-TO-EFFECT

First, a cause-to-effect pattern makes the audience aware of the relationship between some observed occurrence (the effect) and the event leading to that occurrence. For example, a window salesperson first demonstrates the loss of heat from a home and then claims the cause is air leakage around the windows.

CHRONOLOGICAL ORDER

A chronological pattern is especially useful when an executive is tracing the history of a problem or a product. When decisions are being made about the future of some project or product, everyone needs to have the same sense of history about the development of the product. A chronological approach will create a sense of joint ownership of the historical process.

TOPICAL APPROACH

Topical patterns are used when the general topic can be broken into smaller parts to be easily understood. For example, when a new benefits package is being introduced, the subtopics might include health, education, and retirement benefits. This helps the listeners organize their thinking and remember the main points.

PROBLEM-SOLUTION PATTERN

Problem-solution is my personal favorite structure for a speech. Answering these four questions makes the arguments clearer.

What is the problem? It is important that the audience understands early in your talk exactly what issue or problem is being addressed. Most people have a low tolerance for ambiguity.

What are the implications of solving or not solving it? The speaker must create a strong motivation on the part of the audience for solving the problem. There are many problems in the world we cannot solve or don't really care to solve. It is the speaker's job to convince the audience this is not one of those problems.

How can it be solved? Nothing is more frustrating than to listen to someone tell you about a crisis, get you interested in solving it, and then fail to provide any action for you to take. We have enough problems in our daily lives, so we don't want to hear about more of them and then not have any way to help solve them. That's simply too depressing!

What's in it for the people listening if the solution is implemented? The ultimate question the audience will ask is what is the payoff for them personally if they get involved? There are very few, if any, truly selfless persons in this world. We all need to feel we will benefit in some way. Perhaps it will make life more pleasant for our family, and thus ourselves. Perhaps it will make our job easier to do or will make us feel some pride in our affiliation with the company. In any case, it is the speaker's job to convince the audience that they will benefit directly from the speaker's solution to the problem.

Closing the Sale

Recently, I have been actively involved in a university's $100 million campaign for private donations. I meet with alumni and corporate leaders around the country selling the university story. I am quite comfortable telling that story. As a consultant I have never had difficulty selling my services, but in consulting I am usually asked what my fees will be. In development work, if you don't *tell* prospects the amount you want from them, they will never ask. "Making the ask," is the equivalent of the salesperson's closing request for the order, and it is the final step in a persuasive appeal. Unfortunately, it is the very step many people shy away from. They stop their persuasive appeal right before the ask.

I found I had to relearn this principle for development work. In one case, the development officer and I had finished an elegant meal in New York City with an alumnus. We had talked all evening and reminisced about his time at the university, and I had taken an opportunity to detail future plans for the school with him and received good advice for our programs. I was ready to end the evening when the development officer expertly injected the ask into the conversation, which had been the primary goal of this trip! I almost missed making the ask altogether.

Quick (1988) tells the story about the man who prays each week that God will let him win the lottery. After many months without winning, the man adds in desperation the plea, "Lord, give me a break. Let me win the lottery!" From heaven comes a booming voice, "Give me a break, Sam. Buy a ticket." You won't get what you want by waiting for it to happen! You must initiate action yourself.

Strategies

Three thousand years ago, Aristotle identified the three basic forms of appeal to an audience: ethos, logos, and pathos. *Ethos* refers to the speaker's credibility or believability with this audience, *logos* refers to logical and factual appeals, and *pathos* refers to emotional appeals.

Credibility

We *want* to believe people we trust, like, or have respect for. Once credibility is established by the speaker, the audience is ready to listen and believe. How do you establish it? First, the way in which you are introduced to the audience will set the initial impression. As I mentioned earlier, I usually prepare my own introduction for someone to read. The presenters like this because it saves them the trouble of having to pick out those points most notable about your career. You will like it because you will be able to control what is said about you. I have been identified with the wrong organization, had my name mispronounced, had jokes told about me that were not funny, and had such a complete summary of my talk revealed that I wasn't sure there was anything new left to tell them! Be prepared to counter a bad introduction.

Second, the beginning of your speech can indicate your level of training, education, or experience with the topic. You need to establish yourself as an expert without sounding like you are bragging. For example, by saying "Although I have been a communication consultant for over 25 years, I am still amazed at how often major organizational problems are caused by poor human relationships," I have indicated the extent of my consulting experience in an indirect way.

Third, the detail with which you present material will convince the audience that you understand the subject and have something to share with them. It is critical that you find out how much they already know and that you have researched the topic thoroughly enough to be able to present new and interesting information to them.

Fourth, I always try to make personal contact with the audience before I begin so that they see me as a person like them. I may greet audience members at the door as they come in or walk among the audience before the speech begins and introduce myself to themselves. It is amazing how much friendlier the audience is to you if they have shaken your hand before you begin speaking.

Reasoning and Supportive Material

No matter how expert you are at the subject, you will need *strong logic, expert testimony,* and *factual information* to back you up. The speaker presents the data and then makes a claim. The data must be reliable research findings, detailed examples, and information from other experts all taken from sources the audience trusts. The following questions will help you assess the quality of your information:

- Is the support accurate and reliable?
- Is the support directly related to the claims?
- Is the support the best available?
- Is the support information I can understand, accept, and believe?
- Is the support relevant to the needs of the audience?
- Is the support information the audience is likely to recognize, understand, and accept? (Makay and Fetzer, 1984).

Statistical data can be a form of support that is quite impressive or misleading and confusing. When using statistics make sure they are clearly understood by rounding them off, visually displaying them in graphs or charts, and giving them meaning by comparing them to some common example. I have colleagues who have made very effective use of visual aids to clarify statistical information; I have seen others receive snickers from the audience because the visual aid was poorly displayed, presented incorrect information, or was so confusing no one could translate it.

One speaker held up a 2-foot by 2-foot poster in a room with 75 people in it. Only those in the first few rows could read it. I observed another speaker read percentages from a written report that did not correspond to the percentages on the overhead. By the time she was finished, everyone was confused! I have also watched individuals try to explain a chart with a vertical and horizontal axis and get the audience lost in meaningless graphics when the point could have been made simpler.

Reasoning from the data is even more important. If the speaker is not able to help the audience make the connection between the factual information and the actions they should take, then the facts are useless. *Cause-to-effect, either-or reasoning, generalizations,* and *problem-solution* can all be used effectively to make this connection between facts and desired outcomes.

Speakers need to be careful when using cause-to-effect reasoning that they are not simply connecting two effects and assuming that since one occurred before the other, it must have caused the second. The Food and Drug Administration is especially cautious about such reasoning by scientists. Either-or reasoning can be very effective if the speaker has been able to successfully eliminate all other possibilities in the minds of the audience. Then the desired outcome is compared with a less desirable outcome to lead the audience to accept the speaker's solution. Generalizations, either inductively or deductively derived, are common uses of the reasoning process. Demonstrating for an audience that a large category has this characteristic, and since this item is in that category then it too has this characteristic, can be a very appealing deductive reasoning. Inductive reasoning, of course, would take the small examples, add them together, and form a major conclusion. Finally, in a problem-solution pattern the speaker must be careful to discuss how the solution would work, what its benefits would be (especially to audience members), its costs, and advantages.

Nelson and Pearson (1990) suggest these questions to evaluate the validity of the reasoning you are using:

1. Is your evidence consistent with other known evidence?
2. Is there any evidence to the contrary?
3. Does your generalization go beyond your evidence?
4. Is your evidence believable to the audience? (pp. 300–1).

It is my belief, that in presentations of any kind, you are essentially trying to persuade your audience of something. The goal may be to persuade them to adopt an idea or solution you are proposing or simply to accept you and your services. In any case, you are trying to get them to "move" in some direction even if it is only to retain certain kinds of information. Essentially the speaker wants to build the case based on "common ground" with the audience. What ideas and beliefs do they have in common with you? The speaker must build those ideas into the presentation and then slowly indicate where they might diverge.

Emotional Appeal

We are not moved by logic alone. In fact, we often are more persuaded by our emotions, particularly when combined with factual information. Facts may convince us, but emotion will more likely make us take action. Among the emotional appeals that can be used successfully are empathy for a cause or a person, anger at some injustice, conviction to some value or moral principle, and excitement over some change. The ethical speaker will, of course, use emotional appeals along with sound reasoning and factual data. The unethical speaker may use emotional appeals that sidestep factual information and which are contrary to the speaker's goal.

■ *Delivery*

Unfortunately, sometimes how you present something becomes more important than the content of what you are saying. Your goal is to ensure your delivery of the message does not "get in the way" of, or distract from, your message. Your delivery will encourage or discourage the audience from listening.

Obstacles to Effective Delivery

Montgomery (1981) identified several characters that create a poor impression as a public speaker. *Martha Mumbler* is a person who can easily be misunderstood. She swallows her words and speaks too softly. Her voice trails off at the end of the sentences and she mumbles her words. *Roger Rambler* is a person who rambles on and on, never pausing for a reply. He never asks questions, just talks. *Slow-Speaking Sal* is a person who may put you to sleep with her monotone voice and her slow speaking. Your mind can work much faster than she can speak anyway.

Confidential Cal is a person who implies that everything is so important or so secretive that he speaks in a low, confidential tone, not so much hushed as it is muffled. *Nancy Nasal* constantly talks through her nose. It is such an easy, lazy way of speaking it doesn't take much effort at all. *Shifty-Eyed Sam* is honest but his eyes cause others to doubt his sincerity. His eyes are always darting around, a glance at the side, eyes following any movement or sound. *Hesitating Herb* is never sure of himself. He verges on a stutter many times. It could be caused by a lack of confidence in one's own ability or vocabulary but it could also be a bad habit that gets worse with practice (pp. 30–60).

Practicing your speech with a video camera should make you aware of any annoying behaviors you are exhibiting. In a recent presentation I watched, a speaker continually grabbed hold of the speaker's stand. This wouldn't have been so bad except the stand had a movable top and every time he grabbed it, it banged down on the top of the desk. Caught up as he was in his speech, he was completely unaware of the banging sound he was making throughout the speech.

Along with eliminating distracting mannerisms, the speaker must work to make the presentation interesting. You do this through the excitement in your voice, positive facial expressions, and gestures and movement that serve to enhance your speech.

You will also need to check on the preparation of the room. The "Speaker's Checklist" will remind you of some of these details.

Once you have analyzed your audience and adapted to them, caught their attention in the introduction, organized your persuasive appeals into some logical sequence, and practiced effective delivery techniques, you are ready for a little "pizzazz."

Extra Pizzazz

There are techniques which, handled with finesse, add a clever twist to your presentation. Smith (1984) discusses a number of techniques that add "pizzazz" to your talks. Be careful they don't come off as "hokey." Here's one I've seen work.

Tell your audience that you will offer them a chance at a million dollars for their thoughts. Buy ten lottery tickets, tape them on a flip chart in the front of the room, and hand them out to the first ten ideas expressed by the group. It may just be the incentive you need to get discussion going.

Another technique I have seen work was used by a Professional Secretaries International group. Summarize your main points by providing each participant with a "survival kit" that contains representations of the points you are making. Their points were inspirational and included the following:

- a *toothpick* to remind you not to be too picky
- a *lollipop* to help you lick your problems
- a *rubber band* to help you be flexible
- a *paper clip* to help you hold things together
- a *caramel* to help you "chew the fat"
- a *stick of gum* to give you "stick-to-it-iveness"
- a *piece of string* to help tie up loose ends
- a *pin* to help you pinpoint problems

■ THE SPEAKER'S CHECKLIST

Room
Reserved in advance.
Floor plan sent in advance.
Temperature and ventilation.
Coat racks in "secure" location.
Clean up in advance.
Six square feet per attendee?
Excess chairs removed.
Will corner seats in front row be able to see screen clearly?
Adequate clear space up front for you and equipment.
Divide large groups into smoking and nonsmoking.
Close blinds to eliminate distractions.
Must windows be blacked out?
Build speaker's platform with one-foot risers for larger groups.
Wastebasket, trash container.
Tape door latches for silence during late arrivals.
Table for handouts, etc.

Breaks
Refreshments scheduled.
Table for coffee, etc.
Wastebasket.
Restroom locations.
At least one break for every two hours (more frequently in afternoons).

Place Settings
Name tents, pencils, pads, water ashtrays.
Broad felt-tipped markers for name tents (one for every three attendees).
Agenda for longer meetings.
Rolls of mints or candies.

Projector(s)
Who will supply projectors?
Tables or stands supplied.
Plugged in, aligned, and focused.
Any light fixtures in the way?
Lenses dust-free.
Spare bulbs on hand.
Take-up reel available for movie projector.
Extension cords tapes to floor, outlets, and table legs.
Electrical circuits adequate to handle full load plus coffee urn, etc.
Remote control working properly.

Projectionist
Has marked script or cue sheet.
Has signal light or headphone buzzer.
If green, yellow, and red timing lights are used, agree on schedule.
Small light available for projectionist.

Sound
Mike and speakers working.
Practice putting lavaliere mike on.
Feedback problems?
Check levels and set if required.
Do you want talk recorded?

Screen
Large enough for readability.
High enough for visibility. (Bottom of screen should be 4½ feet above floor.)
Fill screen with image.
Does image keystone?
Any hot spots from overhead lights?
Offset for viewgraphs.

(Continued)

THE SPEAKER'S CHECKLIST
(Continued)

Lighting
Adjustable?
Levels checked out and marked.
Who will work the lights?
Will auxiliary lights be required?
Windows adequately draped.

Signs
Room location sign in lobby or
  hall.
Meeting title on room door.
Message board for day-long
  sessions.
"Quiet Please—Meeting in
  Session."

Easel/Chalkboard
Fresh pad.
Fresh markers, varied colors.
Chalkboard cleaned.
Colored chalk.
Eraser.

Lectern
Light working?
Timer working? Noisy?

Water nearby.
Signal to projector/projectionist.
Pointer available.
Props hidden.
Script or cue sheet ready.
Height properly set.
Does it block anyone's view of
  screen?

Handouts
Arranged in order.
Conveniently located.
Evaluation forms or surveys
Current reprints.
Where do you want handouts?
When will you distribute?

Visuals
In correct order.
All right-side up.
Extra blank viewgraph sheets.
Movies or videotapes advanced to
  proper start.

Source: Adapted from T.C. Smith, *Making Successful Presentations: A Self Teaching Guide* (New York: John Wiley & Sons, Inc., 1984).

- a *penny* so that you will have enough "cents" to realize what a valuable asset you are to your profession!

All the items underlined are included in the small bag. I adapted this technique to a speech on team building but you could adapt it in a variety of ways. It was a great success and helped reinforce the points of my talk. The disadvantage is, it takes a good deal of time to prepare and only a very few minutes to present, but I thought it was worth it.

Another "jazzy" technique I have seen used is to have the audience visualize objects around the room. Walk around as if you are telling a story: "If I were in a home, over here might be the TV, next to the bookcase . . . " and so on. At the end have the audience repeat all the objects you identified and where they were located. The first letter of each object stands for a word you are trying to get them to remember. At the end, have them say the object as they visualize it, then the word it stands for, and in five minutes you can demonstrate how they can memorize a dozen or more concepts or ideas.

■ *Consultant's Tips*

- Develop one standard presentation that you can always give on short notice. The topic should be a general "inspirational" topic. Here is the one I give. It is based on the "Four 'Cs' of life: Challenges, Commitment, Creativity, and Choices." The message is: accept challenges, do something with your life you are committed to, allow your creativity to flourish, and remember no one can make you feel a certain way or behave a certain way. We choose how we will react to any situation. Then I tell a story with each word.

   You can pick your own words to base your presentation on: "Success depends on *attitude, anticipation,* and *actions.*" Or, "Keep your sales presentations *short, simple,* and *sincere.*" Your stories may come from your own life experiences. The key is the ideas and stories are so familiar to you that you are able to present them without previous warning. The advantage of having such a speech prepared will be realized the first time you're asked to "say a few words" on the spur of the moment.

- Start with developing the introduction and the ending. These are the most important steps and the most likely to be remembered. I always want to know exactly what the first and last words out of my mouth will be. I have seen too many speakers begin with a few worthless comments and end by mumbling, "I guess that's all I have to say for now." That is a poor way to leave the audience.

- Use examples relevant to the audience. Although your topic could be appropriate no matter what occupation or interests your audience may have, your examples must come from their daily lives. I recently gave a speech to 800 employees of an insurance company. Although I talked about listening carefully to customer needs, the talk was filled with investment product operations language, and their organizational values of service, integrity, adoption to change, accountability, and partnerships. The words used to express these values had been in print in a variety of organization publications and it was critical that my talk be tied to them.

- Practice using video cameras. You will be your own worst judge. Seeing yourself on camera, preferably on a large screen, will tell you better than any person can, what nonverbal distractions you

■ CHALLENGE READINESS INVENTORY

More than 100 business and professional leaders recently surveyed for The Synergy Group business newsletter named the following 16 challenges for today's well-rounded business presenter. Although you need not excel in all areas to succeed, the greater your versatility, the better prepared you will be for success. You might want to take this test to rate your own readiness for a challenge.

For the following 16 questions, rate your comfort level for the given challenges, and circle the appropriate number (0 = totally uncomfortable, 10 = totally comfortable). Then put an asterisk next to the number you would like to reach in the future.

1. Present a complete and concise briefing or report at a staff meeting.

0 1 2 3 4 5 6 7 8 9 10

2. Present a proposal or sales talk with appropriate documentation to a client group.

0 1 2 3 4 5 6 7 8 9 10

3. Meet one-on-one with colleagues, supervisors, employees, clients, community representatives, or reporters.

0 1 2 3 4 5 6 7 8 9 10

4. Deliver a 5- to 10-minute all-purpose, amusing, and motivating talk to groups from 3 to 3000.

0 1 2 3 4 5 6 7 8 9 10

5. Deliver a 30- to 60-minute informative and persuasive talk to groups from 3 to 3000.

0 1 2 3 4 5 6 7 8 9 10

6. Present 12 minutes of legislative testimony on a timely, specific industrial issue.

0 1 2 3 4 5 6 7 8 9 10

7. Participate in a panel discussion on some current controversy.

0 1 2 3 4 5 6 7 8 9 10

8. Participate in a friendly television interview lasting up to 15 minutes.

0 1 2 3 4 5 6 7 8 9 10

9. Participate in an aggressive interview during a crisis.

0 1 2 3 4 5 6 7 8 9 10

10. Introduce a major luminary in your field to 6000 delegates at your international convention.

0 1 2 3 4 5 6 7 8 9 10

(Continued)

215

CHALLENGE READINESS INVENTORY *(Continued)*

11. Present a prepared speech from a text that your boss, delayed in flight, was supposed to deliver.

0 1 2 3 4 5 6 7 8 9 10

12. Work with a speech writer to prepare and present a formal policy statement for your organization.

0 1 2 3 4 5 6 7 8 9 10

13. Present a one-minute television editorial on the benefits your industry brings to society.

0 1 2 3 4 5 6 7 8 9 10

14. Write and deliver three to five humorous comments for a "roast" of a boss, colleague, or friend to celebrate his or her recent accomplishments.

0 1 2 3 4 5 6 7 8 9 10

15. Participate in a lively question-and-answer session after one of your presentations.

0 1 2 3 4 5 6 7 8 9 10

16. Prepare and present a one- to three-hour training session with appropriate material for people just entering your field.

0 1 2 3 4 5 6 7 8 9 10

Now find the total of the numbers circled and the total of the numbers marked with an asterisk. Subtract the total of circled numbers from the total of starred numbers, and read about your score below.

A score of 0 to 20 is Superb! You are close to your productive level of mastery in most areas. You may wish to keep reading to polish your skills and to pick up pointers on how to help other people develop.

A score of 21 to 40 is Good. You are well on your way to full flexibility. A small investment of your time and energy can pay off handsomely.

A score of 41 to 60 is Average. You are sometimes at a disadvantage in a new presenting situation, but you recognize that you can overcome this handicap.

A score of 60+ is Challenging. You have a major project in front of you, and one well worth the effort. Be sure to set small, achievable goals, work toward them regularly over time, and reward your successes along the way.

may be incorporating in your speech. Remember that you will always look heavier, and sound more nasal, on tape than you appear to others (or let's hope so anyway!).

- Know your style and control the situation you get into. For example, if you are not normally a funny person, do not agree to be a stand-up comic after a banquet! If you are not good at extemporizing a speech, do not agree to deliver a speech away from a podium and have to fumble with your notes. Take the "Challenge Readiness Inventory" at the end of this chapter to help you determine what situations you'll be most comfortable with.

- In short, a public speech is like a sales pitch. "Know your product, know your prospect, involve the prospect, ask for action, and be prepared to handle opposition" (Quick, 1988).

- Try these techniques to control your nerves:

    Be prepared. The best defense against nervous stomachs is preparation and constant practice.

    Imagine what the speech will be like. Walk yourself through the speech in your mind, down to the last detail including what the audience will look like.

    Use stress reducers, which include relaxation techniques. Simply moving your shoulders up and down right before you speak will help. I find that 10 minutes of silence, sitting down by myself, does wonders for my concentration and poise.

    Focus on your message. If you really believe in what you are talking about, you will have a much easier time focusing on the message and not on the audience's reaction to you.

- Finally, keep your presentations: *short, simple, and sincere!*

Check your readiness to give a presentation by completing Form 10.1, the "Challenge Readiness Inventory," on pages 215–16.

■ Suggested Readings

Bedrosian, N. M. (1987). *Speak like a pro: In business and public speaking.* New York, NY: John Wiley & Sons, Inc.

Makay, J. J., & Fetzer, R. C. (1984). *Business communication skills: Principles and practice* (2nd ed.). Englewood Cliffs, NJ: Prentice-Hall.

Nelson, P., & Pearson, J. (1987). *Confidence in public speaking* (3rd ed.). Dubuque, IA: Wm. C. Brown.

Smith, T. C. (1984). *Making successful presentations: A self teaching guide.* New York, NY: John Wiley & Sons, Inc.

Chapter 11

CAN THIS GROUP WORK AS A TEAM?

Team-Building Techniques

■■ **READINESS FOR TEAM BUILDING**
When Not to Attempt Team Building
How to Determine Readiness
Readiness of the Organization
Mind-Set of the Group Ready for Team Development

■■ **ADVANTAGES OF TEAM BUILDING**

■■ **CRITERIA FOR EVALUATING TEAMS**
Output
Objectives
Structure
Energy
Atmosphere

■■ **GROUP ROLES**
Schein's Categories
Task Functions
Maintenance Functions
Boundary Management Functions
New Groups

■■ **TYPES OF ORGANIZATIONAL GROUPS**

■■ **TEAM-BUILDING SESSION**
Voluntary Participation
Debriefing Time
Openness and Trust
Guidelines for Confidentiality
Conflict Resolution

"A group usually serves three functions for its members: 1) it satisfies interpersonal needs, 2) it provides support for individual self-concepts, and 3) it protects individuals from their own mistakes."

Hampton, Summer, and Webber (1973)

*F*rancis and Young (1979) defined a **team** as: "an energetic group of people who are committed to achieving common objectives, who work well together and enjoy doing so, and who produce high quality results" (p. 8). The term "energetic" is important. A successful team looks forward to tackling difficult problems and identifying plausible solutions. From this definition, a team might seem to be the ideal approach to solving all of an organization's problems, but that is not always so.

■ *Readiness for Team Building*

One of the most important insights for any consultant or manager to have is to know when team building is not appropriate. One unit head recently solicited my assistance with developing a group of managers to work collaboratively and do a better job of decision making. One of these managers was in the process of being fired, a second was filing suit against the head of the unit, two others were only partially assigned to that unit and had loyalties elsewhere. For the period of time in which two members were on their way out, it seemed obvious to me that this was not a time to build a team. In fact, this group *could not* become a team during that period of time. It is unreasonable to expect an individual who is in litigation against other members of a group to collaborate and sit around a table, helping to reach consensus or compromise on decisions facing that group. The unit head would be much better served to deal with the staff as individuals and avoid bringing them together as a group at all.

When Not to Attempt Team Building

As the facilitator of team building, you will have the job of assessing the need for team building and determining its importance. In the preceding example the need for team building was not strong enough to overcome the barriers. In addition, the timing was the worst. You cannot build a team when other serious issues have to be resolved first.

In another example, a key executive in a group with whom I was working was the main reason for low morale and discontent. He would be gone in three months. This definitely was not a time to build a team with this executive and the rest of his staff.

A third reason for not using team building focuses on the degree to which the climate will or will not support team building. In one organization, the mid-level managers were interested in working more closely together and yet at each step of the process, the unit head pitted them against each other and created a very competitive environment. Team building needs support from the top to be successful.

Do not use team building if teamwork is not necessary to achieve the work group's goals. For example, some projects require individual effort rather than team effort. Also, team building should not be used unless team members understand the purpose and requirements of team building and are committed to the process. The group must first recognize the need to work collaboratively as a team.

A colleague of mine at the vice presidential level in a financial institution was hired to be the quality control vice president and came into a group of top-level executives who did not perceive themselves to be a team but rather as independent and separate entrepreneurs. Often decisions were being made that benefited one individual unit and actually hurt the total effort of the organization. This group did not have any commitment to teamwork.

When the company is undergoing extensive organizational change or when membership or leadership of the team is about to change are additional times when team building seems unwise. Finally, when the particular team is working under an unusually great amount of pressure, team building should not be used. Wait until the crisis passes.

How to Determine Readiness

There are occasions when a large group of very diverse individuals have a common reason for wanting to work collaboratively. This was true of a group of medical affiliated individuals with whom I worked. One group was hospital administrators; the second group was the doctors; the third group was association members who served on the boards of directors of the hospitals. The history of these three groups was they were often in competition or direct opposition to each other and each felt they could survive on their own without the assistance of the others.

At the particular time when I was asked to facilitate a large group setting, they were facing some problems and consequences that demanded they be collaborative. If the doctors, for example, did not send their patients to the hospitals, the hospitals' costs would soar and the institutions would not survive. If the hospitals, on the other hand, did not make the environment conducive and profitable for the doctors, then the doctors had no base of support. The association was interested in maintaining both the hospitals' and doctors' practices because that kept the association alive. These hospitals were facing patient shortages and had empty beds. As the meeting began, the historic relationship among these three groups surfaced, and they remained somewhat separate and antagonistic toward each other. It was critical that they understand the reality of their situation and figure out how they could collaboratively build a team toward the common goal of success in the medical profession.

READINESS OF THE ORGANIZATION

In testing an organization's readiness for team building one should consider the following questions and use them as guidelines:

Do members of the work group in question need to work as a team?

Does the corporate climate support teamwork?

What problems and/or objectives does the work group have? Can the problems be solved and the objectives be met through team building or is some other intervention more likely to be successful?

Do the group manager and members believe team building is needed? Will they approach the activities positively and energetically or consider them a waste of time?

Will the group manager and members take responsibility for conflicts identified by the activities? Will the group be committed to conflict resolution?

Will the group manager and members be willing to change work methods and mind-sets, based on what they learn through team building?

Is now a good time to do team building? Can the company afford to let the group shift their efforts right now from regular work to team building? Are any changes in group membership or leadership expected in the near future?

Is there money in the budget for team building? (Spruell, 1987, p. 1)

These conditions, when met, provide a climate where team building is most likely to occur. Assessing a group's readiness for team development is aided by such self analyses as Shonk (1982) (see Form 11.1).

■ **TEAM DEVELOPMENT QUESTIONNAIRE**

The following questions have been designed to *identify how* you feel *this team is functioning,* specifically, what *areas* you feel *need improvement.* The results will be compiled for discussion at an upcoming team development meeting. You will have an opportunity to review a summary of questionnaire results prior to the team meeting. You should be thinking about discussing your responses and others at this meeting.

Where there are multiple choices, check only one answer. Please be as candid and specific as possible.

Goals

1. List the goals that require members of this team to work together.

_____

_____

_____

_____

_____

2. With regard to the goals of this team, the people on this team are:

_____ Very committed.

_____ Somewhat committed.

_____ Somewhat resistant.

_____ Very resistant.

Team goals that I feel have *low* commitments are:

_____

_____

_____

Team goals that I feel have *high* commitments are:

_____

_____

_____

(Continued)

222

■ **TEAM DEVELOPMENT QUESTIONNAIRE** *(Continued)*

3. To what extent do you know and understand each team member's goals?

_____ Very knowledgeable about team members' goals.

_____ Fairly knowledgeable about team members' goals.

_____ Somewhat vague knowledge of team members' goals.

_____ Very vague knowledge of team members' goals.

Goals I would like to know more about are:

_____

_____

_____

4. The goals of members of this team are:

_____ Strongly in conflict.

_____ Somewhat in conflict.

_____ A little in conflict.

_____ Not at all in conflict.

The key conflicts I see are:

_____

_____

_____

Roles

1. The roles of the members of the team are:

_____ Very clear to me.

_____ Fairly clear to me.

_____ Somewhat unclear to me.

_____ Very unclear to me.

(Continued)

223

■ TEAM DEVELOPMENT QUESTIONNAIRE *(Continued)*

Areas I would like to have clarified concerning my role are:

_____

_____

_____

_____

Areas in which I am unclear about what others expect of me are:

_____

_____

_____

Areas I would like to have clarified concerning others' roles are:

_____

_____

_____

2. Team members' roles overlap:

_____ Very much.

_____ Quite a bit.

_____ Somewhat.

_____ Not at all.

Roles that overlap are:

_____

_____

_____

3. Team members' roles that are in conflict are:

_____

_____

_____

(Continued)

■ TEAM DEVELOPMENT QUESTIONNAIRE *(Continued)*

Procedures

1. The decision-making process on matters that affect more than one member of the team is:

_____ Very clear.

_____ Fairly clear.

_____ Somewhat unclear.

_____ Very unclear.

Decisions that need to be clarified are:

_____

_____

_____

2. Thinking of all the communications within this team, I would say they are:

_____ Good with all members of the team.

_____ Good with some members of the team.

_____ Good with very few members of the team.

_____ Not very good with the majority of the team.

Please specify what subjects you feel need to be better communicated:

_____

_____

_____

3. Team meetings

_____ Are very effective.

_____ Are fairly effective.

_____ Need some improvement.

_____ Need much improvement.

(Continued)

225

■ TEAM DEVELOPMENT QUESTIONNAIRE *(Continued)*

Please specify how you would like team meetings to be improved:

_____

_____

_____

_____

4. I believe the leadership of this team

   a. Is helping the team's performance by:

   _____

   _____

   _____

   b. Could improve the team's performance by:

   _____

   _____

   _____

5. As teams work together, behavior patterns are established that help or hinder the team's performance such as:

   Following up or not following up on decisions.

   Raising or not raising sticky issues.

   Facilitating or delaying decisions.

   Do you feel that there are such patterns that inhibit this team's effectiveness?

   _____ Yes

   _____ No

   If yes, what are they?

   _____

   _____

   _____

(Continued)

■ TEAM DEVELOPMENT QUESTIONNAIRE *(Continued)*

Relationships

1. Conflicts within the team are:

   _____ Openly discussed/resolved.

   _____ Discussed somewhat.

   _____ Very seldom mentioned.

   _____ Not discussed at all.

   A conflict that needs to be resolved to improve the team's performance is:

   _____

   _____

   _____

2. Relationships I would like to discuss are:

   _____

   _____

   _____

3. What is causing stress for you and/or other members of the team?

   _____

   _____

   _____

Environmental Influences

1. What constraints or influences outside of the team keep it from working more effectively? Please explain.

   _____

   _____

   _____

(Continued)

■ **TEAM DEVELOPMENT QUESTIONNAIRE** *(Continued)*

General

1. What do you believe are the team's key strengths?

_____

_____

_____

2. If you could, what would you do to make this team more effective?

_____

_____

_____

Analysis of Key Issues

Please review the attached summary of responses to the team development questionnaire. Use this sheet to list what you believe are the major issues for discussion/resolution and indicate their relative priority. A = High, B = Medium, C = Low. These issues will provide the basis for discussion at an upcoming team development meeting.

1. Environmental Influences

_____

_____

_____

_____

2. Goals

_____

_____

_____

_____

(Continued)

TEAM DEVELOPMENT QUESTIONNAIRE *(Continued)*

3. Roles

_____

_____

_____

_____

4. Procedures

_____

_____

_____

_____

5. Relationships

_____

_____

_____

_____

6. Other

_____

_____

_____

_____

If a team is getting ready for team development, the members will have to find answers to these questions:

1. What are we here to do?
2. How shall we organize ourselves?
3. Who is in charge?
4. Who cares about our success?
5. How do we work through problems?
6. How do we fit in with other groups?
7. What benefits do team members need from the team? (Francis and Young, 1979, p. 8)

These organizing questions help get the group started. You might pose them at the first team-building meeting and ask the group to address them collectively.

MIND-SET OF THE GROUP READY FOR TEAM DEVELOPMENT

In order for any group effort to be successful, everyone connected to the group must have the same mind-set about groups in general. A belief system that assists a team development program begins with the conviction that the group faces significant areas that need improvement and that the team has the power to do something about these issues. Team members must be willing to do a real diagnosis of the problems to identify tangible, achievable short-term results. The members must be committed to the team process. That means that they must accept the importance of feelings and attitudes; they must realize that the motivation for change comes from within; and they must recognize the interdependence of the teammates and be willing to risk new ways of working together (Shonk, 1982, pp. 24–26).

There are many reasons why an organization would want to develop a positive climate for team building. The following lists a few of these advantages.

■ Advantages of Team Building

In a meta-analysis of 63 previous studies, Nicholas (1982) found team-building interventions to be the second most effective intervention on measures of productivity and job behavior after structured laboratory training efforts. Team building had "an impact of 50 percent for every variable category measured" (p. 536). In another meta-analysis study of 126 previous studies, Neuman, Edwards, and Raju (1989) also found team building and lab training to be the most effective means of changing satisfaction and other attitudes. Clearly, team building generates a variety of positive results. "Team development in its best sense is creating the opportunity for people to come together to share their concerns, their ideas, and their experiences, and to begin to work together to solve their mutual problems and achieve common goals" (Dyer, 1977, p. 5).

Clearly, team building generates a variety of positive results for the group as a whole and for the individual members. The group benefits from the breadth of resources the individual members bring to the team. The combined talents and skills of the members allow them to manage complex issues creatively. Mature teams are capable of making better quality decisions than all but the most brilliant individuals. Hence, the use of a team should improve the overall quality of decisions. Furthermore, well-developed teams are capable of responding quickly and energetically.

For the individual member, the collective strength of the team may counteract the common concern that it is hard to influence organizations and make any impact outside the person's immediate area. The team changes this feeling as team members extend their viewpoint to see that they, together, can achieve a great deal. The team can feed the individual's need to have a sense of personal significance, and team processes motivate activity and achievement on the part of the members, together and individually (Francis and Young, p. 15).

■ Criteria for Evaluating Teams

These attitudes about teams on the part of members will help make a team successful. There are other ways to determine a team's success. Responsibility for evaluating the efforts of the team may be the responsibility of the members themselves or the manager to whom they report. In either case the following characteristics are offered by Francis and Young (1979, pp. 7–8, 60–61) as criteria for judging a team's effectiveness.

Output

The test of a team is its capacity to deliver the goods. A team is capable of achieving results that the individuals who comprise it cannot do in isolation.

Objectives

A team needs a purpose that is understood, shared, and felt to be worthwhile by its members. This purpose can be described as the team's mission. The effective team is clear about its objectives. It sets targets of performance that are felt to be stretching but achievable. A goal should be within reach but should stretch the team's capabilities.

Structure

A mature team has dealt with thorny questions concerned with control, leadership, procedures, organization, and roles. The team structure is finely attuned to tasks being undertaken, and individual talents and contributions are utilized without confusion. With well-organized team procedures, roles are clearly defined, communication patterns are well-developed, and administrative procedures support a team approach.

Effective structure implies appropriate leadership. The team manager has the skills and intention to develop a team approach and allocate time to team-building activities. Being a team doesn't mean the group is leaderless. One group I worked with couldn't get past the "polite" stage where no one wanted to step forward and take charge. Statements like, "I'd be happy for you to do it," "I think I'll let someone else take over this time," and "I don't want to step on anyone's toes" go beyond politeness and lead to useless activity. Every team needs leadership.

Every team also needs suitable membership. Team members must be individually qualified and capable of contributing the mix of skills and characteristics that provide an appropriate balance. Team members need to be well-developed individuals, and the team thrives on strong individual contributions. Each member offers something unique.

Energy

Team members need to take strength from one another. Collectively they feel more potent and find that team activities renew their vitality and enjoyment. Together members develop effective work methods, including lively, systematic, and effective ways to solve problems together. Teamwork has to be fun and energizing.

Atmosphere

A team develops a distinctive spirit, a climate in which people feel relaxed, able to be direct and open, and prepared to take risks. This constructive climate allows for openness among members and for their support and simple enjoyment of one another. Team members feel a sense of individual commitment to the aims and purposes of the team. They are willing to devote personal energy to building the team and supporting each other. Team building cannot be done only at the convenience of individual members.

A healthy atmosphere fosters the team's ability to create new ideas through the interactions of its members. Innovative risk taking is rewarded, and the team supports new ideas from members or from outside. Team and individual errors and weaknesses are examined without personal attack to enable the group to learn from its experience. The ability to provide critiques without rancor, to separate the person from the idea so that ideas, not people, can be criticized is a crucial skill for teams and their consultants and managers.

The team must have an open climate, where individuals feel free to raise problems and concerns without fear of being attacked. Individuals must be ready to accept feedback when it is freely given. The scale for rating team development (Form 11.2) included in this chapter can be a useful tool for determining the success of your team-building program.

◼ Group Roles

In order to pull a team together, the facilitator must be keenly aware of the variety of group member roles played out in most group settings. Some of these roles will render the group dysfunctional, while other roles are necessary for success.

Schein's Categories

Schein (1988) has identified group roles in three categories: task functions, building and maintenance functions, and boundary management functions.

Task Functions	Building & Maintenance Functions	Boundary Management Functions
initiating	harmonizing	boundary defining
information seeking	compromising	scouting
information giving	date keeping	negotiating
opinion seeking	encouraging	translating
opinion giving	diagnosing	guarding
clarifying	standard setting	managing entry
elaborating	standard testing	managing exit
summarizing		
consensus testing		

Source: Schein, 1988, p. 50.

■ TEAM DEVELOPMENT SCALE BY WILLIAM G. DYER

1. To what extent do I feel a real part of the team?

1	2	3	4	5
Completely a part all the time	A part most of the time	On the edge, sometimes in, sometimes out	Generally outside, except for one or two short periods	On the outside, not really a part of the team

2. How safe is it in this team to be at ease, relaxed, and myself?

1	2	3	4	5
I feel perfectly safe to be myself, they won't hold mistakes against me.	I feel most people would accept me if I were completely myself, but there are some I am not sure about.	Generally, you have to be careful what you say or do in this team.	I am quite fearful about being completely myself in this team.	A person would be a fool to be himself in this team.

3. To what extent do I feel "under wraps," that is, have private thoughts, unspoken reservations, or unexpressed feelings and opinions that I have not felt comfortable bringing out into the open?

1	2	3	4	5
Almost completely under wraps	Under wraps many times	Slightly more free and expressive than under wraps	Quite free and expressive much of the time	Almost completely free and expressive

4. How effective are we, in our team, in getting out and using the ideas, opinions, and information of all team members in making decisions?

1	2	3	4	5
We don't really encourage everyone to share their ideas, opinions, and information with the team in making decisions.	Only the ideas, opinions, and information of a few members are really known and used in making decisions.	Sometimes we hear the views of most members before making decisions and sometimes we disregard most members.	A few are sometimes hesitant about sharing their opinions, but we generally have good participation in making decisions.	Everyone feels his or her ideas, opinions, and information are given a fair hearing before decisions are made.

(Continued)

■ TEAM DEVELOPMENT SCALE BY
WILLIAM G. DYER *(Continued)*

5. To what extent are the goals the team is working toward understood and to what extent do they have meaning for you?

1	2	3	4	5
I feel extremely good about goals of our team.	I feel fairly good, but some things are not too clear or meaningful.	A few things we are doing are clear and meaningful.	Much of the activity is not clear or meaningful to me.	I really do not understand or feel involved in the goals of the team.

6. How well does the team work at its tasks?

1	2	3	4	5
Coasts, loafs, makes no progress	Makes a little progress, most members loaf	Progress is slow, spurts of effective work	Above average in progress and pace of work	Works well, achieves definite progress

7. Our planning and the way we operate as a team is largely influenced by:

1	2	3	4	5
One or two team members	A clique	Shifts from one person or clique to another	Shared by most of the members, some left out	Shared by all members of the team

8. What is the level of responsibility for work in our team?

1	2	3	4	5
Each person assumes personal responsibility for getting work done.	A majority of the members assume responsibility for getting work done.	About half assume responsibility, about half do not.	Only a few assume responsibility for getting work done.	Nobody (except perhaps one) really assumes responsibility for getting work done.

(Continued)

**TEAM DEVELOPMENT SCALE BY
WILLIAM G. DYER** *(Continued)*

9. How are differences or conflicts handled in our team?

1	2	3	4	5
Differences or conflicts are denied, suppressed, or avoided at all costs.	Differences or conflicts are recognized, but remain unresolved mostly.	Differences or conflicts are recognized and some attempts are made to work them through by some members, often outside the team meetings.	Differences and conflicts are recognized and some attempts are made to deal with them in our team.	Differences and conflicts are recognized and the team usually is working them through satisfactorily.

10. How do people relate to the team leader, chairman, or "boss"?

1	2	3	4	5
The leader dominates the team and people are often fearful or passive.	The leader tends to control the team, although people generally agree with the leader's direction.	There is some give-and-take between the leader and the team members.	Team members relate easily to the leader and usually are able to influence leader decisions.	Team members respect the leader, but they work together as a unified team with everyone participating and no one dominant.

11. What suggestions do you have for improving our team functioning?

TASK FUNCTIONS

As you will recall from Chapter 9, *task functions* are those behaviors that help the group accomplish the job they have to do. For example, *someone* must initiate, or get the conversation started. Giving and receiving information and opinions ensures all group members share common information. Consensus testing is checking to see whether there is agreement among the group members.

MAINTENANCE FUNCTIONS

Maintenance functions are those that help hold the group together. Usually these actions deal with interpersonal relations and help resolve and cope with conflict in the group. "Date keeping" makes group members aware of the difference between attitudes shaped by past experience and those based on current events.

BOUNDARY MANAGEMENT FUNCTIONS

Boundary management functions are those that link this group to others and the organization as a whole. For example, where do the responsibilities for this group begin and end and how can we find other groups to whom we might be related?

New Groups

Schein (1988) identified four problems of the individual entering a new group. First is identity: Who and what am I to be in this group? Second is control, power, and influence: Will I be able to control and influence others in this group? Third is needs and goals: Will the group goals include my own needs? Fourth is acceptance and intimacy: Will I be liked and accepted by the group; how close a group will we be (pp. 41–42)? Those are individual challenges. There are also conditions which are not supportive of group activity. A new group may experience a series of conditions under which team building would *not* work if:

- team members have varied perceptions of overall team goals.
- there is confusion about the roles, responsibilities, and authority of each team member.
- the team lacks effective procedures for planning, problem solving, and decision making.

- members frequently feel tense or bored and members lack commitment to the team.

- members have poor interpersonal relationships and conflict is unmanageable.

- communication is poor and criticism is abusive.

- members feel overly dependent on or rebellious towards the team leader.

- members do not feel an equal importance to the team.

- members believe team authority is distributed unfairly.

- members believe financial or other rewards are distributed unfairly.

- evaluation of team progress is missing.

- evaluation of team procedures is missing.

Any of these conditions can lead to the failure of team development.

Types of Organizational Groups

There are many versions of "teams" in organizations today. One is the "self-managed" team. "**Self-managed teams** are small groups of co-workers (perhaps 8–15) who share tasks and responsibilities for a well-defined segment of work. At best they exhibit the principle of 'whole work'—planning, executing, and measuring whole operations, whether building whole components or providing one-stop shopping services for clients" (Jessup, 1990, p. 79).

Quality circles is another form of teams in modern organizations. **Quality circles** are groups of employees taken from various levels and units in the organization, who meet with a facilitator to solve organization problems and make recommendations to upper management. Despite their initial praise, many report their lack of success. For example, Goddard (1988) reported that 75 percent of all quality circle programs fail because the work culture or management or both are unsupportive. There is no evidence that participative-type programs produce superior organizational performance if the company's overall management style is autocratic. In fact, in an operation where the job is well defined and managers and employees are comfortable with a directive approach, the costs of introducing a participative style may outweigh the benefits (p. 20). Employee-involvement programs must be tied to specific performance objectives (i.e., increased productivity and lower costs).

Bell and Rosenzweig (as reported in French and Bell) listed the essential ingredients for an effective work team:

> Get the *right people* together for a large block of *uninterrupted time* to work on *high-priority problems* or opportunities that they have identified and that are worked on in ways that are structured to enhance the likelihood of *realistic solutions and action plans* that are *implemented enthusiastically* and followed up to assess actual versus expected results (p. 132).

▌ *Team-building Session*

A team-building session (seminar, workshop, retreat) must start with increasing the level of comfort with the group facilitator and with each other. If you are running the group as an outsider, then you will have to take extra time to bridge the gap between being a threatening stranger who may change people's lives for better or for worse, and being a trusted guide who will lead this group through transformations resulting in more effective output.

One of the ways to increase the comfort level of the group is by establishing norms such as those described below.

Voluntary Participation

Anytime I have worked with a "mandatory attendance" group I have spent a great deal of time coping with their frustration. At the very least, I can make their participation voluntary once they are in the group. To the extent possible, you want the group to have chosen to participate in a group effort. Some people simply aren't "group" people and need the freedom and time to work independently.

Debriefing Time

However the facilitator designs activities and group work, there should always be more time devoted to discussing how this activity relates to their work world than to doing the activity itself. Every time I have tried to rush a group because I wanted to squeeze in one more activity or experience, I have regretted it.

Openness and Trust

The concept of reciprocity is acted out in terms of the openness of the relationship. If I am open with you, if I exhibit trust in you, you are much more likely to reciprocate than if I ask you to initiate trusting me first. The communication manager/consultant must maintain some distance and be careful with the type of information he or she reveals (see Chapter 17) because the overture may be misinterpreted and at the same time demonstrate the kind of openness that is *desired* about work related issues.

Guidelines for Confidentiality

Participants have to have a sense of security before they can achieve cooperation. Basic needs must be met first. Therefore, the consultant/facilitator must talk about the importance of leaving what is said inside the session. He or she must also be overly cautious at first not to inadvertently reveal any information shared during early sessions until permission is given by the group and trust has been formed.

Conflict Resolution

Most groups have interpersonal conflicts of one kind or another. Working through those conflicts is a prerequisite for team work. This doesn't mean everyone present has to like or enjoy working with every other person in the team but it does mean that every person present must have at least reached a level of comfort that they can work with every member of the team. Chapter 13 details more information on working with conflict and difficult situations as well as "difficult people"!

Much of the work in organizations is accomplished through the joint efforts of a team. Chapter 9 provided tips for running team meetings. This chapter has covered the importance and characteristics of building teams. Together, they should assist with the understanding of how groups function in organizations. The fact is, groups are used extensively, particularly with the implementation of participative decision making. It is not possible, therefore, to avoid participating in group action unless you lead a life of isolation.

Suggested Readings

American Society for Training and Development (1988). *Practical guide for technical and skills trainers: Vol. 1 & 2,* Alexandria, VA: American Society for Training and Development.

Francis, D., & Young, D. (1979). *Improving work groups: A practical manual for team building.* San Diego, CA: University Associates.

Schein, E. H. (1988). *Process consultation Volume I: Its role in organizational development* (2nd ed.). Reading, MA: Addison-Wesley Publishing Co., Inc.

Chapter 12

HOW DO YOU TELL CLIENTS WHAT KIND OF JOB THEY ARE DOING?

Using Descriptive Feedback

*T*here are appropriate and inappropriate times when one should provide feedback to others. Probably when the wolf is staring intently at Little Red Riding Hood, it is not a good time to provide feedback about his big teeth! Knowing when to provide feedback, as well as the style and manner in which it should be provided, is a critical element for the communication specialist.

> The president of a state utility company came under heavy pressure from the parent corporate office to cut costs. He decided to issue a statement to all employees about the budget cuts and detail exactly what line items would be cut. Among a number of employee benefits that were slated for cuts, one item served as a catalyst for employee frustration at the arbitrary process used to make these cuts. "During the last fiscal year we spent a significant amount of money on donuts at departmental meetings. From this day on, no donuts will be served at company meetings." It seemed a trivial matter to warrant being listed among other more severe cuts and seemed to anger employees the most. Three days later, the president was pictured in the local newspaper with the CEO of the parent company who was on site visiting. And guess what the president had in his hand: a donut and a cup of coffee! This provided the fuel for a humorous form of feedback to him. One anonymous employee cut the picture out of the paper, attached it to the following memo, and distributed it throughout the entire company, including of course, the president's office. The memo was addressed to all employees, ostensibly from the office of the President. (See Figure 12.1)

This was a rather humorous way to provide feedback to the president about the perceived trivial criticism of donut distribution at departmental meetings! In this instance, the employee felt this humorous memo was a

243

Inter-Office Memo

To: All of My Company Buddies

From: Your President

It has come to my attention that there was an alleged picture of me carrying an alleged donut in the alleged 9/29/94 city paper, Section F, Page 1. It is incumbent upon me to reply to these vicious rumors.

First, that was not me in the picture, but a person who looks exactly like me.

Second, I paid for the donut.

Third, I did not get the donut for me, but for my boss, for whom donuts are still legal.

Fourth, you will notice that there is a black mark on my forehead. This bruise came from the recent touch football game and resulted in temporary amnesia. My memory has since recovered and I now recall my donut policy.

Fifth, a close examination of the donut reveals that it is a peanut sprinkle donut, not my favorite chocolate-iced donut; therefore, I could not have even realized full pleasure from this alleged act. In fact, some experts even think that the item is a bagel.

In conclusion, there clearly was no violation of my donut policy indicated in the alleged picture. The "no donut" policy stands until we are through with this budget crunch.

Economically Yours,

Your President.

FIGURE 12.1

safer way to provide the boss with feedback than a face-to-face confrontation.

We all like to receive feedback but are afraid to ask for it. If I asked you to tell me "How am I doing?" you may really tell me and I may not like the answer! Feedback requires active listening and careful description of observed behavior. These two skills are the cornerstones to effective feedback and impactful interventions into human behaviors.

Schein (1988) suggested that most of what the process consultant does when he or she intervenes with individuals or groups is to manage the feedback process. The consultant makes observations that provide information, asks questions that direct the client's attention to the consequences of the individual's behavior, and provides suggestions that have implicit evaluations built into them (i.e., any given suggestion implies that other things that have not been suggested are less appropriate than what has been suggested) (p. 105).

Feedback comes in two forms: information on a person's behavior, and information on what impact that behavior can have on others. Remember that the overall purpose of feedback is to help, not attack. When giving feedback, make sure you can answer yes to these questions.

Timing: Have I checked with the receiver to determine the best time and place to give feedback?

Motivation: Am I being supportive while giving the feedback rather than ridiculing and hurting the receiver?

Language: Am I using positive or neutral rather than derogatory statements?

Tone: Am I using a friendly and caring tone of voice?

Value: Is the feedback useful to the receiver rather than an outlet for my feelings, frustrations, or anger?

Focus: Am I focusing on actions rather than attitudes or personalities?

Specificity: Am I using specific examples of observed behavior?

Information: Am I giving a manageable amount of helpful information rather than overloading the receiver with more information than is necessary?

Questions: Have I asked the receiver questions to ensure that my feedback was clear and helpful? (ASTD, 1988, p.3)

When receiving feedback, check for yes answers to these questions.

Timing: Have I agreed to the time and place for receiving feedback?

Trust: Do I trust the giver to accurately present information concerning my behavior?

Non-defensiveness: Am I prepared to listen to the feedback, rather than argue, refute, or justify my actions?

Specificity: If feedback is vague, am I requesting specific behavioral examples?

Tone: Am I using a neutral rather than a defensive tone of voice?

Questions: Have I asked questions that clarify the feedback?

Feedback is best when it is asked for and when there is a need for impartial knowledge. The client has to understand the difference between wisdom, which is a personal attribute of an individual, and knowledge which is gained from books and facts. It is the consultant's job to be honest, direct, and nonthreatening.

▐ *Types of Feedback*

There are a variety of methods to provide feedback, many of which cause defensiveness. The function of feedback is to describe another person's observable behavior, disclose your thoughts and feelings about that behavior, interpret motives, and prescribe specific remedies. These may be our objectives; however, my experience has been that when people are evaluated they often feel under attack and begin to defend themselves.

Feedback is a way of helping another person to consider changing his or her behavior. It is communication to a person (or group) that gives that person information about how she or he affects others. As in a guided missile system, feedback helps an individual keep his or her behavior "on target" and thus better achieve individual goals.

People give three kinds of feedback to others:

Evaluative: observing the other's behavior and responding with one's own critique of it. "You are always late for everything. You are undependable."

Interpretive: observing the behavior and trying to analyze why the person is behaving that way. "You are late to meetings. I think you are spreading yourself too thin—trying to do too many things at the same time, and consequently you don't do anything really well."

Descriptive: observing the behavior and simply feeding back to the person specific observations without evaluating them, but sharing with the person how her or his behavior affects the speaker. "At the meeting last week you were 30 minutes late, on Monday you came when the meeting was half over, and today you missed the first 45 minutes of the meeting. I am concerned about the information you are missing by not being here."

In the first example, the use of terms like "always" and "undependable" are evaluative terms and create a climate of defensiveness on the part of the receiver. Chances are the person isn't *always* late, and using an all-inclusive term like "always" serves only to make the person angry. The receiver then naturally looks for ways to refute the statement. "I wasn't late to the staff meeting on Friday! You're being unfair."

In the second example the observer is playing dime store psychologist and trying to figure out why someone may be behaving a certain way. Unless you are a trained psychologist, your business is not to analyze and interpret someone else's behavior. You don't know why someone acts a particular way. All you can observe is behavior. You can't observe attitudes, nor should you be critiquing them.

In descriptive feedback we are describing, as specifically as possible, what we have actually observed the individual doing. We present that factual information, without judging the rightness or wrongness of the behavior and without trying to figure why the person may have behaved that way.

■ Effective Feedback

Feedback should describe problematic behavior that the receiver can correct. Ideally, it will be offered in response to the receiver's request, but whether or not it is solicited, effective feedback should be timely, clear, and accurate.

Useful Content

We have already discussed why feedback is more useful if it is descriptive rather than judgmental. Describing one's own reaction to problematic behavior leaves the individual free to use the feedback or not, as the individual sees fit. Avoiding judgmental language reduces the need for the receiver to react defensively. Specific observations are more convincing than general ones. To be told that one is inattentive will probably not be as useful as to be told that: "Just now when we were deciding how to assimilate new employees, you were reading your mail. It made me feel that you were not interested or involved in the discussion."

Effective feedback takes into account the needs of both the receiver and the giver of the feedback. Feedback can be destructive when it serves only the giver's own needs and fails to consider the needs of the person on the receiving end. For example, I may have a need to complain about the lateness of a report. The report writer may not need to hear my complaints because she is already aware of the deadline and cannot change the fact that some missing data from another department prevented her from finishing it earlier. It may make me feel better to "blow off steam" but in this instance it may actually impede the other person's ability to complete the task.

Effective feedback is directed toward behavior which the receiver can do something about. Frustration is only increased when a person is reminded of some shortcoming over which she or he has no control. One receptionist was criticized for her high pitched voice over the phone. She had actually worked with a speech therapist and had improved it as much as possible. To continue to criticize her for something she could not change was not helpful, in fact, it was harmful. If the problem was severe enough, then her supervisor should have discussed other career options, but simply to continue to provide feedback that the problem existed, could do nothing to bring about change.

Feedback is most useful when it is solicited rather than imposed and when the receiver has formulated the kind of questions which those observing can answer. Unfortunately, people don't ask for feedback often enough. Therefore, we should take advantage of those rare opportunities when someone does ask us to take the time to provide it. It is easy to miss opportunities because one may dismiss a request as superficial.

> For example, I recently had someone ask, "How are things going?" (referring to a project she was working on). I said, "Oh, just fine." The answer was, "No, I really mean, *how do you think things are going?*" Then I said, "Oh, you *really* want some feedback about your performance?" If the person had not persisted, I would have missed a very good opportunity to provide this individual with feedback about her work performance at a time when she was actually requesting it!

Timeliness

In general, feedback is most useful at the earliest opportunity after the given behavior has occurred (depending, of course, on the person's readiness to hear it and the support that is available from others). One of the most delayed examples of feedback I have experienced occurred with two female trainers with whom I was working. We were designing a seminar and the two began discussing their earlier work together. Finally, one said, "Let's be sure we get straight what each person's role will be throughout the course of this seminar because we aren't always clear about how much we want someone to be involved." When she was asked to explain further what her point was, she described a workshop the two of them had designed in which she felt her talents were not fully used. In fact, she was unclear about the role she should take. I ended up being the mediator in this discussion, and I asked when this workshop had occurred only to discover it had been eight years earlier! Feedback that delayed is useless and unfair. It is unfair because the person who chose not to provide the feedback closer to the time the behavior occurred had been harboring resentment for a long time. Indirectly she may have been acting on that resentment in her behavior toward the other person, who could do nothing about it.

> Another example of poor timing would be if I asked my husband, during a formal banquet, how he liked my new outfit. To actually give me straightforward feedback, which may have been negative, at that time would have been inappropriate. What I really wanted him to say was, "You look great" whether I did or not! Why? Because there was nothing I could do to correct my appearance at that moment. The next time I was selecting an outfit to wear or buying a new one, when I could make a reasonable decision about how to use this information, would be a more appropriate time to tell me the outfit makes me look unattractive (if he dares to tell me that at all!). To provide such criticism in the middle of a social event could make both of us miserable!

Clarity and Accuracy

One way of checking to ensure clear communication is to ask the receiver to rephrase the feedback to see if it corresponds to what the sender had in mind. In this way too, the sender is training the other person to provide descriptive feedback.

Both giver and receiver should have an opportunity to check with others about the accuracy of the feedback. Is this one person's impression only or an impression shared by others? A teacher knows that an entire classroom of students will not always be happy with the way in which the class is structured. The teacher must therefore check for themes that exist among most of the students. When you get disturbing or confusing feedback, be sure to check it with other co-workers and colleagues. "Have you ever noticed me behaving in this way . . . ?"

Feedback, then, is a way of giving help; it is a corrective mechanism for the individual who wants to learn how well his or her behavior and intentions match and a means for establishing one's identity—for answering "Who am I?" Feedback can be informal or presented in the form of a formal evaluation process, like performance appraisal.

■ Performance Appraisal

Performance appraisal programs are permanent parts of the organization's personnel function. Some organizations have very formalized systems that evaluate employees annually or semiannually. **Performance appraisal** systems are a formalized way of providing feedback to employees about their job performance. This feedback will likely include both positive and negative feedback. Documentation of the evaluation becomes a part of the employee's record and provides a basis for determining merit raises and career advancement.

Traditionally, performance appraisal has been a top-down activity. Employees' performances are evaluated by their supervisors. Many companies today are beginning the process of appraisal from the bottom up. Top-level executives are more uncomfortable about this approach since they have much to lose in the process. However, companies that have tried having employees evaluate their superiors report success with improving the general work climate. It turns out that senior-level managers are hungry for feedback about their performance. In fact, as a consultant, I am often asked by senior management about their style of leading and managing. I find them extremely curious about how others perceive them. They know they have been "successful" because they have acquired a top-level job, but what they may be unaware of is how they come across to others on a one-to-one basis.

Whether the performance appraisal system is top-down or bottom-up, important issues need attention. Stroul (1987) suggested ten questions to be asked during a performance appraisal that will help focus the feedback on significant areas of management:

- Are managers rewarded for developing subordinates? In many organizations, developing subordinates is either not rewarded or is inadvertently punished.

- Do managers receive skill training and assistance in using the system and, specifically, in being helpers or counselors? Often, managers are only given the actual appraisal form and cursory instructions for completing the forms. Managers need training in rating performance objectively and in problem solving and helping skills.

- Are job descriptions or specific job-goal documents based on behavioral or job-relevant standards? Recent legal rulings suggest that performance appraisals are comparable to selection tests, and therefore must be demonstrably related to job content.

- Are employees actively involved in the appraisal process? Generally, systems that incorporate end-user input function more effectively.

- Does mutual goal-setting take place? Research evidence suggests that joint goal-setting is related to performance improvement and improved organizational climate.

- Do appraisal sessions have a problem-solving focus? A problem-solving focus is essential for performance improvement.

- Is the judge role clearly separated from the helper-counselor role? This is a gray issue that is often overlooked because of difficulty in implementation.

- Do the paperwork and technical assistance required by the appraisal system place an unreasonable work load on the manager? This is often overlooked but is a key determinant of success or failure.

- Are peer comparisons a central feature of the appraisal process? **Peer comparison** is a popular notion whereby an employee's work is compared to the performance of others in the work unit. This method must be handled carefully or competition is generated with devastating results.

- Is information needed for administrative action accessible and effectively used? The person conducting the evaluation needs to understand what actions can be taken as a follow-up to the appraisal. This is another feature too often overlooked in designing a successful performance appraisal system.

These questions could be used to generate a performance appraisal system. However, an organization whose employees receive feedback only through this formal system, once a year, is in trouble!

Consultant's Tips

Negative feedback will be misunderstood much more readily than positive feedback. Consequently, go slowly and be descriptive. I prefer never to put negative feedback in a memo. There are too many opportunities to misinterpret the language. I use memos for good news and face-to-face meetings for bad news. I want to be sure people have a chance to ask any questions they might have when I am telling them something they may not want to hear. However, once the negative information has been communicated face-to-face, follow-up written documents are absolutely necessary to maintain a "paper trail."

Positive feedback, when it is too general, has little impact. We shouldn't assume when we tell employees that they're doing a "good job" that the information will positively affect their performance. If they don't know exactly what it is they did well, it is unlikely they will know what to continue doing! In fact, if the feedback is perceived as too general it might also be interpreted as insincere.

Keep feedback impersonal. It is important that the person and the person's actions be separated in discussions. I can like the person, respect the person, but find a particular behavior unacceptable. I love my children deeply, but I dislike intensely their tendency to squabble with each other. It is their behavior I find distasteful, not their person. Thus, when you provide feedback, make it impersonal and attach it to a specific behavior, not to the personality of the individual with whom you are talking.

Tailor the feedback to fit the person. Some people appreciate receiving straightforward, direct feedback about their efforts. Others cannot tolerate such directness and need positive reinforcement before they are prepared to handle any negative information. Others learn best by example. Still others must hear new information several times before they really listen.

Use humor when appropriate. Sometimes it is easier to tease someone and indirectly provide feedback. This works when the relationship is a good one. The humorous memo in the beginning of this chapter was sent anonymously to the president of a company. It would be great if the president had a sense of humor, recognized the criticism as valid, and responded with his own humorous memo (I can imagine a variety of scenarios!). However, many top-level executives might not be able to handle such forms of feedback. In another organization, a short story was written about the head of the unit satirizing a recent series of decisions (or lack of them!). The story was never mentioned by the unit head in public. In private he expressed his inability to accept the feedback in that form.

Sometimes subtlety works best. There are times when direct confrontation over an issue is not the best approach. You may be calling too much attention to a problem others can then trivialize. For example, one woman who was constantly asked to take the minutes at executive meetings simply placed the memo pad in front of the senior member's chair at the next meeting, and then offered to provide him with a pen so he could take the minutes at that meeting. He got the message without her having to make a big deal out of the issue and began rotating this secretarial function among all present.

We know who we are by "bumping up against" other people. Their feedback helps shape our identity, self-esteem, and self-concept. The more feedback we provide for others, the better they are able to perform. The more we *ask* for feedback from others about ourselves, the clearer image we have of how others see us.

Suggested Readings

Cusella, L. P. (1987). Feedback, motivation, and performance. In F. M. Jablin, L. L. Putnam, K. H. Roberts, and L. W. Porter (1987), *Handbook of organizational communication* (pp. 624–78). Newbury Park, CA: Sage.

Downs, C. W., Johnson, K. M., & Barge, J. K. (1984). Communication feedback and task performance in organizations: A review of the literature. In H. Greenbaum, R. Falcione, and S. Hellweg (Eds.), *Organizational communication abstracts* (pp. 13–47). Beverly Hills, CA: Sage.

Laird, A., & Clampitt, P. G. (1985). Effective performance appraisal: Viewpoints from managers. *Journal of Business Communication, 22* (3) (49–57).

Chapter 13 ════════════════════════

HOW DO I COPE WITH DIFFICULT PEOPLE?

Dealing With People and Conflict

"If you can't do anything to improve on the silence, don't disturb it."
                                                        Author unknown

*F*or a manager, supervisor, consultant, or anyone responsible for the activities of others, there are times when silence is preferred to communication! Especially when you are dealing with difficult people or stressful events! My skills as a consultant are most often used when there is conflict or some "difficult" personalities with whom others must deal. One example of a "roomful" of difficult people is the following:

> I had been hired by a CEO to facilitate a top-level decision-making meeting between the budget committee of the organization, and what served as the board of directors, who were external to the organization but had the final say in decision making for that group. I walked into the meeting and noted immediately that the two groups of people had lined themselves up on either side of a long, narrow table. An agenda had been given to me by the CEO prior to the meeting and ground rules were established early on for this to be a goal-setting and objective-writing session.
>
> Ten minutes into the meeting, a large, gray-haired, impressive individual on the right side of the table said to me and the assembled group, "When are we going to get to *our* agenda?" When I asked what he meant, he pulled from his briefcase a second agenda that I had never seen before and proceeded to explain that this agenda had been sent to the CEO prior to the meeting and he understood, as a member of the board of directors, that this would be the agenda discussed for this meeting. The first item on the agenda was misrepresentation of funds and distribution of funds by the chief financial officer (CFO) and his staff. At this point the CEO said, "Well, I am sure Sue DeWine will help the group address those issues, plus others you have raised. I want to turn this meeting over to her now" and he promptly left!
>
> It became clear very quickly, once other individuals jumped into the discussion, that this had been a land mine set for the CFO with the intention of dethroning him. I was supposed to facilitate a col-

laborative discussion between these two groups in setting goals for the future of this organization!

The board of directors was angry, arrogant, and belligerent. The executive committee was stunned and the CFO seemed to be walking blindly into this trap. How could a consultant help these individuals cope with a conflict-ridden agenda and two groups that perceived each other to be difficult people? The only thing I could do was plunge in and list the issues one by one, deal with them matter of factly, and try to deflect the emotional response of individuals on the committee.

After a harrowing four hours' worth of negotiations, we came out of this meeting for a break. I was told by individuals from both sides of the table that they thought I had dealt with them fairly. For the first time they felt their concerns were being heard and understood. I don't know if either side really understood the other, but at least that's what they perceived to be happening.

Some people would describe certain members of that board as "difficult personalities." You can all think of a person in your life who is usually negative, arrogant, or downright mean-spirited. *These are the 10 percent of the workforce who cause 90 percent of the problems!* The American Psychiatric Association (1980) identified such personalities as "difficult" to work with in practically any setting.

■ *Identifying the Difficult Personality*

The American Psychiatric Association (1980) indicated that the **difficult personality** is unable to adapt to the demands of particular interpersonal relationships or social roles. While everyone around them is changing, such people maintain constant, difficult patterns of behavior.

"This is the colleague or superior or subordinate with whom disagreement and strain seem almost inevitable, and who appears to obstruct operations which should proceed evenly and amicably" (Hollwitz, Churchill, and Hollwitz, 1985, p. 1). These people cause distress for others and are generally unresponsive to feedback.

Other authors have suggested that difficult people have three things in common. First, their low self-esteem leads to views of the self as undeserving, unloved, unappreciated, and unsupported. They tend to defend themselves by believing they do not have these needs. Second, they lack the ability to cope with and resolve conflict situations. Instead they attempt to wear the other down or use fear to control others. Third, they have a tendency to use the importance of the relationship as leverage to gain advantage. When they are denied the leverage they tend to redefine the relationship (Brammer, 1993; Monroe and Borzi, 1987).

These individuals have been identified by other authors as: "difficult employees" (Bissell, 1985), "unpleasant people" (Weiss, 1992), "difficult customers" (Deeprose, 1991), or "marginal employees" (Pfeiffer, Goodstein, and Noland, 1986a). They are further characterized as usually blaming someone other than themselves for problems; taking up a good deal of the manager's time; and over-reacting to situations thereby causing more distress for those around them.

Brammer (1993) developed an instrument to identify disruptive communication patterns often exhibited by difficult people. The characteristics of disruptive communication, identified by approximately 300 subjects in six different types of organizations, were the following:

Characteristics of Disruptive Communication

aggressiveness
lack of clarity
poor listening
avoidance
not being approachable
complaining
negative verbal behaviors
apparent compliance, masked resistance
negative nonverbals
uncooperative behaviors
information strategies
conversation management
manipulative behaviors
lack of feedback
defensiveness
alibi
indecisiveness
gossiping

These characteristics are included in a questionnaire (Form 13.1) that asks individuals to identify a person they consider "difficult" and respond to items about that person. We should first see how many might apply to ourselves! Some of the most difficult people I have encountered as a consultant include the following:

"The Machiavellian Manipulator"—This person has a serious problem with control. If manipulators aren't in charge, then they are angry and

■ COMMUNICATION QUESTIONNAIRE

Please read the following statements. Describe the typical communication behaviors of a person with whom you work, i.e., a superior, subordinate, or colleague/peer, by ranking each statement on a scale of 1–7. Think about the person's communication behavior in general, rather than specific organizational communication situations.

Please circle the description of the subject.

Superior	Subordinate	Colleague/Peer
Male Female	Male Female	Male Female

1 = very strong agreement   5 = mild disagreement
2 = strong agreement   6 = strong disagreement
3 = mild agreement   7 = very strong disagreement
4 = neutral feelings or don't know

1. This person tells "tales."
   1   2   3   4   5   6   7

2. This person carries "tales."
   1   2   3   4   5   6   7

3. This person postpones things.
   1   2   3   4   5   6   7

4. This person procrastinates.
   1   2   3   4   5   6   7

5. This person is noncommittal when decisions need to be made.
   1   2   3   4   5   6   7

6. This person accepts responsibility.
   1   2   3   4   5   6   7

7. This person shifts responsibility to others.
   1   2   3   4   5   6   7

8. This person second guesses everyone.
   1   2   3   4   5   6   7

9. This person questions everything.
   1   2   3   4   5   6   7

(Continued)

■ **COMMUNICATION QUESTIONNAIRE** *(Continued)*

10. This person is suspicious of others' actions.

1 2 3 4 5 6 7

11. This person does give positive comments.

1 2 3 4 5 6 7

12. This person makes threats to me and others.

1 2 3 4 5 6 7

13. This person tries to ingratiate him- or herself with others.

1 2 3 4 5 6 7

14. This person says things about me behind my back.

1 2 3 4 5 6 7

15. This person does not play favorites.

1 2 3 4 5 6 7

16. This person has hidden agendas.

1 2 3 4 5 6 7

17. This person attempts to control conversation interaction.

1 2 3 4 5 6 7

18. This person does not stay on the topic.

1 2 3 4 5 6 7

19. This person interrupts me or others in conversations.

1 2 3 4 5 6 7

20. This person does not monopolize conversations.

1 2 3 4 5 6 7

21. This person denies having had conversations.

1 2 3 4 5 6 7

22. This person usually responds to messages (memos, phone calls, reports, etc.) quickly.

1 2 3 4 5 6 7

23. This person lies to me and others.

1 2 3 4 5 6 7

(Continued)

■ COMMUNICATION QUESTIONNAIRE *(Continued)*

24. This person does not distort information.
    1 2 3 4 5 6 7

25. This person withholds information.
    1 2 3 4 5 6 7

26. This person is easy to talk to.
    1 2 3 4 5 6 7

27. This person acts in an authoritarian manner.
    1 2 3 4 5 6 7

28. This person is not moody.
    1 2 3 4 5 6 7

29. This person is dogmatic.
    1 2 3 4 5 6 7

30. This person generally says the right thing at the right time.
    1 2 3 4 5 6 7

31. This person is autocratic.
    1 2 3 4 5 6 7

32. This person is not conceited.
    1 2 3 4 5 6 7

33. This person acts in a parental fashion.
    1 2 3 4 5 6 7

34. This person is difficult to understand when he or she speaks.
    1 2 3 4 5 6 7

35. This person is never condescending.
    1 2 3 4 5 6 7

36. This person uses distracting gestures.
    1 2 3 4 5 6 7

37. This person never scowls.
    1 2 3 4 5 6 7

38. This person expresses his or her ideas clearly.
    1 2 3 4 5 6 7

(Continued)

■ **COMMUNICATION QUESTIONNAIRE** *(Continued)*

39. This person won't make eye contact with me.
1 2 3 4 5 6 7

40. This person never smiles.
1 2 3 4 5 6 7

41. This person is cooperative with me and others.
1 2 3 4 5 6 7

42. This person says one thing and does another.
1 2 3 4 5 6 7

43. This person's writing is difficult to understand.
1 2 3 4 5 6 7

44. This person is a team player.
1 2 3 4 5 6 7

45. This person always follows through.
1 2 3 4 5 6 7

46. This person harangues me and others.
1 2 3 4 5 6 7

47. This person is a good listener.
1 2 3 4 5 6 7

48. This person ridicules me and others.
1 2 3 4 5 6 7

49. This person is picky.
1 2 3 4 5 6 7

50. This person is cynical.
1 2 3 4 5 6 7

51. This person can deal with others effectively.
1 2 3 4 5 6 7

52. This person does not use sarcasm.
1 2 3 4 5 6 7

53. This person does not whine.
1 2 3 4 5 6 7

(Continued)

■ **COMMUNICATION QUESTIONNAIRE** *(Continued)*

54. This person constantly complains.
    1 2 3 4 5 6 7

55. This person pays attention to what other people say to him or her.
    1 2 3 4 5 6 7

56. This person is approachable by me.
    1 2 3 4 5 6 7

57. This person is inaccessible.
    1 2 3 4 5 6 7

58. This person is very communicative.
    1 2 3 4 5 6 7

59. This person typically gets right to the point.
    1 2 3 4 5 6 7

60. This person communicates only through memos.
    1 2 3 4 5 6 7

61. This person hides in his or her office.
    1 2 3 4 5 6 7

62. This person does *not* listen to me or others.
    1 2 3 4 5 6 7

63. This person is sensitive to others' needs of the moment.
    1 2 3 4 5 6 7

64. This person is not articulate.
    1 2 3 4 5 6 7

65. This person is not ambiguous.
    1 2 3 4 5 6 7

66. This person communicates in a vague manner.
    1 2 3 4 5 6 7

67. This person has a good command of the language.
    1 2 3 4 5 6 7

68. This person communicates antagonistically.
    1 2 3 4 5 6 7

(Continued)

69. This person does not use combative remarks.

    1   2   3   4   5   6   7

70. This person uses confrontational remarks.

    1   2   3   4   5   6   7

Adapted from Brammer 1993.

frustrated. Their major goal in any kind of group setting is to be the one that pulls the strings on the puppets.

"The Bullheaded Blocker"—No matter what direction the group heads, no matter what ideas are suggested, this person's goal is to launch an offensive and to make clear why that idea won't work. Blockers must have played tackle in high school because every run seems to be countered by a block on their part.

"The Conciliatory Crab"—This person is disguised as being willing to go along with the group norm and the group idea but really becomes a crab outside the group setting or a complainer about what the group ends up doing. That's why I suggest that the conciliatory crab's true personality is disguised in the group meeting.

"The Alert Analyst"—The alert analyst sits back, remains silent most of the time, and tries to analyze the personality of the group. This person is a careful thinker. He or she sometimes comes up with good insights but most of the time does not contribute to the group process.

"The Backseat Driver"—This individual always wants to second-guess the leader or the group facilitator and without the same access to information believes he or she has a better solution. Backseat drivers don't trust others enough to allow them to utilize their skills.

"The Knowing Know-It-All"—This person appears to be the intellectual or the philosopher of the group. There's nothing you can tell this person that he or she hasn't thought of or read about before.

"The Hidden Agenda Harry"—I find the most difficult type of person to work with is the person who is not direct or obvious about his or her intent. You must always try to figure out in what direction such people are heading next. They come under the guise of working on one problem when they really want something else—something unstated—to happen.

Actually, we have all encountered individuals we would describe as "difficult people." What we aren't as aware of is when *we* are the "difficult person"! As a consequence, when I talk about defusing the difficult person, I am speaking to all of us!

Dealing with the Difficult Person

One of the ways I deal with difficult people in my role as a consultant is by *cutting them off verbally*, saying: "Thanks, Jim, now let's turn to . . ." I also use physical blocks by standing in front of, or next to, the person and physically cutting him or her off or out of the conversation. This technique can work well with those individuals who are trying to dominate the conversation or manipulate relationships.

I have also turned to what I call *limited-impact techniques* whereby I attempt to isolate the person's potential impact on the group by having him or her do a single-person project or get involved in facilitating the group with me. This pulls the person out of the discussion. If all else fails, I will ask the troublemaker to leave the group for a private discussion of the problems that he or she is causing. I use this technique with some of the worst cases listed above, like the blocker or the backseat driver.

It is important to *find a balance* between trying to ignore these people and spending a disproportional amount of time with them! One author suggests, "Avoid trying to ignore them. They will only chase you more, and raise the stakes. . . . If they set off a firecracker, which you act as if you did not hear, they will bring a bomb tomorrow!" (Bissell, 1985, p. 30).

At the same time, they may overreact to minor situations and unless you are careful you will spend a great deal of time fighting fires with them! You need to *be direct, and to the point.* Be sure to indicate what you can and cannot accomplish for them. You also have to let them fight their own battles. Don't become a "protector" for them.

Another author suggests using *"six magic words to defuse anger:* 'I understand (that this is the problem); I agree (that it needs to be solved); I'm sorry (that this happened to you)' " (Deeprose, 1991, p. 6). This kind of direct language takes the form of assertiveness training techniques: describe the situation or behavior, indicate your reaction to it, outline the desired change in behavior, and finally, indicate actions you will take if the behavior does not change.

The best way to lower someone else's temperature is to *remain calm* yourself. The louder the other person gets, the quieter you should become. When a fire loses oxygen, it dies out. When anger has nothing to reflect off of, it fades.

The assertiveness technique of the *"broken record"* works well with some difficult people. Repeating over and over, the same statement about how you intend to respond to some request, rather than becoming upset that someone keeps making the same request, is an effective tool. Statements such as "I don't do any business over the telephone," "We do not deal with telemarketing programs," "I never buy any product by phone," are repeated several times until they end the conversation. In this situation, hanging up works well too!

Dealing with difficult people requires great patience and flexibility. These individuals test our skills in more ways than we can imagine! They are often at the center of conflict situations.

■ *Conflict and Stressful Events*[1]

Besides having difficult people to deal with, we often negotiate stressful or conflict situations. When these conflict conditions occur between you and these difficult personalities, you will need a variety of techniques to help you manage this process!

J.W. Pfeiffer, a communication consultant, used an interesting analogy to explain why conflict so often occurs in an interpersonal relationship:

> In the late afternoon when you observe a sunset, the sun often appears to be a deep red, larger and less intense than it seems at midday. This is due to the phenomenon of refraction, the bending of the light rays as they pass through the earth's atmosphere, and the higher density of dust in the air through which the light passes as the sun goes down. The sun has already moved below the horizon but it is still in sight because its emissions are distorted by the conditions of the medium through which they must travel.
>
> In a similar way the messages which we send to each other are often refracted by intrapersonal, interpersonal, and environmental conditions which contribute to the atmosphere in which we are relating. I may distort my messages to you by giving out mixed messages verbally and nonverbally, and you may distort what you hear because of your own needs and experiences. The two of us may be located in an environment, physical and psychological, which contributes to the difficulty in clearly sharing what we intend. In an atmosphere of suspicion, for example, we may both become unduly cautious in our communication (Pfeiffer, 1973, p. 120).

While it is unlikely that total nonrefracted communication is possible, certainly we can improve our chances of meaningful dialogue by keeping in mind some of the principles of conflict management. This becomes particularly important in the organizational setting, where individuals often use up many hours attempting to resolve some interpersonal conflict.

Types of Conflict

There appear to be two types of conflict in the organizational setting: (1) **content conflict,** which is conflict over the goals of the organization, its structure, policies, or networks and (2) **personal conflict,** which takes the form of emotional and personal differences among the individuals within the organization. A conflict over content or issues might revolve around labor negotiations and pay increases while a personal conflict might focus on a group's inability to talk openly with a dictatorial, unfair supervisor.

Content conflict can be dealt with in rather routine, rational ways.

Usually, the conflict does not get directed toward personalities. However, when a group discusses the organization's goals, often a subtext (unspoken dialogue) exists that deals with personalities. For example, one group was discussing a policy change in the way the sales force wrote up orders. On the surface, the conflict was over what type of procedure would work best but the underlying conflict had to do with a personal conflict between two individuals who had been "at war" for a long time. It did not really matter to either one of them which procedure was adopted. All that mattered was that the other person's position be defeated.

Personal conflict is more difficult to cope with than content issues are. Once people start responding emotionally, then attention shifts from the issue to getting the emotions under control. I find groups so uncomfortable with emotional outbursts that they allow them to sidetrack the discussion. People are so relieved when the yelling has stopped they are willing to live with an unresolved issue rather than risk "stirring things up" again!

CONFLICT-RESPONSE STYLES

Hall (1969, p. 6) has identified five styles of dealing with interpersonal conflict, based on the responses of 387 managers. Individuals may use all five styles at one time or another. Think about which style you tend to use most often when you are in a conflict situation. Certainly there are times when we react to a situation before thinking about the consequences. What we are working toward, according to Hall, is the final style, synergistic.

The *win-lose* style is used when individuals associate winning with status and competence, and losing is seen as losing status. The result is an individual who is aggressive, dogmatic, and inflexible.

The *yield-lose* style is based on the assumption that human relationships are so fragile that they cannot withstand the process of working through differences. Here the person's need for affection and acceptance is most important and causes submissive behavior.

The *lose-leave* style views conflict as hopeless, and thus the individual simply strives for protection from a punishing experience by withdrawing from the situation entirely.

According to the *compromise* style, a little bit of winning and a little bit of losing are better than losing altogether. This strategy attempts to soften the effects of losing by limiting the gains of winning. Often this style results in a climate of suspicion for both parties since neither is completely satisfied with the results.

Finally, there is the *synergistic* style, which is the most desirable style.

Here major importance is attached to the goals of the participants in the relationship and to the well-being of the relationship at the same time. The confrontation of differences in a problem-solving way and a tolerance for differences are key elements in this style.

The synergistic style assumes definite attitudes that may be helpful in managing conflict, such as:

Belief in the existence of a mutually acceptable solution

Belief in the desirability of such a solution

Belief in cooperation rather than competition

Belief that the other person is valuable and trustworthy

Belief that the other person can compete, but can choose to cooperate

A Conflict-Style Instrument

Rosanna Ross and I (Ross and DeWine, 1988) have developed a conflict-style instrument that identifies the way in which individuals handle most conflict situations. The Ross-DeWine Conflict Management Message Style (CMMS) is a self-report instrument designed to assess conflict styles through messages used in interpersonal conflict (see Forms 13.2 and 13.3). CMMS identifies three message types: self-oriented, issue-oriented, and other-oriented messages.

The questionnaire is composed of 18 items, 6 that reflect each of the three styles. Each item uses a 5-point Likert scale from "never say things like this" to "usually say things like this." A respondent receives three subscale scores on this instrument, with scores ranging from 6 to 30. Mean scores on each subscale were determined (n = 116): *self*, 11.21; *issue*, 19.91; *other*, 18.16.

Respondents are directed to interpret their scores by: (1) comparing their scale means with the normative data and with the means of their training group; (b) discussing how the styles apply to specific situations; and (c) determining how they would like to see their own subscale scores change.

A message with a focus on *self* reflects emphasis on the speaker's personal interests. An example of a self-focused item is: "You can't do (say) that to me—it's either my way or forget it!" A message that focuses on *issue* maintains that the problem can be solved without jeopardizing the relationship and emphasizes that both parties must deal with the problem. An example of an issue-focused item is: "This is something we have to work out; we're always arguing about it." A message that focuses on *other* emphasizes overlooking the problem and keeping the other party

■ **CMMS: RECALL OF COMMUNICATION BEHAVIOR IN INTERPERSONAL CONFLICT**

Instructions: Consider situations in which you find yourself in conflict with another person. How do you *usually* respond in this situation? (Please write answers on this sheet.)

Below list some of the ways you often behave, comments you frequently make, and feeling you often have, when you are in a conflict situation:

_____

_____

_____

_____

_____

Instructions: Below you will find messages which have been delivered by persons in conflict situations. Consider each message separately and decide how closely this message resembles messages you have used in conflict settings.

The language may not be exactly the same as yours, but consider the messages in terms of similarity to your messages in conflict. There is no right or wrong answer to this test, nor are these messages designed to trick you. Answer in terms of responses *you make*, not what you think you should say.

Give each message a 1–5 rating on the answer sheet provided according to the following scale. Mark *one answer only*.

1	2	3	4	5
never say things like this	*rarely say things like this*	*sometimes say things like this*	*often say things like this*	*usually say things like this*

In conflict situations, I:

1. ☐ "Can't you see how foolish you're being with that thinking?"
2. ☐ "How can I make you feel better about this?"
3. ☐ "I'm really bothered by some things that are happening here; can we talk about these?"
4. ☐ "I really don't have anymore to say on this . . . (silence) . . ."
5. ☐ "What possible solutions can we come up with?"

(Continued)

269

■ **CMMS: RECALL OF COMMUNICATION BEHAVIOR IN INTERPERSONAL CONFLICT** *(Continued)*

6. ☐ "I'm really sorry that your feelings are hurt—maybe you're right."

7. ☐ "Let's talk this thing out and see how we can deal with this hassle."

8. ☐ "Quit! You're wrong! I don't want to hear any more from you."

9. ☐ "It is your fault if I fail at this, and don't you ever expect any help from me when *you're* in a spot."

10. ☐ "You can't do (say) that to me—support me or forget it!"

11. ☐ "Let's try finding an answer that will give us both some of what we want."

12. ☐ "This is something we have to work out; we're always arguing about it."

13. ☐ "Whatever makes you feel happiest is OK by me."

14. ☐ "Let's just leave well enough alone."

15. ☐ "That's OK . . . it wasn't important anyway . . . You feeling OK now?"

16. ☐ "If you're not going to cooperate, I'll just go to someone who will."

17. ☐ "I think we need to try to understand the problem."

18. ☐ "You might as well accept my decision; you can't do anything about it anyway."

Ross, R. & DeWine, S. (1982). Interpersonal Conflict: Measurement and Validation. Presented at SCA, Louisville, KY.

■ **SCORE SHEET FOR CMMS**

Conflict Management Message Style Instrument

By each item number, list the rating (from 1–5) you gave that item on the previous page. When you have entered all ratings, add total ratings for each column and divide by six. Enter the resulting score (your mean) in the space provided.

	SELF *(Items)*	ISSUE *(Items)*	OTHER *(Items)*
	1. ☐	3. ☐	2. ☐
	8. ☐	5. ☐	4. ☐
	9. ☐	7. ☐	6. ☐
	10. ☐	11. ☐	13. ☐
	16. ☐	12. ☐	14. ☐
	18. ☐	17. ☐	15. ☐
YOUR MEAN	——	——	——
AVERAGE MEANS	(13.17)	(24.26)	(21.00)

The items comprising the SELF focus deal with one's personal interests in the conflict situation. These messages suggest that one's primary concern is in resolving the conflict so that a person's personal view of the conflict is accepted by the other. This is a "win" approach to conflict resolution.

The items comprising the ISSUE focus deal with an emphasis on both parties dealing with the problem. These message statements suggest an overriding concern with the content of the conflict rather than the personal relationship.

The items comprising the OTHER focus deal with neither the conflict issues nor personal interests, but emphasize maintaining the relationship at a cost of resolving the conflict. These statements suggest that one would rather ignore the problem to maintain a good relationship with the other person.

All of us may use one of these styles in different settings and under different circumstances. People do tend to have a predominant style which is evidenced by the kinds of messages sent during conflict situations. The intent of this instrument is to cause individuals to focus on what

(Continued)

■ SCORE SHEET FOR CMMS *(Continued)*

they are communicating in the messages they send during conflict and to make sure that what they are saying is what they intended to say.

The means reported on the preceding page are based on research reported in Ross and DeWine (1983) and are an indication of scores one might expect to receive. Scores that are higher or lower than these means indicate a higher or lower use of this message style than would normally be expected.

Ross, R. & DeWine, S. (1982). Interpersonal Conflict: Measurement and Validation. Presented at SCA, Louisville, KY.

happy. An example of the other-focused item is: "That's O.K. . . . it wasn't important anyway."

The instrument is preceded by a cover page that directs subjects to recall and to describe in writing their most common behavior in conflict. This critical incident–recall is designed to encourage congruity between subjects' responses on the items and their actual behavior. On a second page, respondents are asked to consider each message separately and to decide how closely the message resembles comments that they have made in conflict situations. Respondents are told there are no right or wrong answers.

An individual's score on a given subscale indicates the frequency with which the respondent would select messages similar to those in that subscale. Although no interpretation section accompanies the instrument, the CMMS is designed for training purposes and includes an explanation of the three message styles and their mean scores. (See Ross and DeWine, 1988 for detailed statistical analysis of the instrument.)

This instrument can be used in training sessions, as you work with individuals in small groups, or on a one-to-one basis. It will provide insight for both you and the individual/group about how conflict is currently being handled. If you understand someone's style of resolving conflict you are better prepared to negotiate.

Stages of Conflict

Pondy (1972) has identified five distinct stages of conflict development:

Latent conflict deals with underlying sources of organizational conflict, like competition for scarce resources.

Perceived conflict can occur in either the absence or presence of latent conflict. Perceived conflict occurs if the individuals misunderstand each other's position.

Felt conflict may also be termed the *personalization of conflict* because it is at this stage that conflict actually affects the individual directly.

Manifest conflict is the actual occurrence of conflict, which may range from open aggression to apathy or even extremely rigid adherence to rules.

Conflict aftermath is a function of how well the entire episode or sequence of episodes has been resolved. Perhaps this stage will reveal the basis for a more cooperative relationship, or it might suggest how newly perceived problems might be handled, or it *may* foster more serious difficulties.

Causes of Conflict

Alan Filley (1975) has identified some of the causes of conflict in the organization as follows: ambiguous responsibilities, conflict of interests, communication barriers, need for consensus, dependence of one person on another, suppression of disagreement, and personalization of the situation.

We know people would rather receive negative information than no information at all. Ambiguous situations and a vague understanding of job responsibilities will lead to conflict. Many people are more frustrated by ambiguity than directions and instructions, even when they disagree with those instructions!

It is also evident that majority vote is a much simpler way to solve conflicts than reaching consensus. The criteria for selecting one method over the other is the degree to which commitment to the solution is needed. Consensus takes longer and generates more conflict initially. Majority vote, while quicker and easier, may simply delay the conflict until it is time to implement the decision. It is quite possible the conflict has merely been suppressed, only to be revealed later—like a disaster, waiting for an unexpected moment to strike!

One of the difficulties in resolving or managing conflicts is that the real cause or issue is often not uncovered but remains hidden behind symptoms. A careful analysis of the real cause is a crucial step toward managing the conflict situation.

Analysis of Conflict Situations

The following steps will lead to assessment of the conflict situation in which you find yourself:

1. *Assess immediacy.* A relationship in conflict is an emotionally draining experience. One of the first things a person must decide is whether this relationship is important enough to him or her to warrant the amount of time and energy it will take to resolve the conflict. Once we are committed to the relationship and realize that it will require our energy and attention, we then seem more willing

to try resolution techniques. You must answer these questions: How important is the relationship to me? How willing am I to devote time and energy, in order to cope with the emotional drain, in resolving this conflict?

2. *Identify the type of conflict. Intra*personal conflict exists within a person and may not involve others (e.g., making a decision between two choices). *Inter*personal conflict exists between two or more people. A relationship is not in conflict unless both persons involved are aware that the conflict exists. Conflict is either in the open and everyone knows it exists, or it is hidden and thus not everyone involved is aware of it.

3. *Decide on a basic coping strategy.* Initially, we must decide whether we can merely control the conflict (not let it get out of hand, cool it down but not really resolve it), or we actually are able to work at resolving the conflict. The conflict control strategy is characterized by statements such as, "I feel the conflict cannot be resolved at this time; however, I feel I must maintain the relationship so I choose to merely control the conflict, lower the emotional level, have a cooling-off period, etc."

The decision to resolve the conflict assumes it can and must be resolved, with all issues out in the open and communication skills in use to achieve a solution.

4. *Distinguish symptoms from causes.* We often waste time trying to resolve symptoms instead of the real underlying cause of the conflict. (For example, when a girl complains about her boyfriend always being late for a date, it is possible that their disagreement over the time he arrives is only a symptom of a deeper conflict. They may each have different expectations for the relationship—she may want it to be permanent and he may regard her as just someone to date.) Symptoms let you know a conflict is present; causes of conflict are issues underlying the symptoms.

5. *Identify methods used so far.* We must be aware of our basic coping techniques for handling conflict. What have we already tried to do to resolve the conflict (e.g., ignore the problem, hope it will go away; try to win the argument through persuasion, compromise, give in and let the other person win)? Identify the methods used and the success of each technique.

6. *Brainstorm for available alternatives.* When trying to arrive at solutions to an interpersonal conflict a person must be able to **brainstorm** ideas. He or she must be willing to list as many ideas as pos-

sible without evaluating them, no matter how wild or impossible they may seem. The strategy of brainstorming assumes that eventually some of these ideas may trigger a possible solution.

7. *Evaluate the likely outcome of each alternative.* Often it is difficult for us to imagine the best possible outcome of a behavior. When a relationship is in conflict, we tend to see only the negative results. It is important that we evaluate each alternative negatively and positively, asking: "What is the worst possible outcome if this alternative is chosen?" and "What is the best possible outcome?"

8. *Select the alternative and communication skills needed to resolve the conflict.* Finally, we are ready to determine what communication skills are needed to resolve this interpersonal conflict and put into action all of the communication techniques outlined earlier. We ask ourselves, "What other techniques might I try to resolve this conflict? Where do I go from here?"

Many people avoid conflict at all costs and responding to these two questions helps uncover why they have such strong avoidance tendencies. The preceding format allows the individual to carefully analyze the conflict situation before entering into a battle. These issues are of prime importance if interpersonal conflicts are to be resolved successfully.

As a consultant I frequently use this format to help individuals analyze their fears about resolving conflicts. Describing for a client some of the conflict styles and using the conflict instrument will help your client (as well as yourself) identify the way in which conflict is normally handled and with what impact. Any of these ideas can be presented to the client as a form of analysis for their own particular setting. The most important step is to recognize that a conflict exists. Avoidance behavior permeates most work settings!

The longer individuals delay confronting a conflict, the larger and more pervasive it becomes. It is like that part of the iceberg which is under water. You cannot see it, but it is there, waiting for you to run into it!

Note

1. Portions of this chapter were taken from Tortoriello, Blatt, and DeWine (1978).

■ *Suggested Readings*

Filley, A. C. (1975). *Interpersonal conflict resolution*. Palo Alto, CA: Scott, Foresman & Co.

Hocker, J., & Wilmot, W. (1985). *Interpersonal conflict*. Dubuque, IA: Wm. C. Brown.

Monroe, C., Borzi, M., & DiSalvo, V.S. (1986). Conflict behaviors of difficult subordinates. *Southern Communication Journal, 53,* 311–29.

Ross, R., & DeWine, S. (1988). Assessing the Ross-DeWine conflict management message style. *Management Communication Quarterly, 1* (3), 389–413.

Tucker, R.K. (1987). *Fighting it out with difficult, if not impossible people.* Dubuque, IA: Kendall Hunt.

Chapter 14

HOW CAN PEOPLE GET ORGANIZED WHEN THE RULES KEEP CHANGING?

Understanding Change Processes

The mallet Alice uses is a flamingo which tends to lift its head and face in another direction just as Alice tries to hit the ball. The ball in turn is a hedgehog. Another creature with a mind of its own. Instead of lying there waiting for Alice to hit it, the hedgehog unrolls, gets up, moves to another part of the court, and sits down again. The wickets are card soldiers ordered around by the Queen of Hearts who changes the structure of the game seemingly by barking out an order to the wickets to reposition themselves around the court.

Rosebeth Moss Kanter
Changemasters, *(1983) p. 19*

*R*osebeth Moss Kanter described a croquet game that compels the player to deal with constant change. For Alice, nothing remains stable for very long because everything is alive and changing around her. Kanter suggested that companies in the 1990s are having to enter into contests less like traditional sports and more like the croquet game in *Alice in Wonderland.*

There are days when I feel I have joined Alice in Wonderland! One client I worked with attempted to signify how quickly goals may change by having the company goal statements handwritten on a legal pad and photocopied instead of being typed neatly. No one took him seriously.

On the other hand, I worked with a university committee for one and a half years developing a new plan for a required curriculum. The plan was to be presented to the university community for debate and discussion. The chair of the committee thought he should present this plan in the most professional manner possible so he had it printed in a small booklet. The faculty were outraged since it "looked" like the plan was too permanent and had already been adopted without their consent! They took that document *too* seriously.

Sometimes, as you attempt to deal with constant change, you feel you can't win! Charles Handy suggested in his book *The Age of Unreason* (1989) that the future only holds more change and uncertainty.

The status quo will no longer be the best way forward. The best way will be less comfortable and less easy but, no doubt, more interesting, a word we often use to signal an uncertain mix of danger and opportunity . . .

While in Shaw's day, perhaps, most men and women were reasonable, we are now entering an Age of Unreason, when the future, in so many areas, is there to be shaped, by us and for us . . . for bold imaginings in private life as well as public, for thinking the unlikely and doing the unreasonable (p. 4).

This chapter addresses the issues surrounding change, resistance to change, and strategic planning. Consultants are **change agents,** persons who enter a system and by their very entrance, cause change to come about. Communication specialists (managers), who intervene into an on-going relationship in the organization, are change agents as well.

Types of Change

Watzlawick, Weakland, and Finsch (1974) identified two distinct types of changes that may occur in any organized system: " . . . one that occurs within a given system which itself remains unchanged **(first order change)**, and one whose occurrence changes the system itself **(second order change)**" (p. 10).

An example of first order change is the addition of a new department, such as a new product department, to the organization while the organization itself remains basically the same. However, when the addition of a new department changes the very nature of the entire organization, like a "department" for quality control that affects the entire organization and changes the basic way its business is conducted, second order change, wherein the system itself changes, occurs.

Second order change is of much greater magnitude and more difficult to accomplish, and it is the type usually dealt with by consultants and communication managers. Watzlawick et al. discussed systems that are unable to create second order change by saying,

A system which may run through all its possible internal changes (no matter how many there are) without effecting a systematic change, i.e., second order change, is said to be caught in a game without end. It cannot generate from within itself the conditions for its own change; it cannot produce the rules for the change of its own rules (p. 22).

The consultant must help the client prepare for change because any type of change, even positive change, may be met with resistance. We tend to resist any type of disruption of our routines. The consultant must deal with this resistance before the group allows itself to move forward.

■ Resistance to Change

Resistance to change is experienced at almost every step. Moore and Gergen (1986) identified the fear of taking risks as a key factor in resistance to change " . . . either in those managers who must decide whether to initiate change or those employees who are changed by its implementation" (p. 31). In their model (see Figure 14.1) they identified those environmental factors likely to influence the individual risk taker.

They suggested how organizations can support risk taking:

- Organization expectations must be clear, and people at each level of the organization must be aware of what the expectations mean to their work groups.
- Reward systems, both formal and informal, must be identified and developed.
- Support systems can take many forms, both formal and informal.
- Resources made available to employees can be a budget for a specific project, support staff, a mechanism through which to gather data, or equipment and supplies.

Once necessary risks are identified, employees themselves will be able to identify appropriate rewards and needed resources. Involvement of all employees in the discussion about potential risks to employees is critical to the success of any change effort.

Pasmore, Francis, and Haldeman (1982) suggested the following criteria for reducing employee resistance to change: 1) a well-defined, clearly articulated need for change; 2) support from top management; 3) support from the union leadership; 4) employee involvement and participation; and 5) careful management of expectations about the benefits to be gained from the intervention. Each of these criteria is explained through actual consulting examples.

Explaining the Need for Change

Often we assume it will be obvious to everyone why a change must be made. That assumption may lead to sloppy preparation of the change effort. Managers and consultants who do not take the time to explain the process being used and the reason why some change intervention is necessary, may be met with heavy resistance.

One communication audit project with a social service agency, with

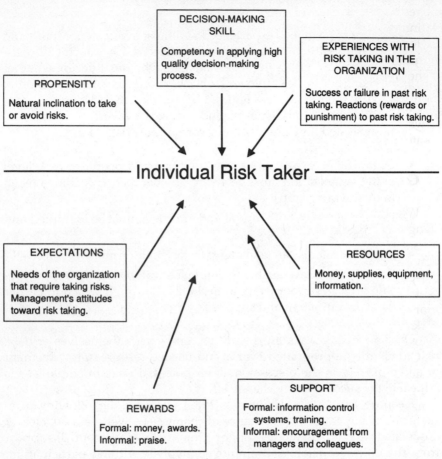

FIGURE 14.1   **The individual risk taker's actions are influenced internally by individual tendencies and externally by organization structure/culture factors.**   Based on Maggie Moore & P. Gergen, Risk Taking and Organization Change in C. N. Jackson (Ed.), *Targeting Change: Organizational Development,* Alexandria, VA: American Society for Training and Development, 1986, p. 33.

which some of my colleagues were involved, stands as a good example. The auditors started interviews without meeting with employees to describe in detail the goals and objectives of the project. First they had a hard time scheduling interviews; it seemed everyone was too busy to fit a 30-minute interview into the work day. Then, of the few they did get scheduled, 80 percent did not show up. The researchers stopped the project and went back to square one.

They planned a meeting with union officials to describe the intent of the research and discovered something they should have found out in the beginning. Two years before, another team of "researchers" had conducted interviews on the apparently innocuous topic of "workplace communication" and jobs were redesigned and eliminated as a result. Many of the current employees' friends and relatives had lost their jobs in the last "purge" through information collected in interviews. No wonder they were met with resistance to participate in yet another round of interviews! Don't assume individuals will understand the method or purpose of interventions into the organizations.

Gaining Support for Change

When middle management and/or line workers try to bring about change without support from top management, chaos is often the result. The same is true for union membership. One lighting manufacturing company hired me to conduct a series of team development workshops. The vice-president for human resources was my contact person. I asked to meet with the president but never succeeded in establishing a meeting prior to the first workshop. It was a mistake for me to continue with the workshop when I had been unsuccessful in assuring top management support. That is a mistake I have never forgotten.

On the Saturday morning when the first workshop was to begin, the president made a surprise visit. I was wondering where my "contact," the vice-president, was when the president told me he had an announcement to make before the workshop was to begin. He stood up and announced that as of 5:00 the previous day the vice-president, my contact, was no longer associated with the company. Then he proceeded to undermine any attempt on my part to make the series of workshops meaningful by saying, "We will continue with the workshops since we have already contracted for them, but the outcome of these discussions is very much in question until we hire a new vice-president and get this company back on track." Thus, I began my first workshop on "team building" and the importance of everyone in the organization feeling like they are part of the decision-making process!

Dealing with Expectations for Change

At the other end of the continuum from having negative expectations of the intervention, employees can also have expectations that are unrealistically positive. In working with another manufacturing company, the president asked me to intervene to discover why employee attitudes and morale appeared to be so low. I began a series of interviews and survey distribution. I received very positive encouragement from employees and had no difficulty getting them to talk with me. It became clear that this group of people saw me as a "savior," one who might be able to bring about the demise of the foreman of the plant. This individual was strongly disliked and feared. He used intimidation tactics to get employees to work harder. He had recently implemented a punishment system on piecework for all employees. It is fair to say they hated him. They fully expected that I would be able to convince the president to fire this individual. Since I had no power to actually bring about any change in personnel, but could only recommend, I had to carefully change their expectations for the outcome of this work. In fact, the president was unlikely to actually fire the foreman because of a relationship to his family. What I could do was recommend structural changes, provide some coping strategies for the employees, and suggest ways for the president to minimize the foreman's impact on the lives of the workers.

Implementing Change

In 1951 Kurt Lewin identified three steps in any change process that are still being applied today: initial "unfreezing" of behavior, "changing," and finally "refreezing" new behavior. During the first step, individuals must be made aware of damaging results from old ways of acting. The client must be stimulated to want to change; thus, results from data collections that reveal the lack of success with old patterns, must be presented in a way to make individuals want to hear more.

In the second stage, new behaviors or changes are introduced, and in the final step, those new behaviors are reinforced and rewarded so that they get "frozen" in the individuals' minds as normal patterns.

Greiner and Metzger (1983) identified three other steps of change implementation: power reinforcement, leadership modeling, and re-education (p. 271). Power reinforcement speaks to the issue of top management support for any change effort. If senior managers are not obviously supporting the change effort, then lower-level employees will see little reason to make changes in behaviors or systems.

Leadership modeling means having top management practice what it preaches. Employees will be watching management, and "if senior executives regard change as the responsibility of everyone but themselves, then the effort will falter" (p. 272).

Finally, re-education means unlearning old skills and acquiring new skills. This step combines the concepts of "unfreezing" and "refreezing," discussed in an earlier chapter. The final recommendations can then be reported to senior management. Greiner and Metzger (1983) cite a case study that clearly demonstrates some of the pitfalls of the final report which might document steps needed to implement change efforts.

> When one of the authors finished a particularly challenging assignment early in his career, he wrote a very incisive, well-documented report, which he felt included sufficient logic for a radical change. It was brilliant. He ordered 25 copies of the report to be printed. His consulting boss at the time stopped the printing and asked why so many copies had been ordered. The author replied that each member of senior management and the board of directors should have a copy. He could see clearly all the follow-up business to be sold as the client was impressed by a brilliant literary work that bordered on a doctoral dissertation.
>
> The author's boss was most understanding and agreed that the report was good. He then began to ask a few innocent questions. Had the client been consulted as to who should get a report? Which members of senior management might become alienated to the consultants if they chose to read the findings as an indictment of their previous management decisions? How much of the sensitive data in the report might be copied by someone and used for his or her own devices? What if someone left the company and took a copy to a competitor. How much damage would be done to the client?
>
> Needless to say, the author quickly contacted the client and asked for his opinion, explaining all the possible risks. The client felt that the report should not be distributed because of "potential sensitivities." The lesson was learned: always check with your client. There may be any number of reasons why the CEO or other key executives don't receive a copy, and a smart consultant won't overlook that (p. 277).

In order for change to take place, both the consultant and the client must be ready to implement it. "The ability of the consultant to effect organizational change is in direct proportion to the client's ability to develop the climate for change and to provide the authority and support for the consultant to effect change" (Ferguson and Ferguson, 1988, p. 542). If the client isn't ready, even a Pulitzer Prize–winning essay won't have any impact.

The consultant acts as the conscience of the client. As consultant, your role is to make sure the individuals see themselves as others see them. "The most useful tool in a consultant's kit to effect organizational change is not a sledge hammer, but a mirror" (Ferguson and Ferguson, p. 543). You must move at a speed with which the client can keep pace. Clients must see themselves in the mirror on their own, not have the mirror smashed over their heads!

Organizations must develop processes for dealing with dramatic changes as well as resistance to such change. Strategic planning is one approach for dealing with organizational change. Often consultants and internal managers are asked to facilitate the development of plans to cope with changing environments and change within the organization.

Strategic Planning

Pfeiffer, Goodstein, and Nolan (1986a,b) defined **strategic planning** as "the process by which the guiding members of an organization envision its future and develop the necessary procedures and operations to achieve that future. 'Envisioning' involves a belief that aspects of the future can be influenced and changed by what we do now" (p. 1).

> Strategic Planning is a reiterative process. Strategic planning and strategic management (which is the day-to-day implementation of the strategic plan) are never-ending tasks. The future, by definition, always faces us; thus, organizations must always be in the simultaneous process of planning and implementing their plans (p. 3).

The fact that strategic planning has no timeframe means organizations are like the painting crew on the Golden Gate Bridge in San Francisco. As soon as they reach the end of the bridge on one side, it is time to begin repainting on the other side. Painting the bridge and strategic planning never end.

Ernest (1985) suggested: "typically, planning within organizations focuses on the external environment alone, with little attention to organizational strengths and weaknesses" and calls for importance being placed on the "cultural dimension as a major component in organizational success . . . There must be a fit between planning and the beliefs, values, and practices within the organization" (p. 49). In order to assess the organization's culture we have to remember that the rules constantly change.

If we consider ourselves to be players of a game who know that the rules are real only to the extent that we have created or accepted them, then we can create a condition under which change can occur. This is an entirely different situation from one in which we feel like pawns in a game with rules we have no control over.

Greiner and Metzger (1983) graphically described the magnitude of the task for a change agent when they said:

> In strategic planning, the consultant must be able to analyze all facts of a client's business from a financial, manufacturing, marketing, personnel, and organizational viewpoint, not to mention an in-depth understanding of the client's industry and competition. If that isn't enough, this compre-

hensive analysis must be performed in a way that crystallizes the key strategic issues and choices facing the client and then proposes realistic recommendations. To change the strategic direction of any corporation is a Herculean task, equivalent to turning a giant oil tanker in heavy seas (p. 91).

Fortunately, in the role of consultant you do not have to know all the information. The client is the expert and in fact, if the plan is to succeed, clients must "own" it, rather than have it "handed" to them by a consultant who has done the analysis independently. The consultant acts as a facilitator of the process, keeping the group on task and making sure all planners have agreed with the analysis and plans.

If the client is prepared for planning, the consultant becomes rather unobtrusive. However, in most organizations with whom I have worked on developing planning documents, there are often communication or interpersonal issues that get in the way of making decisions about the future. Unless those human interaction problems are dealt with first, the group will not move forward but instead may actually move backward (see previous chapter on dealing with difficult people!).

Goals, Objectives, and Action Plans

The goals of planning are to: 1) determine the ability of the company to respond to demands by clients, 2) assess environmental factors external to the organization which will influence that company's success or failure, 3) set long-term goals and objectives, given company resources and future changes in the environment, and 4) determine action steps necessary to attain company goals.

Determining the internal strengths and weaknesses of an organization must be a carefully thought-out process. If those strengths and weaknesses are constantly put in the framework of the customer, they will look quite different from traits identified without the customer in mind. In one organization with which I worked, one department and the head of that department were perceived as being very organized because reports were turned in on time and were complete and detailed. From the customer's viewpoint, however, their careful reporting habits sometimes got in the way of responding to customer requests in a timely fashion. The second goal of planning requires a sensitivity to external environment factors. With the constantly changing world environment, any organization is a candidate for obsolescence unless there's careful attention to environmental change.

Goals are long-term "directions" for the organization, while objectives are specific, measurable, actions to be taken in order to reach the goals. **Objectives** must be *stated in clear language,* must *be measurable,* should *be obtainable* given current resources, and must have *a responsible party assigned* to them with a *time line*. Without these criteria, you do not have a plan, and without a plan, as the fable of the Sea Horse that follows implies, you are likely to end up someplace you don't want to be!

Once broad goals have been set, and objectives identified, then action steps designed to actually take the group from "A" to "B" must be agreed upon. The sample outline in Figure 14.2 identifies the differences between goals, objectives, and action steps.

I worked with a medical association setting objectives for the association for a five-year period. I met with them in October and again in April of the following year. My first question was how many of the action steps had been implemented. When I was met with blank stares, I knew that

---

■ THE SEA HORSE

Once upon a time a Sea Horse gathered up his seven pieces of eight and cantered out to find his fortune. Before he had traveled very far he met an Eel, who said,

"Psst. Hey, bud. Where 'ya goin'?"

"I'm going out to find my fortune," replied the Sea Horse, proudly.

"You're in luck," said the Eel. "For four pieces of eight you can have this speedy flipper, and then you'll be able to get there a lot faster."

"Gee, that's swell," said the Sea Horse, and paid the money and put on the flipper and slithered off at twice the speed. Soon he came upon a Sponge, who said,

"Psst. Hey, bud. Where 'ya goin'?"

"I'm going out to find my fortune," replied the Sea Horse.

"You're in luck," said the Sponge. "For a small fee I will let you have this jet-propelled scooter so that you will be able to travel a lot faster."

So the Sea Horse bought the scooter with his remaining money and went zooming thru the sea five times as fast. Soon he came upon a Shark, who said,

"Psst. Hey, bud. Where 'ya goin'?"

"I'm going out to find my fortune," replied the Sea Horse.

"You're in luck. If you'll take this short cut," said the Shark, pointing to his open mouth, "you'll save yourself a lot of time."

"Gee, thanks," said the Sea Horse, and zoomed off into the interior of the Shark, there to be devoured.

The moral of this fable is that if you're not sure where you're going, you're liable to end up someplace else.

Source: Robert Mager, *Preparing Objectives for Programmed Instruction* (San Francisco: Fearon Publishers, 1962). Reprinted by permission.

While there are any number of ways to define goals, objectives, and action plans, they should include a clear indication of the major issues facing the group, what the group plans to do in response to those issues, and a brief outline of the specific actions they plan to take. These statements should be concise and to the point.

SAMPLE GOALS AND OBJECTIVES FOR THE ASSOCIATION OF COMMUNICATION CONSULTANTS

This hypothetical association recognizes the need to ensure that its members continue to be trained in communication theory so that their consulting practices will provide the most updated interventions to clients based on solid research results. Consequently, their first goal relates to member education:

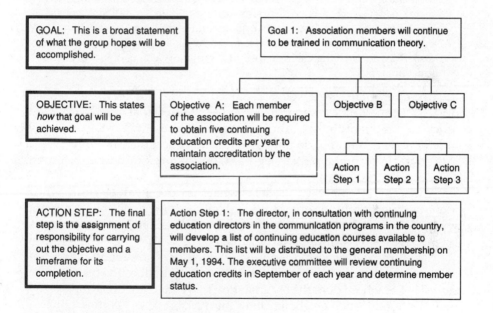

CRITICAL POINTS IN GOAL-WRITING PROCESS

1. Goals are broad statements of issues for the group.
2. Objectives must be measurable.
3. Action steps must assign responsibility and timelines.
4. Goals are not realized without specific objectives and action steps.
5. The group must attempt to reach consensus on all goals. This implies that each group member can "live with" that goal, not necessarily that each goal would be most important to every member.
6. This process takes time and extended discussion.

FIGURE 14.2 Goal Setting for Professional Associations Developed by: COMMUNICATION CONSULTANTS, 190 Longview Heights, Athens, Ohio.

this time around, they had to agree to hold each other accountable or my time and theirs would be wasted. People naturally resist change of any kind.

Planning Model

Pfeiffer, Goodstein, and Nolan (1986a,b) have developed as good a model as anyone which outlines the steps leading to strategic planning to handle change efforts (see Figure 14.3).

> To be successful, a strategic planning process should provide the criteria for making day-to-day organizational decisions and should provide a template against which all such decisions can be evaluated . . . . When a consultant asks managers about their organization's strategic plan, they frequently look pained or embarrassed and begin to search through their desk drawers or filing cabinets to find the plan, which is obviously non-functional (p. 1).

Too often, plans are developed, placed in a file, and left there to collect dust. Thus, the first question asked by the Pfeiffer et al. model is, "How much commitment to the planning process is present?" If the answer is little or none at all, stop, do not pass Go, and cancel plans to move ahead into strategic planning steps! Step back, and figure out how to get more commitment to the idea first.

The second step in their model is what they call a **values audit**, which identifies the significant organizational values that cannot be "tampered with." This includes an assessment of the organizational culture and what type of change can be supported by that culture.

Step three is the mission formulation. Pfeiffer et al. suggest the organization answer these three questions: What function does the organization serve? 2) For whom does the organization serve this function? and 3) How does the organization go about filling this function?

Strategic business modeling is the process by which the organization defines success and is the fourth step in this model. First the organization identifies a quantified business objective (e.g., increased profits) and then lists statements of how the quantified objectives will be achieved.

A **performance audit**, the next step, examines the recent performance of the organization on production, quality, service, profit, return on investment, cash flow, and so on. "The purpose of the performance audit is to provide the data through which the gap analysis—the determination of the degree to which the strategic business model is realistic and workable—can be conducted" (p. 13). The key question the audit must answer is whether the organization has the capability to successfully implement its strategic business plan and achieve its mission.

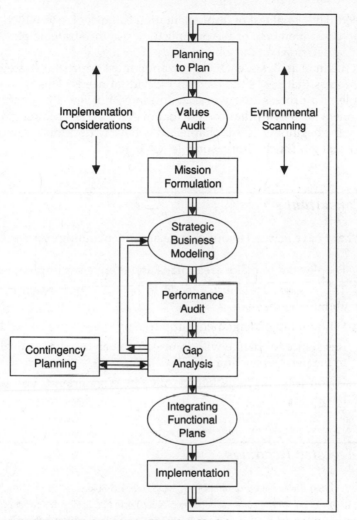

FIGURE 14.3 The Applied Strategic Planning Model From J. W. Pfeiffer, L. D. Goodstein, & T. M. Noland, *Applied Strategic Planning: A How to Do It Guide,* San Diego, CA: University Associates, 1986. Reprinted by permission.

The contingency plan identifies the major opportunities for and threats to the organization. Contingencies are considered because they will necessitate changes if they occur. Contingency planning is placed to the left of the linear phases of the model (see Figure 14.3) "because these contingencies are not based on highest probability events" (p. 15).

The final two steps are integrating functional plans and implementation. This is the place in which action steps are introduced and time lines assigned. The "final test of implementation is the degree to which managers and other members of the organization use the strategic plan in their everyday decisions on the job" (p. 17).

In the final analysis, each organization must apply the strategic planning process that best suits its own individual needs. This model is one example of a process that works with many, but not all, organizations. Everyone who is in a situation like that of Alice in the croquet game, outlined at the beginning of this chapter, may have to develop a new age process to deal with such "unreasonable" change!

■ Consultant's Tips

What I have learned about change and the planning process is:

- People tend to make great plans and then never implement them.
- The *process* of planning tends to help a group reach consensus about who they are.
- Without top management support, any change process is doomed.
- Resistance to change will occur even when the change is of benefit to the person resisting it!
- If you feel you have joined Alice in Wonderland, you probably have!

■ Suggested Readings

Handy, C. (1989). *The age of unreason.* Boston, MA: Harvard Business School.

Kanter, R. M. (1989). *When giants learn to dance.* New York, NY: Simon & Schuster.

Watzlawick, P., Weakland, C. E., & Fisch, R. (1974). *Change: Principles of problem formation and problem resolution.* New York, NY: W.W. Norton & Co., Inc.

PART V

Evaluating Success

*E*valuating the success of a training or consulting intervention is a critical, but often neglected, aspect of the process. Chapters 15 and 16 outline steps that should be taken in order that you and the client may determine the degree to which any approach has been successful. If you don't have a good understanding of what impact you have had in the past, you can't expect to be able to predict with any certainty how successful you will be in the future.

The argument made in these chapters is that evaluation should be a "front-end" activity, meaning it should be a part of the initial planning step, not tacked on after the intervention is completed. You may want to begin the evaluation with the very first introduction of some change in the system. You will need to determine from the beginning how you will measure your success.

Chapter 15

EVALUATING THE IMPACT OF TRAINING

"There is a decreasing willingness to spend money on faith and an increasing pressure to justify training costs. Therefore, it is necessary for those in the field to focus on training evaluation and to adequately demonstrate and communicate to management that training efforts are making worthwhile contributions."

Robert S. Dvorin
ASTD Info-Line, 1986

*A*llocation of funds for training programs are based on an assumption that better trained employees will be greater assets to any organization. It is often difficult, however, to determine specific benefits to the organization as a result of training. Many training programs are not evaluated in any systematic way. A great deal of practical advice about the need for training evaluation has been written (Bakken and Bernstein, 1982; Deming, 1982; Denova, 1970; Digman, 1980; Dopyera and Pitone, 1983; Kearsley, 1982; Peterson, 1979; Salinger and Deming, 1982; and Zenger and Hargis, 1982), but few researchers have attempted to measure different levels of training impact.

Wexley and Latham (1981) suggested:

> The typical approach to training and development is to review a program with one or two vice presidents at the corporate office, various managers in the field, and perhaps a group of prospective trainees. If the program looks good, the organization uses it. In fact, the program may be used again and again until it becomes all but institutionalized. It continues to be used until someone in a position of authority decides the program has outlived its usefulness (p. 78).

This is a typical system for evaluating the impact of training in many organizations. Much of the evaluation is done on the basis of opinion and judgment. In the end, no one really has a good understanding of exactly what the training has accomplished.

■ Obstacles to Evaluation

In a survey distributed by *Personnel*, approximately 75 percent of the companies contacted had no formal methods of evaluating the effectiveness of their training programs, although approximately 30 percent of these companies either recognized the need for developing techniques for evaluation or were attempting to formulate a system (Wagel, 1977). In a more recent survey, nearly one-half of the large industrial corporations surveyed listed a lack of standards and yardsticks as the most pressing problem, weakness, or shortcoming with respect to evaluation of in-house management training programs (Clegg, 1987).

Clearly many organizations still have not implemented formal evaluation procedures. A variety of myths surround the evaluation process, preventing this implementation.

Training Evaluation Myths

Often, individuals do not conduct formal evaluation programs because they believe it cannot be done. One author, Phillips (1987, pp. 2–4), has identified nine myths about evaluation of training that training directors must overcome:

Myth #1 I can't measure the results of my training efforts.

Myth #2 I don't know what information to collect.

Myth #3 If I can't calculate the return on investment, then it is useless to evaluate the program.

Myth #4 Measurement is only effective in the production and financial areas.

Myth #5 My chief executive officer does not require an evaluation, so why should I do it?

Myth #6 There are too many variables affecting behavior change for me to evaluate the impact of training.

Myth #7 Evaluation will lead to criticism.

Myth #8 I don't need to justify my existence, I have a proven track record.

Myth #9 The emphasis on evaluation should be the same in all organizations.

Myth number five becomes a cover for many of the other excuses. If no one has asked for the information, why should I put myself through the extra trouble? Underlying myths numbers 1, 2, 6, and 7 is a lack of confidence or ability to conduct such evaluation programs. Therefore, excuses are invented about the kind of information to collect and the way in which to collect it. Myths numbers 3 and 4 suggest very limited uses of evaluation programs and thus provide an excuse for nonimplementation. Myth number 8 may suggest a false sense of security. If the only reason someone can think of to conduct an evaluation is to justify his or her existence, then it probably does need to be justified!

Inadequate Evaluation Methods

In order to link training to bottom-line results, training directors must show outcome results from the training. The only way to prove the existence of any concrete results from training is to have an evaluation program in place from the beginning of the design process. Even when evaluation programs are put in place, they are often inadequate. Of all the methods that could be used for evaluation of training, companies still list the following as their most frequently used source of information: informal collection of passing comments, evaluation based on attendance records, student participation, end-of-course evaluation sheet, and end-of-course report by instructor. These evaluation methods are subjective and inaccurate. Many people have pointed out these shortcomings:

> With the field of human resource development getting attention from so many quarters, we see a growing need for the field itself to establish consistency and order in how it is counted and measured. The needs range from the evaluation of individual training programs to data development for national policy deliberation. Unfortunately, many decisions in allocation of resources for HRD . . . are being made with only the crudest kinds of information (Craig, 1983, p. 1).

Bunker and Cohen (1977) also concluded that "Training evaluation is one of the most under-researched and neglected areas of industrial/organizational psychology" (p. 525). Summary reviews of training evaluation literature have lamented the lack of organizational support for evaluating training programs (Ball and Anderson, 1975; Campbell, Dunnette, Lawler, and Weick, 1970; Goldstein, 1978; Grant, 1977; McGehee and Thayer, 1961). Thus, while there is a general sense of the positive impact of training on employees, sound evaluation methods have not been developed.

Many authors discuss the need for justifying training programs by "documenting bottom-line results . . . or on-the-job performance" of trainees after training (Cornwell, 1980, p. 289) as well as evaluating the direct cost/benefits of training (Deming, 1982). Types of evaluation devices suggested have been a repertory grid (Smith, 1990), a "pre-then-post" measurement where the participant is asked to rate prior knowledge *after* training, and an extended control group pretest design (Bunker and Cohen, 1977). All of these methods identify different aspects of training. One way to organize an evaluation program is first to decide what aspect or level of training is to be evaluated and then develop the method to be used.

Criteria for Evaluation

What are often missing in evaluation programs are the criteria or standards against which evaluators must compare the training. In an ASTD (1988) publication the following seven questions were posed in order to help evaluators determine what ought to be evaluated.

1. *What questions do you want to answer?* How did participants feel about the training? What did they learn? How did they learn? How did the training affect their attitudes and behavior? What were the organizational results?

2. *How will you measure the items addressed in your questions?* Will you administer paper and pencil test questionnaires and surveys? Will you require participants to demonstrate their new knowledge and skills in a role-play simulation?

3. *What are the objectives of your training program?* Are your evaluation criteria based on these objectives?

4. *Do the criteria indicate improvement between expected and actual performance* when measured against the results of your needs analysis?

5. *What data sources are already available to help you measure results?*

6. *Are there alternative methods for generating these data* such as interviews and on-site observations?

7. *What are the best and most cost-effective methods for measuring the results of the training?*

Background Information

In addition to these typical questions, Sredl and Rothwell (1987) recommended the collection of background information on the program, including the following information.

The context of the program. To investigate this aspect, you might ask the following questions:

1. How many trainees annually attend the program?

2. On average, how many trainees attend each offering (session) of the program?

3. How long does the program last?
4. Where is the program usually held? In how many locations?
5. What do supervisors in the organization think about HRD generally? The HRD department? This program?
6. What is the organization's culture like? Where along a continuum between authoritarian and democratic does it fall?
7. What is the history of this program? What led to its being offered?
8. What organizational policies and/or procedures are related to the program, if any?

Program participants. These questions should be asked:

1. What kinds of people attend the program? (Consider job class, tenure with the organization, and attitudes.)
2. How are these people selected? Is attendance mandatory, voluntary, or negotiated? Why are selection procedures handled this way?
3. When are attendees selected? Is there any special cycle of registration? On what is that cycle based?

How the program is conducted. Ask these questions:

1. What are the instructional goals and objectives?
2. What needs assessment method was used? How was it used?
3. Was a front-end analysis performed?
4. How were the instructional objectives verified?
5. What is the purpose of the program?
6. How is the program structured?
7. How is instruction delivered? How were delivery methods selected?
8. What assumptions are made about entry-level skills of trainees? Are prerequisites specified? How are trainees' knowledge and skill levels screened?
9. How much planning precedes each program offering? To what extent is an attempt made to tailor each offering to needs of the group attending?
10. What exercises and media are used? How were they prepared? Tested?

11. By what methods is the program evaluated?
12. How are results of evaluation used?

Program outcomes. Ask these questions:

1. How well have learners liked the program? What accounts for these attitudes?
2. How well have learners performed in the program? What historical information exists on any trends in test scores? How are demonstrations rated?
3. What evidence exists that the program has changed on-the-job performance in a desirable way? In any way?
4. What evidence exists that the program has contributed to higher productivity, higher morale, lower absenteeism, fewer mistakes?
5. What evidence exists to show that participation in the program increased the value of existing human resources? Contributed to achievement of individual career plans? Contributed to achievement of organizational strategic and HR plans?

Levels of Evaluation: Kirkpatrick's Model

One author developed a theoretical model from which evaluation tools might be developed. Kirkpatrick's (1967, 1979) model for evaluation identifies four levels of training impact. It includes the trainees' reactions or attitudes toward a training event (How well did the trainees like the program?), their learning of new knowledge, skills or attitudes (What principles, facts, and techniques were understood and absorbed?), improvements in job behavior (What changes have occurred in the participants' behaviors?), and organizational results (How have turnover, absenteeism, reduction in grievances, and morale changed?).

Hamblin (1974) divided Kirkpatrick's fourth level into noneconomic organizational variables (e.g., quality, employee morale) and ultimate value or economic variables (e.g., sales, costs, profits). Hamblin explained that evaluation at each of the levels of the hierarchy will help to identify the reasons why successful training outcomes might occur at one level but not at the next higher level. For example, employees' general reaction to the training (Kirkpatrick's Level 1) might be quite positive (e.g., the participants enjoyed the training, thought it was interesting), but they could still score low on a knowledge test (Kirkpatrick's Level 2).

Unfortunately, many people attempt to measure only Level 1, reaction. One author pointed out the major problem with this one-shot approach to evaluation:

> It is often said that assessment or validations of training made at the end of a training event can suffer from a contamination which will cast serious doubts on any results. If the course has been a highly successful and enjoyable experience the learners can be so pleased with themselves and the event that they are in a state of euphoria. In this emotive state, particularly as they are saying goodbye to their fellow students with whom they may have formed particular relationships, views expressed on the training may be clouded (Raye, 1986, p. 125).

Establishing the basic criteria that the training must match will help get past this basic level of "reaction." Once these criteria have been identified, then the task becomes one of developing methods to evaluate training events that match the criteria. The following is a fairly comprehensive review of evaluation methods for training programs.

Evaluation Methods

There are a variety of evaluation methods, including the following:

Paper-and-pencil tests: This method measures how well trainees learn program content. An instructor administers paper-and-pencil tests in class to measure participants' progress.

Attitude surveys: These question-and-answer surveys determine what changes in attitude have occurred as a result of training. Practitioners use these surveys to gather information about employees' perceptions, work habits, motivation, values, beliefs, working relations, etc. Attitude surveys also reveal respondents' opinions about their jobs, the workplace, co-workers, supervisors, policies, procedures, and the organization. If you conduct a program to change attitudes, before and after surveys can assess improvement.

Simulation and on-site observation: Instructors or managers' observations of performance on the job or in a job simulation indicate whether a learner's skills have improved as a result of the training.

Productivity reports: Hard production data such as sales reports and manufacturing totals can help managers and instructors determine actual performance improvement on the job.

Post-training surveys: Progress and proficiency assessments by both managers and participants indicate perceived performance improvement on the job.

Needs/Objectives/Content comparison: Training managers, participants, and supervisors compare needs analysis results with course objectives and content to determine whether the program was relevant to participants' needs. Relevancy ratings at the end of the program also contribute to the comparison.

Evaluation forms: Participants' responses on end-of-program evaluation forms indicate what they liked and disliked about the training. While this is an inadequate form of evaluation if used by itself, it does at least give the program planners the participants' immediate holistic response to the training.

Professional opinion: Instructional designers critique and assess the quality of the program design.

Instructor evaluation: Professional trainers administer assessment sheets and evaluation forms to measure the instructor's competence, effectiveness, and instructional skills.

Cost analysis: The training manager compares costs of instructor's fees, materials, facilities, travel, training time, and the number of trainees to determine the hourly cost of training for each individual participant. (Taken from ASTD, 1988 Info-Line, p. 8)

A review of current evaluation forms reveals a lack of well-developed instruments to measure more than the immediate reaction of participants. As a result I have developed an instrument to measure the impact of training on behavior changes and job performance in more detail.

▋ *Training Impact Questionnaire*

Kirkpatrick's (1979) hierarchy appears to provide the clearest and most comprehensive assessment of training impact. Sredl and Rothwell (1987), developed a model demonstrating ways to evaluate each of Kirkpatrick's levels of assessment (see Figure 15.1). This model served as the basis for the development of the Training Impact Questionnaire (TIQ) included in this chapter. Most organizational training evaluation takes place at the first level, participants' overall reaction to the training program. The amount of knowledge acquired, the second level, can be fairly easily measured with objective tests. Level 4, impact on organizational variables, can be measured with organizational outcome data (e.g., turnover rate, absentee records, etc.).

In Figure 15.1 Kirkpatrick's four levels are identified as well as the additional level recommended by Hamblin. I decided that Level 3, behav-

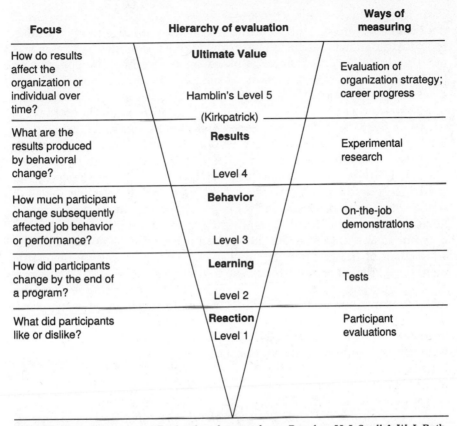

Focus	Hierarchy of evaluation	Ways of measuring
How do results affect the organization or individual over time?	Ultimate Value Hamblin's Level 5 —— (Kirkpatrick) ——	Evaluation of organization strategy; career progress
What are the results produced by behavioral change?	Results Level 4	Experimental research
How much participant change subsequently affected job behavior or performance?	Behavior Level 3	On-the-job demonstrations
How did participants change by the end of a program?	Learning Level 2	Tests
What did participants like or dislike?	Reaction Level 1	Participant evaluations

FIGURE 15.1   Hierarchy of Evaluation Approaches   Based on H. J. Sredl & W. J. Rothwell, *The ASTD Reference Guide to Professional Training Roles and Competencies, 1 & 2*, New York: Random House, 1987.

ioral changes and application to job tasks, would be the focus of this research. Kirkpatrick's Level 3 is similar to Bloom's Taxonomy (Bloom, Englehart, Faurst, Hill, and Krothwohl, 1956). The levels of knowledge as described by Bloom include: knowledge, comprehension, application, analysis, synthesis, and evaluation.

The instrument described here addresses Level 3, behavior. Redding (1984) suggested that an "organization has a right to expect that, as a result of being trained, all trainees will demonstrate at least three behavioral outcomes . . . cooperation . . . comprehension . . . and competence" (p. 9). Competence refers to the obvious fact that the trainees must be equipped with the techniques and the resources to function in their organizational role at an acceptable standard of expertise.

A systematic assessment of behavioral changes after training and the participants' ability to apply those changes to job tasks are a critical part of the evaluation process. At the same time, little evidence exists that this type of evaluation is conducted with any degree of confidence. The instrument described in this chapter is based on participants' perceptions of their ability to apply learned skills to the job compared to a supervisor's assessment of their job performance.

Newstrom (1978) discussed the need for all four levels of Kirkpatrick's model to be included in any evaluation of training. Consequently, while the TIQ is an attempt to go beyond the typical reaction questionnaire used in organizations, it also is designed to include both Level 1 and Level 3 of Kirkpatrick's model. These two levels must be evaluated by the participants and/or their superiors and subordinates while Level 2 (knowledge) must be developed for each unique training experience and Level 4 (organizational variables) must be measured with organizational outcome data. All four levels should be measured for a comprehensive assessment of training impact (see DeWine, 1987, for details on instrument development and reliability and validity tests).

Training evaluation is critical to successful human resource development. Currently, organizations are evaluating the reactions of participants but doing little to assess the impact of communication training on other levels of Kirkpatrick's hierarchy. The TIQ is an attempt to provide a tool with which to measure the application of the perceived level of skill learned on the job as well as the degree to which the participant perceived the skill has been mastered.

Strong internal reliability and validity tests suggest that this instrument can measure these factors successfully. The instrument should be administered 2 to 4 weeks following the training program so that impact and not reaction to training is measured. A specific skill taught during the training is identified and the respondent answers questions regarding that skill. Supervisors, as well as subordinates, are also asked to complete the questionnaire in order to measure observations of the training participants' skill performances (see Forms 15.1 and 15.2 participant's and supervisor's forms of the TIQ). A comparison of supervisors' and subordinates' perceptions of the participants' ability to apply the skill to the job helps to identify the extent to which self perceptions are in conflict with others' observations of behavioral change.

This instrument, as well as the many other forms of evaluation listed earlier, can be used in several different study designs. For example, the evaluator may need to have information about the participants' knowledge of a subject matter prior to the training to determine how much they have learned from the training itself; therefore a before-and-after design would be used. Another way to determine more percisely the impact of training is to compare a group of participants with nonparticipants, or a

■ PARTICIPANT'S TRAINING IMPACT QUESTIONNAIRE

Several weeks ago you participated in the _____ training program. The purpose of this survey is to show how much the program has helped you on the job.

The survey consists of skills that were presented in the program. Feel free to answer honestly. Your answers will be confidential and will be used only for improving the program. Thank you for helping to improve the program.

Instructions

You will be asked to evaluate each skill presented in the training program. The survey lists a skill and then gives a series of statements about that skill. Mark your reaction to each statement on the accompanying answer sheets.

Mark your response as follows:

1—strongly disagree (statement never true)

2—disagree (statement rarely true)

3—sometimes agree and sometimes disagree

4—agree (statement usually true)

5—strongly agree (statement always true)

Please respond to all statements. Thank you.

Skill A: _____

_____

Please fill in the appropriate response for each item on the answer sheet.

1. I use this skill regularly on the job.
2. After this training program I would perform this skill without practicing.
3. I didn't learn this skill in the training program, so I had to learn it on the job.
4. I perform the skill differently on the job because work conditions don't permit me to perform it the way I learned in the training program.

(Continued)

305

**■ PARTICIPANT'S TRAINING IMPACT
QUESTIONNAIRE** *(Continued)*

5. I perform the skill differently on the job because the skill doesn't work the way I learned it in training.

6. I perform the skill differently on the job because my supervisor told me to do it differently.

7. I never perform this skill on the job.

8. The skill isn't part of my job.

9. I get help to perform the skill because I didn't learn it in the training program.

10. I don't perform the skill on the job because the skill is too difficult for me.

11. I don't perform the skill on the job because the skill comes up so rarely that I forget how to do it.

12. I don't perform the skill because I was assigned a different job.

13. I learned to perform the task well in the training program because the program was effective.

14. The skill could be learned from a manual or an instruction sheet as easily as in a training program.

15. I had trouble learning the skill because the training program was confusing.

16. The skill would have been easier to learn with more reference materials.

17. Because of learning this skill I feel more comfortable about doing my job.

18. Because of attending this training program, I feel better about the company.

19. After attending this training program, I am interested in attending other training programs.

20. I think my participation in this training program will help me to advance in the company.

*Reverse score these items: 3,4,5,6,7,8,9,10,11,12,14,15,16

*Sum items for two scores:
   Relationship of skill to the job: 1,2,3,4,10,14,20,21,22,23
   Skill performance: 5,6,7,8,9,11,12,13,16,19

■ SUPERVISOR'S TRAINING IMPACT QUESTIONNAIRE

Several weeks ago one of your employees participated in the _____

_____ training program. The purpose of this survey is to show how much the program has helped him or her on the job.

The survey consists of skills that were presented in the program. Feel free to answer honestly. Your answers will be confidential and will be used for improving the program.

Instructions

The survey lists a skill and then gives a series of statements about that skill. Mark your reaction to each statement on the accompanying answer sheets.

Mark your response as follows:

1—strongly disagree (statement never true)

2—disagree (statement rarely true)

3—sometimes agree and sometimes disagree

4—agree (statement usually true)

5—strongly agree (statement always true)

Please respond to all statements. Thank you.

Skill A: _____

Please fill in the appropriate response for each item on the answer sheet.

1. My employee uses this skill regularly on the job.
2. After training he or she has been able to perform this skill without practicing.
3. He or she didn't learn this skill in the training program, so he or she had to learn it on the job.
4. Work conditions don't allow him or her to perform the skill the way he or she learned it in training, so he or she does the task differently on the job.
5. He or she performs the skill differently on the job because I, as his or her supervisor, told him or her to do it differently.

(Continued)

■ **SUPERVISOR'S TRAINING IMPACT**
QUESTIONNAIRE *(Continued)*

6. He or she never performs this skill on the job.

7. The skill isn't part of his or her job.

8. He or she doesn't perform the skill on the job because he or she didn't learn the skill in the training program, so he or she gets help to do the skill.

9. He or she performs the skill well on the job because the skill is easy for him or her.

10. He or she doesn't perform the skill on the job because the skill comes up so rarely that he or she forgets how to do it.

11. He or she doesn't perform the skill because he or she was assigned a different job.

12. He or she learned to perform the task well in the training program, but could have learned it just as easily from a manual or an instruction sheet.

13. Because of learning this skill he or she feels more comfortable about doing his or her job.

"control" group. The consultant or trainer might administer before-and-after testing of both the participants and the nonparticipants. In any case, the evaluator should plan carefully what evaluation method will be used so that the data are the most meaningful.

Nadler (1982) has called for more research on human resource development programs as well as evaluation of the immediate impact of the training on individuals and the organization. With training programs increasing dramatically, organizations need valid tools by which to measure the impact of these training programs. The TIQ will provide an important mechanism by which to accomplish this task. One thing is quite clear: when no formal, well-developed evaluation of training is in place, the organization has little idea whether the training is helpful or harmful. When billions of dollars are being spent it would certainly seem prudent to ensure those dollars are invested wisely.

■ Suggested Readings

Arnold, W. E., & McClure, L. (1989). Evaluating training programs. In W. Arnold & L. McClure, *Communication training and development* (117–28). New York, NY: Harper and Row.

DeWine, S. (1987). Evaluation of organizational communication competency: The development of the communication training impact questionnaire. *Journal of Applied Communication Research, 15*, pp. 113–27.

Pace, R. W., & Faules, D. F. (1989). The design, conduct, and evaluation of human resource training. In R. W. Pace & D. F. Faules, *Organizational communication.* (2nd ed.) (303–23). Englewood Cliffs, NJ: Prentice Hall.

Chapter 16

STRATEGIES FOR EVALUATING CONSULTING

Once upon a time in the land of Fuzz, King Aling called in his cousin Ding and commanded, "Go ye out into all of Fuzzland and find me the goodest of men, whom I shall reward for his goodness."

"But how will I know one when I see one?" asked the Fuzzy.

"Why, he will be sincere,*" scoffed the king, and whacked off a leg for his impertinence.*

So, the Fuzzy limped out to find a good man. But soon he returned, confused and empty-handed.

"But how will I know one when I see one?" he asked again.

"Why, he will be dedicated,*" grumbled the king, and whacked off another leg for his impertinence.*

So the Fuzzy hobbled away once more to look for the goodest of men. But again he returned, confused and empty-handed.

"But how will I know one when I see one?" he pleaded.

"Why, he will have internalized his growing awareness,*" fumed the king, and whacked off another leg for his impertinence.*

So the Fuzzy, now on his last leg, hopped out to continue his search. In time, he returned with the wisest, most sincere and dedicated Fuzzy in all of Fuzzland, and stood him before the king.

"Why, this man won't do at all," roared the king. "He is much too thin to suit me." Whereupon, he whacked off the last leg of the Fuzzy, who fell to the floor with a squishy thump.

The moral of this fable is that . . . if you can't tell one when you see one, you may wind up without a leg to stand on.

Robert Mager
Goal Analysis, 1972

*I*f you don't know how to tell when you are successful at solving human communication problems, then you may not have a leg to stand on, or a platform from which to launch your activities! You need to be articulate about how the client will know when the problem has been solved.

The evaluation needs to assess the relationship between the consultant or communication manager and the client, the results of intervention into interpersonal relationships in the group, the progress the organization has made toward reaching its overall goals, and how much the group's activities have contributed to that achievement.

Information can be collected from the consultant/manager, the client system, outcome data like attitude surveys or turnover rates, and bottom-line figures. Standard data collecting methods discussed in Chapter 4 are used: observation, interviews, content analysis, questionnaires, personnel and demographic data, and company publications and documents. Using these approaches and methods, how does one go about organizing an evaluation program for consulting?

▌ *Criteria for Evaluating a Consultation*

While there are a variety of methods for evaluating the success of a consultation, the following are the criteria I have found to be the most indicative of success: consultant effectiveness, consultant satisfaction, client satisfaction, and project outcome.

Evaluating the Consultant's Effectiveness

Lippitt and Lippitt (1986) posed the following organizing questions to evaluate the competency of the consultant:

Does the consultant's relationship with the client model interpersonal relations for the group? The consultant must be a role model for the kind of relationships that need to exist for the group to be successful. The way in which you interact with the client speaks volumes about your ability to train others to function as a team.

Does the consultant make sure contractual arrangements are clear from the outset? During the entry stage, the consultant and the client should establish exactly what each is willing to do, when it will be done, and how they will tell when they are done. Expectations of each party to the contract must be clearly identified.

Does the consultant really have the skills needed to help solve the client's problem? One of the worst things a consultant can do is claim talents and abilities that she or he does not possess. To raise expectations and not deliver is worse than doing nothing at all. You need to be very clear about what you can and cannot do.

Does the consultant gain influence in the client organization through appropriate means? The consultant usually does not have the power to change the organization but must convince others to make changes. For that reason it is very important that the consultant have the ear of the decision makers. Employees must feel that what they tell the consultant will be listened to by top management. Often individuals feel the best way to get top management to hear their concerns is to say them through another voice.

Does the consultant track clients to apply what is learned independently rather than rely on the consultant? As an outside consultant, I always assume that my job is to work myself out of a job. If the client is depending on me on a permanent basis to continue to solve problems for the group, then I become an internal employee. It also indicates a lack of talent in the group. I am usually able to identify an individual who has at least some ability to solve human communication problems. I work at having that individual step into my role as an insider. This can also be true of internal consultants since they should not become permanently attached to one particular unit in the organization.

Does the consultant treat others nonjudgmentally and with respect? The consultant's greatest asset is objectivity. This means treating each person with respect. The consultant cannot afford the luxury of identifying the "good guys" and the "bad guys." People sense when you are looking out for your own welfare at the expense of theirs.

Does the consultant keep clients' information to him- or herself? If you want to find out what's going on, you have to be able to reassure people that what they tell you in confidence will not be individually attributed. If something they share with you in private comes back to them through other sources, they will know not to trust you. You must also be careful not to inadvertently pass along private information because even though your intentions may be good, the impact will be the same. People will try giving you less important bits of information to see what you do with it. You will be "on trial," so watch your step!

Can the consultant identify the problem and keep it in focus? Often the client does not know how to identify the problem. It may be disguised as something else. In one case the top manager trusted one assistant but not the other and yet the problem was described as "needing to have clearer job descriptions for the two assistants." It is the consultant's job to help the client articulate the problem and focus on it until some resolution is reached. Clients may try to sidetrack outside consultants because, although they know they may need help, they may also like to avoid the problem, hope it goes away, and when it doesn't get solved, blame the consultant for not solving it!

Does the consultant explain the role the client is expected to play and the contribution the client is expected to make? I recently had a group ask me to interview all members of one unit and then plan a feedback session between top management and the unit members. When it was time for the retreat, unit members said they were afraid the head of the unit would not listen to them. They felt that all he did was talk *at* them about his goals and objectives but that he did not listen to their concerns. I had a meeting beforehand with the unit head and made it clear that during the retreat his role was to listen and if he began talking I would tap him on the shoulder and remind him to listen. I had to do it only twice during the retreat and he got the message. Clients want to know exactly what you expect of them. Their role should always be clearly defined.

Is the consultant willing to undergo an evaluation of his or her services? Good consultants and communication managers want to know how they are doing. Chapter 9 provided tips on giving feedback to others. The consultant may have to train the client in providing feedback, but it certainly should be welcomed.

Evaluating the Consultant's Satisfaction

Some of the questions you might ask yourself in an evaluation of your satisfaction with a particular consulting assignment include:

Did you fully accomplish what you promised in the initial proposal?

In addition to completing work objectives, did your efforts lead to the desired results?

Did the client benefit from your services?

Had you performed your duties differently, would the outcomes have changed?

Did the results occur even though you did not complete the work as promised?

Did the consulting expense exceed the possible benefits?

Were you pleased with the project's conduct and success?

Did you enjoy consulting on the project?

How do you feel about your relationship to the client?

Were you able to establish professional trust and rapport?

Would you consult with this client again? (Kelley, 1981)

You are not the only or necessarily the best source of assessment for your own success. However, these questions are a good place to begin the evaluation. A part of your success depends on your own satisfaction with your work. Next, you must assess your client's satisfaction.

Evaluating the Client's Satisfaction

Holtz (1989) suggested to clients who are hiring consultants, six criteria used to assess the impact of the consultant's work. First, is *enthusiasm*. Enthusiasm indicates the depth and degree of a consultant's interest in the task. Second, *leadership*. In many cases consultants are called upon to lead the client's staff in writing or assembling a proposal, for example. Third, *presentation*. This may refer to a formal presentation to an assembled group or there may be occasions when it refers to instruction of a client's staff by the consultant. Fourth, *efficiency*. When you have a new employee, you may be able to permit that person a few weeks to become oriented and to make a full contribution but you cannot afford that luxury with a consultant. Fifth, *effectiveness*. This is closely related to efficiency and yet it is not the same thing. Effectiveness refers to the degree to which the desired end result is achieved. A consultant may be efficient, in other words finish whatever he or she does with great speed and, yet, not produce the result desired. Finally, *openness*. It refers to the consultant's willingness to share what he or she knows with the client and the client's staff. It means honest and conscientious work but does not hold back information (pp. 185–86).

Evaluating the Project Outcome

Fuchs (1975) suggested three broad areas in which to evaluate the success of the consulting project. First, comparing the performance against the proposal. This includes an assessment of the objectives of the consultant's assignment, a clear understanding of the scope of the undertaking, what findings were to be expected, and results to be accomplished, time schedule and starting date, project costs, staff personnel. These are measurable outcome variables and can be clearly defined. There may be a need to identify some intervening variables that cannot be controlled. For example, even though the client and consultant agree on a starting date, it might be delayed because of external factors that neither the client nor the consultant can control.

Second, the consultant's contribution to the company's financial position is another area for evaluation. This includes a statement of income and expense less sales returns and allowances, cost of goods sold and manufactured, direct labor, selling costs, and accounts receivable. How did the consulting intervention affect these outcomes?

Third is long-term benefits. Rudolph and Johnson (1983) pointed to the problems involved in failing to recognize this criterion. They suggested:

Many beginning communication consultants feel a postseminar/workshop form is adequate, but the form does not measure any end result or impact on the organization. All it measures is the seminar/workshop participants' reactions to the session leaders and the immediate reactions to items asked, such as the number of assignments, amounts of interaction, adequacy of the meeting room, session content, quality of food, and the participants' perception of how useful the information covered in the session will be when they get back to the job. This information is invaluable when it comes to determining success and learning at the session but it does not answer the question about changes stemming from the sessions (p. 53).

Long-term benefits may be the most important measurement of the consulting activity. While actively engaged, the consultant should materially raise the competence level of the people in the organization. This should be accomplished by demonstrating leadership ability that encourages project team managers to perform in a superior manner. The consultant should be the catalyst in making things happen and in reshaping the areas of the company in need of constructive change (pp. 140–41).

While all of the above suggestions provide guidance for the evaluation of a particular assignment, the consultant must judge him- or herself as well. Your own professional development program will identify standards by which to measure your own success.

Professional Development

The consultants or communication specialists are often so busy helping other people improve their skills that they forget to work on their own development in a consistent fashion. You must practice what you profess to be good for others.

Phillips (1987) suggested that a trainer or consultant must have a personal development model that contains three essential elements: a sound grounding and working familiarity with a body of knowledge, research, and theory; a development of skills including listening, presenting, observing, sensing, supporting, challenging, and diagnosing; and the development of self or who one is, one's beliefs, values, and life experiences. Knowledge, skills, and self-confidence are the attributes needed to achieve success.

Bard and Stephen (1987) have produced a professional development checksheet for trainers to be filled out by the trainer and his or her manager. It asks respondents to list the priority of the performance statement as well as the degree of competency the individual has in that area. Form 16.1 lists those competencies. They suggested,

■ THE LEARNING NEEDS ASSESSMENT SCALE

Learning Needs

The Assessment Scale generates two kinds of data: your most important job functions and your present competency level for thirty-seven areas within eight functions. When completing the scale, choose a number from 1 to 5 to rate each; 1 is the lowest rating, 5 the highest.

For the priority rating use the following guide:

0 You do not perform that function.

1 You occasionally perform the function, but it is not critical to the organization now or in the near future.

2 You regularly perform the function, but it is not critical and is unlikely to become so in the near future.

3 You regularly perform the function, and it is necessary and may become more important in the near future.

4 You perform the function occasionally now but may perform it more frequently in the future, and it is critical to your job.

5 You perform the function frequently, and it is critical to your job.

For the competency rating use the following guide:

0 You are not able to perform the function.

1 You can perform the function partially or with difficulty and lack most of the skills and knowledge you require.

2 You can perform the function, but there are significant skills and knowledge you need to acquire.

3 You are competent in performing the function but still need to acquire more knowledge or experience to feel fully confident.

4 You are at mastery level but can still increase your performance by increasing your skills and knowledge.

5 You can perform at a level of excellence and don't need any additional skills or knowledge at this time.

(Continued)

■ **THE LEARNING NEEDS ASSESSMENT SCALE** *(Continued)*

	Ratings (0–5 scale)			
Functions and Performance Statements	**Priority**		**Competency**	
	Mine	Manager's	Mine	Manager's
1. Learning Needs Assessment				
Use competency-based models, performance analysis, and other needs assessment techniques.				
Design and use various instruments, surveys, questionnaires, and other data-collection methods.				
Analyze data and translate into program needs.				
2. Develop Learning Strategies and Designs				
Select best strategies to meet learning needs.				
Use adult learning theory and principles.				
Develop learning objectives and designs.				
Use diverse learning methods.				
3. Provide Learning Materials				
Research and collect information from print and nonprint sources.				
Develop multimedia materials.				
Write and produce case studies, exercises, manuals, and other print materials.				
Evaluate film, software, packaged programs, and other vendor materials for rental and purchase.				

(Continued)

THE LEARNING NEEDS ASSESSMENT SCALE *(Continued)*

Functions and Performance Statements	Ratings (0–5 scale)			
	Priority		Competency	
	Mine	Manager's	Mine	Manager's
4. Facilitate Group Learning Activities				
Use effective presentation methods.				
Use group interaction methods.				
Use full range of learning methods.				
Use audiovisual equipment and materials.				
Use computer-based instruction.				
5. Evaluate Learning Results				
Design and use methods and instruments to collect learning-related data.				
Formulate recommendations for program redesign.				
6. Internal Consulting				
Conduct data collection and problem analysis.				
Formulate strategies and develop plans to solve learning-related problems.				
Contract with in-house clients regarding problem analysis as well as strategies and resources required to solve learning problems.				
Prepare organizational climate for change.				
Work with a wide variety of personalities and styles to implement plans.				
Evaluate effectiveness of strategies and plans.				

(Continued)

■ THE LEARNING NEEDS ASSESSMENT SCALE *(Continued)*

Functions and Performance Statements	Ratings (0–5 scale)			
	Priority		Competency	
	Mine	Manager's	Mine	Manager's
7. Individual Counseling				
Assist individuals to assess learning needs and develop learning plans.				
Provide learning-related information and resources.				
8. Management				
Develop and maintain a positive working relationship with line and upper management.				
Communicate the importance of human resource development to line management and upper management.				
Develop yearly and multiyear training and development plans.				
Develop yearly and multiyear budgets.				
Select competent staff.				
Develop positive work environment for staff.				
Effectively supervise and motivate staff.				
Contract with, manage, and evaluate consultants.				
Schedule and coordinate staff, facilities, materials, and equipment to meet program goals.				

(Continued)

■ **THE LEARNING NEEDS ASSESSMENT SCALE** *(Continued)*

Functions and Performance Statements	Ratings (0–5 scale)			
	Priority		Competency	
	Mine	Manager's	Mine	Manager's
Management *(Continued)*				
Develop and maintain an information system providing performance data to staff, management, and other departments.				
Evaluate individual staff and program performance.				

From Ray Bard & Leslie Stephen, Developing Your Learning Plan, in *The Trainer's Professional Development Handbook* by Ray Bard, Chip R. Bell, Leslie Stephen, and Linda Webster. San Francisco: Jossey-Bass. Copyright © 1987 Jossey-Bass, pp. 27–40. Permission to reproduce granted.

If your plan is to work HRD [Human Resource Development] for a few years as part of your career path, the development of a learning plan can help you focus your professional growth while in the field. You will also find the expertise required in learning how to direct your development will be valuable when you move to other departments in the organization. If you have chosen HRD as your profession, the continued acquisition of new skills and knowledge is one of the essentials of becoming and remaining a competent professional (p. 27).

Lippitt and Lippitt (1986) pointed out the need for all professionals to participate in a professional association, discipline, or education process to maintain competency. All professionals should be engaged in life-long development and learning. In order to bring the best techniques for working with others to the relationship, consultants and communication specialists must constantly be attending workshops and seminars and receiving higher education. Anyone not doing that is in jeopardy of bringing less than his or her best effort to the client system.

These evaluation methods will generate data that must sometimes be statistically analyzed. Knowing when you have meaningful results is critical.

Interpreting the Meaning of Statistics

In Chapter 5 I identified a number of statistical tests that can be applied to organizational data. Statistical tests will tell you if you have a significant result, but they cannot tell you if that result is meaningful.

For example, I worked with a client who wanted to measure the impact of their training program on employee attitudes about the company. We administered a pre- and post-test on employee satisfaction with the company. There were statistically significant differences in participants' scores after the training session. However, the meaningfulness of those results was less clear since the turnover rate and absenteeism did not decrease. Is a 3.4 on a 5.0 scale meaningful? What does it mean when someone checks the midpoint? The respondent may not have an opinion, be undecided, feel both a little positive and a little negative, or simply not have any basis for judgement. Thus, I believe statistical results must always be accompanied with more "rich" data that help explain the statistical analysis and make it meaningful.

Choosing Evaluation Techniques

Figure 16.1 identifies a variety of techniques that can be used for evaluation. It compares the evaluation methods most appropriate for consult-

Kirkpatrick's 4 levels of training evaluation	Consult	Train	Teach	Counsel
Reaction	band-aid stops bleeding	"happy-gram"	teacher evaluations	reduced stress test
Knowledge	internal consultant	objective tests	objective essay/test	self-awareness questionnaire
Behavior	MBO system	DeWine's TIQ	behavioral objectives	client is more competent
Organizational outcomes	problem is solved	turnover rate is decreased	job place-ment is successful	positive impact on family

FIGURE 16.1   Evaluation Methods

ing with those appropriate for teaching, training, and counseling. For example, if the client wants only an immediate reaction to how well the consulting went, then determining whether the "band-aid" stopped the "bleeding" is all that is necessary. In other words, did the brief intervention provide immediate relief? Or if we want to examine the degree to which knowledge has increased, an internal consultant test could be developed which is designed to measure the knowledge base acquired by the internal consultant about the client.

On the other hand, consulting often deals with changing behavior, and a Management By Objectives (MBO) system would help track this. If a change in behavior is the goal, then the manager and the employee would need to identify the change and agree on a way to measure whether it has in fact changed.

Finally, evaluating the success of the consulting intervention in terms of organizational outcomes can be accomplished by determining when the problem is solved and is no longer an issue. The client and the consultant need to agree on the indicators of its resolution.

The techniques listed for training evaluation were discussed in the previous chapter. Teaching and consulting are also listed since these helping professions have many things in common with consulting (see Chapters 2 and 3). Since teaching is a more long-term relationship, the evaluation methods can be more long term as well. The counseling evaluation methods are much more personal. For example, to measure the success of consulting on a "reaction" level, one might measure the amount of reduction in stress an individual experiences, with a pre- and post-intervention measurement.

These techniques can all be valid ways of determining an individual's effectiveness as a consultant as well as the success of a total intervention.

Consultant's Tips

Evaluation is a critical, but often neglected, area of consulting. Usually it is not thought about until the intervention is practically completed. The method of evaluation should be selected during the first step of designing the entire intervention. In other words, evaluation is a front-end activity as well as a terminating ritual.

- Do *some* kind of evaluation even if it is only on the reaction level. Use whatever is available until you are able to infuse the system with a more comprehensive evaluation program.

- *Be sure to ask the right questions.* Several lists of potential questions have been provided in this chapter. Some you must ask of yourself and some must be asked of others. It is always good to check your perception of yourself and your activities with the perceptions of those you are helping.

- *Be responsive to feedback.* If your consulting activities are going to be evaluated then you must be open to suggestions for change or else there is no reason to conduct the evaluation.

- Others will be watching you for guidance as you *handle negative feedback.* As a role model you need to show how action can be taken on suggestions for improvement.

We cannot determine where we should head next if we don't have a good understanding of where we have been. Evaluation must be a planned activity from the beginning of the intervention or one cannot hope to move the group forward.

Suggested Readings

Blake, R. R., & Mouton, J. S. (1989). *Consultation* (2nd ed.). Reading, MA: Addison-Wesley Publishing Co., Inc.

Block, P. (1981). *Flawless consulting: A guide to getting your expertise used.* San Diego, CA: University Associates.

Lippitt, G., & Lippitt, R. (1986). *The consulting process in action* (2nd ed.). San Diego, CA: University Associates.

PART VI

Professional Development for the Consultant

The last section of the book focuses on personal issues for the consultant or communication manager. Chapter 17 addresses issues related to forming friendships and romances in the organization. Since people spend a great deal of time at work, personal relationships will develop. The consultant needs to be aware of the impact of such relationships for two reasons: it may affect the group with whom you are working, and it may affect your own relationships with individuals. I hope this chapter is thought-provoking and provides some insights about how undisclosed relationships can make situations worse.

Chapter 18 deals with professional development topics as well as issues related to starting your own firm: taxes, legal forms, marketing your services, and maintaining clients. This is a very practical chapter that will give you some clear guidance for beginning the job of being a consultant. Much of this information relates specifically to an outside consultant rather than an inside employee.

Chapter *17*

FRIENDSHIPS, ROMANCES, AND WORKING RELATIONSHIPS

"Women are far more likely to form close relationships with one another (at work) than their male counterparts with whom they engage in intimate and sympathetic conversation. Their greater needs for affiliation lead women to open up with a rapport and honesty unprecedented in relationships between male colleagues."

L. B. Rubin
Just Friends: The role of friendship in our lives, *1985*

*F*riendships are formed, romantic liaisons established, and marriages are born, all at work. Men and women working together on challenging, exciting projects are attracted to the work and to each other. They also react differently to friendships which are formed at work. Consultants and managers who are not aware of the importance of these relationships to the organization and to the work, are likely to be caught off guard when they occur.

In particular, the consultants' greatest advantage is their objectivity. When consultants place themselves in a position of friendship or special relationship to anyone in the organization, then their effectiveness is greatly jeopardized. At the same time, the consultant is often attempting to establish teams without knowledge of the personal relationships existing among team members. Not taking these relationships into account may hurt that process.

Kanter (1983) suggested,

> It is in the post-entrepreneurial corporation's interest for its members to have a generalized team feeling and emotional absorption in the work itself, but not to center feelings on particular people. Any strong attachment to something or someone other than the task at hand is likely to pose a threat to the openness, inclusion, collaboration, and trust essential to post-entrepreneurial organizations. It limits the flexibility to redeploy people. It is distracting to both those participating in it and those observing (pp. 284–85).

This belief is shared by many in the organization, and yet to believe we can disallow interpersonal relationships is certainly naive. In fact, recent research suggested that employees are more tolerant of romantic relationships at work than is commonly believed (DeWine, Pearson, and

Yost, in press). What we can do is learn to identify these natural links within the group, help individuals understand when their relationship is hurting the effectiveness of the group, and work with them for some resolution. In this chapter, professional relationships, friendships, and romantic pairs are explored in the context of improving the general climate of the organization.

Professional Relationships

Schindler-Raiman (1987) described a cluster of value changes that have influenced attitudes toward work, including interpersonal relationships in the workplace. The rapidity of change in the modern world has created an environment of uncertainty. This uncertainty has resulted in an acceptance of temporary bonds and multiple loyalties in one's personal and professional life rather than the emphasis on permanent commitments and single loyalties. Respect for authority has changed to confrontation and questioning of authority figures.

The effect of the work environment on individual workers has gained more attention from management as employees have demanded an improved quality of work life and a healthy environment. Instead of conforming to established patterns of time, employees are developing new ways of organizing time to their personal advantage.

All these changes suggest greater recognition of employees as individuals, who relate to each other on a personal basis rather than as interchangeable functionaries, whose relationships can be predicted according to job title. For the consultant or communication manager, recognition of the uniqueness of interpersonal work relationships affects both how one structures organizational communication and how one interacts personally with one's own co-workers.

Gender and Professional Relationships

While women have attacked the "good old boy" system for its discrimination against women, it has provided men with natural links to other professionals who can help them get their job done. Women recognize the value of such professional relationships and resent the fact that they have been denied access to valuable networks that would support their careers and jobs.

When one of my colleagues accepted a top-level executive position in a corporation, she soon learned how difficult it would be to train the previously all-male group of executives to give her access to the same networks they enjoyed. Within the first month of the job, the CEO informed her that he and the other six top-level executives of the company would be taking their annual fishing trip and staying in his condo at Hilton Head. He explained that this "retreat" always helped them work out problems that needed the support of all members to resolve. He apologized that it was too bad she couldn't go. He didn't realize that he had hired an individual who wasn't about to accept things as they had always been.

Her first task was to convince the CEO of the great disadvantage to her if she was left out of this important informal communication. Her second, and perhaps more difficult, task was to assure him that it would not lead to suspicions by the spouses that there would be any suggestion of inappropriate behavior since this would now be a co-ed group. She recommended a talented consultant to work with the group on establishing team behavior, and the impact of a female on their all-male retreat. They decided to rent two condos, bring the consultant (who was also a female) along and make their previously all-male "bonding" trip a high-level team-building session instead.

Knowing that informal settings are important for team-building activities, the consultant suggested developing various activities that all members could participate in. Since the new female executive did not particularly enjoy fishing, she worked toward a compromise.

"John, isn't it true that Roy doesn't like fishing?" Well yes, the CEO agreed that Roy usually found some other activity to participate in by himself on the afternoons they went fishing. "And isn't it true that most of the other executives also play golf?" Yes, that was true. "So why not," she asked, "play golf on one afternoon and go fishing on one other afternoon so that all of the group could participate in at least one of the activities they enjoyed?" and have an opportunity to spend time with the CEO in an informal setting. In the end, he agreed. For the first time this group enjoyed a retreat in an informal setting, where team members could appreciate each other as individuals within a "mixed" group.

Relationships with Bosses and Clients

We all know that more deals get cut on the golf course than in the board room. Those professional relationships make negotiating easier. You work harder to reach a compromise with someone you know and like. While you are negotiating on Friday, it is much more difficult to turn down your golfing partner, whom you expect to see on the course again

Sunday morning. It is much easier to turn away a stranger to whom you have no professional commitment.

At the same time, I believe that sometimes only a fine line separates professional relationships, platonic friendships, and romance. The consultant or manager who socializes with only some of the staff, to the exclusion of others, will pay the price of supposed favoritism. No matter how fair the individual may attempt to be, others' perceptions of that fairness will always be tarnished by their observation of those close, personal conversations that are likely to occur in informal surroundings.

It is difficult to draw that line especially since we are spending so much time at work that it naturally becomes the place where friendships are formed. Joseph Straub (1992) suggested to new executives,

> Keep your distance without losing rapport . . . . As a supervisor, you have to relinquish some of the easygoing relationships you enjoyed before you left the rank and file to join management. When you need a sympathetic ear, try talking to your spouse, friends outside of work, or co-workers at your own level—but not subordinates (p. 3).

I think this is especially true for the consultant. By the very nature of your position, you are an "outsider" hired to provide an objective view of life in an organization. Once you lose that objectivity, you are less useful to the organization. At the same time, individuals must feel they can talk informally with you about problems and concerns and that they will not have to come to your office to do the talking.

Socializing with your boss or client can be an aid to developing trust but it can also backfire. I suggest the following guidelines for conversation with clients or your boss in social settings (DeWine, 1989b):

Take cues from your boss or client. If your boss or client keeps business out of the conversation, it is risky for you to mention office matters. If you are unsure whether something is appropriate, refer to it briefly and watch the reaction. Nonverbal behavior (sitting back, looking away) can be a clue that your boss or client doesn't feel comfortable talking about the subject.

Drink in moderation or not at all. Even if a few drinks don't normally affect you, it's smart to stick to a wine spritzer or a beer if you feel that drinking is appropriate because your boss or client is drinking. Drinking more isn't worth the risk of saying or doing something you'll later regret.

Avoid revealing personal information. No matter what your boss or client chooses to tell you about his or her personal affairs, it is not smart to talk about your marital, family, financial, or health problems. Nor is it advisable to betray any lack of confidence about your professional abilities, your career choice, or your job.

Be cautious in your comments about other staff members. If you are asked your opinion of other employees or what you know about them personally, don't be overly critical. Instead, try to address your boss or client's concern and offer suggestions on how the problem situation could be remedied. If, for example, you are asked whether you have noticed that a colleague has a drinking problem, talk about ways the person might be helped rather than focusing on the times he or she has been late or has botched an assignment.

Keep the socializing "professional" if your boss is of the opposite sex. The more relaxed the setting, the more opportunity there is for misinterpretation of language and behavior. Individuals who suspect that their boss or client's intention may be romantic or sexual are smart to bring up their spouses, "significant others," or family in the conversation.

Don't confuse your role as a colleague with your role as a friend. If your boss or client invites you out more often than your colleagues, don't advertise that fact. Your colleagues may be reluctant to share information or work closely with you if they feel you have access to the boss or client that they don't.

■ *Mentoring*[1]

One type of relationship that bridges the gap between strictly professional relationships and those that are more personal is a **mentoring** relationship. Mentoring relationships can be formalized programs established by the organization to assimilate new employees or can occur naturally between colleagues who develop a close personal relationship as well.

Ever since the Greek poet Homer's "faithful and wise" Mentor first advised Odysseus, wise individuals have counseled, coached, and taught the young. When Odysseus was away from home for many years, he entrusted his son, Telemachus, to his friend and advisor, Mentor. While Odysseus was gone, Mentor served as guardian, teacher, and father figure to his young protégé. Since those ancient times there have been mentors and protégés in virtually every discipline and career area.

Organizations pay close attention to the relationship developing between more experienced employees and their subordinates. These relationships are often credited with adding to the success and satisfaction of an individual's work life. Estler (1977) identified three critical factors that contribute to individuals being screened out of high level managerial positions: competence, compatibility, and mentorship.

Facilitated Mentoring

Many organizations now recognize the value of mentors to newer and younger employees. Wilson and Elman (1990) suggested the principal benefits of organizational mentoring as the transmission of corporate culture and the provision of a "deep sensing" apparatus for top management.

Mentoring can contribute to employee motivation, job performance, and retention rates . . . mentoring provides a structured system for strengthening and assuring the continuity of organizational culture. The existence of a strong corporate culture that provides members with a common value base, and with implicit knowledge of what is expected of them and what they in turn can expect from the organization, can be vital to organizational success and effectiveness (pp. 88–89).

Murray (1991) defined **facilitated mentoring** as "a deliberate pairing of a more skilled or experienced person with a lesser skilled or experienced one, with the agreed-upon goal of having the lesser skilled person grow and develop specific competences" (p. 19). At the same time, other authors acknowledge that mentoring relationships can involve peers (rather than superior and subordinate) and can be designed to accomplish organizational assimilation.

Benefits of Mentoring

In a study of critical incidents of mentoring relationships, we (DeWine, James, and Hale, 1991) discovered that most subjects remembered the mentoring relationship as extremely positive. The most frequently mentioned positive outcome was enhancement of career development. For example, subjects said, "I was able to gain more money and freedom to exert more influence over my position," "My mentor gave me advice on going to conferences as an equal," and "After two years of guiding my career in insurance and benefits and assisting me with my resume, I obtained a management position" (p. 5). They also reported skill development and increased self-esteem as related benefits.

The mentors reported positive outcomes as well, for example: "When my protégé is successful in something encouraged by me, there is some 'reflected glory' involved and the possibility of a sense of accomplishment on my part" (p. 5).

Types of Mentors

In another study of mentoring relationships of women (DeWine, Casbolt, and Bentley, 1983), we identified the following profiles of these relationships:

Parent—By far the most prevalent theme described by protégés is a relationship similar to a father/daughter relationship, where there is great respect for this "older and wiser" person who influences the protégé's life and career significantly. Interestingly, this parental relationship did not seem to exist in the female-female relationship. Women did not tend to see mentors in "mother" roles in this sample of subjects.

White Knight—Many protégés described their mentors in glowing terms as if they were above human error. Usually, there was a point in the relationship when the protégé discovered the mentor had made a "mistake" and at that point the "white knight falls off his horse." Their respect for the mentor is not necessarily diminished but their "awe" of this individual is. One subject said, "I thought he had all the answers at first until I saw him caught short by one of his own managers once. This just made me realize how human he was."

Mentor-to-friend transformation—A large number of mentoring relationships undergo a change from mentor-protégé to friend-friend and vice versa. Often the mentor starts out as a person who sponsors the protégé's entrance into an organization, and then once the protégé is firmly established, this relationship, which was built on "socialization," is no longer needed as a critical part of the protégé's environment. Consequently, the two individuals change their relationship to friendship. This transformation can occur in the other direction, for example, one subject indicated that "We started out as friends but she moved more quickly than I through the organization and soon became my mentor."

The Badger—Some mentors activate their protégés' motivation by "badgering" their charges. This constant challenge and demand for excellence forces some to achieve more than they thought they could. One subject described this type of relationship when she said, "He pushed me into things, he delegated to the extreme and forced me into succeeding. I didn't dare let him down."

The Seductive Manipulator—While the "badger" tries fairly openly to push or shove the protégé into positions of responsibility, the seductive manipulator does so without the protégé really being aware of these activities on her behalf. The mentor merely places opportunities in the protégé's path and indirectly points them out. In some ways it's the old "bait and switch" game. One entry-level manager described this type of interaction in the following way: "She used to offer me increased opportunities for visibility in the corporation as if they had happened by chance. It was only later that I learned that these were all carefully planned for my benefit as well as hers. I didn't really know that I was being prepared for a managerial position until my replacement had already been trained by me!" While there were no examples of sexual harassment in this sample, this type of interaction could be conducive to it.

The Guilt Trip Producer—Often managers identified their feeling of guilt whenever they let their mentor down by not performing to her or his standards or expectations. The theme of "you can be more than you are" was repeated over and over so that to fail that mandate was to admit that you were only as good as your mentor originally found you. "I felt terrible when the first long report I had done under his guidance was not successful. It was as if he had failed too and it was my fault" is typical of this interaction.

The King/Queen—This theme describes an interaction in which the mentor is very dictatorial and authoritarian. Here the interaction is more one of action by decree. "He manipulated me. I ended up watching his kids for him and even became the go-between for him and his wife." In this situation the protégé is told how to go about the business of becoming successful.

The Self-Promoter—This mentor clearly sees advantages to surrounding her- or himself with some of the "best and brightest." In this case the mentor understands the advantage of having successful protégés. In one case, a woman described a male mentor who was extremely negative toward professional women, with the exception of his female protégés. In those instances he clearly saw the advantage of working with the best, "even if they were female."

Cheerleader—Many protégés described their mentors as individuals who either "watched from the sidelines" or "followed from behind," encouraging and cheering them on as they continued to advance. "She told me I could do anything," "He inspired me; I always could turn to him for encouragement even when we were no longer in the same discipline" are examples of this type of interaction. In a "cheerleading" relationship the mentor seems to derive pleasure in watching the success of the protégé.

Groom—Mentors who are in positions of power and have the ability to move a protégé into a higher position of responsibility often are seen as "grooming" their protégé for a particular position. Many protégés indicate that their mentor has groomed them for special assignments, in many cases for the mentor's own job so that the mentor was able to move up.

Overwhelmingly, the women in this study saw their mentor relationships as positive and viewed them with great nostalgia. Even when some of the more negative themes were developed women saw these relationships as useful to their careers. There was a certain percentage of subjects who had had some experiences they saw as being used and manipulated. In all cases, the termination or even some change in the relationship, was difficult to manage.

Termination of Mentoring Relationships

Many of the mentoring relationships described by these subjects continued beyond the study. Others went through normal terminations due to one or the other person in the relationship moving from the area, moving out of the organization, or moving out of the profession all together, and the mentor and protégé were no longer in close contact. The most difficult change was when the participants remained in contact but the nature of the relationship was influenced somehow, and one or both individuals had a difficult time accepting their new role.

Many protégés described the difficulty they had in "breaking away" from a mentor who was still seeing them in the role they played in their initial interactions. Several mentioned teachers who still saw them as students. One said, "I am now 40 years old and am a peer and colleague to one of my mentors, but she still insists on introducing me as one of her former students. I have never been able to change her perception of me as one who is basically still 'learning the ropes.' "

When the advice of the mentor is no longer needed, it is particularly difficult for the mentor to accept this change in the relationship. Even after the mentor-protégé relationship ends there is still likely to be a great loyalty in the once strongly committed relationship between two previous partners, unless there is a serious falling out between them. According to the norm of reciprocity, two demands are expected in relationships. This concept suggests that: 1) one helps those from whom one receives help; and 2) one does not injure those who have helped him or her (Swensen, 1973).

Very few people ever make it alone. We all need someone to lead the way, show us the ropes, tell us the norms, encourage and support us, and make it a little easier for us. Whether that someone is a mentor, friend, supervisor, or a professional colleague, there is an element of friendship present in each case. How you, as the communication manager or consultant, manage that relationship may enhance or hinder your effectiveness in solving communication problems in the organization. The challenge in being a communication specialist is that everyone expects you to model the most effective type of communication on all occasions!

Friendships at Work

Can co-workers be friends? Or must you maintain some distance in your working relationships? By opening up your private life to examination by those you must supervise, be supervised by, or with whom you compete for scarce resources, are you making yourself too vulnerable? Obviously, there is no easy answer. In fact, each person must decide individually the extent to which he or she will consent to be vulnerable.

We do know that there are differences in the ways in which men and women typically handle personal friendships and work. Rubin (1985) summarizes these differences:

> Women, even aspiring women, find themselves enmeshed in the struggle between achievement and affiliation . . . The working world may be dominated by men, but the issues that are at the forefront when women work together are women's issues: affiliation vs. professionalism, jealousy and role confusion, nurturing and autonomy. Men's concerns are professional—getting the job done, being competent, moving up. Many women share these concerns, but they are interlaced with more relational desires—that of liking and being liked, sharing and not sharing, inclusion and isolation. In the nine-to-five of a man's world, we are wrapped up in the female sphere still (p. 56).

Rubin goes on to identify how she perceives women cope with friendship on the job:

> Given the fact that most working environments are patriarchally structured and not particularly nurturing, how do women cope? In large part, by bringing the mountain to Mohammed. That is, by doing men's work in a women's way. Women are far more likely to form close relationships with one another than their male counterparts with whom they engage in intimate and sympathetic conversation (p. 67).

If we agree with Rubin's assessment, males and females will handle friends at work quite differently. The problem I have with Rubin's observations is that they are based on biological differences rather than psychological differences. A person's characteristics may be closer to what is considered typically masculine or feminine, *regardless* of biological gender or sexual preference. We know that for some people in the organization (males *and* females), interpersonal relationships are of prime importance, while to others, work always comes first. Neither approach is right or wrong, simply different. Communication managers and consultants must understand and appreciate the differences. There are also differences in peoples' reactions to romance in the office.

Romance at Work[2]

> People with whom one is working are the people who excite. A day spent launching a project, writing a paper, or running a seminar is more likely to stimulate intellectually and sexually than an evening spent sharing TV, discussing the lawn problems, or going over the kids' report cards (Jamison, 1983, p. 45).

With women moving into more powerful organizational positions, and men and women working as partners on exciting and stimulating projects, love in the office is more prevalent than ever before. The thrill of achievement, and the pleasure of working side by side with bright, competent people, can stimulate seductive feelings. Additionally, an office affair is more intense since the individuals see each other not just evenings and weekends but all day, every day. The couple thus develops an intimate understanding of each other's work world (Quinn and Lees, 1984).

Beliefs about Office Romances

Much has been written in the popular press about this topic, with authors suggesting a variety of coping strategies. This advice has ranged from "dealing with the culprit privately" (Gray, 1984) to "saying no to office romances" (Handley, 1986), to hiring professional consultants to run "gender-awareness" sessions focusing on sexual tensions (Collins, 1983, 1987). One author suggested breaking up office romances by practicing "proactive crisis management instead of reactive damage control" (Braiker, 1988).

Corporate executives' assessment of the impact of office romances in the workplace varies as well. Helen Gurley Brown, editor of *Cosmopolitan* magazine, champions acceptance of affairs on the job and has been quoted as saying, "You can be sure that the more committed people are to their work, the more likely they are to fall for someone they meet on the job." Chester Wright, chief of the Work Force Effectiveness and Development Division for the U.S. Office of Personnel Management concluded, "Sexual attraction is inevitable" (Spruell, 1985, p. 21). Another executive advises, "The best approach is to set in place a policy that restricts that specific situation" (Flax, 1989, p. 16). The outcome can vary from "heading to the altar or [to] the unemployment line" (Luckert, 1989, p. 12). If the individuals involved are "single, not too powerful, and work in areas that don't overlap," then some suggest these relationships may be "tolerated quite well" (McLaughlin, 1988, p. 153). These conditions, however, are infrequently met.

Despite wide talk and increasing impact, few academic studies have examined intimate work relationships. Instead, conclusions have been drawn from case studies, anecdotal evidence, and questionable survey methods. For instance, Jamison (1983) concluded from a single case study, "Careers are damaged, perhaps irreparably" (p. 42). A survey asked college students whether or not they believed sexual intimacy in the workplace would foster better communication between the workers, create a more harmonious work environment, and enhance creativity (Powell, 1986). Individuals who are not caught up in the drama or the consequences of such behavior have little experience on which to base such predictions.

Other surveys asked people to indicate how much of a problem they think romance may be in the office. For example, a study by Mishra and Harell (1989) revealed that managers in Michigan believed workplace romances were a problem in their companies. However, the survey questions were not precise; thus, the reader does not know the exact nature of the problems subjects thought office romances presented. Some researchers have drawn conclusions from "conversations with professional men and women" (Crary, 1987, p. 27) without reporting exactly how many conversations were conducted. Books have been written about the subject (Horn and Horn, 1982 and Westhoff, 1986) but none of these texts review the impact of office romances on the communication structure in the organization. Rather, they deal with the pervasiveness of the problem, raise questions for managers who must supervise the romantic couple, and describe how these relationships may turn into sexual harassment cases.

Studies of the Effects of Office Romances

Mainiero's (1986) lament that research on organizational romances suffers from a lack of methodological rigor and that most of it is an analysis of anecdotal material and/or case studies is not unwarranted. Her comprehensive review of 19 previous studies, starting in 1975, indicated that a number of research questions revolving around the organizational climate need to be asked.

Quinn's 1977 study was one of the first serious attempts to examine intimate relationships at work. One hundred thirty-two descriptive case studies were analyzed to develop a questionnaire that was administered to two hundred eleven individuals. Behavioral changes brought about by office romances ranged from romantic partners being easier to get along with and being more productive to the negative results of gossip, hostility, and loss of productivity. Unfortunately, this study is over 15 years old, and the office environment, as well as the increase in romantic relationships at work, have significantly changed individuals' perceptions of office romance. Quinn's early research led the way for later researchers to examine this issue more closely.

In the field of communication, several scholars have examined romantic relationships at work. Dillard and his associates have conducted a series of studies looking at the impact of office romances (Dillard, 1987; Dillard and Broetzmann, 1989; Dillard and Witteman, 1985). Dillard's research is based on data collected through phone interviews and focuses primarily on motives for intimate relationships and the impact of those motives on romantic involvement, organizational participativeness, and job performance. This research lays the groundwork for a more intense look at the impact intimate relationships have on co-worker communication patterns as well as superior-subordinate communication networks.

A second communication focus on office romance comes from Miller and Ellis (1986) who looked at romantic relationships and the effect of gender, status, and attractiveness of the participants on the attributions of motives. This research was conducted with undergraduates and their perceptions of how these relationships might affect organizational climates. Subjects were given vignettes and asked to assume the degree to which the individuals in the vignettes would do less work, assume more power, lose the respect of co-workers, and become inaccessible. Using undergraduate students plus hypothetical cases resulted in severe limitations on the conclusions.

In spite of this recent research activity, many issues remain dealing with the impact of romantic relationships on co-worker communication behavior and remain to be explored. While Dillard and Broetzmann's research (1989) measured the impact on the organization in terms of absenteeism, tardiness, enthusiasm, complaints, and general job performance, we were interested specifically in the change in interoffice communication as a result of the office romance. Communication behaviors were examined from the point of view of the co-worker as well as participant. Miller and Ellis (1986) suggested that observers of office romance will be affected by their own biases and thus their observations are less valid. However, if we are studying the impact of office romance *on co-workers* then the only way we can understand this phenomenon is to study it from their own perspectives.

Subjects in one study (DeWine, Pearson, and Yost, in press) were asked about changes in their ability to trust, get along with, share information with, influence, and communicate with romantic partners. Besides surveying co-workers' perceptions, those subjects who had participated in an office romance themselves completed additional survey instruments and were separated out for comparison.

We found that the majority of people who completed our survey tolerated, and in most cases accepted, office romance. It did not appear to affect co-worker relationships negatively, but rather, people were fairly neutral toward romantic partners. Office affairs do occur. It's not likely they can be ruled out, thus, we must figure out how to cope with them and limit their negative impact.

Consultant's Tips

- *Develop your closest friendships outside client systems.* Everyone needs someone in whom to confide. Those confidences must not affect the work relationships that already exist. Consequently, they should be shared with individuals not in the immediate work environment (i.e., spouses, close friends not in the organization). Of course you must restrain yourself from betraying the confidentiality entrusted in you. Information shared with friends at work should be more general and specific individuals should not be named.

- *Don't start an intimate relationship unless you are prepared to cope with the consequences.* Those consequences may include one of the partners leaving the company if the relationship interferes with people's ability to work together. Other consequences such as a lack of trust by co-workers, perceived favoritism leading to resentment, and breakdown in relationships among co-workers, may not be so obvious.

- *Become a mentor to someone else; it will be rewarding to both of you.* As a consultant, I often have taken "consultants in training" with me to observe and co-facilitate. One of the best ways to learn how to handle conflict in a group is to observe it; the process is difficult to describe in detail. At the same time, I benefit by having another person to act as a process observer who may pick up things I have missed. The mentor benefits as much as, or more, than the protégé.

- *Recognize that males and females will cope with friendships at work differently.* This difference may not have as much to do with biological sex as psychological sex. One individual will approach the office secretary with friendly overtures, maintaining the relationship first and asking for help second. Others will think first of the work to be done, and only when it is completed will then turn to maintaining the relationship with "small talk." Understanding this difference allows us to be more tolerant of these differences rather than rejecting one approach or the other.

Dealing with human beings in an organization means dealing with relationships. Many of the problems organizations face today are caused by dysfunctional relationships among those who must make decisions about the organization's future.

When I asked one vice-president to allow a team of researchers to study friendships in his organization, his answer was, "We don't have anything like that going on around here. We're here to work." I suspected he thought we would be researching more intimate relationships, but whether he actually thought we would research friendships or romances, they definitely *were* "going on around there" and to believe otherwise was to ignore half the activity of the organization! We live much of our lives at work and we need to be sensitive to all the relationship issues that exist. Not to do so results in ignoring a major portion of our lives and significant influences on our productivity, to say nothing of our general well-being!

Notes

1. Parts of this section were taken from DeWine, Casbolt, and Bentley (May, 1983); and DeWine, James, and Hale (May, 1991).
2. Parts of this section are taken from DeWine, Pearson, and Yost (in press).

■ *Suggested Readings*

Berryman-Fink, C., Ballard-Reisch, D., & Newman, L. (1993). *Communication and sex-role socialization*. New York, NY: Gardland Press.

Horn, P. D., & Horn, J. (1982). *Sex in the office*. Reading, MA: Addison-Wesley Publishing Co., Inc.

Rubin, L. B. (1985). *Just friends: The role of friendship in our lives*. New York, NY: Harper and Row.

Chapter 18

THE BUSINESS OF CONSULTING

Entrepreneurship, Marketing, Ethics, and Career Development

Lawyers who defend themselves have a fool for a client!

Author unknown

So you made it to the end of this book and you are still interested in becoming a consultant or communication specialist? This means you want to be your own boss, maybe practice what you preach on clients and your own employees and colleagues. But just because you are able to help large groups of people establish effective work climates doesn't mean you will be able to do it for yourself. You may be an outstanding facilitator with groups who must make decisions; however, you may know little about how to establish a group of your own! This final chapter is designed to provide you with some practical suggestions about actually starting a consulting business.

A colleague of mine and I taught a small business class in a community filled with creative, talented, and highly educated individuals. Because few large businesses were located in this small community, many people had chosen to start their own business. We were teaching a ten-week course covering financial, legal, and personnel issues related to small businesses.

On the first night of class we discussed why individuals might want to own their own business and the advantages and disadvantages of doing so. One member of the class said he was looking for something new to challenge himself. We cautioned him to think about this carefully before making any big decisions. One week later, at the second class, Jake walked into class all smiles. "I quit my job on Tuesday and bought a restaurant on Wednesday!" In the stunned silence that followed this announcement, my colleague covered her disbelief and asked, "Jake, have you ever owned or even worked in a restaurant before?" "No, but I eat in them a lot and I figured I would learn quickly!"

We hadn't even covered getting a bank loan yet! As the evening went on Jake learned the importance of developing a business plan. We discussed how a business plan outlines potential problems with the new business. Later that week, Jake discovered he had bought

343

the restaurant only, not the parking lot attached to it! In fact, he learned the previous owners had rented the parking lot. One of the reasons the previous owners had decided to sell the restaurant was that the owner of the parking lot had not renewed their lease since he planned to build an office building on it. Jake had bought a restaurant without a parking lot! That's a hard way to learn the importance of a business plan.

This chapter is intended for those readers who are now, or want to be some time in the future, independent consultants, external to any organization. External consulting means being a small business owner. The first step in establishing a small business is the development of a business plan.

The Business Plan[1]

It is a fact that nine out of ten small businesses fail in the first five years. If you are thinking of becoming an independent consultant, be prepared for five years of low, or no, profit. In my experience, identifying clients and business are not the most important problem: cash flow is.

The owner of a small business must be aware of legal ramifications, tax benefits, insurance options, liability issues, and financial plans, as well as maintaining a high-quality product. According to estimates by the U.S. Department of Commerce[2] there are some 10 million small businesses in the U.S., not counting about 2 1/2 million family-owned farms. These 10 million small businesses make up 90 percent of all U.S. businesses. They account for 55 percent of the total domestic employment and 43 percent of the Gross National Product.

One of the primary factors determining the success or failure of any small business is the "business sense" of the owner or operator of that business. Many people become small business owners because they have a creative idea, talent, or a craft which they want to market, but they have little information or experience with business concerns.

Consultants might fall into the same category: a lot of talent but little knowledge of what it takes to run a small business successfully. They may have the talent and skill to be a consultant but not have the knowledge or the experience necessary to set up a consulting firm. The development of a business plan could prove quite useful to any individual considering consulting as a full-time job. Such a business plan would include an analysis of the following types of information.

Parts of a Business Plan

Part one of a business plan should be a *brief statement or definition of the services or products* one intends to market. In the case of a consulting firm, the consultant must be able to describe in simple language the skills and techniques that can be delivered to an organization. Consultants must be able to state in a sentence or two exactly what they could deliver to an organization as a consulting firm.

The second part of the business plan should *define the target market*. By target market I mean who the customers will be, the size of the market, trends in that market, and a description of the competition. One might be wise to target a particular population with which one wishes to work, especially as a start-up business. For example, one consulting firm works entirely with hospital administrations, another works with political campaigns, and yet another communication consulting agency works with industrial top-level management to perfect their public speaking skills. In any case, it is important that you have a specific target in mind when developing your firm and your marketing strategies.

You might want to focus your consulting firm in a particular location, in which case the analysis of your competition will be easier to manage. It is important that you find out what kind of consulting is already going on within the organizations with whom you want to work, who is conducting that training or consulting, the prices they are charging, and how they are marketing themselves. Nothing is less successful than approaching an organization with a consulting contract that has already been completed previously by some other firm. *Know your territory.*

The third part of the business plan is to *develop strategies for new services or product improvement*. This might mean in-servicing yourself by learning new skills and new strategies or it might mean developing packaged programs that could be modified across a variety of organizations.

The next area outlined on the business plan is the *overall marketing strategy*. Marketing strategies are discussed in greater detail later in the chapter and must be included as a part of the overall plan. Some consulting firms take a broad base approach to advertising through some sort of mass mailing campaign. Others prefer a more personalized strategy where hundreds of contacts and interviews are made with potential clients and personal letters are sent to targeted clients in organizations.

The fifth section of the business plan should be an *outline of the organizational structure*. Who will own the firm, who will be participating in its activities besides yourself, and what will the make-up and structure be in the organization? Even though you are running a small business it is just as important for you to determine how that business will operate as it is for the larger organizations with which you may be consulting.

The sixth area to be analyzed as part of the business plan is the *financial procedure* used to support this activity. The potential owner should outline a profit/loss forecast predicting potential income as well as potential loss for a given period of time. All to often people assume that a consulting firm which operates out of a home will have little, if any, cash flow problems. One incurs overhead costs with a home business just as any small business owner might encounter. There are administrative expenses, staff development costs, secretarial fees, and insurance, just to name a few.

All too often the firms with which a consulting agency might deal have long periods of time between delivery of service and payment for service. The consultant must be prepared to cope with this time span. As a part of your financial program you need to develop a break-even chart where you consider fixed and variable costs. Examples of fixed costs are rent or mortgage payments and insurance premiums. Variable costs include material to be used for each client, which would vary according to a particular situation. You might want to prepare a packet of hand-outs for each participant, for example, or slides and overhead transparencies for a talk to a large group.

The previous six areas outlined are a step toward making some important decisions about establishing a consulting firm. Wolfe (1984) also suggested identifying if there is a seasonal or cyclical factor in your business. Do clients need your services more at any particular time of the year or at certain stages in their growth? This could help you determine a more narrow focus for your marketing campaign.

Forms of Ownership

Probably one of the most important initial decisions is which type of legal form your consulting firm will follow. There are three basic types of forms that any small business may use. One may establish a sole ownership or proprietorship, a partnership, or a corporation.[3]

SOLE OWNERSHIP

Sole ownership or proprietorship businesses make up 78.6 percent of the total business concerns in the United States but only 11.3 percent of the total sales. In a **sole ownership** legal form, the business is owned and operated by a single person. The advantages are that this is probably the easiest form of business to establish, thus incurring low start-up costs. Fees to register a sole ownership are minimal. There are few legal restrictions or regulations, and as sole owner you receive all of the profits from the small business. Additionally, the sole owner has complete control over decision making and management policy. Finally, this type of legal form is flexible in order to respond to specific situations.

There are a number of disadvantages incurred with sole ownership. First, assets and liabilities of the proprietorship are merged into the assets and liabilities of the owner. This means that the debts of the proprietorship are the debts of its owner.

Second, income is taxed as income to the individual. You cannot hire yourself as an employee; thus, money taken from the company cannot be deducted as wages to an employee and/or a business expense. Additionally, it is extremely difficult to raise capital, especially long-term financing from banks.

Third, it may create an unstable business life. For example, if the owner dies, the business dies. This is especially important if the owner's goodwill and personal contact with clients have built the business.

Finally, it does provide you with a limited viewpoint since you have only one person's ideas, views, and knowledge as input into decision making for the firm. You must acquire appropriate licenses and permits, open and manage a company checking account, and be responsible for all the functions of your small business, from major financial decisions to janitorial duties.

PARTNERSHIP

The second type of legal form is a partnership. Partnerships make up 7.7 percent of the total businesses in the United States and only 4.4 percent of the total sales. A **partnership** is an association of two or more people to carry on as co-owners of a business concern.

The financial advantages of a partnership legal form are low start-up costs and additional sources of money that may be available through one's partner or partners. Each partner brings personal skills and experience to the business, thus providing a broader management base than a sole proprietor can achieve. However, many new consultants cite the flexibility to make business decisions as one of their primary reasons for establishing a consulting firm of their own. The more partners the business has, the less flexibility any one individual may have.

A major disadvantage to a general partnership is that each partner is personally liable for wrongful acts by any of his or her partners in the operation of the partnership; in essence, you are your brother's keeper. Personal assets of the partners may be used to satisfy liabilities of partnerships but not vice versa. Like proprietorships, representative partners cannot be employees, and wages are not business expenses. Partnerships may create an unstable business life in that the elimination of any partner constitutes automatic dissolution of the partnership.

In order to establish a partnership, a written partnership agreement should be developed, although one may develop out of an oral agreement or business paractice. Specifically, the following are indicated: what the business is and what its goals are; how much each partner will contribute in cash; how each partner shares in profits and losses; procedures for withdrawal of funds and payment of transfers; provisions for continuing the business if a partner dies; and specification of the financial, legal, and managerial powers of each partner.

INCORPORATION

The third legal form is the establishment of a corporation. Corporations make up 13.7 percent of the businesses but 84.3 percent of the sales (see Figure 18.1). A **corporation** is a legal entity which exists separately and distinctly from its owners.

The advantages of a corporation are that liability of the owners is equal to their investment, and ownership is easily transferred; thus, the organization exists beyond the life of its owners. In addition, certain tax advantages are incurred, such as the salary of the owner(s) being deductible as a business expense and the owner being treated as an employee for benefit of retirement. Plus, it is much easier to raise capital from lending institutions. Finally, you have the ability to draw on expertise and skills of more than one person.

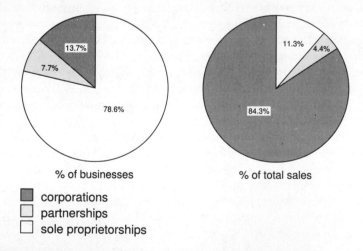

FIGURE 18.1 Forms of Ownership Most businesses in the United States are sole proprietorships, but they account for only 11.3 percent of total sales. Although only 13.7 percent of U.S. businesses are incorporated, corporations bring in 84.3 percent of total sales. Partnerships are the least used form of business and bring in the smallest contribution to total sales.

The disadvantages of a corporation legal form include double taxation of dividend profits as well as corporate taxes and end taxes. Closely regulated by government agencies, the corporation becomes the most expensive form of business to organize, and maintaining the necessary recordkeeping information is costly and complicated.

To incorporate one must develop articles of incorporation which include the nature or purpose of the business to be conducted, description of capital structure, and names and addresses of other corporations similar to your own. There are special types of corporations such as a closely held corporation, in which stock is not available to the public through the sale on any stock exchange, and professional corporations, wherein an individual or group's profession is licensed.

Finally, one could develop a sub-chapter S. Some of the requirements for this special type of corporation are that it may have no more than 15 shareholders; no shares may be owned by other corporations or nonresident aliens; no more than 20 percent of the income may come from passive sources, i.e., rent, royalty, dividends; and finally, no more than 80 percent of the sales income can be generated outside the U.S.

The advantages to this special type of corporation are that there is no double taxation to both the individual and the company, business losses can be carried back to prior years of the owner's income, and the control of the organization is similar to a partnership.

The disadvantages are that it may be confusing and costly to set up and follow necessary rules. Also the IRS may watch the formation of these special corporations very carefully. The incorporation of your firm establishes its credibility to some extent and protects you in terms of any liability to clients for promised services.

Table 18.1 summarizes the advantages and disadvantages of the three basic legal forms of ownership. One of these legal forms will work best for your particular circumstances. An attorney should be consulted to make certain you comply with local, state, and federal laws. Once you have established your firm legally, you next have to let people know you exist!

■ Marketing

Greiner and Metzger (1983) suggested,

To the surprise and frustration of most consultants, marketing is the lifeblood of the industry. Consultants would rather consult than sell; after all, that is what drew them to the field. It is natural for them to assume that effective consulting skills, combined with a few satisfied clients, should lead to an endless stream of new clients. Therein lies the marketing failure of most consultants and consulting firms (p. 41).

■ TABLE 18.1

ADVANTAGES AND DISADVANTAGES OF FORMS OF OWNERSHIP

	Sole Proprietorship	Partnership	Corporation
Simplicity	+ Easiest to start + Low start-up costs + Few legal restrictions	+ Easy to start + Low start-up costs	– Most regulated
Authority	+ Complete authority	+/– Divided by agreement	– Rests with stockholders
Liability	– Personal assets/debts not separate from business assets/debts	– Each liable for actions of all	+ Limited
Taxes	+/– Taxed as individual	+/– Taxed as individuals	– Taxed as employees; business taxed separately
Financing	– May be difficult to get	+/– More resources than individual, fewer than corporation	+ Most likely to attract
Stability	– Dies with owner	– Dissolves with elimination of any partner	+ Has separate life from any of owners

Consultants think of themselves as professionals in some rather narrow definition of the field. When individuals are in the business of consulting, they have to think of themselves as small business owners who must market their services.

Identifying Your Market Niche

It is important that the consulting firm identify the type of firm it is and market itself correctly. Suryanarayanan (1989) has identified five basic types of consulting firms that currently exist:

Pure strategy advisors may be small firms such as the Boston Consulting Group that provide high-cost advice mainly to chief executives.

Traditional management consultants are firms such as McKinsye and Co., Booz Allen & Hamilton, and Arthur D. Little that combine strategy consulting with advice in functional areas such as marketing, manufacturing, and logistics or industry-specific advice in such industries as automotive or consumer electronics. These firms are much more diversified and larger than the pure strategy firms.

Accounting firms are relatively recent entrants into consultation in a purposeful organized manner, although they have engaged in general counsel for many years. Until recently they marketed themselves as computer experts, but soon learned there were ways to serve other needs of the client. With consulting revenues rising at a faster pace than auditing and tax-practice fees, many accounting firms will soon find their earnings from consulting overtaking all other earnings. Examples include Andersen Consulting, Coopers and Lybrand, and Price Waterhouse.

Human resources firms may specialize in developing compensation packages. Most work closely with a client's personnel director or the CEO to develop a strategic human resource policy. Companies in this category include Hay Group, acquired by Saatchi and Saatchi in 1984, and Sibson and Co., a Johnson and Higgins company.

Specialized firms offer advice on specific markets or skills. They are hired by their counterparts in client businesses. Examples include Oliver Wyman and Co., specializing in the financial services industry, and Symmetriz in systems development for operations management. This category also includes university professors and sole practitioners offering specialized services. Competition in this category is fierce.

Once you have identified the type of firm you have developed or will develop, next you must advertise what you have.

Getting the Word Out

There are many ways to make contact with clients and market the service of your company when you want to increase the client pool. Smith (1990) suggested the consulting company can get its message out through its own staff, present and past clients, professional associations, associates in other businesses, suppliers or subcontractors, and other consultants who may not have the same services to offer. The range of tools covers press advertising and articles; talks on radio and television; conferences; teaching institutions; special seminars; research projects; receptions with or without presentations; pamphlets; letters; telephone calls; and personal calls. The client may be reached through his or her staff, the general public, the government, trade unions, shareholders, professional associations, associates, suppliers, and educational institutions. In short, you use every possible contact to get the word out. Two forms of marketing that can be used are indirect and direct.

INDIRECT MARKETING

Most service professionals believe it is easier to keep an old client than attract a new one. Businesspeople who take client retention for granted while they constantly seek new business, may experience serious losses. Most consultants I have worked with, including my own firm, have depended heavily on referrals from satisfied clients. That means that the first principle of marketing for consultants is to satisfy current customers. Begin by getting one client and making that client very happy with your work.

White and Mindiole (1986) suggested the following steps to ensure your clients stay with you:

1. Develop client satisfaction letters, surveys, or meetings in which evaluations of your firm's performance can be gathered.
2. Ensure that more than one key professional from your firm maintains regular contact with significant clients.
3. Implement a client service planning program in which detailed plans for providing additional services to key clients are developed.

Often, I receive consulting contracts by word of mouth. Someone is looking for outside help, mentions it to a colleague, who, it turns out, has worked with me directly or has heard me speak, or read an article I've written and passes my name along. In one case, I conducted a workshop for alumni returning to the university for a weekend. Two days later I received a phone call from a corporate lawyer who was in charge of setting up an in-house employee development program for 1,500 employees of a national insurance company. When I asked how she had acquired my name she replied, "Actually, my parents called me and raved about your workshop they had attended and insisted I must hear you talk. Since I rarely hear them give such glowing compliments, I decided I would follow their advice!"

No matter the size of the consulting firm, the best marketing strategy still remains referral. Richard Ziehm (1989), president of Precision Extrusions, Inc., suggested his criteria for hiring consultants as the following:

I've picked management consultants almost strictly through referrals. I read at least part of most direct-mail pieces, but rarely accept phone calls. I discuss our need with friends in the basic organizations to which I belong

. . . Even my accountants, attorneys, and competitors are good sources of referrals. If I were selling consulting services, having consulted with Precision Extrusions previously, I would hunt for business by selling to the competition of my recent successes. For example, I would send direct mail to other extrusion companies and mention that I had a recent project at Precision Extrusions. This piques interest, arouses curiosity, and appeals to a CEO's sense of insecurity. Can I afford not to learn what this guy taught so and so? (p. 26)

Greiner and Metzger (1983) called this indirect marketing. They claim that

. . . indirect marketing is largely the domain of the biggest and longest established consulting firms . . . These elitist consulting firms perceive little need to advertise or make "cold calls" on clients. They want their quality image to be so pervasive in the market's consciousness that key decision makers in client organizations naturally select them before considering an unknown, though perhaps equally qualified consultant. Above all, the indirect approach is low-key and subtle, to the point where the client does not realize that he or she is the "victim" of hidden persuasion (p. 43).

All of these indirect marketing techniques introduce your services in more informal ways. Direct marketing techniques are more formal, more obvious advertising strategies.

DIRECT MARKETING

Directing marketing can be quite costly. The direct approach recognizes that what is being marketed in consulting is an intangible personal service, much the same as life insurance. Direct sales requires contacting by mail or some form of advertising, to large numbers of people. "For every 20 people contacted five executives' doors are opened. For every five doors opened, one sale is consummated" (Greiner and Metzger, p. 46).

Once you get into the CEO's office, there are three questions that should be asked in the initial interview:

1. What are you especially proud of about your organization in the past several years?
2. What things would you like to change?
3. If you could wave a magic wand, what things would you do that you haven't been able to do because of lack of time or expertise?

These three questions allow you to identify what problems may exist and how you may be able to help. Question one identifies the organization's strengths, question two identifies its weaknesses, and question three helps you determine what has been keeping organization members from solving the problem.

Greiner and Metzger (1983) remind us of the proverb: "Listen and you may learn something new; keep talking and you only espouse what you already know." That is a good principle to remember in that initial and subsequent interviews.

Schrello (1988) suggested the following tips for individuals who are attempting to market seminars or consulting activities. For direct marketing copy he suggests:

1. Capture the readers' interest
2. Describe a need you know they have
3. Show how your product or service can meet that need
4. Establish your credibility to do what you claim
5. Request action now
6. Add a clincher of some kind: a bonus, premium, or added reason to act now (p. 5).

He also suggested that you should set up a problem the customer recognizes, show how your product or service can solve that problem, then prove your solution. Written promotional materials should talk to your readers personally and involve them just as you would face to face. Writing as if for an individual, rather than a group or an organization, is a proven technique.

Speak to emotional needs and the intellectual needs of your readers. Always use "you" never "we." For example, "You will get . . ." rather than "We will give you . . ." Schrello (1988) also suggested that based on studies of persuasive words by the Yale Psychology Department and an analysis of what works best, the 15 words that spell direct marketing success are:

Discovery

Easy

Free

Guaranteed

Help

Introducing

Money

New

Now

Proven

Results

Save

Today

You

Win

In consulting you must continually market your services. Since your skills are the product you are promoting, your attitude toward yourself and what you can provide are critical. Tepper (1987) identified the most important ingredient for a successful consultant: a positive attitude.

> Attitude is critical to the consultant because regardless of your chosen field, you risk rejection more than any other professional. Consultants run an even higher risk of rejection than salespeople. In sales you sell the client a product and/or service. It is delivered, you receive your commission check, and you are on to the next person. In consulting, you sell the prospect on a service, then you have to keep selling the client on your value and ability, on the program, and on the approach you have developed (p. 311).

Marketing your own services is more difficult than marketing some inanimate object. Because you cannot present this service objectively, you must develop ethical guidelines to direct your own behavior.

Ethics

One of my students reported on the following historical event:

> Dora, an 18-year-old, was sent to Sigmund Freud for therapy (Freud, 1901). Her father was a close friend of Freud's and wanted him to "bring Dora to reason." She was having hysterical attacks that annoyed her father. After several weeks of therapy, Freud learned that Dora's father wanted her to have a romantic interlude with his friend so that he could enjoy the company of the friend's young wife. Dora's hysterical outbursts were a direct result of being faced with the dilemma of not wanting to obey her father. The outbursts increased with his persistence.
>
> Considering the father as the client, Freud proceeded to try and convince Dora that the request was not unreasonable. Although

SUE DEWINE
Midwest Associate

Communication Consultants, Inc.
154 Martha Avenue
Centerville, Ohio 45459
(513) 866-7524
or
(513) 433-7804

"Specializing in Optimizing
Human Potential in
Industry and Education"

Using this picture business card early in my career reminded people who I was.

COMMUNICATION
CONSULTANTS,
INCORPORATED

8 York Drive
Athens, Ohio 45701
(614) 594-7539

SUE DeWINE
MIDWEST ASSOCIATE

ORGANIZATIONAL COMMUNICATION
SCHOOL OF INTERPERSONAL COMMUNICATION
OHIO UNIVERSITY
ATHENS, OHIO 45701

This is a rather standard business card I have used for some years with my firm's logo imprinted on it. I also included my university address because I am often making contacts for the university at the same time.

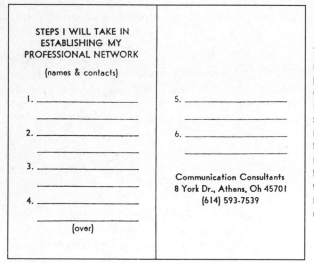

STEPS I WILL TAKE IN
ESTABLISHING MY
PROFESSIONAL NETWORK

(names & contacts)

1. _____

2. _____

3. _____

4. _____

(over)

5. _____

6. _____

Communication Consultants
8 York Dr., Athens, Oh 45701
(614) 593-7539

This is a card I use as part of a networking exercise. I ask participants to fill out the card at the end of a session, listing the names of individuals or goals they want to set for themselves in the next six months. Then I ask them to place the card in their wallet so that they remember these goals every time they reach for their money. They will also be reminded of my firm's name whenever they see the back of the card.

FIGURE 18.2   A business card keeps the consultant's name and service in the client's mind.

356

Freud acknowledged the validity of her perceptions, he decided not to tell her this because he was working in the best interests of her father. Luckily, Dora deduced that Freud was acting on her father's behalf and subsequently dropped out of therapy.

Obligations to the Client

This anecdote raises a serious ethical question: What are the consultant's obligations to the client? Few would deny that the consultant has an obligation to exercise honesty, objectivity, and diligence in the performance of his or her duties and responsibilities or that the consultant owes the client respect, including maintenance of confidentiality. As with most homilies, it is far easier to preach an ethical consultant-client relationship than to practice it.

One must ask, "Who is my client and what interventions are in the client's best interest?" Deetz (1992) would respond that the consultant "should represent the various stakeholders, the total corporation, and any report should be publicly available" (p. 347). In this view, the consultant must be working for the good of the whole, not for a single individual to the detriment of others. Ethical concerns include, but are not limited to, the following issues:

We should consider whether our response to a situation will compromise our personal dignity and integrity or that of our organization and profession. We have an obligation to "give back" to the profession, and thus we should not leave an organization worse off than we found it.

It is unethical to be a "hit and run" consultant who leaves behind injured victims.

Failing to recognize one's professional limitations and exaggerating one's qualifications are clearly unethical and dangerous practices.

The roles of "yes man," a "hatchet," or "dime store psychologist," can also be viewed as unethical roles for a consultant. The consultant is responsible for helping the client identify and resolve a problem by bringing professional expertise and objectivity to the situation.

No consultant should consent to intervene unless there is a commitment to follow-up activities. Otherwise employees will not only mistrust that consultant but are likely to mistrust all interventions in the future and they will resist the implementation of beneficial changes in their organizations.

Consultants must maintain strict standards of confidentiality. Information about the client gained during the course of the consultation relationship cannot be communicated to others unless the client has specifically agreed to such disclosure. This restriction would of course also apply to any research efforts on the part of the consultant. The consultant must keep any results from consulting practices anonymous to protect the consultant as well as the client.

The American Psychology Association suggests that: "information received in confidence is revealed only after most careful deliberation and when there is clear and imminent danger to an individual or to society and then only to appropriate professional workers or public authorities" (as cited in DeWine and James, 1978). Every effort must be made to protect the client's right to privacy, not only on ethical grounds but for legal considerations as well.

Ethics and Professional Behavior

Lippitt and Lippitt (1986) identify as **normative ethics** those basic areas of conduct controlled by the industry: qualifications, contracts, fees, objectivity, and confidentiality. They also recognize that a consultant must develop a personal code of **situational ethics,** that is, behavior guided by each unique situation encountered in professional practice.

Although the professional associations can provide guidelines for appropriate behavior, consultants basically stand alone when faced with ethical dilemmas. We must be able to live with our decision, and standards must be thought out ahead of time if we are to be prepared to make on-the-spot decisions about our own behavior.

Wexley and Latham (1981) identified major categories of behaviors considered improper or unethical for training and development professionals. They include: lack of professional development, violation of confidences, use of cure-all programs, dishonest evaluation of program outcomes, failure to give credit, and abusive treatment of trainees.

It is easy for a consultant to assume that having been trained in communication, management, personnel, psychology, etc., he or she can diagnose the corporate ailment before consulting with the patient. This is as foolhardy as the physician who makes a diagnosis over the telephone and then prescribes medication without seeing the patient. True, it is faster and cheaper, and presents the consultant in an omnipotent pose; but it is neither objective nor unbiased. We do not always possess the remedy for the ills of an organization at our fingertips.

As long as we remember that we are responsible for the decisions we make, the recommendations we advance, and the changes we instigate, and that the responsibility is a lighter burden if we have been as objective and straightforward with the client as possible, then we are effective models of our profession.

Consultants must accept moral responsibility for the consequences of their consulting practices. Consultants need not only ethical standards to govern the effect of outcomes generated by their interventions, but legal protection as well. While it is important that clients take ownership for their part in the problem, consultants must accept responsibility for potentially making the problem worse.

An internal consultant, by virtue of having to live with any actions taken, will be more aware of the result of such action than will an external consultant who can leave the situation. A consultant must be ready to terminate a consulting relationship when it is reasonably clear that the client is not benefiting from it. Finally, consultants need to take their own advice: if it is ethical for clients to be constantly improving their product, then that must be true for the consultant as well.

■ Career Development

In a particularly poignant article, Greiner and Metzger (1983) describe "Stepping Back: How to Stay Sane and Avoid Burnout." It is true that consultants are often least likely to follow their own advice.

> There are hours and hours of sedentary life in planes, airports, cars, client meetings, restaurants, and report writing. Your once youthful figure sinks rapidly to the bottom. To top it off, there are long flights, rough flights, close connections, lost luggage, poorly maintained rental cars, high-sodium and high-cholesterol food, filthy hotel rooms, and extreme climate changes that play Handel's *Messiah* on your sinus cavities.
>
> **Warning: Consulting may be harmful to your health!** (p. 328).
> **Suggestions: Stay away from booze, dancing, junk food, and commuter airplanes!**
>
> Never take yourself or your client too seriously. A sane consultant will maintain perspective, recognizing that all humans, including consultants, are not omnipotent, in fact, that aura of fallibility is what makes the consulting game so interesting and challenging. Clients, just like spouses, lovers, relatives, and friends, often do things for their own selfish reasons, not yours (p. 329).

One colleague arrived at a training program with two different shoes on, one brown and one black. He was very embarrassed and decided to point it out himself before someone else did. What he discovered was that the audience warmed up to him very quickly after his admission! The consultant has to be human too. I always point out my poor spelling before someone else points it out to me. "By the way," I say at the beginning of writing ideas down on newsprint, "I believe Mark Twain's philosophy that people who can spell words only one way are not very creative. I want you to know, you are looking at a very creative person!"

If I take myself less seriously, somehow that allows me to present myself more honestly.

Career Paths for Consultants

A career as a consultant, particularly an outside consultant, can be extremely taxing. Most people do not remain in the field for an entire career. Greiner and Metzger suggested:

> The vast majority (of consultants) perhaps as high as 60 percent, remain as consultants for only three to six years to gain the necessary experience, expertise, and exposure before moving on to that choice job of planning director at International Widgets. Another 30 percent realize that they are doing better financially than in private industry and stick it out for up to ten years until they too, leave for International Widgets as vice president for personnel. The remaining 10 percent are either faculty at universities who consult part-time forever, or they are senior partners in consulting firms who find that they are consulting less, administrating more, and earning in excess of $150,000 per year (p. 332).

These are the kinds of career choices one must make. At the same time, all of us need to achieve balance in our lives.

Bellman (1990) discussed criteria by which a consultant might evaluate the balance within his or her practice. He suggested that the consultant consider such questions as the following: "What is my work schedule?" "How much work do I want to do?" "How effective can one person be, balancing all the parts of the consulting practice?" "How often do I say no to work?" "What should my travel schedule be?" "How long does it take me to work?" "Where should I live and where should I work?" "How should I establish administrative efficiency?" You must be content with your answers in order to stay in the profession.

Financial Rewards of Consulting

Webster and Henderson (1987) reported that "Overall, in the 1980s, average trainers salaries have risen from the low thirties to the high thirties. Unfortunately, women typically earn about 25% less than men in the same positions which results in gaps ranging from $7,000 to $11,000 per year in the average salaries of men and women" (p. 20).

The Northeast and Pacific coast regions tend to offer the highest salaries with the Southeast and West Central regions offering the lowest. However, salaries vary more by type of industry than by geographical location. The best paying industries are manufacturing, transportation, communications, and public utilities. The worst paying industries are health services, finance, insurance, and banking. By position, training managers and specialists in management and in career and organization development tend to earn the highest salaries, while classroom instructors and instructional designers earn the lowest salaries.

Independent consultants can earn anywhere from $400 per day to what I would consider an average of $800–$1,000 per day to $20,000 per half-day lecture for some of the most well-known consultants in the country. The fee depends on what the market will bear, the desire of the consultant, and the consultant's experience level. My fee varies depending on the ability of the client to pay (e.g., I will occasionally work with school systems at a significantly reduced rate because I want to help them) and the inconvenience caused to my life. If it requires travel and extended time away from my home I will charge more per day than I would if the consulting is within driving distance. New consultants look at those amounts and figure they could be making a six-digit salary immediately. However, what they fail to recognize is that consultants do not work every day of the week, every week of the year and that independent consultants have significant overhead charges such as office space and secretarial services.

Future Directions

Since consultants often act as role models for the desired behavior of others, they must have a well-defined professional development program for themselves. The future of the field depends on their ability to adapt to new, innovative ideas and a changing environment and to bring an up-to-date approach to client systems that are also facing change.

Schindler-Raiman (1987) suggested a number of challenges and changes that consultants will have to deal with in the 1990s. They included: 1) doing more with less, 2) the fluctuating national mood (fluctuating between pessimism and optimism and based on the value of the dollar, election results, various world crises, etc.), which affects the people with whom we work, and 3) the speed and complexity of changes (speed of change has led to an overload of information and the constant development of new techniques, knowledge, and technology).

The set of changes that consultants will have to deal with include demographic and population changes. The increasing mobility of the population will require more training of new employees and helping them adjust to a new organization. The aging of the population means fewer young employees and increased competition for jobs by employable persons. This situation will require the consultant to be able to decrease stress for those working in highly competitive systems. As the workforce becomes increasingly multicultural, consultants will be called on to help workers understand and use human resources representing different ages, life stages, and ethnic and racial groups. Keeping individuals abreast of population demographic changes and helping older workers accept and work with younger managers and vice versa will be challenges for the consultant in the contemporary workplace.

Complex communications technology and systems change present another whole new series of challenges for consultants. There will be more emphasis on creative leadership than ever before, which means consultants will have to help long-time leaders change their styles, understand the necessity for such changes, learn to detect conflict and use it as a resource, and become more sensitive to the many realities of their systems. Schindler-Raiman suggested that trainers and consultants must do the following:

- Increase our knowledge and skills with respect to future trends.
- Increase our training methodology tool kits by inventing new, creative training designs.
- Employ the inside/outside team concept and risk teaming with someone else inside or outside the system to increase one's skills and visibility.
- Admit when we do not know something and be able to recruit additional trainers and consultants as resources.
- Enhance what we already know about data collection and the use of resources.
- Understand and learn all about new technologies.
- Be selective in our choices about new technology.
- Learn more effective ways of involving potential participants.
- Find ways to use our time more effectively.
- Learn to confront clients more skillfully when they have legitimate differences of opinion.
- Introduce the possibility of using volunteers in systems.
- Help clients learn modern participative, productive ways of holding meetings, and support clients in recognizing that committing

errors is a component of managing and that one can learn and grow from analysis of both success and mistakes (p. 25).

If you are able to accomplish all of the above, you will definitely need to incorporate since you will have so much business that only that legal form can handle it! All that, still knowing how to lead a balanced personal life without becoming an 18-hour, 7-day-a-week consultant will require your most intense concentration!

Criteria for Evaluating One's Consulting Business

The eight criteria by which Peters and Waterman (1984) identified excellent companies can also be applied to identifying outstanding consultants. These attributes of excellence provide goals for practicing consultants. They are characterized by eight phrases (pp. 13–15):

A bias for action, for getting on with it

Close to the customer

Anatomy in entrepreneurship

Productivity through people

Hands-on, value-driven

Stick to the knitting

Simple form, lean stuff

Simultaneous loose-tight properties

A "bias for action" means being analytical in one's approach to decision making but not paralyzed by that fact. A consultant must take action and demonstrate to the client that the climate can change. Just like an organization, a consultant can end up analyzing a situation longer than necessary, until it's too late to take action.

"Close to the customer" suggests keeping in touch with clients and understanding their needs. Organizations that lose sight of their target population will produce products no one wants. A consultant who loses sight of clients' needs by getting wrapped up in his or her own goals and motivations will not have that client for long.

"Being entrepreneurial" means being innovative and taking risks. Outside consultants must be especially high risk takers because they are on their own, without a parent organization.

"Productivity through people" can occur only if management regards human beings as the single most important investment for the corporation. Believing that human resource development ensures the future of the organization is an attitude that successful consultants embrace themselves and foster in their clients.

"Hands-on, value-driven" is explained by Peters and Waterman as: "The basic philosophy of an organization has far more to do with its achievements than do technological or economic resources, organizational structure, innovation, and timing" (p. 15). A consultant needs to identify what human relationship philosophy drives his or her activities and interventions. This philosophy should define how one believes people are motivated and what techniques will persuade others.

If you "stick to your knitting," you will "never acquire a business you don't know how to run" (p. 15). A consultant should stick to what he or she knows best. Do not expand into product innovation if that is not your expertise.

"Simple form, lean stuff" implies simple but eloquent designs for the system and for operating the organization. I have found that some of the most simple and direct designs for intervening into an organization work best. When I try to design a complex, highly structured innovation, it usually misses the target.

In communication management "simultaneous loose-tight properties" implies an approach to interacting in the organization that includes both centralized and decentralized activities. Some decision-making practices need to be centralized in the hands of a few while others need broad-based support and involvement. The consultant's job is to help the organization distinguish which approach is needed for different decisions.

Just as Peters and Waterman used these criteria to identify excellent companies, we can use them to point out an outstanding consultant. These basic principles about working with customers relate quite well to the client-consultant relationship.

W. Edwards Deming, the father of "quality" in organizations, has indicated that managers and executives are least prepared to deal with human problems. Many managers come from technical training and experiences where a problem can be fixed by replacing a part or a process. With human beings we are constantly molding and shaping and rarely replacing with a small part! I hope this book has helped in some small way to assist you in dealing with the complex human interactions we find not only at work, but at home, in our living rooms.

Notes

1. The section on legal forms is adapted from: DeWine, S. (1987a, November). *Firming up your own communication consulting firm*. Paper presented at the Speech Communication Association Convention, Chicago, IL.

2. Unless otherwise indicated, all statistics are taken from the U.S. Department of Commerce, Washington, D.C.

3. For additional information on various legal forms, consult one of the following references: Baumback, C. & Lawyer, K. *How to organize and operate a small business,* Englewood Cliffs, NJ: Prentice Hall, 1979; Mancuso, J. R. *How to start, finance, and manage your own small business.* Englewood Cliffs, NJ: Prentice Hall, 1978; or Siropolic, N. *How to start your own business, and how to make money.* Boston, MA: Houghton Mifflin, 1977.

Suggested Readings

Bellman, G. M. (1990). *The consultant's calling.* San Francisco: Jossey Bass.

Block, P. (1981). *Flawless consulting.* San Diego: University Associates.

Greiner, L. E., & Metzger, R. O. (1983). *Consulting to management.* Englewood Cliffs, NJ: Prentice-Hall.

THE SILENT TREATMENT: A CASE STUDY

by Sue DeWine and Rita L. Rahoi

"Sue, could you help us with a little personnel problem?"

Thus began a consulting intervention that included training programs, personal counseling, mediation, and team development. The so-called "little personnel problem" was actually a dysfunctional superior-subordinate employee relationship—one so intense that it was affecting the ability of the entire unit to function. These individuals did not have to work as a tightly coupled team and were relatively independent. However, they worked in close proximity to each other, and everyone was keenly aware of the tension between these two people. The fact that they no longer spoke to each other made the problem quite obvious.

Stage I

"We have an annual in-service program coming up and we would like for you to run a communication program for us. We think we can always improve our communication in the office."

A comment from Sue: I often invite colleagues to join me in training programs because I work with a number of aspiring and experienced consultants on a regular basis. Rita Rahoi was an excellent selection for this joint venture because I knew she had some valuable training skills. What I did not know was how insightful she would be in diagnosing the issues in this particular case.

When, as a consultant, you accept an invitation such as this, you are accepting the client's assessment of the problem as well. "We can always improve our communication" is not a very specific diagnosis of the problems confronting this office.

Even though you would rather do a complete needs assessment yourself, often you are not afforded that opportunity. You might find, however, that the best way to work with a client is to begin by conducting some type of training program. This is frequently also an opportunity for the client to assess whether or not to trust you with more serious problems. Our goal is to demonstrate our acceptance of the client as well as the problem. Even though you must consider the client's assessment in planning a training program, you can still conduct your own "mini-needs assessment." In this case, we distributed brief letters to the members of the client organization, asking them to respond to two simple questions: "How could things be better in your office?" and "What is preventing you from improving your office environment?"

The response was overwhelming. We had hoped for some input from employees but anticipated that they would be at best reticent—at worst, reluctant—to share their thoughts. Instead, we were inundated with information: complaints, criticisms, and concerns. Clearly, we had our work cut out for us in planning the initial session.

Reviewing the responses, we looked for themes or concerns that were not only common to many employees but that also could be reasonably addressed in the brief two-hour session we had been asked to conduct. We decided to begin with brief presentations on listening and giving effective feedback, followed by team simulation exercises in which one person in each team was asked to play a person with whom he or she was frustrated (preferably one outside the office, as we hoped to avoid increasing tensions). Their partners were asked to play the role of the frustrated person. This allowed participants an opportunity to practice their new-found listening and feedback skills, since both team members had time and opportunity to play both roles. We also moved from team to team, listening, observing, and providing feedback so that we could model appropriate communication behaviors for participants. These skills were extremely important to these group members because their jobs demand high levels of performance under continual tension and unusually high contact with the public.

Following these exercises, we divided group members into teams to brainstorm suggestions for improved communication and task organization and effectiveness in their workplace. Since we included employees from all organizational levels in each of the two groups, we found that participants were eager to make suggestions. We noted their ideas on large easels and, after approximately twenty minutes of discussion, united the teams to discuss and evaluate the ideas. We carefully avoided associating employees' names with specific suggestions in order to eliminate automatic acceptance or rejection of given comments. They were better able to evaluate ideas objectively when they could see them in print.

A comment from Rita: I was very pleased with our team approach to this initial workshop session. Sue is a wonderful facilitator, and freely shared not only credit but also responsibility. Our personalities and interests also made this a balanced team effort: Sue is very calm and lends an air of authority to coping with dominant managers who threaten group process, whereas I am more vivacious and enjoy encouraging support staff to contribute their comments to discussions. Team approaches do not always work in consulting, but with luck, enthusiasm, and effort, they can be rewarding for both participants and consultants.

We left this initial training program feeling it had been productive and that the response we received from the participants involved was encouraging. This was not the end of the story, however. Several weeks later, we received another call from the director of the organization.

"We really enjoyed your training program and have incorporated many of your suggestions. We still have a serious problem, however, with one pair of employees. Can you help?"

And so, we gathered our notes and prepared for:

Stage II

The "pair of employees" referred to by the organizational director was comprised of a supervisor and assistant who had completely stopped talking to each other. We began by setting up separate meetings with each of the two participants and with their supervisor to gather as much information as possible about the causes and effects of this problematic relationship. To avoid the "good cop, bad cop" trap, enable ourselves to evaluate objectively, and keep from overwhelming the participants with information overload, we took turns as listener-recorder and questioner.

Once we had some idea of the problems involved and which incidents were particularly significant or hurtful to each of the employees, we scheduled a dyadic interview in which the participants were encouraged to listen to each other's comments without immediate feedback, denial, or judgment. We believed this controlled discussion was important, since the power dynamics were imbalanced in this pair (the manager was a dynamic, "workaholic" male, the administrative assistant was a less aggressive woman who had initiated the "silent treatment" as her way of coping).

Unfortunately, it was clear to us that the relationship between these co-workers had deteriorated too far to be repaired. As consultants, we must remember that we are not counselors, and cannot seek to repair whatever problems lie outside, yet contribute to, the climate and culture of an organization. We recognized that one of these employees would probably be happier with a change of employment, and offered assistance in relocation. For the short term, however, our job was to find some way to break the silence barrier and enable these two people to work together effectively until a transfer became possible.

We worked on negotiating baseline behaviors and coping strategies that both parties found acceptable, using a "best-case–worst-case scenario" approach (asking, "What would be your 'best case' of a typical day working with X?" "What are examples of Y's behavior that you absolutely cannot tolerate?"). The negotiated "rules" we ended up with were as follows:

1. X and Y will meet for short periods of time (5–10 minutes) each morning after they are settled in and each afternoon before they leave, each day that their schedules will permit.

2. X will use Y's in-basket for projects rather than stacking them on the desk and will entrust Y to address them, and will ask for materials rather than searching Y's desk.

3. Both will be more responsible for, and aware of, the impact the timing of their communication has (X will not respond to Y's request for sick time by complaining about work yet to be done, Y will greet X courteously in the morning rather than ignoring X).

It seems remarkable that such behaviors needed to be negotiated, but the relationship had progressed—or, rather, regressed—to the point that we believed we would be successful if we only got them to be civil to each other.

We then met with the director of the organization, reviewed our suggestions for the work team and added some suggestions of our own for managing this problem pair:

1. Meet with X and Y to reinforce our recommendations.

2. Be prepared to work proactively, rather than reactively, and intervene before tensions reach this pitch again.

3. Be alert for similar tension building within the department, as the potential for such problems was evident in other staff "teams."

4. Be ready to direct X to participate in any follow-up efforts, as X seems less aware of the effects of X's actions on other staff members and more defensive about performance.

In order to continue efforts to help this organization through what was virtually a day-to-day crisis situation, given the nature of its work, we moved on to:

Stage III

This stage involved efforts to enhance team building among all organizational members. We implemented a training session in which employees submitted their preferences for the type of work and the specific yearly projects to which they would be assigned, listing the tasks to be completed in a group discussion session and using employees' preferences to establish work teams for each project. Since the organization had a set schedule of yearly projects, we knew in advance that tasks could be divided in this manner.

This avoided the slapdash manner in which incoming new employees had been assigned to whatever project was currently in progress and enabled employees to have some sense of direction in their work life. Using this approach also allowed the director to assign the administrative assistant to work with a variety of people in the unit. The tensions resulting from working with only one administrator could then be reduced to some extent.

We also suggested that the director of the organization change his policy of "strongly recommending" that employees attend given organizational functions, ranging from receptions to staff birthday parties. We further noted that attendance might improve if these functions were more casual. Earlier, we discovered these functions were catered by hired wait staff in an uncomfortably formal atmosphere.

Conclusion

Both in our private lives and as consultants, we must make a decision early on about whether it is better to cope with or resolve conflicts. Our intent in this intervention was to provide coping mechanisms that would keep such conflicts from affecting everyone else in the organization.

Several months after the completion of this intervention effort, we heard some encouraging news:

1. Although neither employee has been able to move on to another organization, the two of them are talking (minimally) and have been able to work successfully as members of new teams;

2. The director of the organization has contacted us to discuss other questions or concerns, since, as this person put it, "I don't want things to get this bad again";

3. Employees in the organization continue to talk about their listening and feedback sessions, and referred members of another organization to us for training.

As you read over this case study, we hope you will remember what we keep firmly in mind—that no one set of procedures or programs will give you the answer in every organizational consultation. Just as actors work on "filling their bag of tricks" with techniques, characters, voices, and movement, so we as consultants must be constantly learning in order to provide the most accountable, effective help possible. This case study was as much a learning experience for us as it could ever be for our readers. Should you encounter a similar situation, use our suggestions as guidelines—not as rules—and remember that, as newscaster Diane Sawyer once said, "There is no substitute for paying attention."

REFERENCES

Alderton, S.M. (1983). Survey course in organizational communication consulting: A processual model. *Communication Education, 32,* pp. 413–20.

American Psychiatric Association (1980). *Diagnostic and statistical manual of mental disorders.* Washington, D.C.: American Psychiatric Association.

American Society of Training and Development. (1988). *Practical guide for technical and skills trainers: Vol. 1 & 2.* Alexandria, VA: American Society for Training and Development.

American Telephone and Telegraph Co. (1987a). *The trainer's library: Techniques of instructional development.* Reading, MA: Addison-Wesley Publishing Co., Inc.

American Telephone and Telegraph Co. (1987b). *The trainer's library: Measurement and evaluation.* Reading, MA: Addison-Wesley Publishing Co., Inc.

American Telephone and Telegraph Co. (1987c). *The trainer's library: Planning an analysis.* Reading, MA: Addison-Wesley Publishing Co., Inc.

Anderson, R. L., & Terborg, J. R. (1988). Employee beliefs and support for a work redesign intervention. *Journal of Management, 14,* 493–503.

Arnold, W. E., & McClure, L. (1989). Evaluating training programs. In W. E. Arnold & L. McClure, *Communication training and development* (pp. 117–28). New York, NY: Harper and Row.

Atwater, E. (1992). *I hear you* (revised). New York, NY: Walker.

Baird, L. S., Schneier, C. E., & Laird, D. (1983). *The training and development sourcebook.* Amherst, MA: Human Resource Development Press.

Bakken, D., & Bernstein, A. (1982). A systematic approach to evaluation. *Training and Development Journal, 36,* 44–51.

Ball, S., & Anderson, S. E. (1975). *Practicing in program evaluation: A survey and some case studies.* Princeton, NJ: Educational Testing Service.

Barcus, S. W., & Wilkinson, J. W. (1986). *Management Consulting Services.* New York, NY: McGraw-Hill, Inc.

Bard, R., Bell, C. R., Stephen, L., & Webster, L. (Eds.) (1987). *The trainer's professional development handbook.* San Francisco, CA: Jossey-Bass, Inc.

Bard, R., & Stephen, L. (1987) Developing your learning plan. In R. Bard, C. R. Bell, L. Stephen, & L. Webster (Eds.), *The trainer's professional development handbook* (pp. 27–40). San Francisco, CA: Jossey-Bass, Inc.

Barmash, I. (1985, Sept. 9). A new economic indicator. *Newsweek,* p. 12.

Baum, E. (1991). *Meeting leader's checklist.* Adapted from Higher Education Management Institute, 1979. Unpublished manuscript. Ohio University, Athens, OH.

Baumback, C. & Lawyer, K. (1978). *How to organize and operate a small business.* Englewood Cliffs, NJ: Prentice-Hall.

Bazerman, M.H., & Lewicki, R.J. (1983). *Negotiating in organizations.* Beverly Hills, CA: Sage.

Beckhand, R. (1967). *Organizational development: Strategies and models.* Reading, MA: Addison-Wesley Publishing Co., Inc.

Bedrosian, N.M. (1987). *Speak like a pro: In business and public speaking.* New York: John Wiley & Sons, Inc.

Behof, K. A. (1988, Oct. 24). An identity crisis at Arthur Andersen, *Business Week,* p. 34.

Bell, C. R. (1985). Diagnosis: Frameworks for consultants and clients. In C. R. Bell & L. Nadler (Eds.). *Clients and consultants: Meeting and exceeding expectations* (pp. 152–64). Houston, TX: Gulf Publishing Co.

Bell, C. R., & Nadler, L. (1985). *Clients and consultants: Meeting and exceeding expectations* (2nd ed.). Houston, TX: Gulf Publishing Co.

Bellman, G. M. (1990, Dec.). Balancing your work in your life. *Training and Development Journal*, pp. 50–58.

Bennett, D. (1980). *Successful team building through TA.* New York, NY: Amacom, Division of American Management Assoc.

Berryman-Fink, C., Ballard-Reisch, D., & Newman, L. (1993). *Communication and sex-role socialization.* New York, NY: Garland Press.

Bissell, C. B. (1985). Defusing the difficult employee: How to handle problem people. *Management World, 14* (2), 30–31.

Blake, R. R., & Mouton, J. (1976). *Consultation* (2nd ed.). Reading, MA: Addison-Wesley Publishing Co., Inc.

Blake, R. R., & Mouton, J. S. (1989). *Consultation* (2nd ed.). Reading, MA: Addison-Wesley Publishing Co., Inc.

Blake, R. R., Mouton, J. S., & McCanse, A. A. (1989). *Change by design.* Reading, MA: Addison-Wesley Publishing Co., Inc.

Block, P. (1981). *Flawless consulting: A guide to getting your expertise used.* San Diego, CA: University Associates.

Bloom, B. S., Englehart, M. D., Furst, E. J., Hill, W. H., & Krathwohl, D. R. (1956). *Taxonomy of educational objectives: The classification of educational goals, by a committee of college and university examiners, handbook 1: Cognitive domain.* New York, NY: David McKay.

Boetlinger, H. M. (1969). *Moving mountains or the art and craft of letting others see things your way.* London: Macmillan.

Bolles, R. N. (1971). *What color is your parachute?* Berkeley, CA: Ten Speed Press.

Bowers, D. G., & Stambaugh, L. K. (1986). Making organizational surveys pay off. In C. N. Jackson (Ed.). *Targeting change: Organizational development* (pp. 41–47). Alexandria, VA: American Society for Training and Development.

Boyer, R. K. (1987). Developing consultation skills: A simulation approach. In W. B. Reddy & C. C. Henderson (Eds.), *Training, theory, and practice* (pp. 58–77). San Diego, CA: University Associates.

Braiker, H. B. (1988). The etiquette of office romance. *Working Woman, 13,* 148–52.

Brammer, C. (1993). *Identification of disruptive communication behaviors and instrument development.* Doctoral Dissertation, Ohio University, Athens, OH.

Brownell, J. (1990). Perceptions of effective listeners: A management study. *Journal of Business Communication, 27,* 401–15.

Bucalo, J. P. (1984, December). An operational approach to training needs analysis. *Training and Development Journal,* 80–84.

Bunker, B. B., Nochajski, T., McGillicuddy, N., & Bennett, D. (1987). *Designing and running training events: Rules of thumb for trainers.* In W. B. Reddy and C. C. Henderson (Eds.), *Training, theory, and practice* (pp. 225–39). San Diego, CA: University Associates.

Bunker, K. A. & Cohen, S. L. (1977). The rigors of training evaluation: A discussion and field demonstration. *Personnel Psychology, 30,* 525–41.

Burley-Allen, M. (1982). *Listening: The forgotten skill.* New York, NY: John Wiley & Sons, Inc.

Business Week, (1984, Sept. 10). A consulting maverick goes straight, p. 95.

Campbell, J. P., Dunnette, M. D., Lawler, L. & Weick, K. (1970). *The effectiveness of head resident human relations training.* Doctoral Dissertation, University of Northern Colorado, Boulder, CO.

Caplan, R. E., & Darth, W. H. (1987). Realistic simulations: An alternative vehicle for laboratory education. In W. B. Reddy & C. C. Henderson (Eds.), *Training, theory, and practice* (pp. 137–47). La Jolla, CA: University Associates.

Chenault, J. (1989). Training for changing consultant roles. *Management Consulting, 5,* 48–54.

Christensen, C. R. (1987). *Teaching in the case method: Text, cases, and readings.* Boston, MA: Harvard Business School.

Clampitt, P. G. (1991). *Communicating for managerial effectiveness.* Newbury Park, CA: Sage.

Clegg, W. H. (1987). Management training evaluation: An update. *Training and Development Journal,* 65–71.

Coghlan, D. (1988). In defense of process consultation. *Leadership and Organization Development Journal, 9,* 27–31.

Collins, G. (1983). Managers and lovers. *Harvard Business Review, 61,* 142–53.

Collins, G. (1987, Feb. 1). Men vs. women in the office, *The New York Times.*

Cooper, S., & Heenan, C. (1980). *Preparing, designing, and leading workshops: A humanistic approach.* Boston, MA: CBI Publishing.

Cornwell, J. B. (1980, Aug.). Measuring back-on-the-job performance. *Training,* 289–92.

Craig, R. L. (1983). *Measuring human resource development.* Paper presented at the Senior HRD Management Forum, ASTD National Issues Committee, Washington, D.C.

Crary, M. (1987), Managing attraction and intimacy at work. *Organizational Dynamics, 15,* 26–40.

Culnan, M. J., & Markus, M. L. (1987). Information technology. In F. M. Jablin, L. L. Putnam, K. H. Roberts, & L. W. Porter (Eds.), *Handbook of organizational communication* (pp. 420–44). Newbury Park, CA: Sage.

Cusella, L. P. (1987). Feedback, motivation, and performance. In F. M. Jablin, L. L. Putnam, K. H. Roberts, & L. W. Porter (Eds.), *Handbook of organizational communication* (pp. 624–78). Newberry Park, CA: Sage.

Cypher, B.D., Bostrom, R.N., & Seibert, J.H. (1989). Listening, communication abilities, and success at work. *The Journal of Business Communication, 26,* 293–303.

D'Aprix, R. (1982). *Communicating for productivity.* Cambridge, MA: Harper and Row.

Daniels, T. D., & DeWine, S. (1991). Communication process as target and tool for consultancy intervention: Rethinking a hackneyed theme. *Journal of Education and Psychological Consultation, 2* (4), 303–22.

Daniels, T., & Spiker, B. (1991). *Perspectives on organizational communication* (2nd ed.). Dubuque, IA: William C. Brown.

Davis, M. E. (1986). Problem definition. In S. Barcus & J. Wilkinson (Eds.). *Handbook of management consulting services.* New York, NY: McGraw-Hill, Inc.

Deckhard, R. (1969). *Organization development: Strategies and models.* Reading, MA: Addison-Wesley Publishing Co., Inc.

Deeprose, D. (1991, Sept.). Helping employees handle difficult customers. *Supervisory Management, 6.*

Deetz, S. (1992). *Democracy in an age of corporate colonization: Developments in communication and the politics of everyday life.* Albany, NY: State University of New York Press.

Deming, B. S. (1982). *Evaluating job-related training: A guide for training the trainer.* Englewood Cliffs, NJ: Prentice-Hall.

Dennis, H., Goldhaber, G., & Yates, M. (1978). Review of research systems and procedures in organizational communication research. In B. Ruben (Ed.), *Communication yearbook 2* (pp. 243–69). New Brunswick, NJ: Transaction Books.

Denova, C. C. (1970). *Test construction for training evaluation*. Van Nostrand Reinhold.

DeWine, S. (1980). *Firming up your own communication consulting firm*. Paper presented to the Speech Communication Association, New York, NY.

DeWine, S. (1987a). Evaluation of organizational communication competency: The development of the communication training impact questionnaire. *Journal of Applied Communication Research, 15*, 113–27.

DeWine, S. (1987b, June). Socializing with your boss. *Personal Report*, p. 8.

DeWine, S. (1989). Female leadership in male dominated organizations. *Association for Communication Administrators Bulletin, 67*, 19–29.

DeWine, S., & Daniels, T. (1993). Beyond the snapshot: Setting a research agenda in organizational communication. In S. Deetz (Ed.), *Communication Yearbook 14*, Newbury Park, CA: Sage.

DeWine, S., Casbolt, D., & Bentley, N. (1983, May). *Moving through the organization: A field study assessment of the patron system*. Paper presented at the International Communication Association, Dallas, TX.

DeWine, S. & James, A. C. (1978). *The Hippocratic oath and standards for organizational communication consultants*. Paper presented to the Speech Communication Association, Minneapolis, MN.

DeWine, S. & James, A. C. (1988). Examining the communication audit: Assessment and modification. *Management Communication Quarterly, 2*, 144–69.

DeWine, S., James A., & Hale, C. (1991, May). *Organizational maintenance: Successful assimilation through mentoring relationships*. Paper presented at the International Communication Association, Chicago, IL.

DeWine, S., James, A., & Walence, W. (1985, May). *Validation of organizational communication audit instruments*. Presented at the International Communication Association, Hawaii.

DeWine, S., Pearson, J.C., & Yost, C. (in press). Intimate office relationships and their impact on work group communication. In C. Berryman-Fink, D. Ballard-Reisch, & L. Newman (Eds.) *Communication and sex-role socialization*. New York, NY: Garland Press.

Diamond, M. A. (1986). Resistance to change: A psychoanalytic critique of Argyris and Schon's Contributions to organization theory and intervention. *Journal of Management, 23*, (5), 543–62.

Digman, L. (1980). How companies evaluate management development programs. *Human Resource Management, 19*, 9–13.

Dillard, J. P. (1987). Close relationships at work: Perceptions of the motives and performance of relational participants. *Journal of Social and Personal Relationships, 4*, 179–193.

Dillard, J. P., & Broetzmann, S. M. (1989). Romantic relationships at work: Perceived changes in job-related behaviors as a function of participant's motive, partner's motive, and gender. *Journal of Applied Social Psychology, 19*, 93–110.

Dillard, J. P. & Witteman, H. (1985). Romantic relationships at work: Organizational and personal influences. *Human Communication Research, 12*, 99–116.

Dopyera, J., & Pitone, L. (1983, May). Decision points in planning the evaluation of training. *Training and Development Journal*, 66–71.

Downs, C. (1988). *Communication audits*. Glenview, IL: Scott, Foresman & Co.

Downs, C., DeWine, S., & Greenbaum, H. (in press). Organizational Communication Instrumentation. In R. Rubin & H. Sypher (Eds.). *Instrumentation in Communication*. New York, NY: Longman Press.

Downs, C. W., Johnson, K. M., & Barge, J. K. (1984). Communication feedback and task performance in organizations: A review of the literature. In H. Greenbaum, R. Falcione, & S.

Hellweg (Eds.), *Organizational communication abstracts* (pp. 13–47). Beverly Hills, CA: Sage.

Doyle, M., & Straus, D. (1986). *How to make meetings work.* New York, NY: Berkeley Publishing Group.

Dyer, W. G. (1977). *Team building: Issues and alternatives.* Reading, MA: Addison-Wesley Publishing Co., Inc.

Earley, P. C., Connolly, T., & Lee, C. (1989). Task strategy interventions in goal setting: The importance of search in strategy development. *Journal of Management, 15,* (4), 589–602.

Ernest, R.C. (1985, March) Corporate culture and defective planning. *Personnel Administrator,* 49–60.

Erway, E.A. (1979). *Listening: A programmed approach.* New York, NY: McGraw-Hill, Inc.

Ellis, S. K. (1988). *How to survive a training assignment: A practical guide for the new, part-time or temporary trainer.* Reading, MA: Addison-Wesley Publishing Co., Inc.

Estler, S. (1977). Proceedings of the conference on women's leadership and authority in the health professions. HEW contract #HRA 230-76-0269, 197–217.

Falcione, R., Goldhaber, G., Porter, T., & Rogers, D. (1979, November). *The future of the ICA communication audit.* Paper presented at the meeting of the International Communication Association, Philadelphia, PA.

Farace, R., Monge, P., & Russell, H. (1977). *Communicating and organizing.* Reading, MA: Addison-Wesley Publishing Co., Inc.

Ferguson, S.D., & Ferguson, S. (1988). *Organizational Communication.* New Brunswick, NJ: Transaction Books.

Fiedler, F. E., & Garcia, J. E. (1985). Comparing organization development and management training. *Personnel Administrator,* 35–47.

Filley, A. C. (1975). *Interpersonal conflict resolution.* Palo Alto, CA: Scott, Foresman & Co.

Fisher, A. B. (1989, April 24). The ever-bigger boom in consulting. *Fortune,* pp. 113–34.

Flax, E. (1989). Should you outlaw romance in the office? *Working Woman, 14,* 16.

Francis, D., & Young, D. (1979). *Improving work groups: A practical manual for team building.* San Diego, CA: University Associates.

French, W. L., & Bell, C. H. (1990). *Organization development: Behavioral science interventions for organization improvement.* Englewood Cliffs, NJ: Prentice-Hall.

Freud, S. (1901). Fragment of an analysis of a case of hysteria. In J. Strachey and A. Freud (Eds.), *The standard edition of the complete works of Sigmund Freud, 7,* (pp. 7–122). London: Hogarth Press.

Friedman, P. G., & Yarbrough, E. A. (1985). *Training strategies from start to finish.* Englewood Cliffs, NJ: Prentice-Hall.

Fuchs, J.H. (1975). *Making the most of management consulting services.* New York, NY: AMA-COM.

Furr, R. M. (1985). Surviving as a messenger: Client-consultant relationship during diagnosis. In C. R. Bell & L. Nadler (Eds.), *Clients and consultants: Meeting and exceeding expectations* (2nd ed.). Houston, TX: Gulf Publishing Co.

Gabarro, J. J., & Harlan, A. (1976). Note on process observation. *Teaching.* President and Fellows of Harvard College.

Galagan, P. A. (1989, Jan.). IBM gets its arms around education. *Training and Development Journal,* pp. 34–45.

Gerwig, K. (1991, Oct. 9). Insurer's videoconferencing cuts travel time, boasts training. *Imaging News.,* pp. 6–7.

Gibb, J. R. (1961). Defensive communication. *Journal of Communication, 11,* 142.

Glenn, E.C., & Podd, E.A. (1989, Jan.). Listening self inventory. *Supervisory Management,* 13–15.

Goddard, R.W. (1988, May). Gathering a great team. *Management Weekly,* pp. 20–22.

Goldhaber, G. (1986). *Organizational communication* (4th ed.). Dubuque, IA: Wm C. Brown.

Goldhaber, G., Dennis, H., Richetto, G., & Wiio, O. (1979). *Information strategies: New pathways to corporate power.* Englewood Cliffs, NJ: Prentice-Hall.

Goldhaber, G., & Rogers, D. (1979). *Auditing organization communication systems: The ICA communication audit.* Dubuque, IA: Kendall/Hunt.

Goldhaber, G., Yates, M., Porter, T., & Lesniak, R. (1978). Organizational communication: 1978. *Human Communication Research, 5,* 76–96.

Goldstein, I. L. (1978). The pursuit of validity in the evaluation of training programs. *Human Factors, 20,* 131–44.

Goldstein, I. L. (1989). *Training and development in organizations.* San Francisco, CA: Jossey-Bass, Inc.

Goodall, H. L. (1989). *Casing the promised land: The autobiography of an organization detective as cultural ethnographer.* Carbondale, IL: Southern Illinois Press.

Gordon, T. (1977). *Parent effectiveness training.* New York, NY: Peter H. Wyden.

Gordon, W. J. (1961). *Synectics: The development of creative capacity.* New York, NY: Harper and Row.

Gottmam, J.M., & J.G. (Eds.). (1986). *Conversations of friends: Speculations on affective development.* New York, NY: Cambridge University Press.

Gouran, D.S. (1982). *Making decisions in groups: Choices and consequences.* Glenview, IL: Scott, Foresman & Co.

Grant, D. L. (1977). Issues in the evaluation of training. *Professional Psychology, 8,* 659–73.

Gray, S. (1984, June 18). Romance in the workplace: Corporate rules for the game of love. *Business Week,* 70–71.

Greenbaum, H., DeWine, S., & Downs, C. (1987). Organizational communication measurement: A call for review and evaluation. *Communication Management Quarterly, 1,* 129–44.

Greiner, L.E., & Metzger, R.O. (1983). *Consulting to management.* Englewood Cliffs, NJ: Prentice-Hall.

Gutek, B. A. (1985). *Sex and the workplace: The impact of sexual behavior and harassment of women, men, and organizations.* San Francisco, CA: Jossey-Bass, Inc.

Gutek, B. A., Morasch, B., & Cohen, A. G. (1983). Interpreting social sexual behavior in a work setting. *Journal of Vocational Behavior, 22,* 30–48.

Guzzo, R. A., Jette, R. D., & Katzell, R. A. (1985). The effects of psychologically based intervention programs on worker productivity: A meta-analysis. *Personnel Psychology, 38,* 275–91.

Hale, C. L., Cooks, L., & DeWine, S. (1992, November). *Anita Hill on trial: A dialectical analysis of a persuasive interrogation.* Presented at the Speech Communication Convention, Chicago, IL.

Hall, J. (1969). *Conflict management survey.* Telemetrics International, Conroe, TX.

Hamblin, A.C. (1974). *Evaluation and control of training.* London: McGraw-Hill, Inc.

Hampton, D. R., Summer, C. E., & Weber, R. E. (1973). *Organizational behavior and the practice of management.* Glenview, IL: Scott, Foresman & Co.

Handley, E. (1986). Saying no to office romances. *Bureaucrat, 14,* 35–38.

Handy, C. (1989). *The age of unreason.* Boston, MA: Harvard Business School.

Hansell, S. (1989, Nov.). Andersen's armies. *Institutional Investor, 123*–28.

Hanson, P. G., & Lubin, B. (1987). Assessment of trainer skills by self, peers, and supervisors. In W. B. Reddy & C. C. Henderson (Eds.), *Training, theory, and practice* (pp. 47–58). La Jolla, CA: University Associates.

Harrison, M. I. (1990). Hard choices in diagnosing organizations. *Journal of Management Consulting, 6,* 13–21.

Headrick, G. (1983, Feb.). Let's learn to listen! *Kiwanis Magazine,* pp. 18–20.

Helgesen, S. (1990). *The female advantage: Women's ways of leadership.* New York, NY: Doubleday.

Hill, R. (1986). Role negotiation: Mainlined into the culture of the organization. In C. N. Jackson (Ed.). *Organizational development.* (pp. 19–30). Alexandria, VA.: American Society for Training and Development.

Hirokawa, R. Y. (1987). Why informed groups make faulty decisions: An investigation of possible interaction-based explanations. *Small Group Behavior, 18,* 3–29.

Hocker, J., & Wilmot, W. (1985). *Interpersonal conflict.* Dubuque, IA: William A. Brown.

Hoerr, J. (September 24, 1990). With job training, a little dab won't do ya. *Business Week,* p. 95.

Hollwitz, J., Churchill, R., & Hollwitz, T. (1985, Nov.). *Communication with the difficult personality: Adaptive responses in organizational settings.* Paper presented at the annual meeting of the Speech Communication Association, Washington, D.C.

Holtz, H. (1989). *Choosing and using a consultant: A manager's guide to consulting services.* New York, NY: John Wiley & Sons, Inc.

Horn, P.D., & Horn, J. (1982). *Sex in the office.* Reading, MA: Addison-Wesley Publishing Co., Inc.

Howell, W. S., & Bormann, E. G. (1988). *The process of presentational speaking.* (2nd ed.). New York, NY: Harper & Row.

Huse, E. (1980). *Organization development and change,* (2nd ed.). St. Paul, MN: West.

Iacocca, L. (1984). *Iacocca: An autobiography.* New York, NY: Bantam Books.

Jablin, F.M., Putnam, L.L., Roberts, K.H., & Porter, L.W. (1987). *Handbook of organizational communication: An interdisiplinary perspective.* Newbury Park, CA: Sage.

James, A. C. & DeWine, S. (1990). Shoot out at Midwest Manufacturing. In B. Davenport Sypher (Ed.). *Case Studies in Organizational Communication.* (pp. 177–89). New York, NY: Guilford Press.

Jamison, K. (1983, August). Managing sexual attraction in the workplace. *Personnel Administrator,* 45–51.

Janis, I.L. (1972). *Victims of groupthink* (2nd ed.). Boston, MA: Houghton Mifflin Co.

Jessup, H.R. (1990, November). New roles and team leadership. *Training and Development Journal,* pp. 79–83.

Johnson, P. M. (1990, August). Communicating for commitment and productivity. *Training and Development Journal,* pp. 55–57.

Jones, J. E. & Pfeiffer, J. W. (1979). Role playing. *The 1979 Annual Handbook for Group Facilitators.* San Diego, CA: University Associates.

Kanter, R.M. (1983). *The changemasters.* New York, NY: Simon and Schuster.

Kanter, R.M. (1989). *When giants learn to dance.* New York, NY: Simon and Schuster.

Katz, D., & Kahn, R. (1978). *The social psychology of organizations.* New York, NY: John Wiley & Sons, Inc.

Katz, J. (1982, July 21). It's time to reverse our retreat from reality in teaching college students. *The Chronicle of Higher Education*, p. 40.

Kearsley, G. (1982). *Costs benefits and productivity in training systems.* Reading, MA: Addison-Wesley Publishing Co., Inc.

Kelley, R.E. (1981). *Consulting: The complete guide to a profitable career.* New York, NY: Charles Scribner's Sons.

Keltner, J. W. (1987). *Mediation.* Annandale, VA: Speech Communication Association.

Kirkpatrick, D. L. (1967). Evaluation of training. In R. L. Craig & L. R. Bittel (Eds.), *Training and development handbook.* New York, NY: McGraw-Hill, Inc.

Kirkpatrick, D. L. (1979). Techniques for evaluating training programs. *Training and Development Journal,* 78–92.

Kirkpatrick, D. L. (1987). *More evaluating training programs: A collection of articles from Training and Development Journal.* Alexandria, VA: American Society for Training and Development.

Kreps, G.L. (1989). A therapeutic model of organizational communication consultation: Application of interpretive field methods. *The Southern Communication Journal, 55,* pp. 1–21.

Kurpius, D. (1978). Consultation theory and process: An integrated model. *The Personnel and Guidance Journal, 56,* pp. 18–21.

Kurtz, T. (1990, Sept.). Dynamic listening: Unlocking your communication potential. *Supervisory Management,* p. 7.

Laird, A., & Clampitt, P. G. (1985). Effective performance appraisal: Viewpoints from managers. *Journal of Business Communication, 22*(3), 49–57.

Langdon-Dahm, M. (1986). *Trade secrets: 25 proven success tools for working, dealing and winning with people.* Dayton, OH: Learning Development Systems.

Lewin, K. (1951). *Field theory in social science.* New York, NY: Harper and Row.

Linestone, H., & Turoff, M. (1975). *The delphi method: Techniques and applications.* London: Addison-Wesley.

Lippitt, G., & Lippitt, R. (1986). *The consulting process in action* (2nd ed.). San Diego, CA: University Associates.

Lippitt, G., Lippitt, R., & Lafferty, C. (1984). Cutting edge trends in organization development. *Training and Development Journal,* 59.

London, M. (1989). *Managing the training enterprise: High quality, cost effective employee training in organizations.* San Francisco, CA: Jossey-Bass, Inc.

Luckert, L. M. (1989). Love at the office. *Women in business, 41,* 12–13.

Mager, R. S. (1962). *Preparing objectives for programmed instruction.* San Francisco, CA: Fearon Publishers.

Mager, R. S. (1972). *Goal analysis.* San Francisco, CA: Fearon Publishers.

Mager, R. S. (1984). *Preparing instructional objectives.* Belmont, CA: Lake Publishing.

Maier, M.R., Solem, A.R., & Maier, A.A. (1975). *The role play technique: A handbook for management and leadership practice.* San Diego, CA: University Associates.

Mainiero, L. A. (1986). A review and analysis of power dynamics in organizational romances. *Academy of Management Review, 11,* 750–62.

Maiorca, J. J. (1991). Basic statistics for the HRD practitioner. In W. Pfeiffer & W. Jones (Eds.) *The 1991 Annual: Developing human resources* (pp. 245–65). San Diego, CA: University Associates.

Makay, J.J., & Fetzer, R.C. (1984). *Business communication skills: Principles and practice* (2nd ed.). Englewood Cliffs, NJ: Prentice-Hall.

Mancuso, J.R. (1978). *How to start, finance, and manage your own small business.* Englewood Cliffs, NJ: Prentice-Hall.

Margolies, E. (1985). *The best of friends, the worst of enemies: Women's hidden power over women.* Garden City, NY: The Dial Press.

Maslow, A. H. (revised by R. Frager, J. Fadiman, C. McReynolds, & R. Cox). (1987). *Motivation and personality* (3rd ed.). New York, NY: Harper and Row.

Masoner, M. (1988). *An audit of the case study method.* New York, NY: Praeger.

Masten, R. (1991). *I know it isn't funny but I love to make you laugh.* Carmel, CA: Sunflower Inc.

May, L. S., Moore, C. A., & Zammit, S. J. (1987). *Evaluating business and industry training.* Boston, MA: Kluwer Academic Publishers.

Mayo, G. D., & DuBois, P. H. (1987). *The complete book of training: Theories, principles, and techniques.* San Diego, CA: University Associates.

McCall, M. W., Jr., & Lombardo, M. M. (1979). *Looking Glass, Inc.: The first three years* (Technical Report No. 13). Greensboro, NC: Center for Creative Leadership.

McClelland, D. C. (1965). Toward a theory of motive acquisition. *American Psychologist, 20,* 321–33.

McClelland, D. C. (1987). *Human motivation.* New York, NY: Cambridge University Press.

McGehee, W., & Thayer, P. W. (1961). *Training in business and industry.* New York, NY: John Wiley & Sons, Inc.

McLagan, P. A. (1983). *Models for excellence: The conclusions and recommendations of the ASTD training and development competence study.* Washington, D.C.: American Society for Training and Development.

McLaughlin, P. (1988). An affair to dismember. *Canadian Business, 61,* 153–55.

McNair, M.P. (Ed). (1954). *The case method at the Harvard Business School.* New York, NY: McGraw-Hill, Inc.

Meador, B. D., & Rogers, C. R. (1973). Client-centered therapy. In R. Corsini (Ed.), *Current psychotherapies* (pp. 119–65), Itasca, IL.: F. E. Peacock.

Metzger, R.O. (1989). *Profitable consulting: Guiding America's managers into the next century.* Reading, MA: Addison-Wesley Publishing Co., Inc.

Miller, K., & Ellis, K. (1986, Nov.). *Romantic Relationships in the workplace: Stereotypes and Attributions.* Paper presented at the annual meeting of Speech Communication Association, Chicago, IL.

Mills, G. E., Pace, R. W., & Peterson, B.D. (1989). *Analysis in human resource training and organization development.* Reading, MA: Addison-Wesley Publishing Co., Inc.

Miner, J. (1975). *The management of ineffective performance.* New York, NY: McGraw-Hill, Inc.

Mirvis, P. H., & Berg, D. N. (1977). *Failures in organization development and change: Cases and essays for learning.* New York, NY: John Wiley & Sons, Inc.

Mishra, J. M., & Harell, R. (1989). Managing today's hot workplace issues (drug testing, smoking, AIDS and office romance). *Management World, 18,* 26–29.

Mitchell, G. (1987). *The trainer's handbook: The AMA guide to effective training.* New York, NY: American Management Association.

Moline, T. (1990). Upgrading the consultant. *Journal of Management Consulting, 6,* pp. 17–22.

Monroe, C., & Borzi, M. (1987, April). *The difficult personality: Analytic and strategic concerns.* Paper presented at the annual meeting of the Eastern Communication Association, Syracuse, NY.

Monroe, C., Borzi, M., & DiSalvo, V.S. (1986). Conflict behaviors of difficult subordinates. *Southern Communication Journal, 53,* 311–329.

Montgomery, R.L. (1981). *Listening made easy: How to improve listening on the job, at home, and in the community.* New York, NY: AMACOM.

Moore, M., & Gergen, P. (1986). Risk taking and organization change. In C. N. Jackson (Ed.), *Targeting change: Organizational development.* Alexandria, VA: American Society for Training and Development.

Mosak, H. H., & Dreikurs, R. (1973). Adlerian psychotherapy. In R. Corsini (Ed.), *Current psychotherapies* (pp. 1–34), Itasca, IL: F. E. Peacock.

Mosvick, R. K., & Nelson, R. B. (1987). *We've got to start meeting like this.* Glenview, IL: Scott, Foresman & Co.

Murray, M. (1991). *Beyond the myths and magic of mentoring.* San Francisco, CA.: Jossey-Bass, Inc.

Nadler, L. (1982). *Designing training programs: The critical events model.* Reading, MA: Addison-Wesley Publishing Co., Inc.

Nadler, L., & Nadler, Z. (1987). *The comprehensive guide to successful conferences and meetings.* San Francisco, CA: Jossey-Bass, Inc.

Naisbitt, J. (1982). *Megatrends.* New York, NY: Warner Books, Inc.

Naisbitt, J., & Aburdene, P. (1990). *Megatrends 2000: Ten new directions for the 1990s.* New York, NY: William Morrow & Co., Inc.

Napier, R.W., & Gershenfeld, N.K. (1987). *Groups: Theory and experience.* (4th ed.). Boston, MA: Houghton-Mifflin Co.

Nees, D.B., & Greiner, L.E. (1985). Seeing behind the look-alike management consultants. *Organizational Dynamics,* V. 13, pp. 68–79.

Nelson, P., & Pearson, J. (1990). *Confidence in public speaking* (3rd ed.). Dubuque, IA: Wm. C. Brown.

Neuman, G. A., Edwards, J. E., & Raju, N. S. (1989). Organizational development interventions: A meta-analysis of their effects on satisfaction and other attitudes. *Personnel Psychology, 42,* 461–89.

Newstrom, J. W. (1978). Catch-22: The programs of incomplete evaluation of training. *Training and Development Journal,* 22–24.

Nicholas, J. M. (1982). The comparative impact of organization development interventions on hard criteria measures. *Academy of Management Review, 7,* 531–42.

Nowack, K. M. (1991, April). A true training needs analysis. *Training and Development Journal,* 69–73.

O'Connell, S. E. (1988). Human communication in the high tech office. In G. M. Goldhaber & G. Barnett (Eds.), *Handbook of organizational communication* (pp. 473–82). Norwood, NJ: Ablex.

Osborn, M. (1991, September 17). '90's workers turning page on loyalty. *USA Today,* p. 1B.

O'Shea, T. J. (1986). Presentation of results. In S. W. Barcus and J. W. Wilkinson (Eds.) *Management Consulting Services* (pp. 235–52). New York, NY: McGraw-Hill, Inc.

Pace. R. W., & Faules, D. F. (1989). The design, conduct, and evaluation of human resource training. In R. W. Pace & D. F. Faules, *Organizational communication* (2nd ed.). Englewood Cliffs, NJ: Prentice-Hall.

Pasmore, W., Francis, C., & Haldeman, J. (1982). Sociotechnical system: A North American reflection of empirical studies of the seventies. *Human Relations, 35,* 1179–1204.

Peoples, D.A. (1988). *Presentations plus.* New York, NY: John Wiley & Sons, Inc.

Peters, T. (1988, Spring). Learning to listen. *Hyatt Magazine,* 16–18.

Peters, T. J., & Waterman, R. H. (1984). *In search of excellence: Lessons from America's best run companies.* New York, NY: Warner Communications.

Peterson, R. O. (1979). *Determining the payoff of management training.* Washington, D.C.: American Society for Training and Development.

Pfeffer, J., & Salancik, G. (1978). *The external control of organizations.* New York, NY: Harper and Row.

Pfeiffer, J. W. (1973). Conditions which hinder effective communication. In *The 1973 Annual Handbook for Group Facilitators.* LaJolla, CA: University Associates, p. 120.

Pfeiffer, J. W. (1986a). *Strategic planning: Selected readings.* San Diego, CA: University Associates.

Pfeiffer, J. W. (1986b). Encouraging managers to deal with marginal employees. In W. Pfeiffer, L.D. Goodstein, & T. M. Noland (Eds.), *Understanding applied strategic planning: A manager's guide* (4.17–4.25). San Diego, CA: University Associates.

Pfeiffer, J. W., Goodstein, L. D., & Noland, T. M. (1986a). *Understanding applied strategic planning: A manager's guide.* San Diego, CA: University Associates.

Pfeiffer, J. W., Goodstein, L. D., & Noland, T. M. (1986b). *Applied strategic planning: A how to do it guide.* San Diego, CA: University Associates.

Pfeiffer, J. W., & Jones, J. E. (1971). Intergroup meeting: An image exchange. *A handbook for structured experiences for human relations training III.* La Jolla, CA: University Associates, pp. 81–82.

Pfeiffer, J. W., & Jones, J. E. (1973). Design considerations in laboratory education. In J. E. Jones & J. W. Pfeiffer (Eds.), *The 1973 annual handbook for group facilitators* (pp. 177–94). La Jolla, CA: University Associates.

Pfeiffer, J. W., & Jones, J. E. (1972–1993) *The 1972–1993 annual handbook for group facilitators.* San Diego, CA: University Associates.

Phelps, L. & DeWine, S. (1976). *The Interpersonal Communication Journal,* St. Paul, MN., West. pp. 78–79.

Phillips, C. (1987). The trainer as person: On the importance of developing your best intervention. In W. B. Reddy & C. C. Henderson (Eds.), *Training, theory, and practice* (pp. 29–35). La Jolla, CA: University Associates.

Phillips, J. J. (1983). *Handbook of training evaluation and measurement methods.* Houston, TX: Gulf Publishing.

Pondy, L. R. (1972). Organizational conflict: Concepts and models. In John M. Thomas and Warren G. Bennis (Eds.), *Management of Change and Conflict* (p. 100). Middlesex, England: Penguin.

Poole, N.S., & Hirokawa, R.Y. (1986). Communication and group decision making. In R. Y. Hirokawa & N. S. Poole (Eds.), *Communication and group decision making* (pp. 15–34). Newbury Park, CA: Sage Publications.

Porter, L. C. (1987). Game, schmame! What have I learned? In W. B. Reddy & C. C. Henderson (Eds.), *Training, theory, and practice* (pp. 67–74). La Jolla, CA: University Associates.

Powell, G. N. (1986). What do tomorrow's managers think about sexual intimacy in the workplace? *Business Horizons, 29,* 30–35.

Prince, G. M. (1970). *The practice of creativity.* New York, NY: Harper and Row.

Quick, T. L. (1988). *Power, influence, and your effectiveness in human resources.* Reading, MA: Addison-Wesley Publishing Co., Inc.

Quinn, R. E. (1977). Coping with Cupid: The formation, impact, and management of romantic relationships in organizations. *Administrative Science Quarterly, 22,* 30–45.

Quinn, R. E., & Lees, P. O. (1984). Attraction and harassment: Dynamics of sexual politics in the workplace. *Organizational Dynamics, 13,* 35–46.

Raye, L. (1986). *How to measure training effectiveness.* New York, NY: Nichols.

Redding, W.C. (1979). Graduate education and the communication consultant: Playing God for a fee. *Communication Education, 28,* 346–52.

Redding, W. C. (1984). *Professionalism in training—guidelines for a code of ethics.* Paper presented at Speech Communication Association, Chicago, IL.

Reddy, W. B., & Henderson, C. C. (Eds.) (1987). *Training, theory, and practice.* San Diego, CA: University Associates.

Ribler, R. I. (1983). *Training development guide.* Reston, VA: Reston Publishing Company.

Robbins, S.P. (1989). *Training in interpersonal skills: Tips for managing people at work.* Englewood Cliffs, NJ: Prentice-Hall.

Rogers, E. (1988). Information technologies: How organizations are changing. In G. Goldhaber & G. Barnett (Eds.), *Handbook of organizational communication* (pp. 437–52). Norwood, NJ: Ablex.

Romiszowski, A. J., & deHaas, J. A. (1989, Oct.). Computer mediated communication for instruction: Using e-mail as a seminar. *Education Technology,* 7–8.

Ronstadt, R. (1980). *The art of case analysis: A guide to the diagnosis of business situations.* Dober, MA: Lord Publishing.

Rosenberg, M.J. (1987). Evaluating training programs for decision making. In L. May, C. Moore, & S. Zammit (Eds.), *Evaluating business and industry training* (pp. 57–74). Boston, MA: Kluwer Academic Publishers.

Rosow, J. M., & Zager, R. (1988). *Training: The competitive edge: Introducing new technology into the workplace.* San Francisco, CA: Jossey-Bass, Inc.

Ross, R. S. (1989). *Small groups in organizational settings.* Englewood Cliffs, NJ: Prentice-Hall.

Ross, R., & DeWine, S. (1988). Assessing the Ross-DeWine conflict management message style. *Management Communication Quarterly, 1* (3), 389–413.

Rossett, A., & Arwady, J.W. (1987). *Training needs assessment.* Englewood Cliffs, NJ: Educational Technology Publications.

Rubin, L. B. (1985). *Just friends: The role of friendship in our lives.* New York, NY: Harper and Row.

Rudolph, E.E., & Johnson, B.R. (1983). *Communication consulting: Another teaching option.* Annandale, VA: Speech Communication Association.

Sackman, H. (1975). *Delphi critique: Expert opinion, forecasting and group process.* Lexington, MA: Lexington Books.

Salinger, R., & Deming, B. (1982). Practical strategies for evaluating training. *Training and Development, 36,* 20–29.

Schein, E. H. (1978). *Career dynamics: Matching individual and organizational needs.* Reading, MA: Addison-Wesley Publishing Co., Inc.

Schein, E. H. (1985). *Organizing culture and leadership.* San Francisco, CA: Jossey-Boss, Inc.

Schein, E. H. (1987). *Process consultation Volume II: Lessons for managers and consultants.* Reading, MA: Addison-Wesley Publishing Co.

Schein, E. H. (1988). *Process consultation Volume I: Its role in organizational development* (2nd ed.). Reading, MA: Addison-Wesley Publishing Co., Inc.

Scherer, P. S. (1989). The turnaround consultants steers corporate renewal. *Journal of Management Consulting,* pp. 17–24.

Schindler-Raiman, E. (1987). Risks we must take: Changes, challenges, and choices for consultants and trainers in 1987 and beyond. In W. B. Reddy & C. C. Henderson (Eds.), *Training, theory, and practice* (pp. 17–26). La Jolla, CA: University Associates.

Schrello, D. M. (1988). *How to market training programs, seminars, and instructional materials.* Long Beach, CA: Schrello Direct Marketing.

Schultz, B.G. (1989). *Communicating in the small group: Theory and practice.* New York, NY: Harper & Row.

Sheppard, B. H., & Bazerman, M. H. (1986). *Research on negotiation in organizations, 1.* Greenwich, CT: JAI Press.

Sherwood, J. (1981). Essential differences between traditional approaches to consulting and a collaborative approach. *Consultation,* 1 (1), pp. 52–55.

Shonk, J.H. (1982). *Working in teams: A practical manual for improving work groups.* New York, NY: AMACOM.

Shuster, H.D. (1990). *Teaming for quality improvement: A process for innovation and concensus.* Englewood Cliffs, NJ: Prentice-Hall.

Sigband, N. B. (1987, Feb.). The uses of meetings. *Nation's Business,* p. 11.

Siropolic, N. (1977). *How to start your own business, and how to make money.* Boston, MA: Houghton Mifflin Co.

Skinner, B. F. (1953). *Science and human behavior.* New York, NY: Macmillan.

Smith, B.P. (1990). Marketing of management consulting. *Journal of Management Consulting, 6,* pp. 34–40.

Smith, B.J., & Delahaye, B.L. (1987). *How to be an effective trainer: Skills for managers and new trainers* (2nd ed.). New York, NY: John Wiley & Sons, Inc.

Smith, T.C. (1984). *Making successful presentations: A self teaching guide.* New York, NY: John Wiley & Sons, Inc.

Spaid, O. A. (1989). *The consummate trainer: A practitioner's perspective.* Englewood Cliffs, NJ: Prentice-Hall.

Spechler, J., & Wicker, J. (1980). Internal consulting groups: Catalysts for organizational change. *Management Review, 69* (11), pp. 24–28.

Spruell, G. (1987). First rate technical skills training. *ASTD Info Line* (p. 1). Alexandria, VA: American Society for Training and Development.

Spruell, G. R. (1985). Daytime drama: Love in the office. *Training & Development Journal, 39,* 21–23.

Spruell, G. R. (1987). Team building at its best. *Info-Line* ASTD (v. 701).

Sredl, H. J., & Rothwell, W. J. (1987). *The ASTD reference guide to professional training roles and competencies, 1 & 2.* New York, NY: Random House Professional Business Publications.

Steele, F. (1985). Consultants and detectives. In C. R. Bell & L. Nadler (Eds.), *Clients and consultants: Meeting and exceeding expectations.* Houston, TX: Gulf Publishing Co.

Steil, L.K., Barker, L.L., & Watson, K.W. (1983). *Effective listening: Key to your success.* Reading, MA: Addison-Wesley Publishing Co., Inc.

Steiner, G. A. (1979). *Strategic planning: What every manager must know.* New York, NY: The Free Press.

Straub, J. (1992, April). Keeping your distance without losing rapport. *Supervisory Management,* 3.

Stroul, N. A. (1987, Nov.), Whither performance appraisal? *Training and Development Journal,* pp. 70–74.

Sullivan, R. L., Wircenski, J. L., Arnold, S. S., & Sarkees, M. D. (1990). *The trainer's guide: A practical manual for the design, delivery, and evaluation of training.* Rockville, MD: Aspen Publishers.

Suryanarayanan, S. (1989). Trends and outlooks for U. S. consulting. *Journal of Management Consulting, 5,* pp. 3–9.

Swensen, C. (1973). *Introduction to interpersonal relationships.* Glenview, IL: Scott, Foresman, & Co.

Sypher, B. D. (1990). *Case studies in organizational communication.* New York, NY: Guilford.

Sypher, B. D., Bostram, R. N., & Seibert, J. H. (1989). Listening, communication abilities, and success at work. *Journal of Business Communication, 26,* 293–303.

Tracey, W. R. (1989). *Designing training and development systems.* New York, NY: American Management Associations.

Tepper, R. (1987). *The consultant's problem solving workbook.* New York, NY: John Wiley & Sons, Inc.

Thrash, A.A., Shelby, A.N., & Tarver, J.L. (1984). *Communication and business in the professions: Speaking up successfully.* New York, NY: Holt, Rinehart, & Winston.

Tichy, N.M., & Devanna, M.A. (1986, July). The transformational leader. *Training and Development Journal,* pp. 27–32.

Time management module. Higher Education Management Institute (1979). Cocoa Beach, FL: HEMI.

Timm, P.R. (1986). *Managerial communication: A finger on the pulse.* (2nd Ed.). Englewood Cliffs, NJ: Prentice-Hall.

Tompkins, P. K. (1992). *Organizational imperatives: Lessons of the space program.* Los Angeles, CA: Roxbury.

Tortoriello, T., Blatt, S., & DeWine, S. (1978). *Communication in the organization: An applied approach.* New York, NY: McGraw-Hill, Inc.

Tucker, R.K. (1987). *Fighting it out with difficult, it not impossible people.* Dubuque, IA: Kendall Hall.

Van de Ven, A. & Delbecq, A. L. (1971). Nominal versus interacting group processes for committee decision-making effectiveness. *Academy of Management Journal, 14,* 203–12.

Van de Ven, A. & Delbecq, A. L. (1974). The effectiveness of nominal, delphi, and interacting group decision making processes. *Academy of Management Journal, 17,* (4), 605–21.

Wagel, W. H. (1977). Evaluating management development and training programs. *Personnel, 54,* 4–10.

Warshauer, S. (1988). *Inside training and development: Creating effective programs.* San Diego, CA: University Associates.

Watzlawick, P. (1976). *How real is real? Confusion, disinformation, communication.* New York, NY: Vintage Books.

Watzlawick, P., Weakland, J., & Finsch, R. (1974). *Change: Principles of problem formation and problem resolution.* New York, NY: W. W. Norton & Co., Inc.

Weaver, T. (1971, January). The delphi forecasting method. *Phi Delta Kappan* (January), 267–71.

Webster, L., & Henderson, S. C. (1987). Charting your HRD career. *The trainer's professional development handbook.* San Francisco, CA: Jossey-Bass, Inc.

Weiner, B. (1985). *Human motivation.* New York, NY: Springer-Verlag.

Weiss, D. H. (1992, March). How to deal with unpleasant people problems. *Supervisory management,* pp. 1–2.

Westhoff, L. A. (1986). What to do about corporate romance. *Management Review, 75,* 50–55.

Wexley, K. N., & Latham, G. P. (1981). *Developing and training human resources in organizations.* Glenview, IL: Scott, Foresman & Co.

Whalen, J. (1990, October). Winning presentations: Less talk is more convincing. *Supervisory Management,* 1–10.

White, L., & Mindiole, C. (1986). Marketing professional services. In S. Barcus and J. Wilkinson (Eds.) *Handbook of management consulting services.* New York, NY: McGraw-Hill, Inc.

Wilson, J. A. & Elman, N.S. (1990). Organizational benefits of mentoring. *Academy of Management Executive, 4,* 88–94.

Wolf, W. B. (1990). A parable: The consultant as detective. *Consultation, 9,* 93–94.

Wolfe, L.D. (1984, June). Minding the business of consulting. *Training and Development Journal,* pp. 45–47.

Wolff, F.I., Marsnik, N.C., Tacey, W.S., & Nichols, R.G. (1983). *Perceptive listening.* New York, NY: Holt, Rinehart & Winston.

Wolvin, A.D., & Coakley, C.G. (1985). *Listening.* Dubuque, IA: W. C. Brown.

Wolvin, A.D., & Coakley, C.G. (1991). A survey of the status of listening and training in some Fortune 500 corporations. *Communication Education, 40,* 152–64.

Woodman, R. W. (1989). Evaluation research on organizational change: Arguments for a 'Combined Paradigm' approach. In R. W. Woodman & W. A. Pasmore (Eds.), *Research in organizational change and development* (pp. 161–80). Greenwich, CT.: JAI Press.

Woodman, R. W., & Wayne, S. J. (1985). An investigation of positive findings bias in evaluation of organization development interventions. *Academy of Management Journal, 28* (4), 889–913.

Zemke, R., & Kramlinger, T. (1989). *Figuring things out: A trainer's guide to needs and task analysis.* Reading, MA: Addison-Wesley Publishing Co., Inc.

Zenger, J. H. & Hargis, K. (1982). Assessing training results: It's time to take the plunge. *Training and Development,* 11–16.

Ziehm, R. (1989). How I use management consults. *Journal of Management Consulting,* (4), 25–27.

AUTHOR INDEX

SUBJECT INDEX